Calvinists Incorporated

University of Chicago Geography Research Paper no. 240

Titles published in the Geography Research Papers series prior to 1992 and still in print are now distributed by the University of Chicago Press. For a list of available titles, see the end of the book. The University of Chicago Press commenced publication of the Geography Research Papers series in 1992 with no. 233.

Anne Kelly Knowles

Calvinists Incorporated

WELSH IMMIGRANTS ON

OHIO'S INDUSTRIAL

FRONTIER

The University of Chicago Press / Chicago and London

ANNE KELLY KNOWLES is lecturer in human geography at the Institute of Earth Studies, University of Wales, Aberystwyth.

The University of Chicago Press, Chicago 60637
The University of Chicago Press, Ltd., London
© 1997 by The University of Chicago
All rights reserved. Published 1997
Printed in the United States of America
06 05 04 03 02 01 00 99 98 97   1 2 3 4 5

ISBN: 0-226-44853-3 (paper)

Library of Congress Cataloging-in-Publication Data

Knowles, Anne Kelly.
    Calvinists incorporated : Welsh immigrants on Ohio's industrial frontier
/ Anne Kelly Knowles.
        p.   cm. — (University of Chicago geography research paper ; no.
240)
    Includes bibliographical references and index.
    ISBN 0-226-44853-3 (alk. paper)
    1. Welsh Americans—Ohio—Ethnic identity—Case studies.   2.
Calvinists—Ohio—Case studies.   3. Ohio—Historical geography—Case
studies.   4. Industrialization—Ohio—Jackson County—History—19th
century.   5. Industrialization—Ohio—Gallia County—History—19th century.
6. Capitalism—Ohio—Jackson County—History—19th century.   7.
Capitalism—Ohio—Gallia County—History—19th century.   8. Jackson
County (Ohio)—Economic conditions.   9. Gallia County (Ohio)—Economic
conditions.   10. Cardiganshire (Wales)—Emigration and immigration—
History—19th century.   I. Title.   II. Series.
F500.W4K66   1997
305.891'660771—dc20   96-25769
                                                                              CIP

♾ The paper used in this publication meets the minimum requirements of the
American National Standard for Information Sciences—Permanence of Paper for
Printed Library Materials, ANSI Z39.48–1984.

To my parents

Contents

List of Maps, Figures, and Tables

Guide to Pronouncing and
Interpreting Welsh Place-Names

Welsh is a Celtic language with its own alphabet, including several letters that do not exist in English. The following is a general guide to how to pronounce Welsh words, including a few of those most commonly used in this text. After the pronunciation guide is a list of common elements in Welsh place-names, many of which occur in places mentioned in this text. I hope both will be of assistance to non-Welsh speakers.

A few tips on pronunciation: Welsh vowels are "pure" sounds similar to those in Spanish and Italian. Thus: *a* ("ah"), *e* ("ay" or "eh"), *i* ("ee"), *o* ("oh"). The letters *w* ("oo"), *y* ("ee", "i", or "uh"), and *u* (a deeper "ee") are also used as vowels in Welsh.

Welsh has five consonants that do not occur in English: *ch* (a gutteral sound similar to a German *ch*), *dd* (as "th" in "then"), *ff* (as the English "f"), *rh* (a breathy, rolled "r") and *ll* (a cross between "l" and "s"). A single *f* in Welsh is said like "v" in English. All *r*'s are rolled.

The emphasis in most multisyllabic words falls on the next to last syllable. Thus *dyffryn* is pronounced "DUH-frin" and *capel* is "CAH-pel." *Eglwys* is pronounced "AYG-looees", with the "oo" and "ee" sounded as one smooth syllable. A key location in this book, *Mynydd Bach*, is pronounced "MUHN-ithe BACH," with the *ch* well back in the throat. *Llangeitho* is pronounced "Llahn-GAY-thoh." Two of the Welsh American publications to which the text refers are *Y Cyfaill*, pronounced "uh CUH-vayll," and *Y Cenhadwr*, pronounced "uh ken-HAHD-oor."

Common Elements
in Welsh Place-Names

aber: mouth of	*gwaun:* undulating moorland
afon: river	*gwyn:* white
allt: wood, slope	*hafod:* summer dwelling
bach (fach): small	*isaf:* lower
bedd: grave	*llan:* (church) enclosure
cae: field	*maen:* stone
caer: fort	*maes:* field
capel: chapel	*mawr (fawr):* great, big
carn: cairn	*melin (felin):* mill
carreg: stone	*morfa:* bog, sea-marsh
castell: castle	*mynydd:* mountain
coch: red	*newydd :* new
coetan: quoit	*ogof:* cave
craig: rock	*pen:* head, top
cwm: valley (small)	*pont:* bridge
dinas: hill-fortress	*porth:* harbour
dyffryn: valley (larger)	*rhos:* moorland
eglwys: church	*rhyd:* ford
moel (foel): bare hill	*tref:* town, homestead
glas: blue (or green)	*tŷ:* house
glyn: deep valley	*uchaf:* upper, higher
gwaelod: bottom	*ynys:* island

Acknowledgments

This book is the fruit of many people's labor in addition to my own. A great many friends and strangers who became friends helped me reconstruct the life stories that lie at the heart of the research presented here. Those individuals are listed by name at the end of the Bibliography, and I thank them all. I would also like to give special thanks to those who repeatedly took time to answer questions, to look again for details of family history, and to help me find people and places in order to tell the story of migration from Mynydd Bach to Jackson/Gallia as completely as possible. Eleanor Cole, Evan E. Davis, John Evans, Edwin F. Jones, and James H. Lloyd were extremely generous with their time and hospitality. I hope this book repays them in some measure.

I am also very grateful to the academic colleagues who provided valuable criticism and encouragement. First, I would like to thank those who guided and inspired me during my time at the University of Wisconsin–Madison, including Robert C. Ostergren, David Ward, Yi-Fu Tuan, and David Woodward of the Department of Geography; and Allan G. Bogue, Paul S. Boyer, and Diane Lindstrom of the Department of History. Others whose comments have been very helpful are Kathleen Neils Conzen, Michael P. Conzen, Charles Dean, Robert A. Dodgshon, James A. Henretta, John Hudson, Geraint H. Jenkins, Emrys Jones, Ieuan Gwynedd Jones, William D. Jones, Henry Lamb, Richard Mahon, Richard J. Moore-Colyer, Derec Llwyd Morgan, Gerald Morgan, Mansell Prothero, Richard Wall, John Walton, Robin Whatley, Sandra Wheatley, and the two anonymous reviewers who read the manuscript for the University of Chicago Press. Various portions of this research were presented to the Cambridge Group for the History of Population and Social Structure, the Newberry Library Rural History Seminar, the Geography Department at Pennsylvania State University, the Geography Department at the University of Lancaster, and to my colleagues and students at the Institute of Earth Studies at the University of

Wales, Aberystwyth. Each of those presentations raised questions that helped me rethink the work yet again, and I thank all the participants for their contributions. Derec Llwyd Morgan and Dafydd Jenkins were most helpful in reviewing the longer translations in the text and Appendix C.

I have benefited greatly from working with a number of talented cartographers to design and produce the maps and diagrams. Sara Arscott redesigned and improved many of the maps in the course of producing their initial renditions. David DiBiase, Kenneth J. Parsons, and Onno Brouwer provided expert advice on overall map design and how to visualize the data at hand. Ian Gulley of the Drawing Office at the Institute of Earth Studies plotted and produced map 3.2. Adam Cooper designed and produced figures 1.4 and 4.5 and assisted with final map corrections. Tom Willcockson drew the reconstruction of Jefferson Furnace in figure 4.1. Warm thanks to them all. It has also been a pleasure to work with the highly professional staff at the University of Chicago Press, particularly associate director Penelope Kaiserlian and manuscript editor Carol Saller. Michael P. Conzen first inspired me to study historical geography and has consistently held up a high standard as an editor and friend.

I was fortunate to work at congenial archives throughout the research. My thanks to the patient and resourceful archivists and reference librarians at the State Historical Society of Wisconsin, the Ohio Historical Society, the Minnesota Historical Center, the National Library of Wales, and the Baker Library, Harvard University Graduate School of Business Administration. Special thanks to Mildred Bangert of the Welsh-American Heritage Museum in Oak Hill, Ohio, for being so hospitable and for permitting me to borrow and copy items from the museum collection.

This study has been generously funded by a number of academic and Welsh American organizations. I gratefully acknowledge the Graduate School of the University of Wisconsin–Madison for granting me a WARF Dissertation Fellowship for research and writing in 1991–1992 and for travel grants for work in Wales in 1989 and 1991; the Geography Department of the University of Wisconsin–Madison for a Whitbeck Fellowship in 1989 and several travel grants to present portions of this research at annual meetings of the Association of American Geographers; and the State Historical Society of Wisconsin for an Alice E. Smith Fellowship in 1989. The National Welsh American Foundation provided generous funds for research overseas through an Exchange Scholarship and additional support for cartography. The Welsh National Gymanfa Ganu Association and the St. David's Society of New York State also provided grants that were important to early phases of the research. I would also like to thank HTV-Wales and the Centre for Advanced Welsh and Celtic Studies at the University College of Wales–Aberystwyth for their support through a Lady Amy Parry Williams Memorial Scholarship for research at the National Library of Wales, and the Institute of Earth Studies and the University of Wales, Aberystwyth, for financial support for the final phase of research and for equipment necessary to complete the project. The University of Wales also provided funding to defray production expenses through a Sir David Hughes Parry Award.

Lastly, I would like to thank the dear friends whose constant interest in this work has sustained me over the course of its gestation. Michael T. Struble first drew my attention to Welsh involvement in Ohio's charcoal iron industry. His guided tour of the back roads of Jackson and Gallia counties was the genesis for this study, and he has always freely shared the fruits of his own research. JoAnne A. Simon has always been ready to cheer me up. Mary Mergenthal's personal and professional support as editor of *Y Drych* (The Mirror) helped convince me that it was important to share this research with the Welsh American community at large. Eluned Evans, my Welsh tutor, opened the doors to Welsh literature, the Welsh Bible, and the thoughts of Welsh-speaking immigrants. My debt to her is immense. Larry Knowles has supported and challenged me from the start, for which I cannot thank him enough.

I would also like to acknowledge that an earlier version of chapter 1 was published in *Annals of the Association of American Geographers* 85, no. 2 (1995), 246–66; and portions of chapter 4 appeared as "Charcoal Iron and the Welsh in Southern Ohio, 1850–1880," in *Historical Geography* 23, nos. 1 & 2 (1993): 33–43. Material from the R. G. Dun & Company Collection is reproduced with kind permission from Dun & Bradstreet and the Baker Library, Harvard University Graduate School of Business Administration. Permission to reproduce the Welsh ballad "Cân Newydd" in Appendix C is kindly granted by Brown University Library. All English translations of Welsh texts are my own unless otherwise noted.

Introduction

When I was conducting field research for this study of emigration from rural Cardiganshire, Wales, to southern Ohio, the question I heard most often was, Why did they go? No question is more important to the descendants of European emigrants today or to those of us who study overseas migration professionally. The curiosity to know why people chose to leave their homeland gives rise to many of the questions that form the basis of our field: Why did people leave during one period and not another? Why did some people leave while others stayed behind? Why did they choose one destination rather than another? Were their initial hopes and expectations fulfilled? These questions are compelling because overseas migration before the age of telecommunications and air travel was often, as one of my own Welsh ancestors put it, "a revolution" in the emigrant's life.[1] Tales of the men and women who passed through that revolutionary experience are essential stories in our efforts to understand American history and identity, whether they are mythologized as the American dream or minutely reconstructed in scholarly monographs and family genealogies.

Recent studies of rural European emigration to the United States have addressed the issue of motivation within the context of emigrants'[2] native, local society and economy, in the belief that regional economic conditions and cultural traditions strongly influenced emigrants' decisions and their subsequent experiences in the new country. These case studies have also carefully ana-

---

1. Rev. Benjamin W. Chidlaw, *The American*, trans. Rev. R. Gwilym Williams (Bala: County Press, 1978; originally published Llanrwst: John Jones, 1840), 44.

2. I use three terms for the people in this study: they are "emigrants" while they are considering departure or are on their way to the United States; "immigrants" once they have arrived in the United States; and "migrants" when they are moving within Britain. The latter term also serves to refer generally to people who have migrated.

lyzed the ways in which immigrants' economic status changed in their U.S. settlements, how their increasing wealth and involvement in commercial agriculture altered the division of labor and gender relations on their farms, and how parents' provision of land for their children sustained ethnic territories and certain cultural traditions for long periods of time.[3] With their main focus on the reproduction of the household and ethnic cultural institutions, these studies have fundamentally revised the earlier interpretation that immigrants quickly lost their native culture on the American frontier.[4] They have also shown that the processes of cultural preservation and the creation of ethnic identity proved to be remarkably long-lived.[5] What has not yet been fully explained is how the broadest, most common aim of emigration—migrants' efforts to improve their economic position—influenced immigrant culture and vice versa. In other words, how did immigrant culture respond, whether creatively or defensively, to American capitalism?

Two major fields of study within social history and anthropology offer conceptual models for pursuing these questions. The first is the still contentious debate over the nature and timing of

3. Robert C. Ostergren, *A Community Transplanted: The Trans-Atlantic Experience of a Swedish Immigrant Settlement in the Upper Middle West, 1835–1915* (Madison: University of Wisconsin Press, 1988); D. Aiden McQuillan, *Prevailing over Time: Ethnic Adjustment on the Kansas Prairies, 1875–1925* (Lincoln: University of Nebraska Press, 1990); Jon Gjerde, *From Peasants to Farmers: The Migration from Balestrand, Norway to the Upper Middle West* (Cambridge: Cambridge University Press, 1985); Walter D. Kamphoefner, *The Westfalians: From Germany to Missouri* (Princeton: Princeton University Press, 1987); Kathleen Neils Conzen, "Peasant Pioneers: Generational Succession among German Farmers in Frontier Minnesota," in *The Countryside in the Age of Capitalist Transformation: Essays in the Social History of Rural America*, ed. Steven Hahn and Jonathan Prude (Chapel Hill: University of North Carolina Press, 1985), 259–292; Kathleen Neils Conzen, *Making Their Own America: Assimilation Theory and the German Peasant Farmer*, German Historical Institute Lecture no. 3 (New York: Berg Publishers, 1990), 1–33.

4. Frederick Jackson Turner, "The Significance of the Frontier in American History," in *The Frontier in American History*, ed. Wilbur R. Jacobs (Tucson: University of Arizona Press, 1986), 1–38; Oscar Handlin, *The Uprooted* (Boston: Little, Brown, 1951). In his second edition (1973) Handlin reasserts his fundamental conclusions about immigrant experience in answer to his critics.

5. Kathleen Neils Conzen, et al., "The Invention of Ethnicity: A Perspective from the U.S.A.," *Journal of American Ethnic History* 12 (1992), 3–41; Steven D. Hoelscher and Robert C. Ostergren, "Old European Homelands in the American Middle West," *Journal of Cultural Geography* 13 (1993), 87–106.

rural capitalist transformation in the United States. As Allan Kulikoff has written in summarizing the debate,[6] its main antagonists are neoclassical economists and Marxist and neo-Marxist social historians whose disagreements largely stem from their differing definitions of capitalism. Neoclassical economists generally define capitalism as "a system of exchange 'in which goods are bought and sold,' where individuals produce 'for the market,' purchasing goods from the market in return." From this point of view, anyone who demonstrates profit-maximizing behavior and accumulates wealth for investment is a capitalist, and any economic system characterized by such exchange and accumulation is a capitalist system. American economic historians such as Winifred Barr Rothenberg admit that such a definition is so broad and vague as to be almost meaningless and that more precise indices are required. Rothenberg's analysis of the change from marketplaces to a market economy in rural Massachusetts, for example, deploys a variety of measurable indices to capture economic change, including the synchronicity and convergence of prices, price elasticity, credit networks, the liquidity of investments, interest rates, wage rates, labor productivity, and the composition of agricultural inputs and outputs.[7] Social historians argue that such measurements do not necessarily reveal a system's prevailing mode of production or the structure of labor-capital relations within it, which together constitute the "social formation" that determined whether an economy was capitalist (where labor is free and capitalists control productive property), anticapitalist (as in the unfree labor system of the antebellum slave South), or noncapitalist (which encompasses a wide variety of other forms). These scholars also give credence to the notion of economic *mentalité*. Some of their most forceful arguments are based on distinguishing between precapitalist attitudes that favored noncompetitive, noncommercial exchange, conducted for the sake of securing family subsistence in traditionalist communities, and the aggressive acquisitiveness typical of the capitalist frame of mind.[8]

6. Allan Kulikoff, *The Agrarian Origins of American Capitalism* (Charlottesville: University Press of Virginia, 1992), 1–9, 13–33. See also his article, "The Transition to Capitalism in Rural America," *William and Mary Quarterly*, 3d ser., 46 (1989): 120–44.

7. Winifred Barr Rothenberg, *From Market-Places to a Market Economy: The Transformation of Rural Massachusetts, 1750–1850* (Chicago: University of Chicago Press, 1992).

8. Kulikoff, *Agrarian Origins*, 15–18; James A. Henretta, "Families and Farms: *Mentalité* in Pre-Industrial America," *William and Mary Quarterly* 35 (1978): 3–

There will probably always be disagreement over the best indicators of the transition from a putative precapitalist economy to a recognizably capitalist one. Nevertheless, recent work has approached consensus on one key point. Leading neoclassical economic historians and social historians now agree that any given society could and probably did contain both capitalist and precapitalist forms of exchange for extended periods of time. Depending upon the scale of one's analysis and the kinds of people put under the microscope, one can find all manner of economic relations in rural American communities from the early eighteenth century to the end of the Civil War. For example, James A. Henretta has pointed out that backwoods farmers in New England retained a strong Calvinistic ethos of economic morality and community-based, noncommercial exchange while New England merchants in coastal towns were pursuing profit without restraint. Christopher Clark found great complexity in the gradual change to a market-oriented economy in rural Massachusetts.[9] Rothenberg's study of the same region concluded that so long as different forms of economy coexisted in a given place, members of that society were likely to hold "contradictory and incompatible ideas and ideals simultaneously." These conclusions echo Fernand Braudel's view of the development of capitalism in modern Europe: "This was not one society, but several, coexisting, resting on each other to a greater or lesser degree; not one system but several; not one hierarchy but several; not one order but several; not one mode of production but several, not one culture but several cultures, forms of consciousness, languages, ways of life. We must think of everything in the plural."[10]

32. Rothenberg summarizes economic historians' generally dismissive attitude toward *mentalité* in describing the concept as an "untestable assertion"; *Market-Places to Market Economy*, 32.

9. James A. Henretta, "The Protestant Ethic and the Reality of Capitalism in Colonial America," in *Weber's* Protestant Ethic: *Origins, Evidence, Contexts*, ed. Hartmut Lehmann (Cambridge: Cambridge University Press, for the German Historical Institute, Washington, D.C., 1993), 327–46; Christopher Clark, *The Roots of Rural Capitalism: Western Massachusetts, 1780–1860* (Ithaca: Cornell University Press, 1990).

10. J. P. Cooper, "In Search of Agrarian Capitalism," in *The Brenner Debate: Agrarian Class Structure and Economic Development in Pre-Industrial Europe*, ed. T. H. Aston and C. H. E. Philpin (Cambridge: Cambridge University Press, 1990 reprint), 140, quoted in Rothenberg, *From Market-Places to Market Economy*, 21, note 75; Fernand Braudel, *The Wheels of Commerce*, vol. 2 of *Civilization and Capitalism, Fifteenth–Eighteenth Century*, trans. Sian Reynolds (New York: Harper & Row, Perennial Library edition, 1986), 465.

Recent work in the field of peasant studies supports this complex, multilayered view of economic behavior and attitudes. In peasant societies today, the same people who readily accept cash payment from outsiders may conduct other kinds of exchange with members of their own society. In fact many societies hold double standards of economic morality, using one yardstick with strangers and another with their kith and kin. The introduction of money into a rural economy need not, of itself, quickly turn all transactions into exchanges of money for goods and labor. Anthropologists have found that cash income earned from strangers commonly goes through a social transformation that absorbs its value into the community without allowing it to destabilize the traditional relationships of social reproduction.[11] Even where such transformations do not occur and money does change traditional social relations, it may still be misleading to restrict the label of "moral economy" to noncompetitive, cashless, subsistence-oriented economies because even highly developed capitalist societies make moral judgments about money and the social meaning of exchange. As E. P. Thompson pointed out in his reassessment of the concept of moral economy, every society generates "a particular type of morality in the interests of a particular type of economy." He continued, quoting David Thorner,

> We are sure to go astray, if we try to conceive of peasant economies as exclusively "subsistence" oriented and to suspect capitalism wherever the peasants show evidence of being "market" oriented. It is much sounder to take it for granted, as a starting point, that for ages peasant economies have had a double orientation towards both.[12]

Thompson also warned against sentimentalizing economic relations within traditional agrarian society. He wrote of eighteenth-century England, "Within this habitus all parties strove to maximize their own advantages. Each encroached upon the usages of others." The fact remains, he concluded, that in peasant societies today as in rural communities in the past, some people have re-

11. Jonathan Parry and Maurice Bloch, "Introduction: Money and the Morality of Exchange," in *Money and the Morality of Exchange*, ed. Jonathan Parry and Maurice Block (Cambridge: Cambridge University Press, 1989), 1–32.

12. E. P. Thompson, "The Moral Economy Reviewed," in *Customs in Common* (New York: New Press, 1991), 271 (quoting P. S. Atiyah, *The Rise and Fall of Freedom of Contract* [Oxford: Clarendon Press, 1979], 84) and 272, note 1 (quoting Thorner, "Peasant Economy as a Category in History," in *Peasants and Peasant Societies*, 2d ed., ed. Teodor Shanin [Oxford: Blackwell, 1987], 65).

sisted the ideas and workings of capitalism and expressed their resistance in arguments for a "just price" and for "conceptions of social justice, of rights and obligations, of reciprocity."[13]

The behavior of the Welsh immigrants in this study exemplifies many of these concepts. In their economic dealings they could be characterized as both family-oriented yeomen farmers and competitive entrepreneurs whose investments hastened the development of industrial capitalism in their rural Ohio community. Their deeply conservative religious values both constrained their economic behavior and facilitated their success in the American capitalist system. As immigrants who fit comfortably alongside the mainstream of nineteenth-century American Protestant society while maintaining a distinctive culture, the Welsh Calvinists in Jackson and Gallia counties, Ohio, offer an illuminating example of the ways in which cultural beliefs and institutions could influence the social formation of capitalism in a rural locality. Their story also shows how economic change could influence immigrant culture, particularly as economic success in the American capitalist system came to threaten the moral basis of Welsh identity.

My primary goal in embarking on this study was to understand two key decisions which were turning points for the Welsh who settled in Jackson and Gallia counties during the first half of the nineteenth century; namely, why they emigrated to that particular location and why they decided to form their own charcoal iron furnace companies in competition with American firms. To see these decisions in context, it was necessary to reconstruct the immigrants' culture and economy as fully as possible in Wales and in the United States. Context implies scale, and I have used various scales purposely to focus on various contexts relevant to the main themes.

Chapter 1 lays out the national context of early nineteenth-century Welsh emigration to the United States in order to determine whether those who left for Jackson/Gallia can be considered typical or atypical for their time. This chapter also introduces spatial features of Welsh migration which are explored in greater detail in later chapters, including the relationship between internal migration and emigration and the clustering of migrants from particular parts in Wales in particular settlements. Chapters

13. E. P. Thompson, "Custom, Law and Common Right," in *Customs in Common*, 102; idem, "The Moral Economy of the English Crowd in the Eighteenth Century," ibid., 185–258; "Moral Economy Reviewed," ibid., 341.

2 and 3 examine the regional and local contexts of choice within which rural people in the county of Cardiganshire weighed the alternatives available through internal and overseas migration. Chapter 2 focuses on the development of three long-standing traditions of internal migration that connected Cardiganshire to areas of greater economic opportunity, asking in the end why so few people from one part of the county took part in those migrations. The localized cultural and economic reasons for emigration to Jackson/Gallia are the subject of chapter 3, which also explains the role of religion in structuring social relations and creating a Welsh ethnic landscape in the immigrants' new settlement and their initial economic activities in southern Ohio.

Chapter 4 remains on the scale of the locality. It tells the story of the Welsh settlers' involvement in the charcoal iron industry, which was rapidly developing all around them when their community was taking shape. In this chapter the strands of economy and culture are most closely entwined, for the Welsh-owned charcoal iron companies illustrate the incorporation of Calvinistic religious values and institutions into economic forms which inspired the book's title. Chapter 5 moves between the national and local scales to reflect upon the moral ramifications of the whole range of Welsh Calvinist immigrant experience, from the decision to leave Wales in pursuit of better economic opportunity to the bittersweet results of economic success, as represented in debates carried on in Welsh emigrant literature, in the Welsh American press, and by members of the Welsh community in Jackson/Gallia.

I have used a variety of statistical and qualitative sources for this multiscaled, trans-Atlantic study. The main core of information, however, is a database of individual immigrant biographies drawn from obituaries, community and chapel histories from Wales and the United States, field research, a wealth of family histories generously provided by American genealogists and Welsh local historians, charcoal iron furnace company records, and governmental sources such as the U.S. and British censuses, the Tithe Survey, and land records. The biographical approach to community reconstruction may be useful to researchers working with other European groups who, like the Welsh, did not leave tidy, comprehensive, trans-Atlantic records behind. Extremely detailed local studies of economic transformation, particularly in Sweden, have proved beyond question that we can discern the actual processes of economic change in individual life histories and geographies.[14] I hope that this study indicates how the close study of localized culture can further enrich our understanding of those processes.

14. See, for example, Göran Hoppe and John Langton, *Peasantry to Capitalism: Western Ostergotland in the Nineteenth Century* (Cambridge: Cambridge University Press, 1994); and Robert C. Ostergren, *Patterns of Seasonal Industrial Labor Recruitment in a Nineteenth-Century Swedish Parish: The Case of Matfors and Tuna, 1846–1873*, Report no. 5 from the Demographic Data Base, Umeå University (Umeå, Sweden: Umeå University 1989).

Chapter One

Historical Geography of Welsh Emigration to the United States, 1795–1850

In 1799, the English surgeon and historian George Lipscomb set off from London for a tour of South Wales. He was one of many English gentlefolk who had become fascinated with the wild, picturesque landscapes and peasant societies of the Celtic fringe. While riding near Presteigne in Radnorshire, Lipscomb and his companions "met with a little horde of Welch-men, who, with their wives and children, and all that they had, were quitting their native retirement, the peaceful retreat of innocence and penury, and journeying toward Deptford, to procure employment in the dockyard." The families Lipscomb saw were walking from Cardiganshire to London, following a route that other Welsh migrants and cattle drovers before them had worn smooth. Lipscomb commented in his travel diary, "It is not at all uncommon for the Welch peasantry to emigrate to the neighbouring counties, or even to proceed as far as the metropolis, in search of employment, in gardening and husbandry, early in the spring."[1] Migration from the Welsh countryside to English cities was indeed common by the end of the eighteenth century. At the same time, however, another movement of people out from Wales was beginning to attract attention, as noted by a Cardiganshire landlord named Thomas Johnes. "Vast emigrations are going to America from this County," he wrote to a friend in 1801; "we can but ill spare them."[2]

Emigration to the United States became an increasingly attractive choice for Welsh people as the century progressed. Notices

1. George Lipscomb, *Journey into South Wales . . . in 1799* (London, 1802), 101, quoted in Gwynfryn Walters, "The Tourist and Guidebook Literature of Wales, 1770–1870: A Descriptive and Bibliographical Survey with an Analysis of the Cartographic Content and Its Extent" (Ph.D. diss., University of Wales, 1966), vol. 1, p. 23.

2. Thomas Johnes to George Cumberland, dated Hafod, 21 February 1801, quoted in Richard J. Moore-Colyer, ed., *A Land of Pure Delight: Selections from the Letters of Thomas Johnes of Hafod, Cardiganshire (1748–1816)* (Llandysul: Gwasg Gomer, 1992), 155.

of emigrant ships sailing from Welsh ports marked their departures and the U.S. census recorded their arrival in tallies that grew
from decade to decade right up to 1900. The details of the story,
however, are poorly understood. The aim of this chapter is to establish the spatial patterns of Welsh emigration during the early
nineteenth century, the relation of emigration to internal migration, and the social characteristics of Welsh emigrants at that
time. In addition to filling some of the gaps in knowledge about
the first half-century of significant Welsh emigration, this information helps clarify the origins of rural and industrial emigrations
later in the nineteenth century, for many of the routes and destinations popular with Welsh emigrants after the Civil War were
established as early as 1830–1850.

There were three main periods of Welsh emigration to the
United States: (1) Quaker and Baptist emigration to Pennsylvania
in the late seventeenth and early eighteenth centuries; (2) widespread rural emigration during the early nineteenth century; and
(3) predominantly industrial emigration during the late nineteenth
century. The latter period is by far the best documented and understood, although the two earlier periods' general characteristics
have been known for some time.

The first documented wave of colonial Welsh emigration came
in the last two decades of the seventeenth century, when Quakers
from Merioneth and Baptists from Radnor and the Cardigan-
Pembrokeshire border (see map 1.1) took up land in William
Penn's new colony in Pennsylvania. Some Welsh Dissenters
maintained contact with fellow believers in Wales, nurturing a
connection that brought a trickle of indentured servants, farmers,
and merchants in their wake. As far as we know, however, very
few Welsh emigrated between 1710 and 1794.[3] In the latter year
a Baptist minister and radical democrat named Morgan John
Rhys set out in search of a suitable place to establish a Welsh
colony in the American interior. Rhys's "Beulah land," located at
Ebensburgh in Cambria County, Pennsylvania, and its daughter
settlements in central and southwestern Ohio rekindled interest in
emigration. Between 1794 and 1801, ships picked up hundreds

---

3. Arthur H. Dodd, *The Character of Early Welsh Emigration to the United
States*, 2d ed. (Cardiff: University of Wales Press, 1956), 12–13, 26; Hywel M.
Davies, "'Very Different Springs of Uneasiness': Emigration from Wales to the
United States of America during the 1790s," *Welsh History Review* 15 (1991):
395. On the popular myth that Welshmen were the first Europeans to land on the
North American continent, see Gwyn A. Williams, *Madoc: The Making of a
Myth* (London: Methuen, 1980).

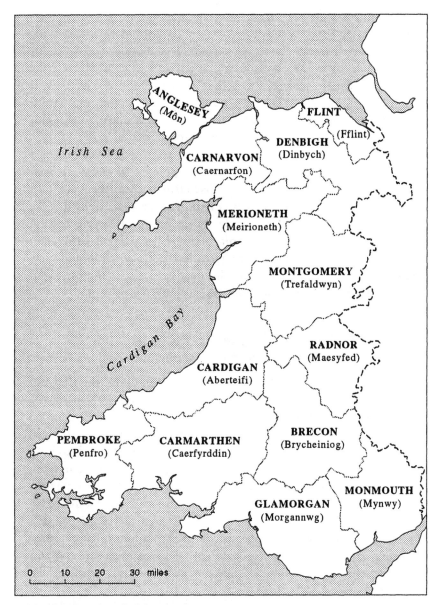

Map 1.1 Counties of Wales

of passengers at Welsh ports, including at least one vessel that was chartered to carry up to three hundred emigrants from the port of Carnarvon to the United States in January 1796.[4]

4. Gwyn A. Williams, *The Search for Beulah Land: The Welsh and the Atlantic Revolution* (London: Croom Helm, 1980); Arthur H. Dodd, *The Industrial Revolution in North Wales*, 3d ed. (Cardiff: University of Wales Press, 1971), 381;

Departures increased again after the conclusion of the Napoleonic Wars in 1815, when Britain resumed normal maritime trade and a severe postwar depression created economic incentives for emigration. By 1831, both newspapers and memoranda to the decennial British census noted that emigration to America was depopulating some rural areas, notably in Carnarvon and Montgomeryshire, and that skilled workers were leaving the coalfields and iron towns of Glamorgan and Monmouthshire for jobs in Pennsylvania. In 1850 the U.S. census recorded 29,868 Welsh natives living in the United States, 89 percent of them in New York, Pennsylvania, Ohio, and Wisconsin.[5] Over the next four decades the Welsh American population more than trebled, to a peak of 100,079 in 1890, while its geographical concentration changed very little. Pennsylvania claimed 38 percent of Welsh-born residents at the turn of the twentieth century; Ohio and New York another 20 percent; and the next six states (Illinois, Wisconsin, Iowa, Utah, Indiana, and Kansas) just 18 percent.[6]

Problems and Issues in Reconstructing Welsh Emigration

Official sources yield little specific information about the flows of Welsh emigrants before the late nineteenth century. Neither the British government nor the Anglican Church compiled detailed or systematic records of population statistics or movements until the end of the nineteenth century. Unlike the state church in Scandinavian countries and the Netherlands, the Anglican Church did not begin to keep comprehensive lists of parishioners' births, marriages, and deaths until the early nineteenth century, and parish authorities rarely bothered to record people's movements between parishes or out of the country. Nineteenth-century church records are probably less complete for Wales than for the rest of Britain because Nonconformists, who formed

---

Dodd, *Early Welsh Emigration*, 23–24; Rev. Robert Williams, Llandudno, to William Owen Pughe, dated 21 January 1796, National Library of Wales ms. 13224B, p. 161.

5. Dodd, *Industrial Revolution*, 385–98; U.S. Bureau of the Census, *The Seventh Census of the United States: 1850* (Washington: Robert Armstrong, Public Printer, 1853).

6. U.S. Bureau of the Census, *Historical Statistics of the United States from Colonial Times to 1957* (Washington, 1960), 99; idem, *Twelfth Census of the United States, 1900* (Washington: U.S. Government Printing Office, 1900), vol. 1, p. 735.

a large majority of churchgoers in Wales by 1838, often did not register life events with their local parish church, either out of neglect or in protest against what they considered an alien authority.[7] The decennial British census did not include place of birth to the level of the county until 1851, limiting its usefulness as a source for migration data before 1861. The lack of early birthplace information and parish-level detail about individuals has prevented British historians from charting internal migration with anything like the thoroughness of studies from Sweden and the Netherlands.[8]

Port records do little to make up for these deficiencies. For most of the eighteenth and nineteenth centuries, British port officials were not required to make detailed lists of ships' passengers, and few of the original, abbreviated lists that recorded the number of outward-bound passengers have survived. Some extant lists include the last residence of emigrants but none specify their place of birth, making it difficult to draw any meaningful conclusions about their cultural background or economic circumstances. The problem is exacerbated for the Welsh by official nonrecognition of their ethnic identity. The Board of Trade did not distinguish Welsh from English passengers aboard emigrant ships until 1908.[9] This may explain the remarkable scarcity of Welsh emigrants in the one detailed registry of emigrants that the British government did create before the twentieth century. In the years leading up to the American Revolution, Parliament became very concerned about the loss of skilled artisans and mechanics to the Colonies. It attempted to clamp down on departures by re-

7. D. V. Glass, "Vital Registration in Britain during the Nineteenth Century," in *Numbering the People: The Eighteenth-Century Population Controversy and the Development of Census and Vital Statistics in Britain* (London: Gordon and Cremonesi, 1973), 181–205; C. J. Williams and J. Watts-Williams, *Cofrestri Plwyf Cymru/Parish Registers of Wales* (Aberystwyth: National Library of Wales and Welsh County Archivists' Group, 1986), xiii–xv.

8. J. Dennis Willigan and Katherine A. Lynch, *Sources and Methods of Historical Demography* (New York: Academic Press, 1982), 123–26; Robert C. Ostergren, *A Community Transplanted: The Trans-Atlantic Experience of a Swedish Immigrant Settlement in the Upper Middle West, 1835–1915* (Madison: University of Wisconsin Press, 1988), 27–30; Jan Lucassen, *Migrant Labour in Europe 1600–1900: The Drift to the North Sea*, trans. Donald A. Bloch (London: Croom Helm, 1987), 264.

9. Dudley Baines, *Migration in a Mature Economy: Emigration and Internal Migration in England and Wales, 1861–1900* (Cambridge: Cambridge University Press, 1985), 3, 5; David Williams, "Some Figures Relating to Emigration from Wales," *Bulletin of the Board of Celtic Studies* 7 (1935): 398.

quiring ships' captains to register every emigrant's name, age, and occupation. The resulting record of 9,364 emigrants for the years 1773–1776 includes only twenty-four individuals identified as coming from Wales,[10] a figure so low as to strain belief.

Various scholars have tried to compensate for the lack of data on British emigration by constructing statistical models and data sets to estimate the flows of English and Welsh internal migrants and emigrants, using place-of-birth information in the decennial British censuses and ships' passenger lists. Although the census-based studies are, of necessity, limited to the period after 1850, their methods and conclusions are significant for early nineteenth-century Welsh migration, for they have framed the theoretical debate about the nature of nineteenth-century British migration and its relationship to the development of industrial capitalism in Britain and the United States.

Between 1930 and 1960, economic historian Brinley Thomas developed the most comprehensive and durable interpretation of British internal migration and emigration that has yet been published.[11] He based his analysis of migration and the North Atlantic economy on Kondratiev's theory that national economic cycles fluctuate in long swings of approximately twenty years' duration. Thomas observed that the long swings in Britain and the United States were out of phase with one another during the nineteenth and early twentieth centuries; that is, construction and railroad-building accelerated in Britain while the same industries were in decline in the United States, and vice versa. The flow of capital and emigrants changed direction accordingly, as investors and workers followed the pendulum swings of economic advantage. Generally, Thomas pictured British migration as a unidirectional flow of people from the countryside to the city, where they stayed when times were good and from which they emigrated when times were bad.

Wales, Thomas argued, was the one region whose economic cycles and migration flows significantly differed from the general pattern for Britain. He found that the long swings of the Welsh economy coincided with those of America. The explanation lay in the dominance of the export coal trade over the Welsh econ-

10. Bernard Bailyn, *Voyagers to the West: A Passage in the Peopling of America on the Eve of the Revolution* (New York: Vintage Books, 1986), 91

11. Brinley Thomas, "Wales and the Atlantic Economy," *Scottish Journal of Political Economy* 6 (1959): 169–92; idem, *Migration and Economic Growth: A Study of Great Britain and the Atlantic Economy* (Cambridge: Cambridge University Press, 1954).

omy. The fact that conditions in the coal industry tended to rise and fall in concert with swings in the American economy meant that Welsh workers generally emigrated when the American economy was strong, and stayed at home or sought work in England when the Welsh economy declined. Furthermore, the employment opportunities generated by the Welsh coal industry greatly dampened emigration from Wales as a whole. An important secondary result of the concentration of Welsh-speaking migrants in industrial South Wales was the creation of a vibrant, new, industrial Welsh culture. In his most controversial conclusion, Thomas asserted that the redistribution of the native Welsh population by internal migration to the coalfields actually saved the Welsh language from extinction. Had South Wales not been transformed by heavy industry, he wrote, "the surplus rural population which was Welsh to the core (nearly 400,000 in the sixty years up to 1911) would have had to go to England or overseas; these people, together with their descendants, would have been lost to the land of their birth for ever."[12]

In his elaborate reconsideration of birthplace data in the British census, Dudley Baines tested the statistical basis of Thomas's argument and found it deeply flawed.[13] For one thing, he argued, British migration patterns were much more complex than Thomas made them appear. The rate and timing of migration flows varied too much from region to region and county to county to support a theory of national flows tied to international economic cycles. Baines found that Thomas had grossly underestimated the numbers of British emigrants as well. He also showed that half or more of all British emigrants in the late nineteenth century had been born in urban, not rural, places. Only in South Wales was there substantial evidence of stage migration in which rural folk passed through urban centers before emigrating.

On most points, Baines argued, Thomas had seriously misrepresented the situation in Wales. The growth of the coal industry

12. Brinley Thomas, "Migration into the Glamorganshire Coalfield, 1861–1911," *Economica* 30 (1930), 275–94; idem, "A Cauldron of Rebirth: Population and the Welsh Language in the Nineteenth Century," *Welsh History Review* 13 (1987): 418–37; idem, "Wales and the Atlantic Economy," 189. Gwyn A. Williams endorses the image of industrial Wales developing a culture that was "Welsh to the core" during the mid–nineteenth century in *The Merthyr Rising* (London: Croom Helm, 1978).

13. Dudley Baines, *Migration in a Mature Economy: Emigration and Internal Migration in England and Wales, 1861–1900* (Cambridge: Cambridge University Press, 1985), 18, 38–42, 221–26.

did not significantly restrain emigration. Between 1861 and 1900 "more than 100,000 natives of the rural Welsh counties went overseas (net of returns) or the equivalent of more than 12 percent of the young adult population." Nor did Welsh internal migration exclusively focus on South Wales. Baines calculated that industrial South Wales attracted only one-third of rural Welsh migrants between 1851 and 1911. Sixty percent of rural Welsh people who left their homes migrated into England or moved overseas. "Welsh migration was not distinctive," Baines concluded, "but [was] integrated into the main pattern of English migration. This means that the rate and pattern of Welsh migration provide no evidence for the existence of the so-called 'Welsh economy.'"[14]

Where Thomas in essence saw "little hordes" of Welsh emigrants, Baines found "vast emigrations." Charlotte Erickson and William Van Vugt have used ships' registers from American ports to determine what sort of Welsh people were emigrating to the States and why they left when they did.[15] Like many other immigration historians, Erickson and Van Vugt categorized emigrants at the most general level as either rural-agricultural or urban-industrial. These categories are often associated with certain social characteristics: rural agriculturalists moved as family groups, settled in rural areas, nurtured traditionalist values, and avoided involvement in industry except when factory wages could help them buy land; urban industrial workers usually migrated as individual men and women or young couples, they settled in American cities, were less conservative than their rural counterparts, and they provided the cheap labor that made rapid industrialization possible during the nineteenth century.[16] Erickson's and Van Vugt's midcentury studies show that English, Scottish, and Welsh emigrants were all making the transition from rural to

14. Ibid., 271, 278.

15. Charlotte Erickson, "Emigration from the British Isles to the U.S.A. in 1831," *Population Studies* 35 (1981): 175–97; idem, "Who Were the English and Scottish Emigrants in the 1880s?" in *Population and Social Change*, ed. D. V. Glass and R. Revelle (London: Edward Arnold, 1972), 347–81; William Van Vugt, "Welsh Emigration to the U.S.A. during the Mid-Nineteenth Century," *Welsh History Review* 15 (1991): 545–61; idem, "Running from Ruin? The Emigration of British Farmers to the U.S.A. in the Wake of the Repeal of the Corn Laws," *Economic History Review*, 2d ser., vol. 41 (1988): 411–28.

16. Bernard Bailyn refines the two types as "metropolitan" emigrants (mainly young men) and "provincial" emigrants (families, many of them farmers, with children) in *Voyagers to the West*, 98–203. The categories are also clearly reflected in immigration historiography's division into rural and urban studies.

urban-industrial migration between 1831 and 1851. Erickson found that half of all British emigrants in 1831 were skilled industrial workers but that most emigrants at that time, regardless of occupation, went overseas in family groups. By 1851, according to Van Vugt, only about one-quarter of British male adult emigrants were farmers or agricultural laborers and the proportion was even lower among the Welsh. He concluded that Welsh emigration was "primarily industrial by 1851," consisting mainly of young, single, rootless men. He also found that Welsh farmers showed "remarkable reluctance to emigrate."[17]

The timing of the transition from rural to urban, agricultural to industrial emigration is an important index of economic change within the sending country. An early phase of heavy agricultural emigration signals that capitalist economic relations had penetrated the countryside, typically through the enclosure of common lands, commercialization of agriculture, and the decline of cottage industry, all of which had the effect of displacing rural people from their customary occupations and places of residence, thus precipitating urban migration and a general shift out of rural employment into urban-industrial employment. Growing numbers of industrial emigrants indicate the onset of a second phase of response to industrial development in the sending country, particularly factory workers' distress during periodic economic contractions that were characteristic of industrial capitalism.[18] This model fits England particularly well; it was, after all, the world's leading industrializing nation throughout the nineteenth century. But how well does it explain events in Wales?

The statistical studies I have summarized here do not fully answer this question. One aspect of the relationship between industrialization, internal migration, and overseas emigration that particularly vexed Dudley Baines was the lack of knowledge about the geography of emigrant origins. He believed that the local context or series of contexts in which emigrants lived must

17. Erickson, "Emigration from the British Isles," 188 and passim; Van Vugt, "Running from Ruin?" 415–16; and "Welsh Emigration to the U.S.A.," 560, 550, and passim.

18. The seminal article is Robert Brenner, "Agrarian Class Structure and Economic Development in Pre-Industrial Europe," reprinted in *The Brenner Debate: Agrarian Class Structure and Economic Development in Pre-Industrial Europe*, ed. T. H. Aston and C. H. E. Philpin (1985; reprint, Cambridge: Cambridge University Press, 1990), 10–63. See also John Bodnar, *The Transplanted: A History of Immigrants in Urban America* (Bloomington: Indiana University Press, 1985), chap. 1.

have influenced their decisions. Studies of other European emigrants have repeatedly shown that local conditions could prompt or retard emigration and that local ties often strongly influenced the choice of destination, yet very little is known about the local origins, stages of intermediate movement, or destinations of Welsh emigrants.[19] Baines also rightly pointed out that neither his own study nor Thomas's work fully explained the relationship between internal migration and emigration. Did migration to cities or industrial South Wales make Welsh people more likely to emigrate, as such moves predisposed some other rural Europeans to emigration? Was Thomas correct in positing that South Wales industry prevented mass emigration from the Welsh countryside by retaining great numbers of rural people who otherwise would have moved overseas? Lastly, Thomas's emphasis on relative economic advantage as the key factor in emigrants' decisions scarcely considered the possible influence of cultural factors.[20]

Welsh immigrants in the United States themselves created a source that provides more detailed answers to these questions than do official British records. In thousands of obituaries printed in Welsh American religious magazines, immigrants recorded the life journeys of their loved ones and friends. In addition to revealing the geography and chronology of early nineteenth-century Welsh emigration, these obituaries suggest that long-term economic cycles were less influential than local circumstances in prompting and sustaining Welsh emigration up to 1850. The obituaries also show that the transition from rural to industrial emigration was far from complete at midcentury and that the Welsh may have had more in common with rural emigrants from continental Europe than with emigrants from their closest neighbor, England.

By the late 1830s, enough Welsh immigrants had settled in the United States to support a lively Welsh-language press based in

19. Baines, *Migration in a Mature Economy*, 42, 89, 119–20, 142, 166–67. Van Vugt made the same observation in "British Emigration during the Early 1850s, with Special Reference to Emigration to the U.S.A." (Ph.D. diss., University of London, 1985), 269. Frank Thistlethwaite first urged immigration historians to examine the regional origins of emigrants in "Migration from Europe Overseas in the Nineteenth and Twentieth Centuries," an essay delivered to the Eleventh International Conference of Historical Sciences, Stockholm, 1960, most recently reprinted in *A Century of European Migrations, 1830–1930*, ed. Rudolph J. Vecoli and Suzanne M. Sinke (Urbana: University of Illinois Press, 1991), 17–49.

20. Bodnar, *The Transplanted*, 3.

Fig. 1.1 Title page of *Y Cyfaill*. Each issue of *Y Cyfaill o'r Hen Wlad* (The Friend from the Old County) greeted readers with images that symbolized their journey to the United States. This engraving from 1847 shows a newly arrived Welshman being helped ashore by one friend while two others (one with the tools of his miner's trade) read the latest news. A man and woman converse under an arbor to the right, seated on a traditional Welsh settle with elegant French doors behind. A fine sailing vessel is moored on placid seas in the distance. Over all the American eagle spreads its protective wings, radiating optimism and strength. The combined effect is tremendously reassuring: come to America, the images say, where you can find work among friends and a high standard of living. (By permission of the National Library of Wales)

New York City and Utica, New York. As in Wales, Nonconformist religious denominations took the lead in publishing monthly periodicals, beginning with the Calvinistic Methodists' *Y Cyfaill o'r Hen Wlad* (The Friend from the Old Country) in 1838 (see fig 1.1). The Welsh Congregationalists followed with *Y Cenhadwr Americanaidd* (The American Missionary) in 1840. Two short-lived Baptist monthlies appeared during the next decade, called *Seren Orllewinol* (The Western Star) and *Y Beread* (probably a reference to the biblical people of Berea). In addition to offering spiritual guidance through sermons and moral essays, these nationally circulated magazines reported on job opportunities at iron works and coal mines, the nature and price of farmland, and the nature of religious provision in new settlements.

Every issue also included notices of births, marriages, and deaths sent in from Welsh communities across the United States.

The level of detail in the obituaries varies from just the name of the deceased to detailed life histories that often convey personality as well as crucial facts such as occupation and age upon emigration. The more complete obituaries are unparalleled sources of geographical information about the emigration and settlement of ordinary Welsh men and women. About half of the several thousand obituaries I read for this study specified individuals' home parishes and farm names in Wales and the county or neighborhood where they settled in the United States, making it possible to plot their origins and destinations quite precisely. A smaller number of obituaries also named one or more places where an individual had stopped en route, providing a glimpse of his or her movements before and after leaving Wales.

I gathered all of the geographical and biographical information contained in obituaries that were published in the four journals mentioned above and entered it into a database of individual immigrants. I limited collection to the years 1838 through 1853 for the sake of manageability and because after 1853 the obituaries in *Y Cyfaill* and *Y Cenhadwr* increasingly show a bias in favor of socially prominent adults, conspicuously slighting less wealthy and younger immigrants. The resulting database includes every individual whose obituary named at least one place in both Wales (specified to at least the level of the county) and the United States (specified to at least the level of a state or port of entry). Purged of a small number of duplicate and dubious entries, the survey yielded 1,772 individuals whose trans-Atlantic migration can be traced between at least two locations. The earliest emigrant in the data set left Wales in 1791, several more in 1795. Thus the data span a period of over sixty years, covering two generations of emigration activity.

The obituaries have their flaws as a source of information. Like any source based on recollection, they may contain factual errors, although the dates of landmark events such as emigration were probably deeply engraved in family memory. (Most of the dates that I have been able to cross-check to other sources have proved accurate to within a year.) The possible underrepresentation of certain groups is the obituaries' most significant bias. Because each journal reported mainly on members of its own denomination, the sporadic publication of Baptist journals during the period under study may result in the underrepresentation of Welsh

Baptists in the migrating population. Since the Baptists were a leading denomination in industrial districts, this may mean that the data do not fully represent immigrants from industrial areas of South Wales.[21] The obituaries mention few Welsh Anglicans and Wesleyan Methodists, and they include only a handful of the Welsh Mormons out of the many hundreds who emigrated to Utah with the Welsh missionary Captain Dan Jones in 1849 and 1853. Their small numbers generally reflect their proportion within the Welsh immigrant population and their peripheral contact with the main settlements. Anglican and Wesleyan Methodist churches accounted for less than 10 percent of all Welsh American congregations at midcentury. Most Welsh Mormons tarried briefly in "Gentile" Welsh settlements or bypassed them entirely by landing in New Orleans and traveling directly to Utah.[22]

The obituaries' great advantage lies in the kinds and amount of detail they contain which other sources omit, most importantly information about emigrants' geographical origins, their routes of travel, and their actual (as opposed to intended) destinations. While cross-sectional studies based on passenger lists and national censuses have revealed a great deal about the magnitude, demography, and occupational structure of British emigration, they give a coarse, generalized impression of its geography and therefore of the contexts within which emigrants made their decisions to leave. Welsh immigrant obituaries take us much closer to understanding those contexts.

Origins of Welsh Emigrants

Emigration from northwestern Europe was typically a localized phenomenon throughout the nineteenth century. As a growing number of detailed case studies have shown, the intensity of emigration varied greatly from place to place, largely because of chain migration's characteristic focus on a few sending areas and

21. Willigan and Lynch, *Historical Demography*, 109–21; T. M. Bassett, *The Welsh Baptists* (Swansea: Ilston House, 1977), 210–11.

22. Edward Jones, *Y Teithiwr Americanaidd: Neu Gyfarwyddyd i Symudwyr o Gymru i'r America* (The American Traveler: Or Advice to Emigrants from Wales to America) (Aberystwyth: E. Williams, 1837); Rev. Benjamin W. Chidlaw, *The American*, trans. Rev. Gwilym Williams (Bala: County Press, 1978; originally published in Llanrwst by John Jones, 1840); Kate B. Carter, comp., *The Welsh in Utah* (N.p.: Daughters of Utah Pioneers, Central Company, Lessons for October 1949); Ronald D. Dennis, *The Call of Zion: The Story of the First Welsh Mormon Emigration* (Provo, Utah: Brigham Young University Press, 1987).

their associated receiving communities.[23] The obituaries show the same kind of localized emigration from Wales. They also reveal differing chronologies of departure. Each of four main emigration regions in Wales had a distinctive time signature. Only one of them corresponded closely to the tempo of major swings in the national economy.

Map 1.2 plots the first known residence of each migrant whose obituary specified place of origin to at least the level of the parish, namely 1,548 out of the total of 1,771 migrants. Four regions dominate the map: (1) Pen Llŷn, the tip of Carnarvonshire's Llŷn Peninsula; (2) the region between Bala and Llanbryn-mair; (3) central Cardiganshire; and (4) the iron district in north Glamorgan and Monmouthshire, including the town of Merthyr Tydfil. These four regions correspond to known centers of early nineteenth-century emigration. They also include the counties that registered the greatest numbers of emigrants during the first five months of 1841, when census takers made a rare attempt to tally the number of emigrants leaving Britain.[24]

Table 1.1 records the shift in distribution from first known residence to place of departure, reflecting the information about internal migration that the obituaries contain. Although only 237 of the obituaries mention moves prior to emigration, they clearly indicate two basic kinds of internal migration. Short-distance moves predominated in northwest Wales, particularly in Carnarvon, Merioneth, and Montgomeryshire. These relocations, which accounted for 60 percent of all pre-emigration moves in the obituaries, typically coincided with marriage, apprenticeship, or a period of employment as an agricultural laborer. A different pattern dominated internal migration in South Wales, for almost all moves by natives of Carmarthen, Brecon, Glamorgan, and Monmouthshire took them to industrial districts in Glamorgan and Monmouthshire. The iron works in Monmouthshire drew the greatest number of internal migrants. This pattern matches the evidence of internal migration in the 1851 British census, which

23. Bodnar, *The Transplanted*, 4; Jon Gjerde, "Chain Migrations from the West Coast of Norway," in *A Century of European Migrations, 1830–1930*, ed. Rudolph J. Vecoli and Suzanne M. Sinke (Urbana: University of Illinois Press, 1991), 159.

24. Williams, "Figures Relating to Emigration," 401–2. The best overviews of Welsh American settlement are Edward G. Hartmann, *Americans from Wales* (New York: Octagon Books, 1983); and Rowland Berthoff, "Welsh," in *Harvard Encyclopedia of American Ethnic Groups*, ed. Stephen Thernstrom (Cambridge: Harvard University Press, 1980), 1011–17.

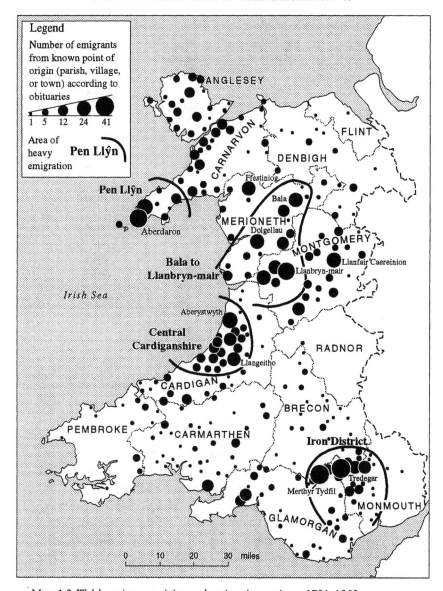

Map 1.2 Welsh emigrant origins and emigration regions, 1791–1853

shows that in 1851 over 60 percent of all migrants living in the iron district had been born in one of the adjoining Welsh counties (Glamorgan, Monmouth, Carmarthen, or Breconshire) and that only 5 percent came from North Wales.[25] The obituaries also include a handful of individuals who migrated long distances to England or the continent before traveling to the United States.

25. Census of Great Britain, 1851, *Population Tables*, pt. 2, vol. 2, "Birth-Places of the People," p. 892.

Table 1.1 Origins and places of departure of Welsh emigrants

Place of origin/ departure	First known residence	Place of departure	Net change
North Wales			
Anglesey	119	111	- 8
Carnarvon	264	260	- 4
Denbigh	70	77	+ 7
Flint	22	21	- 1
Merioneth	172	169	- 3
Montgomery	264	258	- 6
South Wales			
Cardigan	293	273	- 20
Carmarthen	115	89	- 26
Pembroke	35	30	- 5
Radnor	5	6	+ 1
Brecon	67	57	- 10
Glamorgan	182	197	+ 15
Monmouthshire	145	194	+ 50
England	18	24	+ 6
Continental countries	0	5	+ 5
Totals	1,771	1,771	

Source: Welsh immigrant obituaries.

Internal migration thus appears to have pooled future emigrants from South Wales in the industrial region of Glamorgan and Monmouthshire while scarcely altering the overall distribution of those who left from the northwest. The core emigration regions remain the same when internal migration is taken into account. The obituary data thus confirm Brinley Thomas's observation that the industrial district was a magnet for internal migration from counties in South Wales as early as the 1830s, while qualifying his overarching conclusion that the rise of Welsh industry prevented heavy emigration from Wales. The evidence here suggests that the three main regions of rural emigration—namely the Llŷn Peninsula, the region between Bala and Llanbryn-mair, and central Cardiganshire—were virtually untouched by migration to the iron district up to 1850 but that they may have lost significant numbers of people to emigration.

The three northwestern emigration regions shared a number of characteristics. They were among the least economically developed regions of Wales, the slowest to industrialize, their economies most firmly anchored in traditional agriculture. They were strongholds of Welsh Nonconformist religion during the eighteenth and nineteenth centuries as well as the heartland of the

Welsh language. These regions were also insulated from contact with England by barriers of mountains and moorlands and by infamously poor roads. At the same time, they were close to the sea and two of them (Pen Llŷn and central Cardiganshire) had long histories of small-scale maritime trade.[26]

Despite their common culture and material basis, each of the rural emigration regions had a distinctive historical geography that reflected the influence of local factors (see fig 1.2). In the case of Pen Llŷn, the coincidence of emigration with enclosures points to a local crisis over access to resources that were necessary for subsistence. The Llŷn peninsula ends in an exposed headland of heathy moors and scree-covered hillsides. In the early nineteenth century it was populated mainly by cottagers who supplemented the meager produce of their rented land with fishing, coastal trading, and the fuel and grazing for livestock that were available on extensive common lands.[27] People in the fishing village of Aberdaron and the surrounding countryside faced a serious threat to their traditional way of life and indeed their survival when landlords succeeded in winning a series of Parliamentary enclosure acts on Pen Llŷn between 1802 and 1812, engrossing a total of 22,000 acres. Under the act to enclose Aberdaron common, for example, the expenses of enclosure were to be paid "out of the sale of portions of the common lands" and the act prohibited the grazing of sheep on all enclosed lands for seven years. Only 300 of the 6,000 acres to be enclosed were allotted as turbary to provide peat as fuel for local inhabitants. It is likely that the early surge of emigration from Pen Llŷn was prompted by the threat of these enclosures.[28] The obituaries

26. Dodd, *Industrial Revolution*; Gerald Morgan, "Adeiladu Llongau yng Ngogledd Ceredigion/North Cardiganshire Shipbuilding 1700–1880," Occasional Papers in Ceredigion History, no. 2 (Aberystwyth: University of Wales, 1992); J. Geraint Jenkins, *Maritime Heritage: The Ships and Seamen of Southern Ceredigion* (Llandysul: Gomer Press, 1982); Aled Eames, *Ships and Seamen of Anglesey, 1558–1918*, Modern Maritime Classics reprint no. 4 (1973; reprint London: National Maritime Museum, 1981).

27. T. Jones Hughes, "The Social Geography of a Small Region in the Llŷn Peninsula," in *Rural Welsh Communities*, ed. Elwyn Davies and Alwyn D. Rees (Cardiff: University of Wales Press, 1960), 121–84.

28. John Chapman, *A Guide to Parliamentary Enclosures* (Cardiff: University of Wales Press, 1992); Ivor Bowen, *The Great Enclosures of Common Lands in Wales* (London: Chiswich Press, 1914), 19–20. The obituaries include a total of thirty-eight emigrants from the districts affected by the enclosures at Rhoshirwaun, Llanbedrog, and Aberdaron. This compares with just two emigrants from Nefyn,

record the onset of emigration from Pen Llŷn in 1795 and the peak of departures in 1818, earlier than any of the other emigration regions. With as many as seven per thousand leaving Pen Llŷn annually around the turn of the century, the magnitude of departures may have matched the heaviest periods of emigration from Sweden, Germany, and other parts of northwestern Europe later in the century, as well as rates during the peak of emigration from industrial South Wales.[29] It is also possible that emigration itself cleared the way for enclosures by removing discontented residents from the region.

In the hilly region between the village of Bala, Merionethshire, and the Montgomeryshire parish of Llanbryn-mair, emigration also began in 1795 but it recurred in more regular cycles over a longer period of time. Here the driving forces appear to have been a combination of an exceptionally political view of emigration, the influence of local leaders who espoused that view, and the decline of the region's cottage textile industry. Emigration had a venerable history in these parts dating from the late seventeenth century, when Quakers who had suffered some degree of religious persecution in Merionethshire decided to join William Penn's colony in America. They and other dissenters from Radnor and Pembrokeshire originally hoped to establish an independent "Welsh tract" in Pennsylvania. One hundred years later, two young men from Llanbryn-mair named Ezekiel Hughes and Edward Bebb led a party of settlers to the settlement that Morgan John Rhys had founded in central Pennsylvania. Hughes and Bebb continued on to southeastern Ohio and established the first Welsh settlement west of Pittsburgh, near the new town of Cincinnati. The name of their settlement, Paddy's Run, soon became familiar in Llanbryn-mair, as dozens of families from the region emigrated to the fertile Miami Valley.[30]

---

where a negligent commissioner failed to implement enclosure until at least 1833; see Dodd, *Industrial Revolution*, 68–69.

29. Ostergren, *Community Transplanted*, 125, 130–32; Jon Gjerde, *From Peasants to Farmers: The Migration from Balestrand, Norway, to the Upper Middle West* (Cambridge: Cambridge University Press, 1985), 3–4; Williams, *Beulah Land*, 129.

30. Dodd, *Early Welsh Emigration*; Williams, *Beulah Land*; Rev. Benjamin W. Chidlaw, "The Welsh Pioneers in the Miami Valley," *Cambrian* (1884): 248–51; Clare Taylor, "Paddy's Run: A Welsh Community in Ohio," *Welsh History Review* 11 (1983): 302–16. W. Ambrose Bebb fictionalized the saga of the 1795 emigration from Llanbryn-mair in *Dial y Tir* (The Land's Revenge) (Llandybïe: Llyfrau'r Dryw, 1945).

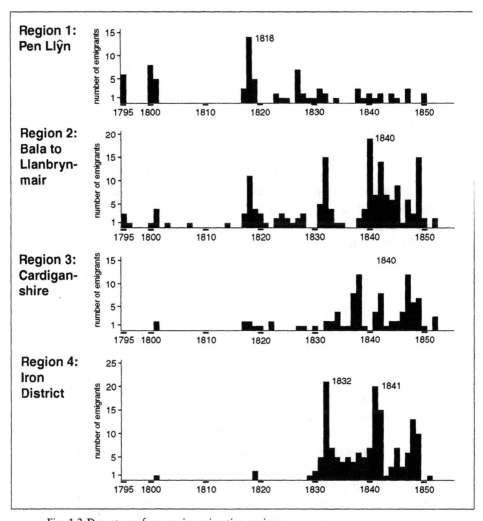

Fig. 1.2 Departures from main emigration regions

The notion that emigration could somehow preserve Welsh culture and achieve political independence for the Welsh can be traced back to the writing of William Jones (1726–1795) of Llangadfan, a village near Llanbryn-mair. His dream of establishing an independent Welsh homeland was an important influence upon the Bebb and Hughes party in 1794–1795.[31] The idea crystalized into a public campaign from the late 1840s through the U.S. Civil War. The movement's chief spokesman, Michael D.

31. Geraint H. Jenkins, "'A Rank Republican [and] a Leveller': William Jones, Llangadfan," *Welsh History Review* 17, nos. 3 (1995): 365–86; National Library of Wales ms. 13221E.

Jones (a distant cousin of Ezekiel Hughes and a Congregational minister), argued to audiences in Wales and the United States that only by establishing a Welsh *Gwladfa*, or homeland, on some overseas frontier would Welsh culture be safe from foreign (i.e., English) influence. After abandoning early plans to organize settlements in Ohio and Wisconsin, he decided that the remote shores of Patagonia would best serve the cause. In 1865 the first boatload of Welsh farmers, laborers, and industrial workers set off on what would become the most dramatic episode in Welsh emigration history, for the colony nearly perished in the Patagonian desert and struggled for years to establish viable farms.[32] Samuel Roberts, another Congregational minister from Llanbrynmair, hatched another utopian scheme to settle a Welsh colony in the backwoods of Tennessee on the eve of the Civil War, but through mismanagement of the land transactions involved and his failure to attract antislavery Welshmen and women to the area, the settlement never got off the ground. Roberts also fueled the discontent of Montgomeryshire tenant farmers by writing inflammatory tracts that urged them to emigrate rather than improve their land only to the profit of avaricious landlords.[33]

The man who most directly influenced emigration from the Bala/Llanbryn-mair region, however, was less of an ideologue than Michael D. Jones or Samuel Roberts, although he also had very definite ideas about the purpose of emigration. Benjamin W. Chidlaw emigrated from Bala with his parents in 1810 and became a bilingual preacher in Ohio. In 1835 and 1839 he returned on preaching tours to North Wales, where he polished his Welsh while urging rural folk to seek better opportunities in the American west. He published his advice in 1840 in a handbook for Welsh emigrants titled *Yr American* (The American).

32. Michael D. Jones, his supporters, and his opponents carried on a lively, sometimes vicious debate about the merits and viability of the *Gwladfa* in the national Welsh American newspaper *Y Drych* (The Mirror). See, for example, Jones's front-page appeal in *Y Drych* 3, no. 20 (16 May 1857): 153. On the history of the *Gwladfa*, see Glyn Williams, *The Desert and the Dream: A Study of Welsh Colonization in Chubut 1865–1915* (Cardiff: University of Wales Press, 1975); and idem, *The Welsh in Patagonia: The State and Ethnic Community* (Cardiff: University of Wales Press, 1991).

33. Wilbur S. Shepperson, *Samuel Roberts: A Welsh Colonizer in Civil War Tennessee* (Knoxville: University of Tennessee Press, 1961); Clare Taylor, *Samuel Roberts and His Circle: Migration from Llanbrynmair, Montgomeryshire, to America, 1790–1890* (Aberystwyth: Privately published, 1974); Samuel Roberts, "Ffarmwr Careful," in *Gweithiau Samuel Roberts* (The Works of Samuel Roberts) (Dolgellau: Evan Jones, 1856).

Chidlaw's greatest impact came rather unexpectedly during a chapel service he led in Llanuwchllyn, a village on the shores of Bala Lake, one crisp autumn evening in 1839. The congregation had only recently mended a deep rift among its members. They came to Chidlaw's worship service in a state of heightened emotion, eager to meet the American preacher and to renew their faith as a united congregation. Prayers, confessions, and cries of *haleliwia* carried on late into the night, and the worshipers persuaded the amazed Chidlaw to continue the meeting early the next morning. It was the young preacher's first experience of a genuine revival. His message of salvation had two meanings in that highly charged atmosphere—salvation through repentance of sin, and hope for a better life in the new world. A number of local people and others from as·far away as Cardiganshire accompanied Chidlaw when he returned to the United States at the conclusion of his tour. He noted in his memoirs fifty years later that many other people who had been present at the Llanuwchllyn revival "had emigrated to distant parts of the world."[34]

The decline in cottage textile production was a contributing factor in the prolonged cycles of emigration from Montgomery and southern Merionethshire. Bala was the leading center for the knit stocking trade in Wales, while Llanbryn-mair was one of the leading parishes in Montgomeryshire's rural weaving industry, with eight small-scale woolen mills and 500 outworkers circa 1840. Competition from the massive and far more efficient textile mills in Lancashire forced most of the region's spinners, weavers, and small fulling mills out of business by about 1860 and undercut knitters' profits as well. Although the obituaries identify only one weaver among the emigrants from this region, its peak of emigration in the 1840s may reflect the impact of lost textile employment, which was a major spur to emigration from the Dutch lowlands and other centers of cottage textile production.[35]

The third rural emigration region, central Cardiganshire, showed yet another pattern of departures. Although a few fami-

34. Rev. Benjamin W. Chidlaw, *The Story of My Life* (Privately published by the author, 1890), 100–110; obituary of John Lloyd, *Y Cyfaill* (June 1840): 183; obituary of Richard Pugh, *Y Cenhadwr* (October 1850): 320.

35. John Davies, *A History of Wales* (London: Allen Lane/Penguin, 1993), 320–23; Dodd, *Industrial Revolution*, 249–80; Wilbur S. Shepperson, *British Emigration to North America: Projects and Opinions in the Early Victorian Period* (Oxford: Blackwell, 1957), 84; Yda Saueressig-Schreuder, "Dutch Catholic Emigration in the Mid-Nineteenth Century: Noord-Brabant, 1847–1871," *Journal of Historical Geography* 11 (1985): 48–69.

lies left villages along the lower Teifi River around 1800, the core area north of the Aeron River did not become an active source of emigration until 1818 and it did not peak until 1840. Neither enclosure, ideology, nor declining rural industry explain the slow but steady development of an emigration tradition in Cardiganshire. Tenant farmers and smallholders here violently—and successfully—resisted enclosure early in the century, and the region's conservative Calvinistic Methodist preachers were more likely to have argued against emigration than for it. Central Cardiganshire's gradually increasing involvement in emigration illustrates the classic development of chain migration in an isolated region. Chapters 2 and 3 will explore in depth the role that personal contacts and local circumstances played in emigration from this part of Welsh Wales.

The fourth emigration region, the iron district of southeast Wales, was a strikingly different place with an economy very different from that of the rural northwest. Beginning in the 1760s, English capitalists came to the region to exploit its wealth of natural resources for making iron, including good-quality ore, convenient limestone outcrops, rich veins of coal, and plentiful water power, all in close proximity to one another. The region rapidly developed into one of Britain's leading industrial districts, specializing during the early nineteenth century in the production of pig iron and iron manufactures. Most men and many of the women in this region worked at the furnaces, rolling mills, and collieries that flourished along the upland valleys.

The iron district is the only emigration region where the chronology of departures clearly followed swings in Welsh and American industry, which were not always synchronized with one another in the first half of the century. The sudden onset of emigration from this region in 1830 coincided with acute depression and labor unrest in the Welsh iron industry, as did the surge of departures in 1832 and 1841. At the same time that industrial workers were facing unemployment and falling wages in South Wales, new iron and coal works in the United States were actively seeking skilled workers. In 1830, the Delaware and Hudson Railroad recruited seventy Welshmen to introduce sophisticated mining techniques at Carbondale in northeastern Pennsylvania. By 1833 Carbondale had enough Welsh residents to support three Welsh churches. Welsh iron workers also found work quickly at Pittsburgh's rolling mills and forges, one of which, the Kensington mill, was dubbed "little Dowlais" after one of the

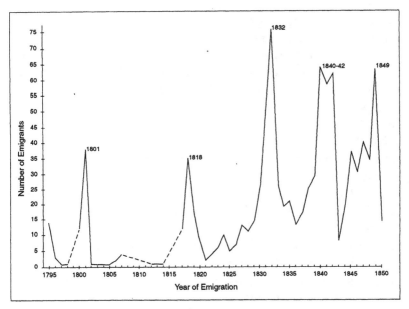

Fig. 1.3 Aggregate chronology of emigration

leading iron works in Merthyr Tydfil, Glamorganshire. Where Welsh foremen went, skilled Welsh work crews followed, creating flows of emigrants out of the iron works and mines in South Wales to new industrial settlements in eastern Pennsylvania, northwestern Maryland, industrial sites around Pittsburgh, and down the developing industrial corridor along the Ohio River.[36]

I have argued up to this point that local circumstances best explain the timing of emigration from particular Welsh regions. Yet if all the data on emigrant departures are combined, as shown in figure 1.3, it appears that Welsh emigration did indeed follow national economic trends, as Brinley Thomas claimed for the second half of the century. The peaks of departures for Wales as a whole correspond to economic depressions and recoveries as surely as an EKG records a patient's heartbeat. Between 1790 and 1802 there were periodic acute shortages of grain due to crop failures and inadequate distribution policies by the government. The Napoleonic Wars (1802–1814) drove up agricultural prices and gave a tremendous boost to the domestic iron industry, including the furnaces and forges in South Wales. After the wars,

36. Philip Riden, "Iron and Steel," in *Atlas of Industrializing Britain, 1780–1914*, ed. John Langton and R. J. Morris (London: Methuen, 1986), 129, map 15.3; letter from Emrys Emrys to the editor, *Seren Gomer* (1832): 238; David Williams, *Cymru ac America/Wales and America* (Cardiff: University of Wales Press, 1975), 81–83.

the sudden oversupply of labor as soldiers returned home, combined with wretched weather (1816 was called "the year without a summer"), made the immediate postwar period miserable for farmers and industrial workers in Wales and England. The iron depression registers clearly in the sudden increase in departures from Wales in the 1830s, as do the crop failures of 1839 and 1841.[37]

Which is the correct interpretation, that Welsh emigration followed national economic swings or that it was prompted by localized circumstances? As ever, the scale of analysis influences the results of that analysis. What the obituary evidence makes clear is that both scales of analysis should be employed wherever possible, because national trends can cloak regional factors that may have weighed heavily in emigrants' decisions. More importantly, the different historical geographies of emigration regions suggest that before 1850, rural economies in Wales were poorly integrated with the industrial economy of South Wales and the larger English economy. Finally, the regional figures show that particular rural areas sustained significant losses of population in the first half of the nineteenth century. If Wales as a whole did not lose a large proportion of its population to emigration during that period, emigration was significant from particular rural localities, perhaps even to the point of seriously weakening local society in places such as Llanbryn-mair.

Why did the Welsh leave these places and not others? Geography again provides some answers. According to the obituaries, the areas that lost few emigrants included high moorlands and mountainous districts with sparse and scattered populations— Snowdonia in the north, the Cambrian Mountains to the east, the Black Mountains and Prescelly range to the south. Areas with little evidence of emigration also include some of the most densely populated parts of Wales, regions where commercialized agriculture, industry, and urban development were rapidly changing the economic landscape and creating appealing new destinations for

37. Davies, *History of Wales*, 332–33; David Williams, *A History of Modern Wales* (1950; reprint, London: John Murray, 1969), 197–200; Arthur H. John, *The Industrial Development of South Wales, 1750–1850* (Cardiff: University of Wales Press, 1950), 32–36; Trefor Boyns, Dennis Thomas, and Colin Barber, "The Iron, Steel, and Tinplate Industries, 1750–1914," in *Glamorgan County History*, vol. 5, *Industrial Glamorgan*, ed. Arthur H. John and Glanmor Williams (Cardiff: Glamorgan County History Trust, 1980), 108; David Howell, *Land and People in Nineteenth-Century Wales* (London: Routledge & Kegan Paul, 1978), 5–6.

internal migration. For example, few emigrants are recorded from the industrial districts of Denbigh and Flintshire, the agricultural lowlands of the Clwyd Valley and the Vale of Glamorgan, or port towns along the southern coast. In addition to offering a greater range of employments than the rural northwest, these regions were among the most anglicized parts of Wales.[38] Of course, it is possible that many people from these areas did emigrate to the United States. Dudley Baines estimated that thousands of natives of Radnor, Brecon, and Pembrokeshire emigrated in the second half of the century. However many people did emigrate from anglicized, economically more developed parts of Wales, it appears that few of them settled in the Welsh-speaking communities that maintained communication through the Welsh American press. The obituaries best represent emigration from Welsh Wales to the communities that retained Welsh language and culture in the United States.

Destinations of Welsh Immigrants

Regional emigrations created a number of Welsh settlements with distinctive regional identities in the United States (see map 1.3 and table 1.2). Generally speaking, the older the settlement, the more likely it was to be dominated by immigrants from a particular part of Wales. For example, obituaries from the community in Oneida County, New York, show that it was predominantly a North Wales settlement with strong representation from Carnarvonshire. Settlers from Pen Llŷn first reached the area in 1795, three years after the first American pioneered a farmstead there. Remsen and Steuben townships soon became the core of a rapidly growing Welsh community. An American minister visiting the area in 1802 reckoned that "one-third of the inhabitants of Steuben are Welsh."[39] By the mid-1830s Utica was a center for Welsh American publishing and the first stop on many immi-

38. W. T. R. Pryce, "Migration and the Evolution of Culture Areas: Cultural and Linguistic Frontiers in Northeast Wales," *Transactions of the Institute of British Geographers* 65 (1975): 79–107; idem, "The Welsh Language 1750–1961," in *National Atlas of Wales*, ed. Harold C. Carter (Cardiff: University of Wales Press, 1988), plate 3.1.

39. Millard F. Roberts, *A Narrative History of Remsen, New York, Including Parts of Adjoining Townships of Steuben and Trenton, 1789–1898* (1914; reprint, Interlake, N.Y.: I-T Publishing, 1985), 14. David M. Ellis dates the first Welsh land purchases to 1804; "The Assimilation of the Welsh in Central New York," *Welsh History Review* 6 (1973): 426–27.

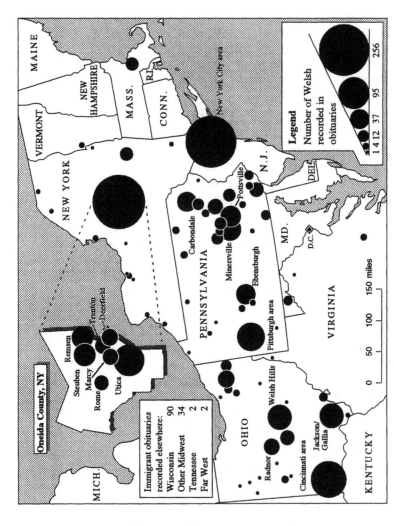

Map 1.3 Welsh-American immigrant destinations, 1791–1853

Table 1.2 Regional concentrations of Welsh immigrants by place of origin

	New York	Pennsylvania	Ohio	Elsewhere	Totals
		Place of death			
North Wales					
Anglesey	74 (62.2%)	15 (12.6%)	11 (9.2%)	19 (16.0%)	119
Carnarvon	180 (68.2%)	35 (13.3%)	12 (4.5%)	37 (14.0%)	264
Denbigh	24 (34.3%)	17 (24.3%)	18 (25.7%)	11 (15.7%)	70
Flint	11 (50.0%)	4 (18.2%)	—	7 (31.8%)	22
Merioneth	102 (59.3%)	15 (8.7%)	24 (14.0%)	31 (18.0%)	172
Montgomery	97 (36.7%)	46 (17.4%)	94 (35.6%)	27 (10.2%)	264
Totals	489 (53.7%)	132 (14.5%)	159 (17.5%)	131 (14.4%)	911
South Wales					
Brecon	11 (16.4%)	35 (52.2%)	15 (22.4%)	6 (9.0%)	67
Cardigan	59 (20.1%)	67 (22.9%)	140 (47.8%)	27 (9.2%)	293
Carmarthen	32 (27.8%)	48 (41.7%)	25 (21.7%)	10 (8.7%)	115
Glamorgan	48 (26.4%)	77 (42.3%)	26 (14.3%)	31 (17.0%)	182
Monmouth	10 (6.9%)	102 (70.3%)	17 (11.7%)	16 (11.0%)	145
Pembroke	10 (28.6%)	8 (22.9%)	11 (31.4%)	6 (17.1%)	35
Radnor	4 (80.0%)	—	1 (20.0%)	—	5
Totals	174 (26.2%)	337 (71.9%)	235 (59.6%)	96 (42.3%)	842
Outside Wales	6 (33.3%)	4 (22.2%)	4 (22.2%)	4 (22.2%)	18
Overall totals	669 (37.8%)	473 (26.7%)	398 (22.5%)	231 (13.0%)	1,771

Note: Sums greater or less than 100% due to rounding.

grants' journeys to settlements further west. The early Llanbryn-
mair settlements at Ebensburgh, Pennsylvania, and Paddy's Run,
Ohio, continued to attract immigrants from Montgomeryshire
throughout the first half of the century. Pittsburgh and Cincinnati
became popular destinations for immigrants from Mid Wales,
while so many of the Welsh in Jackson and Gallia counties,
Ohio, came from Cardiganshire (nearly 76 percent, according to
the obituaries) that the area became known as "little Cardiganshire" among the Welsh American community.[40]

Enduring regional connections were perhaps the single most
common characteristic of rural and urban European immigrant
settlements throughout the nineteenth century. Residential clusters of immigrants from the same county, parish, village, and
street were the geographic manifestation of chain migration, the

40. William Harvey Jones, "Welsh Settlements in Ohio," *Ohio Archaeological
and Historical Publications* 16 (1907): 194–227; Daniel Jenkins Williams, *The
Welsh of Columbus, Ohio: A Study in Adaptation and Assimilation* (Oshkosh,
Wis.: Privately published, 1913), 20–28; Alan Conway, ed. *The Welsh in
America: Letters from the Immigrants* (Minneapolis: University of Minnesota
Press, 1961), 65.

process by which communication back and forth across the
Atlantic guided emigrants to particular destinations in the United
States. The same process directed much of Welsh migration
within Britain, as migration traditions developed between North
Wales and Liverpool, Mid Wales and Shrewsbury, Cardiganshire
and London. The "friction of distance" per se may not have influenced emigrants' choice of routes across the Atlantic and the
American continent, but the principle of following the path of
least resistance—or least uncertainty—clearly did.[41]

Farming settlements that were established after 1840 in Wisconsin, Iowa, Minnesota, and states farther west tended to have
residents from a greater variety of regions, as smaller numbers of
immigrants coming directly from rural Wales mingled with immigrants who had already spent some time in the American
East.[42] Urban settlements also had more mixed Welsh immigrant
populations than did the older rural communities. The significance of the figures for urban settlement obtained from the obituaries is difficult to assess. For example, New York City had only
one Welsh chapel in 1851. Despite having what appears to have
been the largest concentration of Welsh immigrants in the country, New York in fact had a scattered Welsh population with little
cohesion or sense of ethnic identity in this period.[43] The large
numbers of obituaries from New York City, Pittsburgh, and
Cincinnati indicate less the actual proportion of their resident
Welsh immigrant population than the cities' importance as en-
trepôts for immigrants of all nationalities, as well as, perhaps,
their higher rates of immigrant mortality. For example, the Welsh
obituaries record the impact of shipboard diseases on immigrants
newly arrived in New York as well as a spate of deaths due to a
cholera epidemic in Cincinnati in 1849. The significance of these

41. Colin G. Pooley, "Welsh Migration to England in the Mid-Nineteenth
Century," *Journal of Historical Geography* 9 (1983): 287–306; D. B. Grigg, "E.
G. Ravenstein and the 'Laws of Migration,'" *Journal of Historical Geography* 3
(1977): 42–54.

42. Anne Kelly Knowles, "Welsh Settlement in Waukesha County, Wisconsin,
1840–1873" (M.S. thesis, University of Wisconsin-Madison, 1989), 21–24;
Phillips G. Davies, "The Growth and Assimilation of the Welsh Settlements in
Iowa," *Iowa State Journal of Research* 60 (1985): 107–28; Revs. Thomas E.
Hughes and David Edwards, and Messrs. Hugh G. Roberts and Thomas Hughes,
eds., *History of the Welsh in Minnesota, [and in] Foreston and Lime Springs,
Iowa* (Privately published, in Welsh and English, 1895).

43. R. D. Thomas, *America: neu Amrywiaeth o Nodiadau am yr Unol
Daleithiau,* translated as *America: or Miscellaneous Notes on the United States*
by Clare Thomas (1852; reprint, Aberystwyth: National Library of Wales, 1973).

cities to Welsh immigration needs further research.

There were intriguing clusters of immigrants from particular regions in several urban and industrial occupations. Anglesey milk sellers cropped up repeatedly in New York City, for example. Carnarvonshire slate miners appear to have gravitated to Peach Bottom (also known as West Bangor), Pennsylvania, and Glamorganshire iron workers to the Tredegar Iron Works in Richmond, Virginia, named after the original Tredegar works in Monmouthshire. Early emigrations to industrial locations in Pennsylvania established enduring links with the iron and coal districts of South Wales. These routes became virtual highways of immigrant traffic after the Civil War as Welshmen filled U.S. industry's need for skilled anthracite miners.[44] Despite high proportions of immigrants from Glamorgan and Monmouthshire in Pennsylvania, the state's industrial settlements had a more mixed population, according to region of origin, than did most rural settlements. This was partly because many of those who emigrated from Merthyr Tydfil, Tredegar, and other industrial towns before 1850 had been born and raised in various rural counties. It was also because iron works and coal mines on both sides of the Atlantic were stopping-off places for Welsh people whose ultimate destination was a farm or independent business in the rural United States, a point to which I shall return.

The tenacity of regional connections vexed some Welsh immigrant leaders. Richard Edwards complained of his countrymen in Oneida County:

> I am not against the Welsh living together in a Welsh settlement in this country and I am not against them keeping their own language either, but I am against them settling in mountainous districts where the land is covered with snow for five months of the year, when the fertile lands of the Mississippi are much cheaper and have a more pleasant climate.[45]

Benjamin Chidlaw was baffled by Cardiganshire farmers' preference for settling in the Appalachian foothills of southern Ohio when much better land was available in the Mississippi Valley. He tried to dissuade them in his guidebook, writing, "The Welsh tend to remain unfortunately in the old settlements, choosing high and rugged land; but having left their homes as well as the

---

44. William D. Jones, *Wales in America: Scranton and the Welsh, 1860–1920* (Cardiff: University of Wales Press, 1993), 13–18.

45. Conway, *Welsh in America*, 68.

religious facilities they once possessed, they might as well endeavor to secure a good place and productive land, since the district is certain to flourish and religious amenities will follow."[46]

But would they be the right kind of amenities? Like the Dutch, rural Welsh immigrants most fully recreated and preserved their traditional way of life in a limited number of fairly large, inward-looking communities.[47] Sustained access to affordable land was particularly important to the Welsh because they came in relatively small numbers even during peak periods of immigration. Whatever affinity the Welsh may have felt for rugged, hilly land, the more important factor was that Americans and wealthier European immigrants usually bought up the best land on the agricultural frontier, leaving islands of unclaimed or lightly developed inferior ground that were nevertheless no worse than what the Welsh had coped with in their native country. For example, Welsh immigrants to Jackson County, Ohio, were still able to buy government land for $1.25 per acre and improved farms for $7.50 or less per acre in 1850, over thirty years after the first Welsh families settled in the area.[48]

Chidlaw also failed to appreciate that good farmland might not be the sole desire of immigrants from rural Wales. One of the most interesting conclusions to emerge from the obituaries is that Welsh immigrants were interested in both agriculture and industry and that some moved quite freely between the two. This raises important questions about the individual and group characteristics of the Welsh in contrast to other Europeans of their day. Were the Welsh fundamentally different from other emigrants

46. Chidlaw, *Yr American* (Llanwrst: John Jones, 1840), trans. Rev. Gwilym Williams as *The American* (Bala: County Press, 1978), 42–43.

47. Robert P. Swierenga, "Dutch Immigration Patterns in the Nineteenth and Twentieth Centuries," in *The Dutch in America: Immigration, Settlement, and Cultural Change*, ed. Robert P. Swierenga (New Brunswick, N.J.: Rutgers University Press, 1985), 15–42; idem, "Local Patterns of Dutch Migration to the United States in the Mid–Nineteenth Century," in *A Century of European Migrations, 1830–1930*, ed. Rudolph J. Vecoli and Suzanne M. Sinke (Urbana: University of Illinois Press, 1991), 134–57. The exceptions tend to prove the rule. Dutch Catholics who settled in Green Bay, Wisconsin, rather than forming more isolated rural communities, more rapidly assimilated with other immigrant groups; Yda Saueressig-Schreuder, "Emigration, Settlement, and Assimilation of Dutch Catholic Immigrants in Wisconsin 1850–1905" (Ph.D. diss., University of Wisconsin–Madison, 1982).

48. Abstracts of title, Recorder of Deeds, Jackson County Courthouse, Jackson, Ohio; Ohio State Board of Equalization, *Proceedings of the State Board of Equalization*, 7 November 1859 (Columbus, Ohio: 1860), 205–7.

Table 1.3 Estimated age at emigration

Age	No. in sample with calcuable age (%)	Percentage in Welsh census, 1841
0–14	148 (14.6%)	36.8%
15–29	368 (36.3%)	26.8%
30–44	261 (25.8%)	17.1%
45–59	155 (15.3%)	10.8%
60+	81 (8.0%)	8.5%
Totals	1,013 (100.0%)	100.0%

Sources: Welsh immigrant obituaries; Census of Great Britain (1854).

Table 1.4 Estimated age in each period of emigration

Period of emigration	Estimated age at emigration				
	0–14	15–29	30–44	45–59	60+
1791–1819	8.5%	40.1%	36.6%	13.4%	1.4%
1820–1829	12.3	32.1	33.3	17.3	4.9
1830–1839	11.9	34.8	25.7	19.0	8.7
1840–1849	12.7	38.6	22.9	14.4	11.4
1850–1853	25.0	28.6	25.0	17.9	3.6
Overall average	12.2%	37.0%	26.6%	15.8%	8.4%

who traveled in separate rural and industrial channels to the United States? Or are our definitions of those channels too restrictive?

Group Characteristics and Individual Life-Paths

As I mentioned previously, one of the standard indicators used to gauge the character of a group of immigrants is their demography. It is possible to estimate age at emigration for 1,103 individuals in the database, accounting for 62 percent of the obituaries (see tables 1.3, 1.4).[49] Compared to their shares of the total Welsh population, children were greatly underrepresented among the immigrants throughout the period of study except for the last few years, while young adults were considerably overrepresented. This would normally be taken to indicate an industrial emigration. Yet people aged 30–59 were also overrepresented, and the elderly were present at nearly their proportion in the general population. Thus the overall structure of the emigrant

49. Where the obituary records the immigrant's age at death and date of emigration, I used those figures to calculate the age at emigration. Where the contents of the obituary clearly indicate the person's age category upon emigration, I entered the category. No uncertain ages were included.

population best matches the profile of a family migration. This interpretation gains support from the exceptional maturity of adult Welsh emigrants (those aged 15 or older). Adult males emigrated at an average age of 36.6 years and women at 36.7 years. The average age at emigration for those who died in industrial locations in the United States was older still—38.5 years for men and 39.1 years for women. As one point of comparison, the English and Scottish farmers whom Bernard Bailyn traced to New York and North Carolina on the eve of the American Revolution averaged 32.4 years in age when they emigrated, which Bailyn considered an "exceptionally high" age for rural immigrants. The sex ratio of 1.4 Welsh males to every female is also well within the standard range for overseas family migrations.[50]

The underrepresentation of young children in the obituaries is probably due to a bias inherent in the source. Children's deaths were generally less commonly reported to publications such as the Welsh denominational magazines than were deaths of adults. Supplemental biographical evidence further suggests that where rural Welsh settlements actually had few young children during the settlements' early years it was due to the advanced life-cycle stage of the immigrant families. For example, the families who founded the agricultural settlement in Waukesha County, Wisconsin, included more unmarried adult children and grandparents than did the households of other immigrant and American settlers.[51] This may indicate that young Welsh adults stayed with their parents in order to pool family income toward emigration and an initial purchase of land, and that many deferred marriage until the family was well established in the new country.

The final point we can draw from the obituaries' demographic information is that an emigrant's age did not necessarily predict whether he or she would first settle in a rural or an industrial location. Table 1.5 shows that middle-aged and elderly immigrants slightly favored rural areas, while young adults were somewhat more likely to settle initially in an industrial location. The trend is not sufficiently clear, however, to support the conclusion that there was a decisive shift toward a more industrial and youthful migration by 1850.

Occupational information would greatly help clarify the characteristics of the immigrants, but unfortunately only a small propor-

50. Bailyn, *Voyagers to the West*, 224; Ostergren, *Community Transplanted*, 124–26.

51. Knowles, "Welsh Settlement in Waukesha County," 62–65.

Table 1.5 Aggregate number of rural versus urban places of death, by age

Age	Rural (%)	Industrial and/or Urban (%)	Ocean or unknown (%)
0–14	72 (48.6%)	67 (45.3%)	9 (6.1%)
15–29	185 (50.3%)	170 (46.2%)	13 (3.5%)
30–44	137 (52.5%)	115 (44.1%)	9 (3.4%)
45–59	85 (54.8%)	65 (41.9%)	5 (3.3%)
60+	44 (54.3%)	6 (44.4%)	1 (1.2%)
Totals	523 (51.6%)	453 (44.7%)	37 (3.7%)

Notes: N = 1,011; totals 99.9% due to rounding.

tion of the obituaries mention the occupation of the deceased. This may again reflect biases inherent in the source, for the ministers and relatives who wrote detailed obituaries usually focused on the individual's final hours and his or her religious experiences rather than the secular events of their lives. Of the 271 individuals with known occupations, 101 were engaged in industrial work of some kind, compared to just 8 farmers (see table 1.6). The obituaries actually identified more ministers than farmers. Yet the absence of agricultural occupations from the obituaries does not mean that farmers and farm laborers did not emigrate during this period; quite the contrary. The distribution of origins and places of death from the obituaries clearly shows that Welsh people continued to leave rural Wales and to settle in rural America throughout the first half of the century. Community histories and the U.S. manuscript censuses of 1840 and 1850 reveal that most settlers in rural Welsh communities worked in agriculture, as one would expect. Occupational information may have been omitted from the obituaries of rural settlers because the Welsh saw no need to state the obvious. All of the immigrants identified as farmers were founders of agricultural settlements, such as Edward Bebb and Ezekiel Hughes, individuals who in Wales would have had the status of squires or gentlemen farmers.

The occupational figures do confirm that a transition was under way during the middle third of the century, as Van Vugt and Erickson suggested. Of those individuals with a known occupation and a known date of emigration, over 81 percent in skilled industrial trades and 92 percent of unskilled industrial workers emigrated after 1832. The argument for a sea change in the composition of Welsh emigration circa 1830 is also supported by the obituary evidence regarding county of departure (see table 1.7), which takes into account the effect of internal migration. As the data show, emigration from Glamorgan and Monmouthshire was

Table 1.6 Occupations listed in the obituaries

		Known date of emigration	
Occupation	Total number	Number (%) through 1829	Number (%) 1830–1853
Industrial, skilled	85	2 (3.8%)	51 (96.2%)
Industrial, unskilled	24	1 (7.7%)	12 (92.3%)
Nonindustrial craft	85	10 (20.4%)	39 (79.6%)
Service or retail	51	6 (23.1%)	20 (76.9%)
Professional (including clergy)	44	13 (36.1%)	23 (63.9%)
Agriculture	12	7 (70.0%)	3 (30.0%)
Miscellaneous	16	6 (66.7%)	3 (33.3%)
Totals	317	45 (23.0%)	151 (77.0%)

Table 1.7 Emigration from rural and industrial counties by date of departure

	Welsh counties		England and	
Date of departure	Rural[a]	Industrial[b]	the Continent	Totals
1791–1829	211 (89.8%)	22 (9.4%)	2 (0.8%)	235
1830–1839	217 (67.2%)	101 (31.3%)	5 (1.5%)	323
1840–1849	335 (74.6%)	103 (22.9%)	11 (2.4%)	449
1850–1853	27 (81.8%)	2 (6.1%)	4 (12.1%)	33
				1,040
All obituaries, including those without known date of departure:				
	1,353 (76.4%)	391 (22.1%)	27 (1.5%)	1,771

[a]All Welsh counties except Glamorgan and Monmouthshire.

[b]Glamorgan and Monmouthshire.

negligible before 1830, but thereafter contributed a very significant portion to the national total of emigrants. The question is, how many of them traveled strictly within an "industrial corridor," as William D. Jones has described the strongly channeled emigration from South Wales industries to the coalfields and iron towns of Pennsylvania in the second half of the century.

Attempting to answer this question takes us back once again to the obituaries' evidence of internal migration. It suggests that people who migrated to industrial places in Wales were more likely to emigrate to industrial destinations in the United States than those with no prior experience of industry. Of the ninety-six individuals who migrated to an industrial location in South Wales, thirty-two lived in at least one industrial place in the United States. Four went first to a rural location and thirteen ended their journeys in a rural place. Trans-Atlantic industrial connections of course make sense, since men who spent time in Welsh industry learned extremely valuable skills for which there was an eager market in American industry. Welsh coal miners who emigrated to Scranton, Pennsylvania, after the Civil War were always struck by how much it resembled the colliery towns in South Wales. They felt they were coming home.[52] The obituaries also show that people whose internal migration was limited to their native rural district were most likely to emigrate directly to an agricultural settlement in the United States. Here again, one cannot say on the basis of the obituaries alone whether local migration predisposed individuals or their families to emigrate.

Overseas connections between industrial districts and rural districts do not tell the whole story, however. Of the 352 obituaries that mention one or more moves within the United States, only 34 involve migration to an industrial location. Most of those industrial migrants were members of families whose wage earners shuttled between jobs in the coalfields of eastern Pennsylvania. The dominant direction of internal U.S. migration was toward agricultural areas. Among the Welsh immigrants known to migrate within the United States, over 90 percent moved from an industrial to a rural location or between rural settlements. As Alan Conway put it, employment in Welsh or American industry was often a "knight's move" toward the ultimate goal of owning land.[53]

A Typology of Emigrant Life-Paths

Detailed life-paths of individual immigrants give substance to the general patterns I have discussed thus far, particularly when supplemented by additional biographical information. The following typology of emigrant life-paths is drawn from representative cases in the obituaries, two of which I have been able to supplement from the biographical database of immigrants to Jackson and Gallia counties, Ohio, to which I will return in chapters 3 and 4. Figure 1.4 graphically depicts the four basic kinds of lifetime migration patterns that these biographical data sets reveal. The typology is not meant to represent all immigrants but to suggest the diverse personal geographies of immigrant experience.

Thomas J. Jones, Cooper, exemplifies type A, strictly rural migration. Jones was born on a small tenant farm near the village of Llangeitho in central Cardiganshire in 1810. His parents moved

---

52. Jones, *Wales in America*, 2.

53. Alan Conway, "Welsh Emigration to the United States," *Perspectives in American History* 7 (1973): 226.

Type A: Rural migration   Thomas J. Jones, Cooper

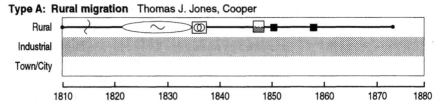

Type B: Industrial migration   Mary Evans

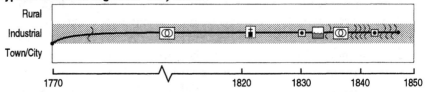

Type C: Mixed rural/industrial migration   John Lot Davies

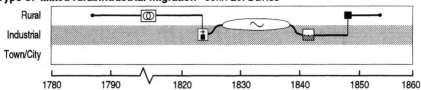

Type D: Itinerant migration   Rev. John T. Griffiths

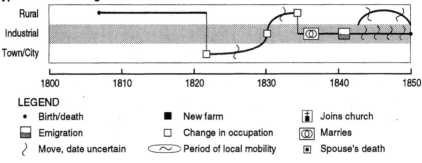

LEGEND

• Birth/death	■ New farm	Joins church
Emigration	□ Change in occupation	Marries
⟩ Move, date uncertain	～ Period of local mobility	Spouse's death

Fig. 1.4 Typical life-paths of Welsh immigrants

to a slightly larger tenancy during Thomas's childhood. He worked as an agricultural laborer and carpenter on neighboring farms until 1836, when he married Elizabeth Morgan, a local woman, and moved to her father's farm. Seven years later the couple finally obtained their own eight-acre tenancy on moorland above Llangeitho. In 1848 the family and a group of neighbors emigrated directly to the rural Welsh settlement in Jackson County, Ohio. There they stayed until 1856, when they made their final move to the prairie/forest frontier in Blue Earth County, Minnesota.

The life of Mary Evans illustrates type B, migration to strictly industrial locations. Mary was born in Swansea in 1770. She moved with her husband William Phillips to the iron district of Monmouthshire, where he worked at iron furnaces in Blaenafon, Pen-y-cae, and Nant-y-glo. After William died in 1830, Mary, who was then sixty years old, decided to join those of her children who had emigrated to the United States. She arrived in Carbondale, Pennsylvania, in 1832 but soon migrated to Pottsville, another coal mining town, where she married Thomas Evans. Although Mary and Thomas lived mainly in the Susquehanna Valley, she traveled frequently to visit her children elsewhere in Pennsylvania and in Maryland and southern Ohio. After moving to Coalport, Ohio, in about 1840 and losing her second husband there, Mary began her last journeys, traveling from the home of one child to another until her death in Pottsville in 1847.

The third and fourth types represent varying degrees of movement within and between rural, urban, and industrial locations. John Lot Davies exemplifies type C, mixed rural-industrial migration. Little is known of John's early life in the hamlet of Abermeurig, Cardiganshire, where he was born in 1787. By 1822 he, his wife Ann, and one child were living in a cottage just north of the Aeron River, within an hour's walk of Abermeurig. He may have migrated seasonally to the iron district; his obituary records that he was converted to Calvinistic Methodism in Merthyr Tydfil in 1823. In 1841 John, Ann, and their two teenage sons emigrated to Pittsburgh, where they stayed for seven years. The family migrated one last time in 1848 to Jackson County, Ohio, where John became a farmer and his eldest son became manager at a nearby charcoal iron furnace. John died in 1853, one year before his sons and other Cardiganshire immigrants organized their own charcoal iron furnace.

Itinerant migration, type D, includes the greatest number and variety of moves. Welsh ministers, represented here by John T. Griffiths, best exemplify this type, but it also applies to young men who tried various occupations before settling down, and to families whose breadwinners followed itinerant trades. Griffiths was born in the rural parish of Llansawel, Carmarthenshire, in

1808. At fourteen he moved to the market town of Carmarthen, where he lived with an uncle and worked as secretary in a notary's office. By 1829 he had taken up the post of schoolteacher in Ystradgynlais, an industrial village on the Glamorgan-Breconshire border. There he converted to Calvinistic Methodism and was inspired to preach. His career as an itinerant preacher began in 1833 in the rural hamlet of Ystradfellte. He then moved to Dowlais in the heart of the iron district, where he wed Susannah Morgans in 1836. They emigrated to Pennsylvania in 1841 and followed John's callings to a succession of Welsh industrial communities, including Pottsville and Danville. He also ministered briefly in Utica, New York, the rural hearth of Welsh immigrant settlement.

Because fewer than 20 percent of the obituaries include details on internal migration, they alone do not provide a sufficient basis upon which to determine whether one of these patterns was dominant at any given time or for any particular sending or receiving region. Nor do they give conclusive evidence about the importance of occupation as an influence over immigrants' movements, since location of origin or destination does not necessarily indicate occupation. By linking thè obituary data to other sources, however, it becomes possible to approach the level of detail achieved in studies of other European groups. Chapters 2 and 3 will explore in much greater detail the geographical patterns and individual life-paths of Cardiganshire migrants, particularly the immigrants who settled in Jackson/Gallia. At this point I will simply suggest that, even if the proportion of type C migrants was small, they may have been important as carriers of technological skills and urban sophistication whose influence may have outweighed their numbers.

Rethinking the Rural-Industrial Transition

The midpoint of the century does appear to have been a watershed in Welsh emigration history. Rural Welsh American communities from Ohio to Wisconsin experienced sharp declines in the number of new immigrant arrivals after 1850. At the same time, the volume of migration from the Welsh countryside to industrial South Wales increased markedly. The industrial valleys' sphere of influence also expanded beyond the proximate counties of Glamorgan, Monmouth, Brecon, and Carmarthenshire to encompass the whole of Wales in the second half of the nineteenth century. The expansion of the steel and coal industries in South Wales and, to a lesser degree, of the slate industry in Carnarvon and Merionethshire created a growing demand for labor that rural Welsh people were eager to fill. Native industries dampened the magnitude of emigration throughout the century, but there is little evidence that they diverted the flow of emigrants to the degree that Thomas suggests until after 1850. And as Dudley Baines has emphasized, migration to the southeast did not account for all internal Welsh migration.[54] There were also strong traditions of migration from Wales to England during the nineteenth century, as the next chapter will demonstrate.

The evidence presented here highlights the value of a life-path approach to migration history. Reconstructing emigrants' movements over their lifetimes facilitates detailed analysis of the local economic and cultural contexts in which they reached their decisions. The method also introduces a level of complexity into the analysis of migration patterns that raises intriguing questions, particularly in relation to rural emigrants' involvement with industrial capitalism. As Van Vugt hypothesized, the same man who boarded an emigrant ship as an industrial worker may have been raised in the countryside and eventually returned to an agricultural way of life in later years. The Welsh may have been more likely to move between occupational and residential categories than other ethnic groups because of their proximity to heavy industry in their native country. If the personal histories contained in Welsh immigrant obituaries portray a rural-industrial transition, however, it was a prolonged process with many variations on the theme.

The word "transition" itself, like "transformation" and other words commonly used to refer to major changes in social and economic relations, can tend to reinforce our proclivity to think of history as "a succession of stable states separated by revolutionary transitions" or, to borrow a phrase from evolutionary biology, as a punctuated equilibrium.[55] Yet as Fernand Braudel stressed in his explorations of the long history of capitalism, it

54. Baines, *Migration in a Mature Economy*, 277–78.

55. Göran Hoppe and John Langton, *Flows of Labour in the Early Phase of Capitalist Development: The Time-Geography of Longitudinal Migration Paths in Nineteenth-Century Sweden*, Historical Geography Research Series no. 29 (London: Institute of British Geographers, August 1992), 2; S. J. Gould and N. Eldredge, "Punctuated Equilibria: The Tempo and Mode of Evolution Reconsidered," *Palaeobiology* 3 (1977): 115–51.

becomes problematic to speak of a transition when the change in question does not clearly take place in a particular period. This study shows that Welsh immigration to the United States had a strong rural component through 1850. Dudley Baines thought that the transition to industrial migration was not complete until 1891, while Erickson and Van Vugt placed it between 1831 and 1851. Each of us looked at the same phenomenon through the lens of a different source. Our combined research shows that the rural-industrial transition continued to be an important feature of Welsh American migration throughout the nineteenth century.

Kathleen Neils Conzen recently proposed that immigration historians should rethink the metaphors they use to describe immigrants' adaptation to American society. Rather than the crucible or melting pot, the salad or smorgasbord, she suggested that we think of the process of adaptation as the valley of a braided river, "where there is a main channel, to be sure," but where the diversity of immigrant responses to new environments also created alongside the mainstream many "side channels that flow with it through time and space, moving in the same direction, constrained by the same bluffs on either side of the broad valley, borne along by the same deep currents and mingling their waters at floodtime."[56]

The image of braided streams is even more appropriate to the process of migration itself. As the obituaries show, not all Welsh immigrants traveled in strictly confined channels. Those who figuratively jumped the banks, experiencing various social and economic contexts, may have been important catalysts in immigrant society. Immigrants' movement between agriculture and industry warrants further study, particularly in the context of the early stages of capitalist development in rural areas. Studies of rural capitalist transformation have, until now, focused on the conflicting values of rural people rooted in place and the outsiders (capitalist farmers and industrialists) whose arrival constituted a kind of economic invasion.[57] In many places this scenario undoubtedly transpired. But in other places, particularly those with little evident conflict, the thrust for change may have come from

56. Kathleen Neils Conzen, "Mainstream and Side Channels: The Localization of Immigrant Cultures," *Journal of American Ethnic History* 11, no. 1 (1991): 16.

57. See, for example, Steven Hahn and Jonathan Prude, eds., *The Countryside in the Age of Capitalist Transformation: Essays in the Social History of Rural America* (Chapel Hill: University of North Carolina Press, 1985).

within rural society itself. Among early nineteenth-century communities, both in Europe and in the United States, the impact of those who moved back and forth between industrial and rural locations may explain aspects of rural change that are not explained by capitalists' efforts to improve agricultural productivity or to develop rural industry. These fainter trails—the life-paths of ordinary people who experienced the personal revolution of overseas migration—may lead us to a new appreciation of the historical geography of capitalist development.

Chapter Two

The Context of Choice: Internal Migration

The mental map of the world that each of us forms in his or her imagination naturally differs quite radically from physical reality. In our minds, places close to home fill the center of the map with rich detail and seem somehow larger than they are because we know them intimately, while distant places are disproportionately small or disappear entirely from the map unless we have some particular knowledge of them. The notion that people's mental maps are skewed according to their knowledge of the world is the spatial corollary of an idea that has long been applied to the study of migration, namely that the imperfections in people's awareness of economic opportunities significantly influence their choice of migration destinations.[1] Across rural Europe in the early nineteenth century, the information people possessed about places outside their native regions was far from perfect. The distant localities of which would-be migrants were most aware were either those of national importance, such as a capital city, or those with which their home region was traditionally connected by commerce and migration. Awareness did not always determine choice, of course, but the obvious advantages of migrating to places where one could reasonably expect assistance, shelter, and comradeship created a strong bias in favor of such destinations. When sustained over time, the outcomes of such biased choices become migration traditions.

Returning to the image of the mental map, one can picture migration traditions as the routes of an imagined road network that are marked by the heaviest lines. For country people contemplating migration, these were the roads most commonly traveled out of rural poverty in search of higher wages, greater variety of employment, and a future less constrained by want. In the case of

---

1. Peter Gould and Rodney White, *Mental Maps*, 2d ed. (Boston: Allen & Unwin, 1986); J. Richard Peet, "The Spatial Expansion of Commercial Agriculture in the Nineteenth Century: A Von Thunen Interpretation," *Economic Geography* 45, no. 4 (1969): 283–301.

Cardiganshire, three enduring migration traditions within Britain offered distinct alternatives to local agriculture and rural crafts. Each one involved particular terms of engagement with the capitalist economy, not only because each offered certain kinds of employment but also because each destination provided a way of life with particular social and, for some, moral expectations. Internal migration has often been considered an important element in individuals' pre-emigration history, particularly in support of the argument that the experience of migrating to wage labor in commercial agriculture or industry predisposed people to emigrate overseas.[2] To understand the motivations behind emigration from a given region, therefore, one must first examine the range of possibilities most readily available to, and likely to have been considered by, people who needed or wanted to change their living situations, as well as the economic and social conditions that constrained their choices.

Constraints and Poverty in Cardiganshire Agriculture

Farmers everywhere have a reputation for being conservative and tight-fisted with money. In Wales, Cardiganshire ("Cardi") farmers have the dubious honor of often being singled out as the greatest of penny-pinchers. Any truth in this stereotype may derive from several facts of nineteenth-century Cardiganshire agriculture. First, an exceptionally high proportion of farmers in the county were small freeholders in the late eighteenth and nineteenth centuries. Unlike many continental European countries and some parts of England, Wales was predominantly a land of tenant farms before sweeping land reforms were instituted at the end of the nineteenth century. In North Wales, where a few large estates owned the lion's share of land, as little as 5 percent of farms in some parishes belonged to freeholders. Tithe Commission surveys in the 1830s and 1840s found that in many Cardiganshire parishes small freeholders owned from 20 to 35 percent of all farms, a proportion similar to the 21.6 percent owner-occupation of farms in Cardiganshire tallied by the first national survey of land tenure in 1887. Because most large farms were let as tenancies, rural Welsh society generally accorded higher status to established tenant farmers than to small freehold-

2. Ewa Morawska, *For Bread with Butter: The Life-Worlds of East Central Europeans in Johnstown, Pennsylvania, 1890–1940* (Cambridge: Cambridge University Press, 1985).

ers, whose farms, often heavily mortgaged, were often located on marginal, less fertile ground.[3] If any farmers had reason to be extremely careful with their money and resources, it was small freehold farmers trying to eke a subsistence from marginal land.

Second, farmers in Cardiganshire generally were averse to taking risks because of their long, hard experience of the land's physical limitations. Cardiganshire hills are not very tall but can be quite steep; the topography that makes modern tractors dangerous today made farmers in the nineteenth century prefer the "time-honored sledge" to wheeled carts.[4] Although fertile loam covers some of the county's gentler, better-drained slopes, most of Cardiganshire's soils are ill suited to intensive agriculture. Heavy clays along watercourses and valley bottoms are difficult to work and prone to become waterlogged, while terminal moraine severely impedes drainage in the upper Teifi Valley. Upland soils are particularly acidic and prone to form peat.[5] Only a limited number of crops are suitable for such growing conditions. Oats grow fairly well in the county's wet, cool, acidic soils, but many of the crops that were promoted by eighteenth- and nineteenth-century improvers do not. Landlords who tried to persuade their tenants to adopt modern crop rotations and other innovations, whether by example, instruction, or proscriptive clauses in tenants' leases, were invariably frustrated. Thomas Johnes (1748–1816) was Cardiganshire's most determined improver and among

3. John Davies, "The End of the Great Estates and the Rise of Freehold Farming in Wales," *Welsh History Review* 7 (1974–1975): 212; Trefdraeth [Anglesey] Poor Rate Book, 1838; Richard J. Moore-Colyer, "Farmers and Fields in Nineteenth-Century Wales: The Case of Llanrhystud, Cardiganshire," *National Library of Wales Journal* 26 (1989–1990): 36–37; David Jenkins, *The Agricultural Community in South-West Wales at the Turn of the Twentieth Century* (Cardiff: University of Wales Press, 1971),145–56. Thanks to Lloyd G. Owens for permission to use the Trefdraeth Poor Rate Book.

4. Richard J. Moore-Colyer, "Landscape and Landscape Change," typescript, 1976, ms. p. 19.

5. B. W. Avery, *Soil Classification for England and Wales* (Harpenden: Soil Survey, 1980); L. F. Curtis, F. M. Courtney, and S. T. Trudgill, *Soils in the British Isles* (London: Longman, 1976); "Soils of Wales," Soil Survey of England and Wales, 1983 (scale 1:250,000); Harold C. Carter, ed., *National Atlas of Wales* (Cardiff: University of Wales Press, 1988), map 1.5, "Soils"; Ministry of Town and Country Planning for the Ordnance Survey, comp., "Rainfall, Annual Average, 1881–1915" (scale 1:625,000), Great Britain Sheet 2, 1949; British Geological Survey, "Llanilar: Solid and Drift" (scale 1:50,000), England and Wales Sheet 178, 1994; Richard J. Moore-Colyer, "Some Aspects of Land Occupation in Nineteenth-Century Cardiganshire," *Transactions of the Honourable Society of Cymmrodorion* (1981): 80.

its most charitable landlords. Welsh-born but unable to speak the language, Johnes struggled for over thirty years to bridge the gap between his vision of Cardiganshire's agricultural potential and his tenants' habitual conservatism. In addition to experimenting with silviculture and animal breeding, Johnes tried to induce Scottish farmers to take up tenancies at his Hafod estate in hopes that they would inspire the Welsh tenants to adopt progressive methods. But Johnes failed to convince his tenants, let alone other local farmers, even after having his book, *A Cardiganshire Landlord's Advice to his Tenants* (1800), translated into Welsh and distributed free of charge.[6]

Third, Cardiganshire's distance from urban markets and the poor condition of the county's roads were structural disincentives to the development of commercial agriculture. The county had few paved roads until the late nineteenth century, and the unpaved tracks and narrow footpaths that laced most parishes did not easily accommodate wheeled traffic. Not until 1864 did a railroad line reach Aberystwyth, the main market and port town for northern Cardiganshire. Throughout the early nineteenth century, the only agricultural products worth exporting from the county were livestock on the hoof, woolen goods, and small amounts of butter and cured pork. Even coastal shipping was too costly to make grain exports worthwhile; at midcentury, most ships leaving Aberystwyth harbor carried lead ore, oak bark, or ballast.[7] All of these constraints meant that Cardiganshire farming had small margins of profitability and that farmers were chronically short of capital. In the view of historian David Howell, lack of capital to invest in improvements was the root cause of agricul-

6. Richard J. Moore-Colyer, ed., *A Land of Pure Delight: Selections from the Letters of Thomas Johnes of Hafod (1748–1816)* (Llandysul: Gwasg Gomer, 1992), 4, 6, 23–35, 52–58. Moore-Colyer estimates that the annual cost of growing turnips amounted to £6 4s per acre, a heavy investment for a farmer short of capital; "Landscape Change," 17. On the patterns of cropping in early-nineteenth-century Wales, see David Thomas, *Agriculture in Wales during the Napoleonic Wars* (Cardiff: University of Wales Press, 1963), 79–95, esp. figs. 24–29. Moore-Colyer discusses the poor standards of manuring on Cardiganshire farms in "Of Lime and Men: Aspects of the Coastal Trade in Lime in South-West Wales in the Eighteenth and Nineteenth Centuries," *Welsh History Review* 14 (1988): 54–77.

7. David W. Howell, "The Impact of Railways on Agricultural Development in Nineteenth-Century Wales," *Welsh History Review* 7 (1974): 45; W. J. Lewis *Ceredigion: Atlas Hanesyddol* (Cardiganshire: An Historical Atlas) (Aberystwyth: Cyngor Sir Ceredigion, 1955), 44; Lewis Lloyd, "The Port of Aberystwyth in the 1840s," *Cymru a'r Môr/Maritime Wales* (1980): 43–61.

tural backwardness throughout Wales. Most farmers reasoned that it was better to secure subsistence production, which provided a monotonous if reasonably nutritious staple diet of barley bread, leek broth, potatoes, peas, cheese, buttermilk, cabbage, and occasionally pork or herring,[8] than to risk crop failure in bad weather.

The lack of capital in the rural Cardiganshire economy was also evident in the persistence of labor exchange and the county's exceptionally low agricultural wages. As in Ireland, the truly poor in Cardiganshire came to depend on the potato as their main source of calories and commonly exchanged their labor at harvest time for sets of potatoes on a large farm. This arrangement, called the "work debt" or "potato duty," guaranteed farmers an adequate workforce while sparing them the need to lay out cash wages or invest in expensive harvest machinery. It is a telling indication of how slowly agriculture became mechanized in the county that cottagers were still fulfilling their potato duty by harvesting grain manually with reaping hooks as late as 1912.[9] Throughout the nineteenth century, Cardiganshire's agricultural wages fell into the bottom rank of pay for rural labor in Wales. The standard wage for male agricultural laborers early in the century was one shilling a day during the winter and 1s 3d during the summer harvest. They received less money if their wages included food. An experienced serving woman on a farm received as little as £5 for a year's labor, about one-quarter of what a man could earn in the course of a year.[10] Many young workers received no cash wages at all, as families commonly exchanged the labor of their children for food or the use of a neighbor's farm implements.

8. David Howell, *Land and People in Nineteenth-Century Wales* (London: Routledge & Kegan Paul, 1978), 18, 91–92; R. N. Salaman, *The History and Social Influence of the Potato* (Cambridge: Cambridge University Press, 1949), 417–18.

9. David Jenkins, *The Agricultural Community in South-West Wales at the Turn of the Twentieth Century* (Cardiff: University of Wales Press, 1971), 51–53. Jenkins points out that terms varied regionally: the arrangement was called *dyled gwaith* (work debt) or *dyled cynhaeaf* (harvest debt) in south Cardiganshire, *dyled tatw* (potato debt) or duty *tatw* (potato duty) in north Cardiganshire. Women exchanged their work gathering and binding sheaves of hay for "quantities of butter known as 'debt butter' (*dyled menyn*)." Ibid., 52, 53.

10. Alun Eirug Davies, "Wages, Prices, and Social Improvements in Cardiganshire, 1750–1850," *Ceredigion* 10 (1984): 35, table 1; Howell, *Land and People,* 100.

Wages also remained low in the first half of the century because of labor surpluses caused by the unprecedented growth of the rural population. Between 1801 and 1851, the population of Cardiganshire increased by 59.3 percent. Southern parishes grew most rapidly during the first three decades of the century, northern parishes slightly later. Research has not yet determined whether the increase in population was mainly due to greater fertility associated with younger age at marriage, or to declining mortality associated with improved health and nutrition. The consequences of increasing population, however, were very clear. In addition to keeping wage levels depressed, the amount of land available to new families declined, in some parishes by as much as 50 percent, between 1801 and the census year of peak population.[11]

Competition for freeholds and tenancies also intensified during this period because of changes in the system of land tenure. The tremendous inflation of land values during the Napoleonic Wars prompted landlords across Wales to convert traditional leases for three lives to short-term or annual tenancies. Although many landlords in Cardiganshire continued to honor the tradition of life-long tenancies and of passing holdings from father to son, sometimes for many generations,[12] the fact that tenancies now had to be regularly renewed gave landlords greater leverage in tenurial relations. Landlords in financial trouble found the move to short-term leases especially advantageous, as large rent increases could provide capital rather quickly to cover their debts. This was precisely the situation of Cardiganshire's three wealthiest families, who owned the Nanteos, Trawsgoed, and Gogerddan estates. Mismanagement and living beyond their means had brought all three families to the edge of bankruptcy during the closing years of the Napoleonic Wars. They resorted to doubling and trebling rents to recoup their losses. When agricultural prices plummeted during the postwar depression, these gentry landlords found it increasingly necessary to grant rent abatements (perhaps the last vestige of the old system of paternalism) and to accelerate the sale of portions of their estates, hastening the development of

11. Census of Great Britain, 1851, *Population Tables*, pt. 2, vol. 2 (London, 1854), "Birth-Places of the People," Division 11, Monmouthshire and Wales, pp. 2, 22–39.

12. Richard J. [Moore-]Colyer, *The Welsh Cattle Drovers: Agriculture and the Welsh Cattle Trade Before and During the Nineteenth Century* (Cardiff: University of Wales Press, 1976), 2–3.

a new class of petty landlords among the county's professional and business elite.[13]

While the county's generally poor agricultural conditions provided sufficient cause to seek supplemental income off the farm, the acute rural distress caused by the postwar depression made it mandatory for many families. One of the easiest ways for people in rural Cardiganshire to earn a little cash was to knit stockings. The growth of urban-industrial centers in South Wales and England in the late eighteenth and early nineteenth centuries created a demand for cheap, durable work clothes, including stockings made from coarse Welsh wool. In Merionethshire, hundreds of female and male knitters brought their stockings to the weekly market in Bala for sale to traveling agents.[14] Cardiganshire did not have a central market for the trade, although the town of Tregaron, best known as a gathering place for cattle drovers, had 176 hosiers (most of them women) in 1851.[15] The 1841 census of Caron (the parish including Tregaron) and a neighboring upland parish, Gwnnws Uchaf, listed more knitters than any other female occupation except for farm servants. For many rural women in this region the pittance they earned by knitting stockings kept them above the destitution of those with the third most common occupation, namely paupers. Knitting stockings required no capital, nor did knitters have to own sheep, since women and children could glean wool from roadside hedges and the moors where sheep pastured in the summer months. Even at the end of the nineteenth century, cottagers from as far away as the coast of Cardigan Bay still came to glean wool from the

13. Richard J. Moore-Colyer, "The Gentry and the County in Nineteenth-Century Cardiganshire," *Welsh History Review* 10 (1981): 497–535; idem, "The Pryse Family of Gogerddan and the Decline of the Great Estate, 1800–1960," *Welsh History Review* 9 (1979): 406–31; idem, "Nanteos: A Landed Estate in Decline, 1800–1930," *Ceredigion* 9 (1980): 58–77; Crosswood Deeds mss., ser. 2, no. 676, affidavit of Mr. Young, sworn 25 April 1816; Geraint H. Jenkins, *The Foundations of Modern Wales: Wales 1642–1780*, vol. 4 in *History of Wales* (Oxford: Clarendon Press, 1987), 267–70; David W. Howell, *Patriarchs and Parasites: The Gentry of South-West Wales in the Eighteenth Century* (Cardiff: University of Wales Press, 1986), 85; G. E. Mingay, *Land and Society in England, 1750–1980* (London: Longman, 1994), 128–29.

14. J. Geraint Jenkins, *The Welsh Woollen Industry* (Cardiff: National Museum of Wales, 1969), 210, 212.

15. Emrys Jones, "Tregaron: The Sociology of a Market Town in Central Cardiganshire," in *Welsh Rural Communities*, ed. Elwyn Davies and Alwyn D. Rees (Cardiff: University of Wales Press, 1960), 74.

rugged highlands above Tregaron and Pontrhydfendigaid. Knitting was also an appealing by-employment because it could be done in spare moments or even while walking.[16]

Spinning and weaving were also important by-employments and full-time occupations in Cardiganshire. Unlike Montgomery and Merionethshire, however, Cardiganshire never developed an extensive putting-out system for textile production. Each rural community and town had weavers, just as it had shoemakers and tailors, making goods for local consumption. Weavers commonly worked in exchange for farm produce, trading a length of flannel for a few pounds of salty butter or a sack of potatoes. They obtained yarn from local spinners and sent lengths of cloth to be finished at the nearest *pandy* or fulling mill. The mills were usually very small operations tucked alongside a fast-flowing stream that provided water power to run the simple machinery (see fig. 2.1). Many were accessible only by long treks along muddy footpaths and rutted, stony tracks.[17]

Cardiganshire's textile industry began to mechanize shortly after the end of the Napoleonic Wars, when small carding and spinning factories were built along the lower Teifi River at Drefach. Mechanized looms did not appear in the county until after 1850, when new, larger mills producing work shirts and flannel underwear for industrial workers in Glamorgan and Monmouthshire made the area around Llandysul the most profitable and productive textile center in Wales. Although the mills made cottage spinning obsolete in southern Cardiganshire by about 1840, industrialization did little to alter the dispersed cottage industry in the rest of the county until the railroads brought cheap imported textiles to local shops.[18]

To earn significantly higher income, one had to look beyond cottage industry to heavy industry or the greater world outside Cardiganshire. The search for higher wages has long been one of the basic motives for migration. To take one of many examples, poor farmers in western Ireland found it worthwhile to trek all

16. Census of Great Britain, 1841, Enumerators' Returns, Public Record Office, London (hereafter [date] PRO HO) 107/1374 (Gwnnws), 1376 (Caron); Jenkins, *Woollen Industry*, 251; Rev. E. Edwards, *Byr Hanes am Blwyf Nantcwnlle* (Privately published, 1930), 15–16; John Rees Jones, *Sôn am y Bont* (Speaking of Pontrhydfendigaid), ed. E. D. Evans (Llandysul: Gwasg Gomer, 1974), 69–71.

17. Jenkins, *Woollen Industry*, chap. 6, quotation on p. 263; Moore-Colyer, "Landscape Change," 80.

18. Jenkins, *Woollen Industry*, 252–62.

Fig. 2.1 Mill near Aberystwyth. The exact location of this small woolen mill is unknown, as is the name of the artist who painted it. He was probably an Englishman who lived in northern Cardiganshire, and his paintings generally date from the 1840s. Whatever his identity, his naive watercolors capture the isolation and limited economic development of the area. Charming as this scene would have been to English visitors and, at times, to the inhabitants, the very small scale of the textile industry and the difficulty of traveling on dirt roads like the one leading away from the mill meant economic hardship for rural people in the county. (By permission of the National Library of Wales)

the way to England to work as seasonal agricultural laborers, for the comparatively high wages on English farms earned them enough cash to pay the increasingly high rents demanded for their tenancies in the early nineteenth century. Internal migration was their preferred strategy to sustain traditional attachments to a "home patch" of land.[19] Migration served a similar function for rural Cardiganshire people. Their search for higher wages developed three well-worn paths out of the most populous parts of the

19. Lynn Hollen Lees, *Exiles of Erin: Irish Migrants in Victorian London* (Ithaca, N.Y.: Cornell University Press, 1979), 23–24, 40–41. As Jan Lucassen points out, Irish agricultural laborers coming to England could earn the cash they needed for rent even when rents became inflated because of the growing demand for holdings, which itself was caused in part by the availability of outside, seasonal employment. Jan Lucassen, *Migrant Labour in Europe 1600–1900: The Drift to the North Sea*, trans. Donald A. Bloch (London: Croom Helm, 1987), 113.

county. For many, the destination closest to home was Cardiganshire's own lead-mining district in the northeastern highlands around Pumlumon, the county's highest peak. The second path led southeast to employment in the iron works, coal mines, shops, and private homes of industrial north Glamorgan and Monmouthshire. The third path followed the drovers roads across the Cambrian Mountains and the English lowlands to London. I will begin with the shortest route.

Cardiganshire's Lead District

The highlands of Pumlumon are a strangely forbidding zone of broad, boggy moors, precipitous waterfalls, and steep-sided valleys cloaked in native oak forest. Romans were the first to mine the veins of lead and silver in the deeply folded hills here. Cardiganshire silver supplied the Royal mint as early as 1624, and King Charles I moved the mint itself to Aberystwyth to produce his soldiers' pay safely beyond the reach of rebel forces during the Civil War in the 1640s. Lead mining first attracted significant private investment in the late 1740s, when a detailed report by the Anglesey-born surveyor Lewis Morris drew attention to the rich deposits south of Pumlumon.[20]

The industry's greatest period of growth in Cardiganshire came between about 1835 and 1870, when new capital investment and managerial talent multiplied the number of mines and increased their efficiency (see map 2.1). This growth attracted large numbers of migrants to the area. For example, the population of Gwnnws Uchaf, a parish on the southern reaches of the lead district, including the Esgair-mwyn mine, grew from 270 to 642 between 1801 and 1851. At least half of this increase was due to inmigration to Esgair-mwyn and the other mines in the parish. Industrial workers greatly outnumbered the farm population in the heart of the lead district, as in Melindwr parish, which had 311 lead miners, mine laborers, and ore dressers compared to just 101 farmers and farm laborers in 1851.[21] In addition to

20. John Davies, *A History of Wales* (London: Allen Lane/Penguin, 1993), 263–64; William Waller, *An Essay on the Value of the Mines, Late of Sir Carbery Price* (London, 1698); George C. Boon, *Cardiganshire Silver and the Aberystwyth Mint in Peace and War* (Cardiff: National Museum of Wales, 1981), 39–41, 46–52; David Bick and Philip Wyn Davies, *Lewis Morris and the Cardiganshire Mines* (Aberystwyth: National Library of Wales, 1994).

21. Census of Great Britain, 1851, *Population Tables*, pt. 2, vol. 2, "Birth-Places of the People," p. 39; 1851 PRO HO 107/2486 (Melindwr), quoted in

providing wage employment, the mines created local demand for agricultural produce and occasional employment for farmers hauling ore to Aberystwyth, which paid as much as 6s a day.

Historian David Williams argued that the mines brought sufficient prosperity to northern Cardiganshire to keep it peaceful during the Rebecca Riots, a series of violent rural protests from 1839 to 1844 that were confined mainly to Carmarthenshire, Pembrokeshire, and the middle Teifi Valley along the Cardiganshire border.[22] While the mines no doubt helped stabilize the region's economy by providing off-farm employment, I doubt that they were as important as Williams suggests. Despite the lead district's rapid rate of growth in the middle third of the century, its industrial population remained much smaller than the workforces of northeast and southeast Wales, owing to both the structural limitations of the industry in Cardiganshire and its modest wages. The district's remote location and lack of coal deposits made on-site ore smelting unprofitable in the nineteenth century, so that the scale of operations remained smaller than the agglomerated works in northeast Wales. Most Cardiganshire lead ore was hauled down to Aberystwyth and shipped out to be smelted at Swansea and other Welsh ports.[23] Wages for Cardiganshire mine workers were generally higher than prevailing agricultural wages but lagged well behind rates of pay for lead workers elsewhere in Britain. Cardiganshire miners received as little as 1s a day in 1800 and 1s 8d to 2s a day in 1826. By 1846 a highly skilled miner could receive up to 16s a day, but most skilled positions went to experienced miners and engineers from Cornwall and Devon. These English-speaking Wesleyan Methodists constituted a distinctly foreign element in the rural population. Native Welsh lead miners typically earned no more than £3 a month as late as the 1870s.[24]

The poverty of the surrounding countryside created a sufficient economic gradient to attract "plenty of labour . . . at low wages,"

Alwyn E. Benjamin, "Melindwr, Cardiganshire: A Study of the Censuses 1841–71," *Ceredigion* 9 (1983): 331.

22. W. J. Lewis, *Lead Mining in Wales* (Cardiff: University of Wales Press, 1967), 269, 282; David Williams, *The Rebecca Riots: A Study in Agrarian Discontent* (Cardiff: University of Wales Press, 1955), 269.

23. Lewis, *Lead Mining*, 173 and 286, fig. 11; 174–80; Davies, *History of Wales*, 328. For a brief overview of lead mining's role in the economy of northern Cardiganshire, see A. J. Parkinson, "Wheat, Peat, and Lead: Settlement Patterns in West Wales, 1500–1800," *Ceredigion* 10 (1985): 111–30.

24. Lewis, *Lead Mining*, 269, 286–88, 265–73.

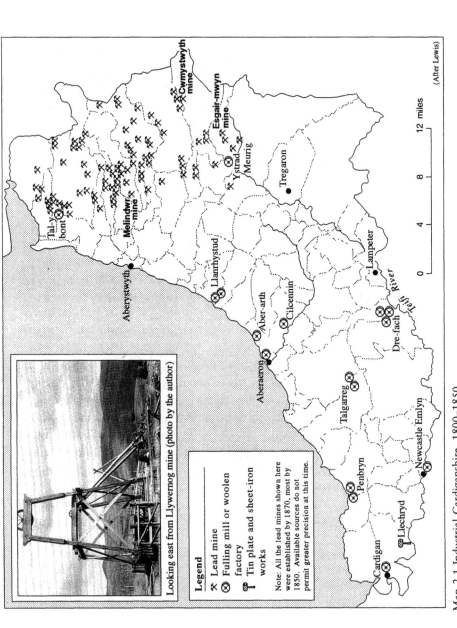

Looking east from Llywernog mine (photo by the author)

Legend

✕ Lead mine

⊗ Fulling mill or woolen factory

⚒ Tin plate and sheet-iron works

Note: All the lead mines shown here were established by 1870, most by 1850. Available sources do not permit greater precision at this time.

Tal-y-bont

Melindwr mine

Cwmystwyth mine

Esgair-mwyn mine

Ystrad Meurig

Tregaron

Aberystwyth

Llanrhystud

Aber-arth

Cilcennin

Lampeter

Aberaeron

Teify River

Dre-fach

Talgarreg

Penbryn

Newcastle Emlyn

Llechryd

Cardigan

0   4   8   12 miles

(After Lewis)

Map 2.1 Industrial Cardiganshire, 1800–1850

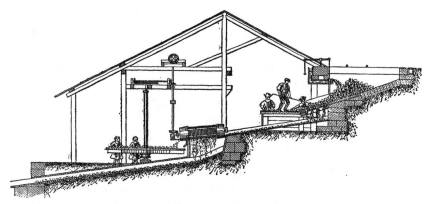

Fig. 2.2 Washing kiln and sizing trommel at a Cardiganshire lead mine. The device pictured in this 1884 engraving from Hunt, *British Mining*, was used at Frongoch mine. Although it may be somewhat larger and more elaborate than was sorting equipment earlier in the century, it performed the same functions with the same workforce: ore deposited at the upper end of the shed was first washed, then raked onto tables, where girls and women sorted clean ore from waste to be discarded and dredge ore to be crushed. This picture shows the process divided into two stages, with a second, rotating sorting table receiving ore that passed through a cylindrical trommel that would either wash or sort the stone by size.

but not from great distances.[25] Various sources indicate that the lead mines drew casual and unskilled labor mainly from their immediate hinterland. The *Mining Journal* of 1843 mentions mine employees coming from a radius of about fifteen miles. Notes to the 1851 census mention "the removal of families to the adjacent [i.e., lead] mining district" from Aberystwyth and Llanychaearn, parishes that lie about fifteen miles from Cwmystwyth, where the largest mines were located.[26] Workers also commuted from hill farms to work at the mines part-time, the men and boys as miners, haulers, and laborers; the women and girls in "crushing sheds" where the ore was washed and sorted (see fig. 2.2). A teenage child's income could add several shillings a week to the family coffers. The manuscript census for 1851 identifies children as young as nine years old as mine workers. Edward T. Porter, an American genealogist who has extensively studied the lead district, estimates that children under the age of fifteen

25. Ibid., 288. Although wages were low, Cardiganshire companies did not compound workers' poverty by paying them with scrip that they could redeem only at the company store, probably because companies needed to minimize disincentives in order to retain workers. Ibid., 273.

26. Cited in Lewis, *Lead Mining*, 269 and note 85; Census of Great Britain, 1851, *Population Tables*, pt. 2, vol. 2, "Birth-Places of the People," note on p. 39.

walked up to 2.5 miles to work at a mine but that the majority of young mine workers lived within 1.5 miles of where they worked.[27]

While lead mining in Cardiganshire provided important income to rural families and attracted significant numbers of migrants, it was a poor man's industry. Many male miners lived in crude, filthy barracks. Underground, men and boys worked in damp conditions and routinely inhaled lead particles and silica dust, which increased their vulnerability to tuberculosis. Women and girls tended ore-crushing machinery in unheated sheds and suffered the din of the crusher's pounding, monotonous roar. Positions of any kind, however, were relatively difficult to obtain in the 1830s and early 1840s, when a depression in pig lead prices reduced investment in Cardiganshire's mines and set some mines idle for months or years at a stretch. The period of greatest activity and in-migration to the lead district came after 1850 and peaked in the 1870s.[28] Earlier in the century, seasonal and long-term migration to Glamorganshire and London offered Cardiganshire residents both higher wages and more appealing living and working conditions than the lead mines. Both of these migration traditions began with the seasonal journeys of agricultural workers but developed into very different kinds of permanent settlement by the middle of the nineteenth century.

The Iron District of Southeast Wales

The migration tradition connecting Cardiganshire with Glamorganshire probably began with the seasonal migrations of agricultural laborers to the Vale of Glamorgan, a fertile region in the southern part of the county where laborers could earn up to double their usual wage. The earliest reported Cardiganshire har-

---

27. 1851 PRO HO 107/2486–7; 1861 PRO HO RG9/4198–9, 4201; 1871 PRO HO RG10/5566, 5568; Lewis, *Lead Mining*, 275. I am grateful to Ed Porter for providing this data and for estimating the distances to work, based on tithe map information.

28. Lewis, *Lead Mining*, 283–85, 175–77, 287; Emrys G. Bowen, "A Clinical Study of Miners' Phthisis in Relation to the Geographical and Racial Features of the Cardiganshire Lead-Mining Area," in *Studies in Regional Consciousness and Environment, Essays Presented to H. J. Fleure*, ed. Iorwerth C. Peate (Oxford: Oxford University Press, 1930), 189–202. A moving turn-of-the-century account of poverty in the lead district appears in W. Jones-Edwards, *Ar Lethrau Ffair Rhos* (On the Slopes of Ffair Rhos) (Aberystwyth: Cymdeithas Lyfrau Ceredigion, 1963), 15–17.

vest gangs in the eighteenth century were farmers "who, after gathering in their own hay crops, came to Glamorgan 'to earn money to pay their rent and pay their winter expenses.'" They also had gleaning rights in the fields they harvested, which could yield fifteen to sixteen bushels of grain per family. According to oral tradition, the workers walked south and commonly slept for free in their employer's barn or granary.[29]

New developments in the northeastern highlands of Glamorgan began to attract migrant laborers by the late 1750s, as English capitalists built new iron works at the Heads of the Valleys (*y Blaenau*), a region that had previously supported only a scattered agricultural population. The entrepreneurs leading this development were experienced ironmasters from southern Glamorgan, Shropshire, and Staffordshire who bought up leases for vast tracks of land from local gentry. They recognized the productive potential of the region's outcroppings of coal, iron ore, and limestone. Before the turn of the nineteenth century, the village of Merthyr Tydfil was encircled by four of Britain's largest iron complexes, which together employed at least 2,000 men, women, and children. By 1850 the area had eight integrated iron works with a total of forty-one blast furnaces and a workforce of roughly 30,000 people. Merthyr itself had a metropolitan population of over 60,000 at that time, making it the largest urban place, and the center of the largest industrial conurbation, in all of Wales.[30]

Merthyr Tydfil was by no means the only iron town in South Wales. By 1800 northwest Monmouthshire had no fewer than six major iron works producing nearly the same volume of iron as Merthyr's Cyfarthfa and Dowlais works, each supporting a

29. Moelwyn I. Williams, "Seasonal Migrations of Cardiganshire Harvest-Gangs to the Vale of Glamorgan in the Nineteenth Century," *Ceredigion* 3 (1957): 156–59; quotation on p. 156 comes from the *Glamorgan Gazette*, 18 August 1911.

30. Chris Evans, *"The Labyrinth of Flames": Work and Social Conflict in Early Industrial Merthyr Tydfil* (Cardiff: University of Wales Press, 1993), 10–20, 25–29; Davies, *History of Wales*, 328–30; John Langton and R. J. Morris, eds., *Atlas of Industrializing Britain, 1780–1914* (London: Methuen, 1986), 129, map 15.3; Richard Lawton and Colin G. Pooley, *Britain 1740–1950: An Historical Geography* (London: Edward Arnold, 1992), 72, table 5.5; Harold Carter and Sandra Wheatley, *Merthyr Tydfil in 1851: A Study in the Spatial Structure of a Welsh Industrial Town*, University of Wales Board of Celtic Studies, Social Science Monograph no. 7 (Cardiff: University of Wales Press, 1982), 8 (citing population for the parish of Merthyr Tydfil) and 18, table 2. The 1851 census gives a total population of 63,080 for the town without specifying the parishes this figure includes; Census of Great Britain, 1851, *Population Tables*, pt. 2, vol. 2, "Birth-Places of the People," p. 892.

rapidly growing population. Five years later, the South Wales iron district as a whole produced 30 percent of total British iron output, a proportion it maintained for over forty years. Very early in the development of the Welsh iron district, however, Merthyr gained almost legendary status because of the aggressive innovations carried out by its resident ironmasters and the tremendous concentration of productive capacity located in and around the town. Welsh historians have focused disproportionate attention on Merthyr's tumultuous labor history, in part because records from the town's iron works happened to survive while others were lost, but also because Merthyr was a fascinating exception in Welsh history, namely a trend-setting industrial town that nurtured a dynamic, Welsh-speaking culture and working class.[31]

The champion of this view, Gwyn A. Williams, declared "Merthyr and its neighboring communities" to be "as much a 'shock city' as Manchester was to England and the world at large."[32] Williams was using "shock city" in the sense of a place whose sudden, explosive growth characterized the transforming impact of a particular industry, and which became a hub of regional development and population increase. While Merthyr never approached the size or economic influence of Manchester or Birmingham, its boomtown quality gave it comparable force in the Welsh imagination. The transformation of the countryside also made a powerful impression upon English visitors, who wondered at the lurid glow the iron works cast against the night sky and the roar of furnaces in blast, punctuated by the deafening crash of immense forge hammers.[33] In daylight one could see that Merthyr's manufactories and residential quarters were densely packed along the valley floor, while sheep continued to graze the hills which flanked the town on three sides (see figs. 2.3 and 2.4). The unusual mix of people drawn to the town made it a worldly, exciting place to rural migrants. On census day in 1851, for example, Merthyr's "visiting" population included a Swiss hardware dealer, "hawkers in sponge" from Paris and Amster-

---

31. Evans, *The Labyrinth of Flames*. For an introduction to the most extensive and revealing manuscript collection for a South Wales iron works, see Madeleine Elsas, ed., *Iron in the Making: Dowlais Iron Company Letters, 1782–1860* (Cardiff: Glamorgan County Council, 1960).

32. Gwyn A. Williams, *The Merthyr Rising* (London: Croom Helm, 1978), 21.

33. George Borrow, *Wild Wales: The People, Language, and Scenery* (London: J. M. Dent & Sons, 1906), 588; *Leigh's Guide to Wales and Monmouthshire* (London: M. A. Leigh, 1833), 299; Evans, *Labyrinth of Flames*, 31–33.

Fig. 2.3 Dowlais Iron Works as ironmasters saw them, circa 1825. In this view, orderly factories constantly produce iron while the peaceful countryside, groomed by diligent servants (note the man edging the grass at lower right), remains a delight for gentlemen setting off on a morning ride. Two farmhouses are visible in the middle distance. The painter, Penry Williams, was the son of an ironmaster at Dowlais and a close associate of the Guest family, owners of the works. (By permission of the National Library of Wales)

dam, a man from Berlin selling rhubarb, a Moroccan steel-pan salesman, and an itinerant Russian jeweler.[34]

Merthyr offered rural migrants a potentially dramatic improvement in their standard of living. An able-bodied man who earned 1s a day as an agricultural laborer in Cardiganshire could pocket 22s to 27s a week hewing coal in Glamorganshire. If he rose through the craft system in the iron works he could earn 30s to 35s a week as a puddler. Industrial wages were very volatile; they rose and fell in direct relation to the state of the iron market, which could fluctuate wildly over short periods of time. The higher cost of food and material goods in Merthyr eroded workers' actual buying power, and it could take years to attain the coveted status of a highly skilled job. Nevertheless, industrial wages gave the working class of Merthyr a standard of living envied by rural laborers. On holidays, a working man could join his

34. 1851 PRO HO 107/2458–9 (Merthyr Tydfil); Williams, *Merthyr Rising*, 52.

Fig. 2.4 Dowlais Iron Works as workers saw them, 1840. Much of furnace work was hard manual labor in dangerous conditions. In this watercolor by George Childs, two men work in the foreground, perhaps filling a barrow with coal or iron ore that the woman, a "filler," will push to a loading platform atop one of the furnaces where it will be dumped into the stack as part of the "charge" for another blast. (Welsh Industrial and Maritime Museum)

fellows parading through the streets "dressed in coat and trousers of finest black cloth, elegant waistcoat, fine shirt, beaver hat, Wellington boots and a fine silk handkerchief in his pocket."[35] Williams writes that what impressed the English Jacobin John Thelwall on his visit to Merthyr around 1830 "was the sheer *pride* of ironworkers, the overweening pride of skilled men, the secretive pride of those thousands of men and women who nursed their craft lore in an industry which counted about 40 separate 'trades.'" Observers from the period also noted "that

35. Davies, "Wages," 35, table 1; John Davies, "Agriculture in an Industrial Environment," in *Industrial Glamorgan from 1700 to 1970*, vol. 5 in *Glamorgan County History*, ed. Arthur H. John and Glanmor Williams (Cardiff: Glamorgan County History Trust, 1980), 284; Ivor Wilks, *South Wales and the Rising of 1839* (Urbana: University of Illinois Press, 1984), 56, table 4.3; Arthur H. John, *The Industrial Development of South Wales, 1750–1850* (Cardiff: University of Wales Press, 1950), 83–84, 87; quotation on p. 87 is from A. R. Wallace, *My Life* (London, 1905).

characteristic phenomenon of working-class South Wales, the open door; traditional community and conviviality, of course, but it was also open to show off the new mahogany inside."[36]

While Merthyr attracted workers from throughout Britain and even from the European and American continents, its population up to the middle of the century came predominantly from South Wales. In 1840 G. S. Kenrick of the Varteg Iron Works in Monmouthshire wrote that "there are many who come from Cardiganshire to the ironworks, for five to seven months in the winter season, live economically while here, and take home from £15 to £20 to their families, which pays the rent of their little farm, and purchases for them clothing and a few luxuries." Other observers noted the same kind of seasonal migration from poor districts of west Carmarthenshire.[37] In the early nineteenth century both counties lay at the outer fringes of the iron district's laborshed (the geographical area from which significant numbers of workers came), the extent of which is evident in the birthplace information in the 1851 census. Merthyr's pulling power faded noticeably beyond a radius of about thirty miles. According to the 1851 census, 57 percent of Merthyr's population had been born outside the city. Fifty-five percent of incomers came from elsewhere in Glamorganshire or from the adjoining counties of Carmarthen and Breconshire. Pembrokeshire and Cardiganshire together accounted for another 15 percent, while 6 percent came from Monmouthshire. All other Welsh counties added just 5 percent more. Most of the remaining 19 percent of incomers came from English counties along the border of South Wales.[38]

36. Williams, *Merthyr Rising*, 28.

37. G. S. Kenrick, "Statistics of the Population of the Parish of Trevethin (Pontypool) . . . and Inhabiting Part of the District Recently Disturbed," *Journal of the Royal Statistical Society* 3 (January 1841): 370; John, *Industrial Development*, 170.

38. Census of Great Britain, 1851, *Population Tables*, pt. 2, vol. 2, "Birth-Places of the People," p. 892. Migration from England greatly increased in the second half of the century, eroding the dominance of Welsh as the language of the home and workplace in industrial towns. Up to midcentury, however, Merthyr Tydfil and the other iron towns along the *Blaenau* were far more Welsh than English, an important factor in their appeal to Welsh-speaking rural migrants. Dudley Baines, *Migration in a Mature Economy: Emigration and Internal Migration in England and Wales, 1861–1900* (Cambridge: Cambridge University Press, 1985), 276–77; John, *Industrial Development*, 63–64. Baines points out that migrants from central Wales mainly went to the West Midlands while most of those from North Wales went to the Liverpool area; *Migration in a Mature Economy*, 278.

The same pattern of declining numbers of migrants over distance is evident all along the periphery of the laborshed, including Cardiganshire. Map 2.2 plots the birthplaces of Cardiganshire natives who were recorded in the 1851 census for the Merthyr Tydfil area.[39] It shows that considerably more people from southern Cardiganshire were present in Merthyr on census day than were natives of central or northern parts of the county. The census lists almost no one from the lead-mining district. The greatest number of Cardiganshire natives were from small towns and farming communities along the Teifi River, stretching from Aberteifi (Cardigan) to Llanbedr Pont Steffan (Lampeter). Migration was generally lighter and more scattered north of an arc formed by the Aeron River and the upper reaches of the Teifi.[40] Parishes south of this geographical divide accounted for 71.9 percent of Cardiganshire migrants of known origin, compared to 43.8 percent of the county's population in 1841.[41]

The census figures, of course, are a snapshot in time that recorded individuals' whereabouts on a single day, with no reference to residential status except for those individuals who were identified as visitors. It is possible that greater numbers of Cardiganshire migrants were congregating in other iron towns. The census enumerators' notes, however, suggest that Merthyr was generally a favored destination and that the zone from which migrants came was only gradually expanding to include portions of Cardiganshire beyond the Teifi Valley. In 1831, enumerators observed that migration to southern industry was affecting northern Carmarthenshire and had reached "some way into southern Cardiganshire." In 1851, they cited "removal of labourers to Merthyr-Tydfil Iron-works" as the leading cause of depopulation in several parishes along the middle and lower Teifi Valley, indicating that by that date migration had developed into permanent resettlement for significant numbers of southern Cardiganshire natives.[42]

39. The census parishes of Merthyr Tydfil, Cyfarthfa, Plas-y-coed, hamlet Heol Hornwood, and the chapelry of Dowlais.

40. The parishes and census subdivisions marking the northern edge of the north-south divide are Llannerch Aeron, Henfynyw, Ciliau Aeron, Llanfihangel Ystrad, Gartheli, Betws Leucu, and Llanddewibrefi.

41. 1851 PRO HO 107/2458-9 (Merthyr Tydfil); for districts listed in note 39; Census of Great Britain, 1851, Population Tables, pt. 2, vol. 2, "Birth-Places of the People," pp. 34-41.

42. John, Industrial Development, 64; Census of Great Britain, 1851, Population Tables, pt. 2, "Birth-Places of the People," notes on pp. 35-39.

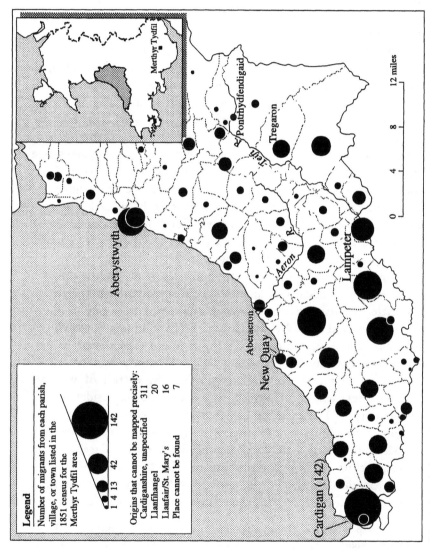

Legend

Number of migrants from each parish,
village, or town listed in the
1851 census for the
Merthyr Tydfil area

1 4 13   42   142

Origins that cannot be mapped precisely:

Cardiganshire, unspecified	311
Llanfihangel	20
Llanfair/St. Mary's	16
Place cannot be found	7

Merthyr Tydfil

Pontrhydfendigaid

Tregaron

Teifi

Aberystwyth

Aeron R.

Lampeter

Aberaeron

New Quay

Cardigan (142)

0   4   8   12 miles

Map 2.2 Birthplaces of Cardiganshire natives living in Merthyr Tydfil area, 1851

Until railroads radically improved overland transportation in Europe, emerging industrial locations typically had a "natural hinterland" from which most of their labor came.[43] The textile mills in Lancashire initially recruited most of their labor from a geographical area comparable in extent to Merthyr's hinterland at midcentury. Most of the men who worked in Carnarvonshire's slate industry before the railroad age came from parishes within a fifteen-mile radius of the quarry where they worked. Jan Lucassen described the same phenomenon of migration traditions constrained by distance during three hundred years of labor migrations from Germany to the Netherlands. One of the critical constraints throughout the prerailroad era was how far a worker could travel before the expenses of migrating (travel costs plus the value of lost work time at home) consumed an unacceptable proportion of his or her earnings. Living within twenty to twenty-five miles of one's birthplace also made it possible for workers to walk home for at least occasional visits on weekends or holidays. Thus the concept of a laborshed conveys both the sense of geographical limits that influenced workers' migrations and the catchment area defined by sustained flows of labor toward a center of relatively high-wage employment.[44]

Another aspect of internal migration, as with overseas migration, was the tendency of migrants from a particular home region to settle in close proximity to one another. For example, Philip N. Jones found that Welsh migrants to coal mining communities in south Glamorganshire in the 1870s and 1880s settled in "intense concentrations" according to their county and parish of origin, so that one would find boardinghouses full of workers from a single village and streets with a majority of residents from one county.[45] The same processes that created this clustering by region in coal mining towns were at work earlier in the century in Merthyr Tydfil. The 1851 census listed most migrants from Cardiganshire in the neighborhood of the Dowlais iron works, which overlooked the northern edge of Merthyr (see table 2.1). The only exception to this general pattern was the clustering of

43. Philip N. Jones, *Mines, Migrants, and Residence in the South Wales Steamcoal Valleys: The Ogmore and Garw Valleys in 1881*, Occasional Paper in Geography, no. 25 (Hull: Hull University Press, 1987), 183.

44. Peter Ellis Jones, "Migration and the Slate Belt of Caernarfonshire in the Nineteenth Century," *Welsh History Review* 14 (1989): 621–26; Michael Anderson, *Family Structure in Nineteenth-Century Lancashire* (Cambridge: Cambridge University Press, 1971), 34–39; Lucassen, *Migrant Labour*.

45. Jones, *Mines, Migrants, and Residence*, 66–77.

Table 2.1 Locations of Cardiganshire migrants from selected towns, villages, and parishes

Place of birth	Parish of Merthyr Tydfil	Chapelry of Dowlais	Cyfarthfa	Other [a]
North				
Aberaeron	2	9	—	—
Aberystwyth	20	39	13	5
Llanafan	1	2	12	—
Llanrhystud	6	21	1	—
Lledrod	7	10	1	—
Tregaron	15	17	—	—
South				
Cardigan area [b]	127	61	11	13
Lampeter	19	30	3	2
Llannarth	8	68	1	9
Llandysiliogogo	2	38	—	—
Llandysul	8	66	1	—
Llanfihangel Ystrad	1	21	—	—
Llanwenog	16	64	—	2
Total for migrants of known origin	378	744	71	57

[a]Gelly Du, Heol Hornwood, Plas-y-coed

[b]Cardigan town, Mount, St. Mary's, St. Dogmaels (Pembrokeshire), Llangoedmor, Llechryd, Ferwig, Cilgerran (Pembrokeshire). The Pembrokeshire districts are included here and in other tallies because they are just over the border and were identified as Cardiganshire in the census—presumably an indication that those migrants considered themselves to be Cardis.

Source: 1851 PRO HO 107/2458-9 (Merthyr Tydfil, including Cyfarthfa, Plas-y-coed, hamlet Heol Hornwood, Gelly Du, and chapelry of Dowlais).

migrants from around Cardigan town in the parish of Merthyr. However inexperienced they were in industry and city ways, rural migrants did not arrive in the South as total strangers. Many of them entered the new industrial world with places to stay and a job already arranged through the help of family and friends.

The importance of personal networks to obtaining work offers the best explanation for the sharp occupational differences between migrants from north and south Cardiganshire (see tables 2.2, 2.3, and 2.4). In comparison to northern Cardiganshire migrants, men and women from southern parishes held a disproportionately high number of jobs in heavy industry and 5.5 times more positions in highly coveted skilled occupations related to iron processing. The industrial craft system was very strong in Merthyr Tydfil. Gaining entrance to the ranks of skilled workmen as an apprentice usually depended on personal contacts in the

Table 2.2   Regional representation of Cardiganshire migrants by occupation

Occupational category	North N/Percentage of known origin	South N/Percentage of known origin	Origin unknown	Totals
Industrial, skilled	74 / 23.7%	238 / 76.3%	88	400
Industrial, unskilled	44 / 19.5%	182 / 80.5%	52	278
Nonindustrial craft	56 / 30.6%	127 / 69.4%	46	229
Service or retail	44 / 44.9%	54 / 55.1%	38	136
Wife	70 / 28.5%	176 / 71.5%	67	313
Miscellaneous	21 / 35.6%	38 / 64.4%	21	80
No occupation given	43 / 33.6%	85 / 66.4%	32	160
Totals	352 / 28.1%	900 / 71.9%	344	1,596

Note: See Appendix A for a complete list of the occupations in each category. I have counted all carpenters, smiths, and masons as nonindustrial craft workers except those who were specifically listed as working at a forge, rolling mill, or other heavy industrial plant.

Source: 1851 PRO HO 107/2458-9 (Merthyr Tydfil).

iron works or coal mines. Southern migrants surely benefited from the fact that nine of the ten Cardiganshire-born iron founders in Merthyr in 1851 came from their part of the county, for Welsh founders—like skilled tradesmen in the Lancashire mills—commonly hired work crews from their families and home neighborhoods.[46] Prior experience does not appear to have been as significant as regional connections in gaining entry to skilled employment. Personal contacts, enhanced by southern migrants' earlier connections to Merthyr, were probably the decisive factors that helped southern migrants and hindered northern migrants from getting the most desirable industrial jobs.

Two other factors may help explain northern Cardiganshire migrants' relative lack of involvement in industrial occupations. The first is the possible relationship between distance from the iron works and the labor needs of the iron industry, particularly as regards skilled labor. A. H. John noted in his studies of South Wales industry that migration patterns in the region confirmed E. G. Ravenstein's observations regarding industrial migration during the late nineteenth century, for during the rise of South Wales iron "the characteristic movement of skilled labour was a short-distance movement." Long-distance migration of skilled workers happened only when men with particular abilities were recruited to fill a "special need." Lucassen further observed that iron making was not amenable to migratory labor because the industry

46. Anderson, Family Structure, 112, 121–23.

Table 2.3 Regional representation in selected male occupations

	Northern migrants	Southern migrants
Iron industry		
Iron processing[a]	16 (15.4%)	88 (84.6%)
Founder	1 (10.0%)	9 (90.0%)
Ore miner	2 (6.7%)	28 (93.3%)
Iron laborer[b]	14 (19.4%)	58 (80.6%)
Totals	33 (15.3%)	183 (84.7%)
Coal and other industries		
Coal miner	4 (40.0%)	6 (60.0%)
Collier	20 (33.9%)	39 (66.1%)
High-skilled underground[c]	2 (12.5%)	14 (87.5%)
Miner, unspecified	25 (35.7%)	45 (64.3%)
Laborer, unspecified	13 (16.9%)	64 (83.1%)
Hauler	12 (35.3%)	22 (64.7%)
Totals	76 (28.6%)	190 (71.4%)
Clothing and retail		
Maker of clothing or shoes[d]	28 (35.0%)	52 (65.0%)
Shopkeeper or merchant[e]	20 (76.9%)	6 (23.1%)
Totals	48 (45.3%)	58 (54.7%)

[a]Drawing out in forge, finer, iron baller, finer, heater, roller, rougher, shearer, straightener; moulder; nail straightener; pattern maker; puddler; rail dresser, filer, passer, presser, shearer, straightener; railman; shearer.

[b]Filler, hauler of iron or mine (ore), laborer in iron works or iron mine, tipper.

[c]Archer, fireman, pit sinker.

[d]Hosier, cobbler/cordwainer/shoemaker, tailor.

[e]Bookseller, carrier of goods for sale, draper, grocer, hawker, stationer, tea dealer, tinker.

Source: 1851 PRO HO 107/2458-9 (Merthyr Tydfil).

operated year-round. The locational stability of the iron industry's labor force was very different from the seasonal migrations typical of industries such as brick making, peat cutting, bleaching, and construction.[47] The craft ladder reinforced this tendency of iron workers to stay within a particular district by rewarding local men and long-time residents with the best-paying positions. The 1851 census shows, for example, that of the 48 percent of iron puddlers and founders in Merthyr who were natives of Glamorganshire, 77 percent had been born in the town itself.[48] If indeed southern Cardiganshire's closer proximity meant the earlier development of a migration tradition to the iron

47. John, *Industrial Development*, 61–62; Lucassen, *Migrant Labour*, 76–86.
48. 1851 PRO HO 107/2458-9 (Merthyr Tydfil).

Table 2.4 Regional representation in selected female occupations

	Northern migrants		Southern migrants	
Industrial				
Laborer	1		10	
Filler or tipper	3		7	
Cleaning[a]	1		2	
Collier or miner	1		4	
Other[b]	2		12	
Totals	8	(18.6%)	35	(81.4%)
Clothing, Service, and Retail				
Servant	13		14	
Housekeeper	1		8	
Cleaning[c]	5		15	
Sewing[d]	5		6	
Other[e]	1		2	
Totals	25	(35.7%)	45	(64.3%)
Wife	70	(28.5%)	176	(71.5%)

[a]Cleaning blast engines, ore.

[b]Breaker of stone, brickfiller/brick woman, coal layer, coal unloader, limestone woman, mine gatherer, mine girl, patcher of mine, piler.

[c]Charwoman, cleaner of chapel, laundress, washerwoman, washing girl.

[d]Dressmaker, knitting stockings, milliner, seamstress.

[e]Grocer, publican, shop assistant.

Source: 1851 PRO HO 107/2458-9 (Merthyr Tydfil).

district, and if longer involvement with iron increased the number of permanent migrants (assertions which do require further examination), then distance may in part explain the relative dominance of southern Cardiganshire migrants in the ranks of skilled labor.

People from northern Cardiganshire may also have had positive reasons to avoid industrial occupations. The two categories of work in which migrants from northern Cardiganshire were relatively dominant in Merthyr Tydfil were service (including a disproportionate share of female domestic servants) and retail occupations. The greatest difference was the proportion of northern men engaged in retail trades. More men from northern Cardiganshire were listed as shopkeepers, merchants, and hawkers than were listed as skilled iron workers. Casual laborers and traveling merchants did enjoy some advantages over industrial workers. They could pick up additional income when it suited them without depending on openings for particular kinds of employment. Skilled positions required greater work discipline, including regular attendance on the job and the investment of months or years of training as an apprentice. Once a man was established in a skilled trade he might move frequently from one works to another but was likely to stay within the industrial district. Thus becoming a skilled iron worker or miner usually precluded a man's continued presence on the family smallholding or tenancy, although his wages, if repatriated, could help secure the holding for those who stayed behind. Northern Cardiganshire had areas where common land was still relatively plentiful in the early nineteenth century. The possibility of being able to carve new smallholdings and garden plots out of the common may have inhibited permanent migration to the South even as it promoted seasonal migration and occasional journeys to sell farm produce, stockings, or homespun. Migrants from southern Cardiganshire, in contrast, may have been more inclined to settle permanently in the South because they had less access to common land.

Traveling merchants and the drovers who took Welsh livestock to markets in South Wales and England created vital links between the rural economy and urban and industrial centers. Until the railroad era, drovers facilitated the exchange of goods, capital, and information between city and countryside, providing essential services for many rural communities in Wales. They were entrusted with families' salable goods (from knit stockings to livestock on the hoof) and returned with cash payment and news from the outside world.[49] Other travelers carried victuals from Cardiganshire farms to the industrial towns. One such man was David Griffiths, who farmed a small tenancy in Nancwnlle parish just north of the Aeron River. As young men in the 1840s, Griffiths and his two brothers established a regular trade carting sides of cured bacon and ham to market in Merthyr Tydfil. The journey by pony cart took two days each way, provided the weather was good. Decades later, a Cardiganshire poet named James Thomas, writing under the pen name "Sarnicol," memorialized David Griffith's travels in a verse-map that charts each stage of the journey from the Griffiths brothers' farms to "Dowlais Top" (see map 2.3):

> There he goes in the early morn
> In his cart to Merthyr, calling farewell,

49. Philip Gwyn Hughes, *Wales and the Drovers* (1943; reprint, Carmarthen: Golden Grove Editions, 1988), 27–79.

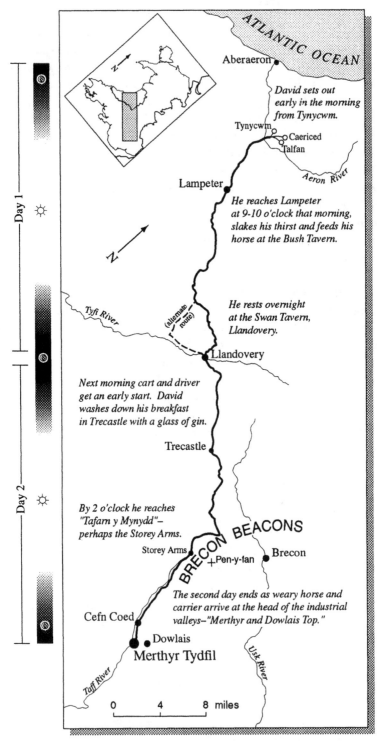

ATLANTIC OCEAN

Aberaeron

David sets out
early in the morning
from Tynycwm.

Tynycwm ○ Caericed
Talfan

Aeron River

Lampeter

He reaches Lampeter
at 9-10 o'clock that morning,
slakes his thirst and feeds his
horse at the Bush Tavern.

Day 1

N

Tyfi River

(alternate route)

He rests overnight
at the Swan Tavern,
Llandovery.

Llandovery

Next morning cart and driver
get an early start. David
washes down his breakfast
in Trecastle with a glass of gin.

Trecastle

Day 2

By 2 o'clock he reaches
"Tafarn y Mynydd"–
perhaps the Storey Arms.

BRECON BEACONS

Storey Arms   Brecon
          +Pen-y-fan

The second day ends as weary horse and
carrier arrive at the head of the industrial
valleys–"Merthyr and Dowlais Top."

Cefn Coed

Dowlais
Merthyr Tydfil

Taff River   Usk River

0   4   8 miles

Map 2.3 Journey of David Griffiths, carrier, to Merthyr Tydfil

> From Talfan, Caericed, or Tynycwm,
> With a heart so light and a heavy load.[50]

Griffiths was one of many West Wales farmers who developed a profitable long-distance business selling provisions to industrial workers. Abel Thomas was another. He traveled six days a week carrying butter from Lampeter to sell in the industrial port town of Neath. When considering the nature of rural people's involvement with capitalism it is important to remember those like Griffiths and Thomas who traveled constantly between the two worlds. "This human connexion," wrote D. J. Williams, "kept in continual touch with each other the life of the countryside and that of the growing industrial town."[51] In addition to selling their own and neighbors' produce for valuable currency, carriers brought news from home to urban-industrial migrants and conveyed information about job opportunities and working conditions to rural communities. They and seasonal migrants lessened rural isolation even as their work helped sustain the rural way of life.

London

The third major destination for Cardiganshire migrants had a unique place in the imaginations and ambitions of rural folk throughout Britain. London was the capital of England, of Britain, of a growing empire. If offered unparalleled opportunities to anyone sufficiently clever and resourceful to turn them to advantage. By the middle of the eighteenth century, London was effectively the expatriate capital of Wales, home to more Welsh business-

---

50. *Dacw fe'n mynd yn y bore bach / Yn y cart i Ferthyr tan ganu'n iach, / O Dalfan, Caericed, neu Dynycwm, / A'i galon yn ysgawn, a'i lwyth yn drwm.*

"Sarnicol" composed the poem "Siwrnai'r Carier i Ferthyr" (The Carrier's Journey to Merthyr) for the 1918 songfest in Llanycrwys parish; the poem was published in Dan Jenkins, ed., *Cerddi Ysgol Llanycrwys* (Poems of Llanycrwys School) (Llandysul: Gwasg Gomer, 1934), 78. It was later set to music and recorded by the Welsh folk group Seithenyn on the album "Cwlwm Pedwar." I am grateful to Rev. Stephen Morgan for sharing his research on the life of David Griffiths.

51. D. J. Williams, *The Old Farmhouse*, trans. Waldo Williams (1961; reprint, Carmarthen: Golden Grove Book Company, 1987), 26–27, quotation on p. 27. On the role of drovers as carriers of news and currency see Hughes, *Wales and the Drovers*, chap. 3; and Richard J. [Moore-]Colyer, *The Welsh Cattle Drovers: Agriculture and the Welsh Cattle Trade Before and During the Nineteenth Century* (Cardiff: University of Wales Press, 1976), 42–46.

men, shopkeepers, and intellectuals than any city or market town in Wales itself. (Cardiff blossomed as the financial center of Wales only in the last decades of the nineteenth century and was not named the official capital until 1956.) The same celebrated late-eighteenth-century renaissance in Welsh intellectual life that gave birth to the modern Eisteddfod (a competitive Welsh festival of the arts, with an emphasis on literature and music) saw the first concentrated efforts to preserve and promote the Welsh language, which also took place in London among Welsh literati.[52] One of the leading voices in London-Welsh literary circles, William Owen Pughe, summed up the city's symbolic importance when reflecting upon his own perceptions as a boy in rural Merioneth-shire. Long before he moved to the capital city in 1776, he had been "[f]amiliar with the name of London . . . from its being, in our rustic conversations, the primary point in the geography of the world."[53]

Significant numbers of Welsh may first have migrated to London in the wake of Henry Tudor's ascent to the throne in 1485. By 1550 there were 169 Welshmen employed at court under his granddaughter, Elizabeth I. A century later, people of Welsh origin or extraction may have accounted for up to 7 percent of the city's population. Between 1841 and 1851, the first decade for which it is possible to make reasonable statistical estimates, roughly 330,000 people moved to London from elsewhere in Britain.[54] Like most rural migrants, the Welsh who came to London were chiefly attracted by the city's superior wages and range of employments. The city's universal economic appeal was reflected in the fact that significant numbers of migrants came there from all parts of Wales, roughly in proportion to the population of each county.[55] If the preaching tours of

52. On the invention of Welsh traditions during this period, see Prys Morgan, "From Death to a View: The Hunt for the Welsh Past in the Romantic Period," in *The Invention of Tradition*, ed. Eric Hobsbawm and Terence Ranger (Cambridge: Cambridge University Press, 1983), 43–100.

53. Glenda Carr, "William Owen Pughe yn Llundain" (William Owen Pughe in London), *Transactions of the Honourable Society of the Cymmrodorion* (1982): 53–54, quotation on p. 54.

54. Emrys Jones, "The Welsh in London in the Seventeenth and Eighteenth Centuries," *Welsh History Review* 10 (1981): 462–66; Francis Sheppard, *London 1808–1870: The Infernal Wen* (Berkeley: University of California Press, 1971), 2.

55. In 1851 London had fewer migrants from Cardiganshire than from any other Welsh county save Merioneth and Anglesey, but even so, they ranked as a higher proportion of the Welsh population there than in Liverpool, Chester, Manchester, or Bristol. Colin G. Pooley, "Welsh Migration to England in the

Welsh evangelist Howel Harris (1717–1773) are any indication, some of the largest clusters of Welsh migrants in the early eighteenth century were located along the western fringes of the city where farms and market gardens produced much of the city's food. In 1739 Harris preached on numerous occasions in Fetterlane, Westminster, and Lambeth, and he frequently returned to preach in London over the next thirteen years. Minutes from the Lambeth meeting noted in 1772 that "[t]he Welch are very numerous in and about Town at this time and many of them tho: they understand a little—yet not English a nough to understand a sermon." The growing number of Welsh in west London worried the meeting's lay leaders, for they saw a crying need to establish churches with Welsh-speaking ministers to keep newcomers from straying into the evil ways of city life.[56]

So many Welsh came to Lambeth that the annual agricultural and hiring fair became known as "Taffy's Fair," "Taffy" being English slang for a Welshman.[57] By the mid–eighteenth century, a good share of the Welsh seeking work in Lambeth's vegetable and fruit gardens were young women, as were many Welsh agricultural laborers elsewhere around London. The Swedish botanist and traveler Pehr Kalm noted during his 1748 visit to southeast England that Irish harvest crews working in Kent were all male, while the Welsh were mostly women and girls. In the nineteenth century, *merched y gerddi*, Welsh garden girls, gained a reputation for being industrious, clean, and well-clad, like the young women depicted in an engraving in the *Illustrated London News* in 1846 (see fig. 2.5).[58] The commentary accompanying this engraving, extracted from Sir Richard Phillips's *Walk from*

Mid-Nineteenth Century," *Journal of Historical Geography* 9 (1983): 293–95.

56. Gomer M. Roberts, *Y Ddinas Gadarn: Hanes Eglwys Jewin Llundain* (The Strong City: A History of Jewin Church, London) (London: Pwyllgor Dathlu Daucanmlwyddiant Eglwys Jewin, 1974), 12; *Cymry Llundain Ddoe a Heddiw* (The Welsh of London Yesterday and Today) (London: Undeb Cymdeithasau Diwylliannol Cymraeg, 1956), 37–38; Meurig Owen, *Tros Y Bont: Hanes Eglwysi Falmouth Road, Deptford a Parson's Hill, Woolwich, Llundain* (Over the Bridge: A History of the Churches of Falmouth Road, Deptford and Parson's Hill, Woolwich, London) (London: Eglwys Jewin, 1989), 9–10, quotation on p. 15.

57. Hugh Clout, ed., *The Times London History Atlas* (New York: Harper Collins, 1991), 78; Owen, *Tros y Bont*, 12.

58. John Williams-Davies, "'Merched y Gerddi'—Mudwyr Tymhorol o Geredigion" ("The Garden Girls"—Seasonal Migrants from Cardiganshire), *Ceredigion* 8 (1978): 292; William Linnard, "Merched y Gerddi yn Llundain ac yng Nghymru" (The Garden Girls in London and in Wales), *Ceredigion* 9 (1982): 260–61 and plate 7.

Fig. 2.5 *Merched y gerddi* (garden girls), circa 1846. The women in the engraving are "pottling" strawberries, putting the fruit, which they themselves probably picked, into small baskets to sell to ladies and gentlemen passing by on the road from Richmond to Hammersmith Bridge. The initials "R. E." burned or painted onto the side of one of the large baskets may mark it as property of the farm where the berries were picked. (By permission of the National Library of Wales)

London to Kew, notes that strawberry season attracted hundreds of female migrants, "for the most part, . . . Shropshire and Welsh girls, who walk to London, at this season, in droves, to perform this drudgery, just as the Irish peasants come to assist in the hay and corn harvests." Their net daily pay (after deducting the costs of transportation and food) was 5s a day, yielding about £10 total for the forty-day season. "After this period," Phillips continued, "the same women find employment in gathering and marketing vegetables, at lower wages, for . . . sixty days, netting about £5 more. With this poor pittance they return to their native country, and it adds either to their humble comforts, or creates a small dowry towards a rustic establishment for life."[59]

John Williams-Davies claimed that most of the women who weeded and harvested produce in London were cottagers from

59. *The Illustrated London News* (27 June 1846), 421.

northern Cardiganshire who migrated to the capital every spring. While this surely is an exaggeration, the local stories on which Williams-Davies bases his conclusion do suggest that a strong tradition linked northern Cardiganshire to London's gardens. As he tells it, "Small groups of about half a dozen girls from Tregaron would start out at midnight on Sunday (so as not to break the Sabbath) and they crossed the mountain to Abergwesyn by breakfast Monday morning. There they met with other parties from Llanddewibrefi and Llangeitho who had come by a different road." For much of the two-hundred-mile, seven-day journey they walked along drovers' roads; in fact Williams-Davies and others locate the origin of the women's migration in the region's long droving tradition (see map 2.4).[60] Oral tradition from the parish of Nancwnlle, a few miles west of Llangeitho, recalled local women walking to London in the summer to do weeding for several weeks in the market gardens, returning home with £2 or £3 in their pockets. The recorder of this tradition included a piece of doggerel composed by Cardiganshire poet Daniel Ddu (1792–1846):

O na bawn i fel colomen
Ar ben Sant Paul yng nghanol Llundain,
I gael gweled merched Cymru
Ar eu gliniau'n chwynu gerddi.

(Oh, were I to be, as were a pigeon
Atop St. Paul's in central London,
For to see the women of Wales
On their knees in gardens weeding.)[61]

More permanent migrations of rural Welsh workers and their families may have become a widespread phenomenon for the first time in the 1790s, when a series of acute harvest failures undermined the subsistence base of Welsh agriculture. This was the period when George Lipscomb observed the "little horde of Welch-men ... their wives and children" walking east from Presteigne, headed for the dockyards in east London. The Welsh generally settled first in working-class areas of central London, such as Bermondsey, Whitechapel, Southwark, and Deptford, where wholesale food markets, municipal construction projects,

60. Williams-Davies, "Merched y Gerddi," 291–99, quotations on pp. 294, 299; Philip Hughes, *Wales and the Drovers*, 53.
61. Edwards, *Nantcwnlle*, 16.

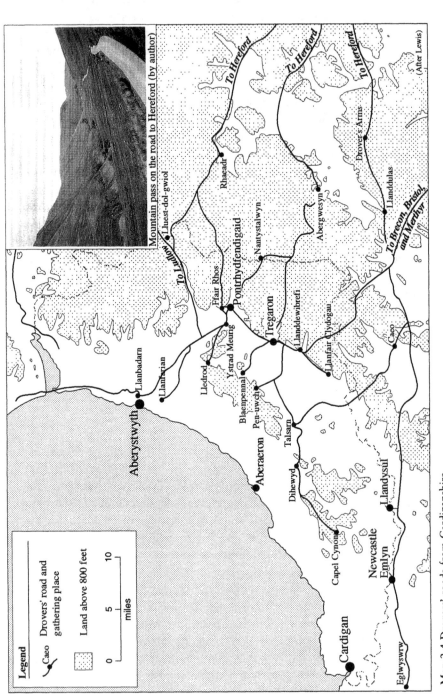

Map 2.4 Drovers' roads from Cardiganshire

Legend

⌒Caeo Drovers' road and
gathering place

▧ Land above 800 feet

0 5 10
miles

Mountain pass on the road to Hereford (by author)

(After Lewis)

To Llanidloes
To Hereford
To Hereford
To Hereford
To Brecon, Bristol, and Merthyr

Aberystwyth
Llanbadarn
Llanrhian
Lledrod
Ystrad Meurig
Ffair Rhos
Lluest-dol-gwiol
Rhaeadr
Pontrhydfendigaid
Nantystalwyn
Blaenpennal
Pen-uwch
Tregaron
Llanddewibrefi
Abergwesyn
Aberaeron
Llanfair Clydogau
Drover's Arms
Llandulas
Talsarn
Caeo
Dihewyd
Capel Cynon
Newcastle Emlyn
Llandysul
Cardigan
Eglwyswrw

and the navy docks offered jobs for unskilled laborers.[62] Male agricultural laborers further swelled the ranks of Cardiganshire migrants after 1820, as they found their traditional employment as harvesters in Hereford and Shropshire being undercut by competition from Irish laborers who were willing to accept even lower wages than they.[63]

Like the Irish who came to London early in the century, Welsh migrants established "a string of settlements tucked into the tumbledown corners of working-class London."[64] The corners inhabited by most Welsh, however, were not quite so tumbledown as the poorest Irish slums, called "rookeries." The Welsh also appear historically to have been more dispersed than other ethnic groups in the city. Emrys Jones mapped likely Welsh households in the seventeenth century (based on surname evidence) and found them living throughout London with no marked concentrations. Peter Clark came to the same conclusion for the eighteenth century, with the exception of a noticeable Welsh presence in the Clerkenwell neighborhood. The 1851 census reveals a similarly dispersed pattern. That census recorded 17,500 Welsh natives throughout the city. They were more numerous in the most populous parts of the city, but even in these quarters there was no parish that one could call predominantly or even distinctively Welsh.[65] Evidence from chapel membership lists suggests further that the London Welsh did not live in clusters along individual streets, as did migrants from particular counties and

62. Sheppard, *Infernal Wen*, 12, 6; Clout, *London History Atlas*, 136–37; Rev. John Thickens, "Hanes ac Atgof" (History and Recollection), in *Dathliad Agor Capel Newydd Eglwys Jewin, Trefn y Gwasanaeth* (A Celebration of the Opening of the New Jewin Church, Order of Service) (London: Eglwys Jewin, 961), 10; Owen, *Tros y Bont*, 16, 19, 161–62; Lees, *Exiles of Erin*, 56–57, 66–71.

63. Edwards, *Nantcwnlle*, 16; Arthur Redford, *Labour Migration in England, 1800–1850*, 2d ed., ed. and rev. W. H. Chaloner (Manchester: Manchester University Press, 1964), 133, 143–44.

64. Lees, *Exiles of Erin*, 56–57, quotation on p. 56.

65. Jones, "Welsh in London in the Seventeenth and Eighteenth Centuries," 465–66, 476; Peter Clark, "Migrants in the City: The Process of Social Adaptation in English Towns, 1500–1800," in *Migration and Society in Early Modern England*, ed. Peter Clark and David Souden (Totowa, N.J.: Barnes & Noble, 1988), 274; Census of Great Britain, 1851, *Population Tables*, pt. 2, vol. 1 (London, 1854), "Birth-Places of the People," Division 1, London, pp. 32–35. See also Owen, *Tros y Bont*, 26–33, 53–54; Emrys Jones, "The Welsh in London in the Nineteenth Century," *Cambria* 12 (1985): 151, 156–57.

parishes in the South Wales coal valleys.[66] The distribution of Cardiganshire natives in London parishes gives a representative picture of this dispersed geographical pattern (see map 2.5).

Many factors could help explain the dispersal of Welsh-born migrants across London, including their relatively small numbers, their coming as small family groups and individuals, the relatively easy acceptance they enjoyed as one of the more desirable kinds of migrants, and the popularity of reputedly docile, respectable Welsh women as household domestics. The dispersal of Welsh families throughout the city may also have been reinforced by the geographical logic of a particular business in which significant numbers of Welsh families took part; namely, the dairy business. Producing and selling milk, butter, and cheese was an ideal economic niche for migrants with pastoral experience, few industrial or artisanal skills, and little capital. From early in the eighteenth century until around 1840, milk was sold by individual vendors, a trade "said to have been dominated by Welsh girls, by the wives and daughters of Irish labourers, and by other elements of the immigrant poor." Milkmaids were gradually replaced by petty entrepreneurs who changed the trade into one of family businesses in which the women and girls ran the dairy counter while the men and boys drove small carts and pony traps on a daily round of neighborhood deliveries. Itinerant milk sellers could enter the business for the £1 cost of a yoke and pails or a perambulator. If a young couple wanted to set up a shop or join an existing operation, they could turn to friends and relatives for loans to get started.[67]

By 1837, London had 314 cowkeepers and dairymen. (Both cowkeepers and dairymen sold milk, but the latter did not keep

66. Record of members' contributions at Charing Cross Road Chapel, London, 1849–1861, Calvinistic Methodist Archives, E139/1, National Library of Wales (hereafter cited as Calvinistic Methodist Archives); list of members' contributions, Crosby Row Chapel, London, 1851–1878, Calvinistic Methodist Archives, ms. 13,015; list of names of those who came with tickets [i.e., letters of transfer] to Nassau Street Church, Soho, London, 1862–1875, Calvinistic Methodist Archives, ms. E139/18; Jones, *Mines, Migrants, and Residence.*

67. Jones, "Welsh in London in the Nineteenth Century," 152–55; P. J. Atkins, "The Retail Milk Trade in London, c. 1790–1914," *Economic History Review*, 2d ser., 33 (1980): 523, 529, 535, quotation on p. 523; Gwyneth Francis-Jones, *Cows, Cardis, and Cockneys* (Borth, Dyfed: Privately published, 1984), 37–44, 54–55.

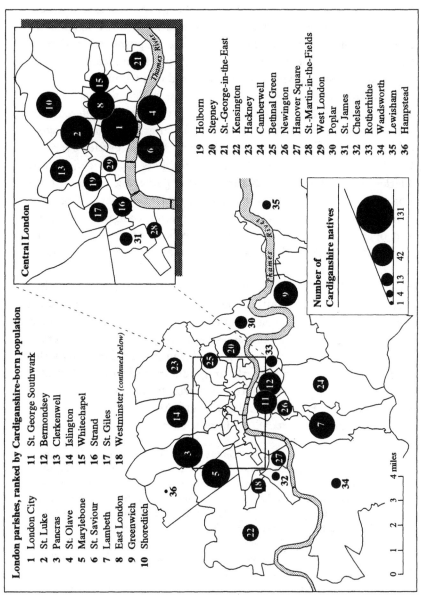

London parishes, ranked by Cardiganshire-born population

1	London City	11	St. George Southwark
2	St. Luke	12	Bermondsey
3	Pancras	13	Clerkenwell
4	St. Olave	14	Islington
5	Marylebone	15	Whitechapel
6	St. Saviour	16	Strand
7	Lambeth	17	St. Giles
8	East London	18	Westminster *(continued below)*
9	Greenwich		
10	Shoreditch		

19	Holborn
20	Stepney
21	St.-George-in-the-East
22	Kensington
23	Hackney
24	Camberwell
25	Bethnal Green
26	Newington
27	Hanover Square
28	St.-Martin-in-the-Fields
29	West London
30	Poplar
31	St. James
32	Chelsea
33	Rotherhithe
34	Wandsworth
35	Lewisham
36	Hampstead

Map 2.5 Distribution of Cardiganshire natives in London, 1851

cows on the premises.)[68] The trade that afforded access to so many Welsh migrants also required them to live apart from one another. Each milk seller had a territory whose extent was determined mainly by his or her mode of transport. Until the business became fiercely competitive late in the century, sales territories rarely overlapped completely and so worked against the clustering of Welsh households. So long as pushcarts and pony traps dominated the trade, there were typically no more than ten milk-delivery shops within a one-mile radius in London.[69]

Contemporary writers suggest that the Welsh were an important part of the London milk trade. Emrys Jones considered their involvement in the trade to be a natural outgrowth of the long-established tradition of Welsh drovers taking cattle over the Cambrian Mountains to the cattle markets at Smithfield and Clerkenwell, which both became noted gathering places for the London Welsh.[70] Anecdotal evidence and folk memory say that many—some claim a majority—of London's dairies were owned and operated by natives of Cardiganshire.[71] An enduring migration tradition may indeed have connected northern Cardiganshire to London through a succession of cattle droving, the garden girls, and the milk trade. In 1933 a number of Cardiganshire men, many of them milk sellers, organized the Cardiganshire Society of London. The first issue of the new organization's magazine listed the names, addresses, and origins of all members.[72] The distribution of their homes, displayed in map 2.6, shows that a striking preponderance of the migrants came from north-central Cardiganshire, particularly from an area bounded by Aberaeron, Llanddewibrefi, Pontrhydfendigaid, and Aberystwyth.

Personal accounts recalling family stories from the late nine-

68. George Laurence Gomme, *London in the Reign of Victoria* (Chicago: Herbert S. Stone, 1898), 223, quoting Robson's *London Directory* (1837), which listed employers only, and therefore significantly undercounted the number of individuals actually involved in the milk trade at that date; Jones, "Welsh in London in the Nineteenth Century," 151–52; "The Milk Exiles," television documentary directed by David Lloyd, broadcast by HTV Wales on 26 February 1982.

69. Atkins, "Retail Milk Trade," 532–34, 535; "The Milk Exiles," HTV Wales, 26 February 1982. According to the latter, the last Welshman to sell milk from a pushcart in London was still at work in 1982.

70. Jones, "Welsh in London in the Nineteenth Century," 151, 154–55.

71. Francis-Jones, *Cows, Cardis*, 20; interview with Jean Williams at her home, Tŷ Capel Jewin, London, 21 June 1992.

72. "Rhestr o'r Aelodau" (List of the Members), *Cylchgrawn Cymdeithas Ceredigion Llundain* (Journal of the Cardiganshire Society of London) 1 (1934–1935): 42–55.

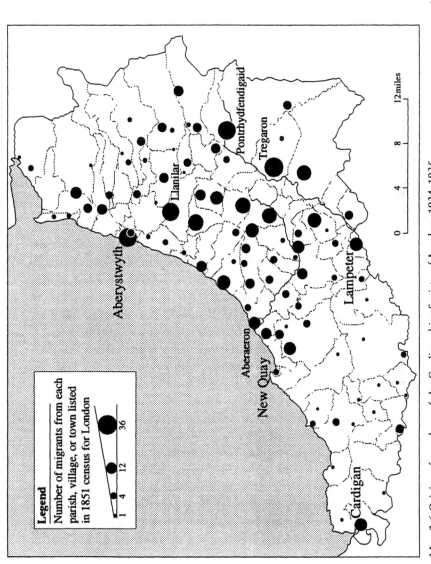

Legend

Number of migrants from each
parish, village, or town listed
in 1851 census for London

1 4   12   36

Aberystwyth

Llanilar

Pontrhydfendigaid

Tregaron

Aberaeron

New Quay

Lampeter

Cardigan

0   4   8   12miles

Map 2.6 Origins of members of the Cardiganshire Society of London, 1934–1935

teenth century describe a cycle of outgoing and returning migrations which resembled long-term rural-urban connections elsewhere in Europe. As one memoirist recalled, young couples from
Cardiganshire would leave their home farms to work with relatives in London; some stayed in the city and eventually set up
their own shops with the help of family capital and labor; families
with children took their annual vacations back in Cardiganshire;
and old couples gathered up their lifetime savings to retire in
Tregaron, Llan-non, or Aberystwyth. Whether the time away was
five years or forty, Cardiganshire remained home.[73] Similar cycles
connected peasant families in rural Auvergne to Paris. Young
Auvergine men left the Massif Centrale to find construction work
in Paris and Auvergine families ran small shops in the city. Many
of these migrants stayed in Paris for most of their adult lives, yet
most of the men returned to the Auvergne to marry local women,
and elderly couples planned on retiring in the countryside which
they always considered to be home.[74] Only gradually, over a
period dating from before 1800 and ending with World War II,
did Parisian Auvergines become permanent urbanites, and even
the postwar generation continued to harbor an emotional attach-
ment to the home district that sometimes motivated a final return.

It is difficult to say to what extent this pattern applied to
Cardiganshire migrants in the early nineteenth century. Evidence
from the manuscript census, city directories, and chapel records
suggests that Cardiganshire migrants did not constitute a significant proportion of milk tradesmen and women until the last two
or three decades of the century. My efforts to trace dairymen with
typically Welsh names in the London Post Office trades directories of 1841 and 1851 to the manuscript censuses of those years
yielded only two definite matches, neither of whom was Welsh-
born.[75] This is hardly conclusive evidence, of course, for recent
migrants to the city may either have been unable to afford having
their names listed in the trade directory or may have been working for London-born employers. If many Welsh families were
working in the dairy trade during the middle of the century,
however, it seems odd that the register of births and baptisms of

73. Francis-Jones, *Cows, Cardis*, 47, 51–55; Jones, "Tregaron," 79.

74. Anne C. Meyering, "Did Capitalism Lead to the Decline of the Peasantry?
The Case of the French Combraille," *Journal of Economic History* 43 (1983):
121–28.

75. *Post Office London Directory*, vol. 2 (1841), pp. 699–700; *Post Office
London Directory 1851*, vol. 3 (1851), *Trades*, pp. 1196–1200; 1841 and 1851
Censuses of Great Britain and indexes, Public Record Office, London.

the London Welsh community's leading Calvinistic Methodist congregation at Jewin Crescent does not list a single dairyman or woman for the period 1799–1837.[76] Yet, however small their numbers, *dynion llaeth* (milk men) left an indelible stamp on the history of migration from Cardiganshire to London, for it was the exigencies of their business which reputedly raised a moral tempest in the Jewin congregation, the heart of London's Cardiganshire migrant community.

Nonconformist chapels were the primary institutions that bound together the dispersed Welsh community in nineteenth-century London. Migrants with strong religious convictions found spiritual sustenance in the Sunday services, midweek prayer meetings, and the all-important *seiat* or society meeting where lay elders guided members through the spiritual self-examination and renewal that lay at the heart of Welsh Calvinism. All of these meetings were conducted in Welsh, giving those in attendance regular practice in the formal, literary language of the Welsh Bible and popular theological commentaries. For all members of the Welsh community, the chapel was also a place to meet with friends, catch up on the latest gossip, and arrange business deals while enjoying the freedom and comaraderie of speaking one's native dialect. Surviving membership lists from London Welsh chapels indicate that migrants from certain parts of Wales tended to congregate at particular chapels. For instance, most of the new members who joined the Nassau Street Church in Soho in 1862 came from North Wales.[77] Jewin chapel, which grew out of the first Calvinistic Methodist congregation in London (located originally on Wilderness Row) was known as the mother church of Cardiganshire migrants in London. It was built in 1823 in what is now the Barbican district. Over one hundred years later, Jewin still seemed to its members to be like "the little village chapel—or rather, the village itself, and that a village in the depths of the Cardiganshire countryside." Emrys Jones called Jewin "a veritable 'pool of Welshness' in a metropolitan desert."[78]

76. David Oliver, comp., *Index to the Register of Births and Baptisms of the Welsh Chapel of the Calvinistic Methodist Denomination at Wilderness Row, Clerkenwell, in the Parish of St. John, afterwards at Jewin Crescent ...*, transcribed from Public Record Office RG4/4400 (London: London Branch, Welsh Family History Societies, 1995). My thanks to David Oliver for kindly providing me a copy of this publication.

77. Listings for 1862, Calvinistic Methodist Archives, ms. E139/18.

78. Dafydd Jenkins, "Dyddiadur Cymro" (A Welshman's Diary), *Heddiw* 6 (1941): 236; Jones, "Welsh in London in the Nineteenth Century," 164. My

Practicing their religion in the company of friends refreshed Welsh migrants, who spent most of their time straining to make a living in a crowded, bustling, alien city. Calvinistic Methodism represented the countryside and the past for these people. Religion's profound associations with home endowed it with a healing comfort. Those same associations conferred upon the chapel the status of defender of all that was traditional in Welsh society against the powerful competing values embodied in the secular, English society that confronted believers as soon as they stepped outside the sanctuary door.

The Jewin congregation first registered changing attitudes and an unwillingness to be governed by church leaders based in Wales in 1829, when four of the chapel's members signed a declaration in support of a national law that proposed extending the franchise to British Catholics. The declaration argued that Nonconformist leaders' opposition to the bill was inconsistent with their own campaign to win Nonconformists the right to vote, a long battle that had finally brought success just one year before. While avoiding any expression of sympathy for the Catholic religion, which was generally anathema to Welsh Nonconformists, the declaration asserted that "every legislative interference upon religious matters is unreasonable, unjust, . . . and an insult to the whole community."[79] Not only did the declaration boldly defy the express position of Calvinistic Methodism's ruling ministers, but the men who signed the document identified themselves as members of the Jewin congregation, by implication lending the declaration the weight of the largest Welsh church in London. John Elias (1774–1841), leader of the Methodists in Wales, promptly excommunicated the four men. Elias's rigid insistence upon obedience to doctrine had long before earned him the nickname of "Elias the Law" (see fig. 2.6). Although Jewin honored his ruling, its severity divided sentiment in the congregation. The four excommunicated men continued their protest through the press, publishing attacks against Jewin's seated minister, James Hughes ("Iago Trichrug" from Nancwnlle), mocking "the pope of Anglesey and his servants in Jewin Crescent."[80]

The policy of excommunicating those who traduced church policy came under a more serious and widespread challenge a few years later, when the orthodoxy represented by John Elias

---

thanks to Dafydd Jenkins for providing a copy of his article.

79. Davies, *History of Wales*, 358–59, quotation on p. 359.

80. Thickens, "Hanes ac Atgof," 14.

Fig. 2.6 John "the Law" Elias. This portrait of the Calvinistic Methodists' ruling authority was published in *Y Cyfaill* to commemorate his death in 1841. Elias was a man aptly described by the evocative Welsh word *cadarn*, which connotes strength, hardness, holding fast, and being very certain of oneself. (By permission of the National Library of Wales)

ran afoul of Welsh migrants' economic interests. One of the cardinal principles of Calvinistic Methodism was keeping the Sabbath. All members of the Methodist Association were to ensure "that they and their families keep holy the Sabbath-day by an holy resting from all such worldly employ as may be lawful on other days, such as buying, selling, and all worldly transactions; all unnecessary words and works about worldly employments and recreations; idle talk, and idle visits; all vain and foolish conversation." The entire day was to be spent "in public and private exercises of devotion."[81] The rule was relatively easy to follow in

81. *The History, Constitution, Rules of Discipline, and Confession of Faith, of the Calvinistic Methodists, in Wales*, 3d ed. (Mold: H. & O. Jones, 1840), 35. The Calvinistic Methodists broke away from the established church in 1811, later than any other Welsh Nonconformist denomination. *The Rules of Discipline and*

rural Wales, where only a break in bad weather during harvest season would seriously tempt orthodox believers to defy the Sabbath. But the pressures of economic competition in London made every Sunday a test of faith for Welsh migrants involved in retail trades, particularly those who sold milk. Jewin historian Gomer Roberts explains that in the 1830s,

> A growing number of London Welsh were selling milk, and had to go door to door on Sunday as on any other day of the week [or risk losing their customers]. The zealous felt that everyone who sold milk on Sunday should be excommunicated and as a consequence 'the Church divided in opinion and feeling and was not made whole for many years' . . . 'Elias's law,' as it was called, came into power around the year 1835, and from then on those who marketed on Sunday were not suffered to be members of the Church. This was a cause of great bitterness in Jewin Crescent, and the decision left its mark on the life of the Church for many years.[82]

John Elias had personal connections at Jewin. He had preached the inaugural sermon when the chapel opened its doors in 1823 and returned frequently to preach.[83] For years he had preached vehemently, in writing and from the pulpit, against violation of the Sabbath. Excommunication was a harsh judgment, however. Elias may well have decided to make Jewin an example to the rest of the expatriate Welsh community. James Hughes wrote in his diary in 1842 that the majority of the congregation opposed the strict discipline that the church's puritanical elders had been enforcing since their election in 1837. Only after Elias's death in 1841 could Hughes openly begin the work toward reconciliation. His support of more moderate leaders soon alienated the shrinking number of diehard conservatives, who may have organized the schism of 1843–1844 in which sixty-seven members reportedly left Jewin on the same day to join the Welsh chapel in Grafton Street.

The moderates at Jewin elected representatives from their own ranks as a new class of ruling elders in 1844, including the artist Hugh Hughes, one of the four "radicals" who had signed the

---

than any other Welsh Nonconformist denomination. *The Rules of Discipline and Confession of Faith* were first published in 1823. David Williams, *A History of Modern Wales* (1950; reprint, London: John Murray, 1969), 155–56.

82. Roberts, *Y Ddinas Gadarn*, 72.

83. *Cymry Llundain Ddoe a Heddiw*, 39.

profranchise declaration in 1829. A congregational vote in 1845 allowed those who sold milk on Sunday to be reinstated as full members. When the conservative minority appealed angrily to Wales for help, they received the noncommittal reply that representatives of the ruling body of the denomination "would be sent to London upon request." The congregation never found a moral justification for conducting trade on the Sabbath, but once the moderate elders were in power, no one dared confront the offenders. The "subject of milk" (*pwnc y llaeth*) continued to cause bitter resentment until the late 1850s, and I was told that older members of the congregation today can still distinguish between families in the church according to who did and did not abide by the Sabbath rule 150 years ago.[84]

Morality and Economy in Internal Migration Decisions

The exigencies of petty capitalism forced some Welsh families in London to choose between financial survival and their faith, between independent action and the good opinion of their friends and relatives. Back in Cardiganshire, people undoubtedly heard about the battle over trading on Sunday. Sabbath restrictions touched the lives of those still in Cardiganshire as well, though usually in less destructive ways. David Griffiths, carrier to Merthyr, was reputedly punished for breaking the Sabbath when he wheeled his cart home in the early hours of a Sunday morning. A tailor in the neighborhood who was sitting up late finishing a garment heard Griffiths passing by and reported him to the chapel elders. Foolishly, when they asked him how he knew of Griffiths' transgression, he answered honestly. Both men were found guilty of breaking the Sabbath and were briefly suspended from taking communion.[85] Neither the milk controversy nor the earlier conflict over granting Catholics the vote would in themselves have prevented migration to London, but both conflicts would have highlighted issues of concern to rural people. Those of orthodox beliefs would have been troubled by the liberal attitudes and lack of respect for authority that the Jewin rebels ex-

84. Thickens, "Hanes ac Atgof," 14–15, 17; Roberts, *Y Ddinas Gadarn*, 89, 108–9, quotation on p. 89; interview with Jean Williams at her home, 21 June 1992.

85. Anne Knowles, "History in a Song," *Y Drych* (The Mirror) (November 1991): 8. Thanks to the Rev. Stephen Morgan for sharing this local anecdote with me.

Fig. 2.7 Nant-y-glo, Monmouthshire, circa 1840. The iron works of Monmouth and Glamorganshire were the "dark, satanic mills" of early-nineteenth-century Wales. This engraving shows one of the earlier iron complexes where Welsh migrants found high-paying, if dangerous work. This moody image looks desolated, but there are signs of continuing construction and ample room along the river banks and nearby hills for the works to expand and coal mines to be added, as they were in the next decade. (By permission of the National Library of Wales)

pressed, while those who desired both Welsh community and full access to economic opportunity in London may have worried about the Elias faction's harsh sentence on milk sellers and the resulting schism in London's largest Cardiganshire community.

Moral concerns may also have weighed in assessments of industrial destinations in Southeast Wales, particularly for devout Nonconformists. By about 1830–1840, "the South" was well on its way toward earning a reputation in rural Wales as a seat of corruption, immorality, and sinfulness. The same qualities that made the industrial region alluring and exciting for some rural people made it appalling and vicious to others. It carried a double stigma as an urban region that harbored all the sins associated with the big city and as an intensely industrial place whose satanic appearance made manifest the dangers of overweening pride, alcohol, and ungodliness (see fig. 2.7). Nonconformist critics, echoing the sentiments of English romantics, portrayed the new urban-industrial Welsh landscapes as scenes of physical and moral degradation. Instead of mountains

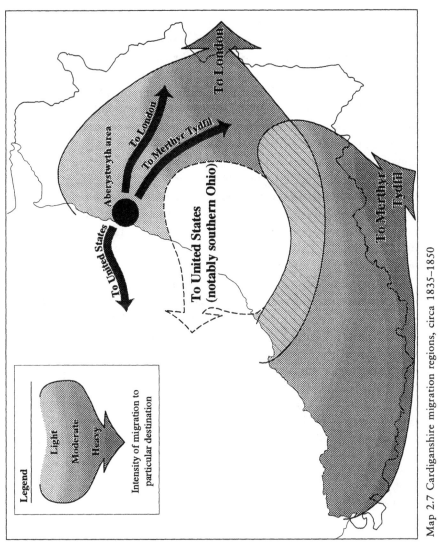

Map 2.7 Cardiganshire migration regions, circa 1835–1850

swept bare, with no residence save human, rural dwellings, and the scattered flocks of mountain sheep, [one now saw in Monmouthshire nothing except] the valleys crowded with expansive works and populous towns; every valley sounding as if it housed a million blacksmiths' shops, and every valley smoking like the plain of Sodom and Gomorrah.[86]

Negative moral attitudes toward life in the South and in London may have made people of certain religious beliefs avoid those destinations, particularly during periods of relatively high industrial unemployment and industrial unrest, as in the Welsh iron industry in the early 1830s. The kinds of employment available in the iron and lead industries and in the capital city also would not have appealed to potential migrants who aspired to own land. Combining the distributions of internal migrants' origins that have been considered in this chapter (see map 2.7) makes it apparent that people in north-central Cardiganshire tended to stand aloof from internal migration to destinations offering wage employment. The obituary data analyzed in chapter 1 highlight the same region as an area of relatively heavy emigration in 1835–1850. The admittedly sketchy geographical data considered in this chapter suggest that distance from both the South Wales iron district and Cardiganshire's lead mining region partly explain the lack of evidence of internal migration from this area. Economic conditions in both industries may have generally slowed internal migration to both destinations during the period when people from this area began to emigrate. The moral controversy over "the battle of milk" (brwyder y llaeth) may also have had a particular impact there because James Hughes, Jewin's minister, was a native son of the region. A more complete answer lies in a closer examination of the particular historical and geographical circumstances of this remote part of coastal Mid Wales.

86. Hywel Teifi Edwards, Arwr Glew Erwau'r Glo: Delwedd y Glowr yn Llenyddiaeth y Gymraeg, 1850–1950 (Brave Hero of the Coal Fields: The Image of the Miner in Welsh Literature, 1850–1950) (Llandysul: Gwasg Gomer, 1994), xx, quoting from an Eisteddfod essay of 1865.

Chapter Three

The Context of Choice: Emigration and Settlement

People in north-central Cardiganshire apparently remained relatively uninvolved with the county's internal migration traditions, yet the Welsh immigrant obituaries analyzed in chapter 1 showed exceptionally high numbers of people from the region emigrating to the United States between 1835 and 1850. Why? To answer the question we must change the scale of analysis from the county as a whole to the locality from which the emigrants came, namely the region physically defined by a high ridge of moorland known as Mynydd Bach. In a few important respects, this region's agricultural economy and religious culture differed from other parts of Cardiganshire and gave it a distinctive place in Welsh history. Historical accident also played a part in precipitating emigration from Mynydd Bach, although no single event can precipitate action unless, like a substance in supersaturated solution, the crystals of change are ready to form. Having grasped the essential character of the region's society and identified the emigrants in their native context, we can then follow them to southern Ohio to discover in what ways their initial settlement pattern, social structure, and economy replicated or differed from the society from which they came.

Topography and Agriculture on Mynydd Bach

Virtually all of the Cardiganshire folk who settled in Jackson and Gallia counties, Ohio, between 1835 and 1850 came from a ten-square-mile region encompassing fourteen rural parishes (see map 3.1). The region begins a few miles south of Aberystwyth in the parish of Llanychaearn, follows the coast of Cardigan Bay to just north of Aberaeron, cuts inland across the coastal plateau to the village of Pennant and then slips down to the Aeron Valley, which it follows east to the river's source in the moorlands along the border of Llangeitho and Blaenpennal parishes. The central

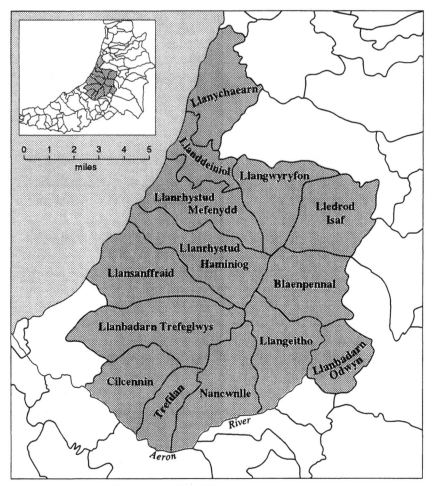

Map 3.1 Study parishes in Mynydd Bach area

physical feature of the region is Mynydd Bach, a curving backbone of rock thinly clad with cotton grass, purple moor grass,
gorse, and heather. Today, along its exposed upper slopes one
can see wind-bent shrubs, remnants of old hedgerows, leaning
hard to the east as the prevailing westerlies have pushed them
over the years. Bogs and two small lakes fill depressions on the
top of the ridge. Down its sides, rough pasture and farmland fall
away like the folds of a heavy skirt whose hem touches the sea to
the west and swings along the arc of the Aeron River. Although
much of the land here is still used for agriculture, it is far less intensively farmed than it was in the early nineteenth century.
Hillsides and valleys that now carry stands of conifers and copses

of native oak, ash, and beech were almost entirely deforested in the 1830s, when surveyors working for the Tithe Commission noted that there was "scarcely any timber to be seen" in the region (see fig. 3.1).[1]

Like other parts of highland Wales, Mynydd Bach is wet and windy, particularly in the winter. Heavy rains saturate the ground, leaching it of nutrients, while sea breezes desiccate the topsoil on exposed hillsides.[2] Where these conditions made arable farming impossible in the nineteenth century, as it is in most places above 200–250 meters in elevation, farmers traditionally grazed sheep. The only highly productive land in this region lies along the coastal plain at Llan-non, a unique remnant of a planned medieval landscape in Cardiganshire, where smallholders and tenants nurtured the soil for centuries with seaweed, manure, and various mulches. The acidic glacial till and heavy clays elsewhere in the region were both less well drained and far less intensively manured than the slangs at Llan-non. On most farms in the early nineteenth century, arable accounted for less than one-third the total acreage and was used mainly to grow barley, oats, clover, and potatoes. The remaining land was a mixture of meadow and rough pasture. Lowland farmers also made customary use of extensive commons of open wasteland on Mynydd Bach to graze their sheep and cattle in the summer.[3]

The changes in land tenure that were gradually transforming agriculture throughout Cardiganshire were particularly pronounced in the Mynydd Bach region, where enclosure of the commons by encroachment resulted in exceptionally high proportions of freeholders and rentier landlords. By the early 1840s, up to 40 percent of farm operators in the region's upland

1. Tithe files, Public Record Office, London, mss. IR/18, for parishes Llanrhystid (13872), Blaenpennal (13985), Cilcennin (13991), Llanbadarntrefeglws (14009), Llanbadarn-odyn (14010), Llanddinol (14011), Llangeitho (14025), Llangrwyddon (14027), Llansaintfraed (14034), Nantcwnlle (14041), Trefilan (14048) quotation from Llanbadarntrefeglws, no. 14009 (mispellings in originals).

2. "Soils of Wales," Soil Survey of England and Wales, 1983 (scale 1:250,000); Harold C. Carter, ed., *National Atlas of Wales* (Cardiff: University of Wales Press, 1988), map 1.5, "Soils"; Ministry of Town and Country Planning for the Ordnance Survey, comp., "Rainfall, Annual Average, 1881–1915" (scale 1:625,000), Great Britain Sheet 2, 1949; J. A. A. Jones, "Climate," map 1.4 (scale 1:500,000) in *National Atlas of Wales*.

3. Tithe files; Richard J. Moore-Colyer, "Some Aspects of Land Occupation in Nineteenth-Century Cardiganshire," *Transactions of the Honourable Society of Cymmrodorion* (1981): 79–81.

Fig. 3.1 Scenes from Mynydd Bach. The stone walls that once marked the bounds of small fields are still visible on the rocky, heavily grazed highland of Mynydd Bach (*top*), although they are now succumbing to grass and the occasional untamed hedge tree (note the wind-bent specimen behind the sheep). Tabor chapel (*bottom*) stands just outside the village of Llangwyryfon. This view of the chapel looks southeast toward the backbone of Mynydd Bach to where cottagers fought "the war of the Little Englishman." (Photos by the author)

Table 3.1 Land tenure in study parishes

| Parish | Freehold | | Tenancy | |
	Number/ proportion	Average acres	Number/ proportion	Average acres
Cilcennin	17 (21.0%)	52.9	64 (79.0%)	37.2
Llanbadarn Odwyn	32 (34.4%)	23.2	61 (65.6%)	49.4
Llanbadarn Trefeglwys	37 (22.8%)	29.3	125 (77.2%)	37.0
Llangeitho	27 (40.3%)	27.1	40 (59.7%)	35.4
Llangwyryfon	38 (32.2%)	9.7	80 (67.8%)	39.7
Nancwnlle	38 (27.1%)	13.3	102 (72.9%)	34.8
Trefilan	4 (8.0%)	24.9	46 (92.0%)	43.9
Totals	193 (27.1%)	23.0	518 (72.9%)	39.0

Sources: Tithe apportionment schedules for Cilcennin (1840), Llanbadarn Odwyn (1845), Llanbadarn Trefeglwys (1839), Llangeitho (1839), Llangwyryfon (1842), Nantcwnlle [*sic*] (1839), Trefilan (1838).

parishes owned their own land and a growing proportion of landlords were either newcomers or petty landholders rather than members of the established local gentry.[4] Mynydd Bach's freehold farms were also more substantial than in many parts of Wales. Some lowland freeholds in the parishes of Cilcennin, Llanbadarn Trefeglwys, and Llansanffraid had from 100 to 225 acres of pasture and arable. Freehold farms were, on average, smaller than the average tenant farm in most parishes (see table 3.1), yet only in Llangwyryfon and Nancwnlle was the average freehold farm smaller than twenty acres.

Those two parishes played an important part in the agricultural and emigration histories of Mynydd Bach. They straddle the top of the ridge, Nancwnlle overlooking the Aeron Valley to the south and Llangwyryfon including rugged wasteland around two lakes, Llyn Eiddwen and Llyn Fanod. The people in these and neighboring parishes mounted sustained, sometimes violent resistance to parliamentary enclosure, marking Mynydd Bach as a rough neighborhood in the early nineteenth century. Their actions directly resulted in local people having continued access to the vital resources of summer grazing and peat on the common when enclosures elsewhere in Wales were forcing rural people to consider emigration as a solution to land scarcity.

In 1815, Parliament sold 840 acres atop Mynydd Bach to an Englishman named Augustus Brackenbury, who planned to develop the land as a hunting estate for visiting gentry. Bracken-

4. Census of Great Britain, 1841, Enumerators' Returns, Public Record Office, London, HO 107/1373 (Cilcennin, Llanbadarn Trefeglwys, Llangwyryfon, Trefilan, 1376 (Llanbadarn Odwyn, Llangeitho, Nancwnlle).

bury's new property included the small ridgetop community of Trefenter and several hundred acres of unfenced common.[5] Trefenter was a fairly new settlement in 1815, although it was sufficiently developed socially to have a Sunday school. Its residents were a mix of farm laborers, craftspeople, and farmers. Most of them were squatters who had occupied their holdings for fewer than twenty-one years, the time required to claim land as a freehold.[6]

When Brackenbury arrived in 1820 to take up his claim, he no doubt expected to be rid of the illegal occupants of his land in short order. But the people he tried to dispossess put up stiff resistance to the man they dubbed "the Little Englishman." Residents of Mynydd Bach repeatedly threatened to destroy Brackenbury's house and the fences he erected to mark the enclosure. The threats were carried out late one night when twenty to thirty people surrounded the house, seized Brackenbury, and set fire to his home. "In all the reminiscences," wrote historian David Williams, ". . . it is recorded that Brackenbury was held over the fire and roasted until he promised to depart, never to return, and the confirmatory detail is added that the metal buttons on his coat became so hot that they could not be touched." Brackenbury omitted the roasting from his own recounting to the authorities.[7] Whether true or apocryphal, the story nicely conveys the community's pride in driving the devil from their midst.

Brackenbury tried a different strategy when he returned in 1826. This time he built an ostentatious stone house mimicking a medieval castle, with a round lookout tower and a square moat eight feet wide and three feet deep. He hired guards to chase away anyone who attempted to cut peat from his hillsides. Once again the locals organized an attack, this time hundreds strong (one story puts it at a thousand men). The crowd descended on the castle en masse. They waited while a group of delegates persuaded Brackenbury to leave, then razed the building. One of the

5. Interview with Dai Morris Jones at his home, Blaen Beidiog, Trefenter, 13 May 1992. Dai is known locally as the last man to cut peat on Mynydd Bach. He told me that some peat bogs on the mountain yielded high-quality peat that dried into dark, coal-like bricks, but that all such peat had been exhausted; only light, friable, smokey peat is left and is not worth the digging.

6. Richard Phillips, *Dyn a'i Wreiddiau: Peth o Hanes Plwyf Llangwyryfon* (Man and His Roots: Some of the History of Llangwyryfon Parish) (Privately published by the author, 1975), 20–28.

7. David Williams, "'Rhyfel y Sais Bach': An Enclosure Riot on Mynydd Bach," *Ceredigion* 2 (1952): 39–52, quotation on p. 41.

rioters was brought before the Court of Great Sessions but was acquitted of all charges by a sympathetic Welsh jury. When Brackenbury returned a third time in 1828 he made no effort to prevent local people from using his land. Near the castle ruins he built a modest stone house called Cofadail. The Englishman lived in the house unmolested for two years. In 1830 he sold the land in twelve parcels and disappeared forever from Cardiganshire.[8]

Rhyfel y Sais Bach (the War of the Little Englishman) was an unusual case of rural Welsh people violently resisting parliamentary enclosure. Their success was evident in the persistence of unenclosed common on Mynydd Bach. Llangwyryfon parish, which includes Trefenter, still had 230 acres of common in 1842. Llanbadarn Odwyn and Nancwnlle had 574 and 521 acres, respectively. Even Cilcennin and Trefilan, lower-lying parishes bordering on the Aeron River, had a little common land left in 1840.[9] More significantly, the number and proportions of freeholds on Mynydd Bach continued to rise in the wake of Brackenbury's defeat, most notably in upland parishes. In 1830, land tax records showed freeholds to be 19 percent of holdings in Nancwnlle and 17 percent of those in Llangwyryfon. When those parishes were surveyed for reapportionment of tithes in the early 1840s, freeholds had risen to 27 percent of holdings in Nancwnlle and 32 percent in Llangwyryfon.[10]

The people of Mynydd Bach again resisted enclosure when a local tenant farmer named Isaac Jennings tried to exercise his rights to the parcels of common land he bought from the Crown in 1847. Jennings was an elder at Llangwyryfon's Calvinistic

8. Richard Phillips, "Amgáu Tir ar Fynydd Bach" (Enclosing Land on Mynydd Bach), *Ceredigion* 6 (1971): 350–63.

9. In *The Great Enclosures of Common Lands in Wales* (London: Chiswich Press, 1914), 47–56, Ivor Bowen notes the following enclosures in the Mynydd Bach region after *Rhyfel y Sais Bach*: Nancwnlle (1850), Blaenpennal (1851), Llangeitho common (1856), and Llanddewibrefi (1863). The National Library of Wales possesses three original enclosure awards for the area, which are identified and dated as the Pen-uwch area in 1857 (probably Bowen's Nancwnlle); the Llangeitho common in 1860; and Blaenpennal in 1864 (probably Llanddewibrefi); National Library of Wales, Cardiganshire C.C. 10–12. Acreage of commons is listed in the tithe apportionment schedules for each parish; see source note to table 3.1.

10. Roberts and Evans Collection/Cardiganshire Land Tax Assessments, 1830, Nancwnlle no. 62/61/1–15, National Library of Wales (hereafter cited as Roberts and Evans Collection); Ibid., Llangwyryfon no. 60/44/1–32. The tax assessment records for other parishes show the proportion of freehold properties varying less than 4 percent between 1830 and the date of the parish's tithe survey.

Methodist chapel, Bethel, and was remembered in the neighborhood as an "uncommonly godly and respectable man." But according to oral tradition, local people repeatedly pulled down by night the walls that Jennings built to enclose his property, to the point where the harassment literally sickened him to death; the poor man died in 1849 at the age of forty-nine. Nor did Jennings's heirs succeed in fencing off the property, which was still open pasture as late as 1975.[11]

Continued access to the common for grazing and settlement also helps explain the continued population growth of Mynydd Bach parishes. With the exception of the lead mining region, most rural parishes in Cardiganshire registered their peak population in the 1821 or 1831 census. The median date for peak population on Mynydd Bach was 1841, and four parishes peaked in 1851 (see table 3.2). As the population grew, the line of settlement pressed further and further up the slopes of Mynydd Bach as people built *tai unnos* (traditionally, houses built in one night), which staked the builders' claim to traditional squatters' rights on a small parcel of land. Even after these temporary shelters were improved and enlarged into cottages and farmhouses, their names savored of their physical circumstances and history. The 1839 tithe apportionment schedule and map for Nancwnlle parish include smallholdings with names such as *Blaen-y-gors* (bog's edge), *Caermynydd* (mountain field), *Lluest-y-pwdel* (summer house by the puddle), and *Tan-y-llethr* (under the slope). None of these properties appears in the parish land tax assessment rolls up to 1830, which suggests that they may have been *tai unnos* built between that date and the tithe commissioners' visit ten years later.[12]

The upland settlements of Trefenter, Blaenpennal, and Penuwch all developed as squatters' communities during the first half of the century. When the Tithe Commission surveyors mapped the region between 1838 and 1845, freeholdings in Trefenter ranged in size from less than one acre to thirteen acres. Many were cottages with no land except a garden plot. Nearly 64 percent of freeholds and 40 percent of tenant farms in Trefenter were smaller than ten acres. Although new holdings on the common reduced the amount of summer pasture and peat avail-

11. Phillips, *Dyn a'i Wreiddiau*, 235–37, quotation on p. 235.
12. Tithe apportionment schedule and map of Nancwnlle parish (1839); Roberts and Evans Collection, Nancwnlle no. 62/61/1–15.

Table 3.2 Population increase, Mynydd Bach and Cardiganshire

Parish	1801	1811	1821	1831	1841	1851	1801/peak
				Acres per person			
Blaenpennal[a]	331	403	473	543	503	505	12.40 / 7.56
Cilcennin	530	546	551	695	647	640	6.42 / 4.90
Llanbadarn Odwyn	312	401	467	558	504	492	14.18 / 7.93
Llanbadarn Trefeglwys	756	879	920	982	1,045	965	8.31 / 6.01
Llanddeiniol	215	250	219	254	273	251	9.66 / 7.61
Llangeitho	250	279	332	377	431	442	8.60 / 4.86
Llangwyryfon	430	539	601	533	642	595	8.94 / 5.99
Llanrhystud	1,148	1,230	1,375	1,525	1,608	1,516	7.64 / 5.45
Llansanffraid	777	1,016	1,172	1,206	1,222	1,286	7.01 / 4.23
Llanychaearn	497	538	630	688	666	538	8.41 / 6.08
Nancwnlle	457	569	635	686	774	783	10.07 / 5.88
Trefilan	226	214	278	313	317	308	9.74 / 6.94
Upper Lledrod	308	149[b]	485	481	501	534	10.91 / 7.77[c]
All parish totals:	6,237	7,013	8,138	8,841	9,133	8,855	
Cardiganshire	61,290	70,067	81,765	90,690	96,002	97,614	

[a]Chapelry of Blaenpennal.

[b]This figure may be a typographical error in the original source.

[c]Combined average for Upper and Lower Lledrod.

Source: Census of Great Britain, 1851, *Population Tables*, pt. 2, vol. 2 (London, 1854), "Birth-Places of the People," Division 11, Monmouthshire and Wales, pp. 36–39.

able to established farmers, they provided a crucial foothold for young families in their home district.[13]

That the land on Mynydd Bach was good for little besides grazing native Welsh sheep and cutting peat no doubt lessened its appeal to would-be enclosers, but they may also have been put off by the native community's determination and their willingness to use rough justice to defend what they considered their land.[14] Resistance to enclosure clearly signaled strong feelings about controlling land and continuing an agricultural way of life, whether as tenant or freeholder. This may help explain why the region was not more heavily involved with migration to industrial areas in southeast Wales, since industrial work often required a man's permanent removal from his rural home, particularly if he wanted to climb the craft ladder to well-paying positions. At the same time, however, population pressure on land and other resources was becoming acute on Mynydd Bach by the late 1830s, exactly the period when significant emigration began.

The number of rentier landlords on Mynydd Bach was another factor that distinguished this region from other parts of Cardiganshire. By 1830 the great families of the county owned less than 10 percent of tenancies in the fourteen study parishes. Most tenant farmers on Mynydd Bach rented their land from professional men like Dr. John Rogers of Abermeurig or Francis Saunders, Esq.; from well-to-do clerics such as Cilcennin's vicar, Timothy Evans; or from minor gentry such as the Gwynne family of Mynachdy, whose patriarch, Alban Thomas Jones Gwynne, built the harbor and town of Aberaeron in 1807. These were the local aristocracy

13. Evan Jones, *Y Mynydd Bach a Bro Eiddwen* (Mynydd Bach and the Eiddwen Neighborhood) (Aberystwyth: Cymdeithas Lyfrau Ceredigion, 1990), 8–19, 22–25; Phillips, *Dyn a'i Wreiddiau*, 280–81; tithe apportionment schedules, Llangwyryfon, Cilcennin, Llanbadarn Odwyn, Llanbadarn Trefeglwys, Llangeitho, Nancwnlle, and Trefilan. At the time of tithe apportionment, as when enclosure laws were passed, the law granted freehold status to any holding that had been continuously occupied by the same residents for at least twenty years. Bowen, *Great Enclosures*, 19.

14. It is interesting that none of the accounts of *Rhyfel y Sais Bach* mention means by which rural Welsh people traditionally administered rough justice, such as men dressing as women (in part to conceal their identity) or a crowd forcing the object of their attack to ride a wooden horse (the *ceffyl pren*). On traditions of community justice in Wales, see Rosemary A. N. Jones, "Women, Community, and Collective Action: The *Ceffyl Pren* Tradition," in *Our Mother's Land: Chapters in Welsh Women's History 1830–1939*, ed. Angela V. John (Cardiff: University of Wales Press, 1991), 17–41.

to whom children were taught to raise their caps in respect.[15] Certain parishes also had large numbers of lesser landlords who rented out small farms, cottages with gardens, or individual fields to supplement their own freehold or tenancy income. In 1839, this class of petty landowners held 46 percent of all holdings and 40 percent of the total acreage in Llanrhystud parish.[16] I found no evidence suggesting that rentier landlords made life difficult for tenants on Mynydd Bach by, for example, charging higher rents than gentry landlords or being less lenient when times were hard. The growing number of petty landlords is socially significant, however, for it indicates a somewhat unusual proclivity among local people to invest their money in small purchases of land, a step toward petty entrepreneurial enterprise which was much more difficult to make in parts of Wales where enclosures and large estates, like those in North Wales, kept land off the market. Comparing emigrant biographies to tax assessment lists and tithe schedules, I find no emigrants who were landlords. As we will see a little later in this chapter, many of them either fell just short of achieving rentier status in their native district or chose to save surplus income toward future expenditure on less expensive and perhaps better land elsewhere.

Welsh Calvinists' Jerusalem

While access to land and determination to keep it distinguished the people of Mynydd Bach in ways that are important to this study, religion was what made the region notable in the emigrants' own day. From the middle of the eighteenth century, the small village of Llangeitho, located near the headwaters of the Aeron River, was one of the cradles of Welsh Calvinistic Methodism. The legacy of revivals in this region, led by the man generally considered to have been Wales' most charismatic preacher, left an enduring stamp on the religious imaginations of those who

15. Roberts and Evans Collection, Cilcennin no. 56/12/1–30; Llanbadarn Odwyn no. 58/26/1–19; Llanbadarn Trefeglwys no. 58/27/1–32; Llangeitho no. 60/40/1–17; Llangwyryfon no. 60/44/1–32; Llansanffraid no. 61/55/1–32; Nancwnlle no. 62/61/1–15; Ben A. Jones, Y Byd o Ben Trichrug (The World from Atop Trichrug) (Aberystwyth: Cymdeithas Lyfrau Ceredigion, 1959), 63, 36, 12.

16. Richard Moore-Colyer, "Farmers and Fields in Nineteenth-Century Wales: The Case of Llanrhystud, Cardiganshire," National Library of Wales Journal 26 (1989–1990): 34.

came to faith within the penumbra of Llangeitho.

Llangeitho's symbolic importance is evident in the number of immigrants who claimed it as their home despite their actually living up to five miles from the parish of Llangeitho and up to eight miles from the village of that name. The same kind of geographical exaggeration led Congregationalists in central Montgomeryshire to identify themselves as coming from Llanbrynmair, the seat of several of the denomination's most influential preachers during the late eighteenth and early nineteenth centuries. [17] Referring to these well-known places as home was a shorthand way to establish one's religious credentials. In late-eighteenth-century and early-nineteenth-century Cardiganshire, "going to Jerusalem" meant going to chapel in Llangeitho. The fame and spiritual importance of the village and parish of Llangeitho grew from the preaching of one man. Daniel Rowland (1713–1790) was born in Nancwnlle and became curate after his father at the parish church in Llangeitho. In 1735, Rowland was converted to Methodism by Gruffydd Jones, Llanddowror, an early Welsh Methodist who was most famous for establishing a system of circulating Sunday schools throughout Wales. Although Rowland initially accepted invitations to preach to distant congregations, riding the rural circuit as Welsh preachers commonly did, he soon ceased traveling almost entirely and settled into his living at Llangeitho.[18] In that secluded place, an unremarkable village on the southwestern flank of Mynydd Bach, Rowland developed into a preacher of unparalleled force and charm.

Physically, Rowland was said to be "a striking personage . . . with sinewy frame and glowing imagination, he could play alike the athlete or the orator"[19] (see fig. 3.2). At his peak he preached fluently, freely, in a Welsh that gripped his congregation. By 1770 his monthly communion services were attracting two to four thousand people, compelling Rowland to move the service outdoors and preach from the hillside. People came from

---

17. Immigrant obituaries mapped to Ordnance Survey Pathfinder series (scale 1:25,000), various dates, for north-central Cardiganshire and central Montgomeryshire.

18. Rev. Joseph Evans, *Biographical Dictionary of Ministers and Preachers of the Welsh Calvinistic Methodist Body* (Carnarvon: D. O'Brien Owen, 1907), 277–88.

19. Edward Matthews and J. Cynddylan Jones, *Cofiant y Parchedig J. Harris Jones* (Biography of Rev. J. Harris Jones) (Llanelli, 1886), quoted in Derec Llwyd Morgan, "Daniel Rowland (?1711–1790): Pregethwr Diwygiadol" (Daniel Rowland . . . Revivalist Preacher), *Ceredigion* 11 (1991): 229.

Fig. 3.2 Daniel Rowland. Rowland stands, open Bible in hand, on the small hill where he may have preached to throngs of pilgrims and curious onlookers on communion Sundays. The statue's stern visage recalls a description of Rowland by the Welsh hymn writer, William Williams, Pantycelyn: "There is Daniel preach - ing / In the mist, the smoke and fire / All at once a thousand praising / Halleluia is the song." (Photo by the author)

as far away as Anglesey to hear him. One Anglesey couple were so captivated by Rowland's preaching that they moved to Llangwyryfon parish in order to attend his sermons every Sunday.[20] The hymnist Morgan Rhys (1716–1779) watched "Llangeitho pilgrims" from southwest Wales pass by Llywele in northern Carmarthenshire on their way to hear Rowland and wrote of the revivalist,

> Your hands and feet were tireless
> In serving the King's children.

20. David Williams, *A History of Modern Wales* (1950; reprint, Cardiff: University of Wales Press, 1969), 150; Derec Llwyd Morgan, "Taith i Langeitho, 1762" (Journey to Llangeitho, 1762), in *Pobl Pantycelyn (Pantycelyn's People)*, ed. Derec Llwyd Morgan (Llandysul: Gwasg Gomer, 1986), 2–15; obituary of Elizabeth Jones, *Y Cyfaill* (February 1846): 88.

Your eyes beheld them coming
Over vast mountains.
Early and late under the cloud
Came the saints to Llywele.[21]

Contemporary descriptions of Rowland's preaching style suggest a man who combined evangelical zeal with the meditative depth of a genuine theologian. His style of exhortation set the standard for Welsh *hwyl*, the mesmerizing, half-chanted, half-sung preaching for which Welsh audiences developed an insatiable appetite. As imaginatively reconstructed by Welsh religious and literary scholar Derec Llwyd Morgan, Rowland was a master of pulpit oratory:

> He drops his voice for a few moments, relaxing his hold on the people, collecting renewed energy; but see his great nature once again red hot, he raises his strong feelings as flames in his voice; and as the temperature rises, the light grows apace; his understanding strengthens as his heart expands—a deep river of the most excellent thoughts flows out of his soul in the most mellifluous melody; and in the middle of the deluge of light and warmth, the congregation loses its self-possession, old white-haired people forget their weakness, travelers from the distant counties lose their weariness, the respectable women lose their politeness—and behold, leaping, weeping, singing, shouting, praising! Hundreds raving under the influence of the Word, having drunk the sweet wine of the new Covenant till they forget the body and its needs, the world and its pain, time and its troubles.[22]

This emotional, physical response among early Calvinistic Methodists led to their being called "Welsh Jumpers"—"from their . . . custom of 'leaping for joy' at their meetings."[23] In ad-

21. D. J. Williams, *The Old Farmhouse*, trans. Waldo Williams (1961; reprint, London: Golden Grove, 1987), 69, quoting Morgan Rhys's elegy to Esther Sion.

22. Morgan, "Daniel Rowland," 230.

23. R. Geraint Gruffydd, "Diwygiad Llangeitho a'i Ddylanwad" (The Llangeitho Revival and Its Influence), *Y Traethodydd* 146, no. 619 (1991): 99–100, quoting *The Oxford Dictionary of the Christian Church*. E. I. Spence witnessed the Calvinistic Methodists' enthusiasm during a visit to Wales around the turn of the nineteenth century. Speaking of a Welsh preacher he saw in Glamoraganshire, he wrote, "His ranting can only be compared to that of a madman. This sect, I understand, is called the *jumping methodists*; they are like the quakers, moved by the spirit, when this enthusiastic madness seizes them, they jump up and down to a considerable height, tear their clothes, howl, and in short act as if they were frantic, screaming and jumping all the way home, however long the distance."

dition to exhortations from the pulpit, early Methodists found great inspiration in Welsh hymns, especially the vivid images that hymnist William Williams, Pantycelyn, set to popular melodies. The combination of a good Rowland sermon and a packed congregation singing Pantycelyn's original setting of "Guide me, O Thou great Jehovah" made for a thrilling religious experience.[24]

The memory of revivals at Llangeitho created a thirst that many Welsh preachers failed to satisfy. Rowland himself was a less magnetic preacher as an old man, although people whom he converted in the late 1780s carried a special aura as last witnesses to the great evangelist's power. Calvinistic Methodist leaders recognized that congregations craved stimulating sermons. They also had to admit that revivals were the surest way of gaining converts, even if the unleashing of passionate emotion made the more sedate ministers of the early nineteenth century distinctly uncomfortable. Thomas Charles of Bala, leader of the Calvinistic Methodists at the turn of the nineteenth century, summarized the dilemma when he wrote, "Unless we are favored with frequent revivals . . . we shall in a great degree degenerate and have only 'a name to live.'"[25]

The jubilant expression of faith remained a hallmark of Calvinistic Methodists around Llangeitho for at least two generations after Rowland's death. Chapel histories from the region portray recurrent local revivals as the lifeblood of religion and passionate worship as the sign of true faith. In the late 1850s a preacher who came to Blaenplwyf chapel in Llanychaearn parish found himself encouraged by chapel member William Rowlands's "fiery Amens . . . When his heart would begin to warm, he would leap to his feet, the Amens would be doubled and

---

Summer Excursions, vol. 2 (1809), quoted in Cylchgrawn Cymdeithas Hanes y Methodistiaid Calfinaidd 43 (Journal of the Calvinistic Methodist History Society) (Carnarvon: Connexional Printing Press, 1958), 70.

24. "Arglwydd, arwain trwy'r anialwch, / Fi, bererin gwael ei wedd . . ." On Pantycelyn's influence on Welsh revivalism, see Derec Llwyd Morgan, Y Diwygiad Mawr (The Great Revival) (Llandysul: Gwasg Gomer, 1981), trans. Dyfnallt Morgan as The Great Awakening in Wales (London: Epworth Press, 1988); idem, "Pantycelyn a'i Gynulleidfa: Yr Emynydd a Mirandus" (Pantycelyn and His Congregation: The Hymnist and Mirandus), in Meddwl a Dychymyg Williams Pantycelyn (The Mind and Imagination of Williams Pantycelyn), ed. Derec Llwyd Morgan (Llandysul: Gwasg Gomer, 1991), 82–101; and Meredydd Evans, "Pantycelyn a Thröedigaeth" (Pantycelyn and Conversion), in Meddwl a Dychymyg Williams Pantycelyn, 55–81.

25. Gruffydd, "Diwygiad Llangeitho," 101–2.

trebled, and it would have the effect of putting the congregation in a new frame of mind, by giving them to understand that things of importance were being discussed." Edward Evans of Ty'n Grug, Llangwyryfon, "was really exceptional in prayer ... He was often in uncommon *hwyl* during services in the chapel; and often he would make his way home, praising, his voice like an organ echoing through the valleys."[26]

Such emotional intensity was also typical of the Methodist revivals that swept through rural communities in the United States during the early nineteenth century. Like frontier American evangelists, early Welsh Calvinistic Methodists offered fire and brimstone, remorse and salvation. Where the intellectualism of Old Dissent in Wales gave people religion for the head, as Williams, Pantycelyn, put it, Methodism gave them religion for the heart (*nid crefydd y talcen, ond crefydd y galon*). Calvinistic Methodism adopted the Methodist institution of the fellowship society to serve the needs of the dispersed Welsh rural population. The *seiat* (a Welsh corruption of "society") was well established in southern Cardiganshire as early as 1750, and by 1790 ten had made the transition from meeting in members' homes to forming congregations and building chapels.[27] The main purpose of the *seiat* was to provide a forum where fellow believers could share and reinforce their religious experiences, but it also created the organizational nucleus for a future chapel. Elders presiding over the *seiat* were responsible for probing believers' experiences to see whether they were genuine. They also performed the role of moral police, ensuring that those who professed faith were behaving appropriately. Because ultimate authority and inspiration came from Scripture, it was important for the men and women who participated in a *seiat* to be able to read and understand the Welsh Bible, as Gruffydd Jones recognized in organizing his mission for Welsh Sunday schools.

26. Rev. Robert Roberts, *Cofiant am y Diweddar William Rowlands, Cwrt-y-cwm, Plwyf Llanychaiarn, Sir Aberteifi* (Biography of the Late William Rowlands, Cwrt-y-cwm, Llanychaiarn Parish, Cardiganshire) (Aberystwyth: Philip Williams, 1861), 4; David Samuel, manuscript history of Tabor chapel, Llangwyryfon, North Cardiganshire Presbytery Records, no. 24(c), ms. p. 12, National Library of Wales. My thanks to John R. Morris, Glan Carrog, for sharing his copy of the Rowlands biography with me.

27. Eryn M. White, *"Praidd Bach y Bugail Mawr": Seiadau Methodistaidd De-Orllewin Cymru* (The Mighty Shepherd's Little Flock: Methodist Societies in South-West Wales) (Llandysul: Gwasg Gomer, 1995); David R. Barnes, *People of Seion* (Llandysul: Gwasg Gomer, 1995), 70–75.

The Calvinistic Methodist *seiat,* Sunday school, and chapel borrowed a number of traditions from Old Dissent, including theological debates in men's Sunday school classes and the memorization of vast portions of the Bible by women and children. The role these traditions played in maintaining orthodoxy was most evident in congregational examinations called *y Gymanfa Bwnc,* literally the topical assembly, in which the minister quizzed members of the congregation on their understanding of the Bible. The highlight of these catechizing sessions were group recitations of Bible verses in haunting, rhythmic cadences. In some congregations, Sunday schools "sang" these verses in a uniquely Welsh style called *llafar-ganu,* a forceful speaking-singing in which the tones are pitched in minor harmonies. Both *llafar-ganu* and unsung recitation united participants in ritual performance unlike anything experienced by English Nonconformists.[28] In the less formal setting of the *seiat,* individual believers found their own style of expression in extemporaneous prayer, which became a valued kind of performance for gifted men and a few powerful women.

Aside from distinctive rituals such as *y Gymanfa Bwnc,* Calvinistic Methodism differed from contemporary American evangelical Protestantism mainly in its attitude toward authority. Unlike the anticlerical, profoundly democratic strain of thought espoused by American Baptists and Methodists, Welsh Calvinistic Methodism emphasized obedience to governmental and church authority.[29] Daniel Rowland set the tone by refusing to sever his official ties to the Church of England even after the Church denied him his living because of his overtly Methodistic message and style of preaching. Thomas Charles and other leaders of the Calvinistic Methodist movement in the late eighteenth century shared Rowland's reluctance, continuing to see their role as renewing the Church from within rather than forming a separatist movement. They did not incorporate as an independent religious body until 1811 and did not publish their own *Rules of*

28. John Ballinger, "Further Gleanings from a Printer's File," *West Wales Historical Records* 11 (1926), 219–25; idem, "Holi'r Pwnc" (Examining the Subject, i.e., catechism) *West Wales Historical Records* 12 (1927): 225–31. *Holi'r Pwnc* survives today only in a few Welsh Baptist congregations in northern Pembrokeshire and *llafar-ganu* only in the Rhydwilym circuit, where it was still performed annually at Whitsun as late as 1993.

29. On the anticlericism and democratic impulse of the Second Great Awakening, see Nathan O. Hatch, *The Democratization of American Christianity* (New Haven: Yale University Press, 1989).

Discipline until 1823, after nearly one hundred years of quasi-official existence.[30] During the formative early decades of the century, liberal and conservative leaders struggled to control the heart and future of the denomination. Their debate hinged on whether Calvinistic Methodism would embrace the antinomian and arminian notion that anyone could be saved through God's grace, or would stand fast in the Calvinist conviction that God preordained who would and would not be saved. By 1830 the High Calvinists had won the theological battle.[31] At the same time, the culture of Calvinistic Methodism was taking a decided turn toward discipline and orthodoxy, cultivating a Puritanical strictness that cast a heavy mantel over Welsh society as the denomination claimed growing numbers of converts and as the Welsh Congregationalists and Welsh Baptists adopted the moral imperatives of Calvinism.

The people of Mynydd Bach experienced these developments firsthand. The region's most important religious leader after Daniel Rowland was a preacher and later ordained minister named Ebenezer Richard (1781–1837). Richard's vigor and gift for organization contributed greatly to the institutional development of Calvinistic Methodism. From his base in the market town of Tregaron, four miles east of Llangeitho, he traveled constantly throughout Wales and to Welsh chapels in London in his capacity as secretary of the South Wales Methodist Association, keeping minutes for regional assemblies, preaching, and drafting rules to govern various aspects of denominational life, including the behavior of itinerant preachers. Richard believed that religion should be "as near as possible to people's homes"; to that end, he "possessed the upper part of the county of Cardigan for Christ under the banner of Methodism" by founding small chapels in almost every rural neighborhood.[32]

30. Williams, *Modern Wales*, 155–56; Barnes, *People of Seion*, 67.

31. John Davies, *A History of Wales* (London: Allen Lane/Penguin, 1993), 329–30; R. Tudur Jones, *Duw a Diwylliant: Y Ddadl Fawr, 1800–1830* (God and Culture: The Great Debate, 1800–1830), pamphlet, originally delivered as lecture at Hen Gapel, Tre'r-ddôl, 22 September 1984 (Welsh National Folk Museum, 1986).

32. Evans, *Biographical Dictionary*, 254–57, quotations on p. 256. The National Library of Wales has a number of Richard's diaries in its manuscript collection, as well as many of his notes from Association meetings. He was a fine writer in Welsh and English. Some of the English minutes from the monthly Cardiganshire Association meetings are reprinted in *Cylchgrawn Cymdeithas Hanes y Methodistiaid Calfinaidd* (Journal of the Calvinistic Methodist History Society) (Carnarvon: Connexional Printing Press), vol. 27, no. 1 (March 1942); vol. 27,

Richard was also the first Calvinistic Methodist preacher in central Cardiganshire to perform the sacrament of baptism and to cease the tradition, established under Rowland, of basing chapel services on the Anglican Book of Common Prayer. The long-standing amity between Anglicans and Nonconformists in the region, which Rowland had nurtured precisely by refusing to declare himself a Methodist, smoothed the way for these important changes. Richard himself deserved credit for being a "dexterous and inoffensive" leader whose deportment and diplomacy minimized the threat Calvinistic Methodism posed to local Anglican clergy and landlords. He was a model of the new generation of Welsh Nonconformist ministers, well-educated, temperate, "every adornment of the outer man a true portrait of the princely superiority of the inner man," as one of his elegists wrote.[33]

Richard made his greatest impression upon Mynydd Bach as a preacher and as the founder and examiner of Sunday schools. His earthy metaphors made religion and religious obligation vividly real for farm people. For example, in 1832 he came to preach at Bethania chapel near Llan-non to help raise funds for enlarging the sanctuary. Knowing the congregation needed a push to contribute toward the cause, Richard directed his message at the richest member of the congregation. "When men go to wash sheep," he said, "what they need to do is throw the strongest ram first into the lake, so that the others may follow; and we shall do that tonight. I am calling upon you, John Davies, [to be] the first." In another story, Richards questioned an embarrassed Sunday school in Lledrod about the biblical passage "For it is filthy to recite the things that they did in secret." He made them declare over and over that the only fitting end for filthy acts was to bury them, then concluded, "Because this little school has come together to bury filthy things, let us all go to the funeral, in order to heap enough dirt upon them so that they will never be seen again."[34]

no. 3 (September 1942); and vol. 28, no. 2 (June 1943). On Ebenezer Richard, see E. W. and Henry Richard, *Bywyd Ebenezer Richard* (The Life of Ebenezer Richard) (London: W. Clowes, 1839).

33. Rev. John Evans, *Hanes Methodistiaeth Rhan Ddeheuol Sir Aberteifi o Ddechreuad y "Diwygiad Methodistaidd" yn 1735 hyd 1900* (The History of Methodism in Southern Cardiganshire from the Beginning of the "Methodist Revival" in 1735 to 1900) (Dolgellau: E. W. Evans, 1904), 100–101; inscription upon Richard's grave, as printed in *Y Cyfaill* (December 1843): 181.

34. Evans, *Hanes Methodistiaeth*, 132, 144.

As one of the authors of the *Rules of Discipline,* Richard strove to inculcate proper behavior in his followers on Mynydd Bach. The Calvinistic Methodist code of behavior forbade a long list of sins of which English and American fundamentalists also disapproved, including marriage outside the faith, drunkenness, gluttony, dancing, gambling, vain dress, and foul language. Calvinistic Methodists were also to forswear "foolish talking and jesting," bickering over prices in the market, and "speaking evil of dignities." Members were to devote the Sabbath to divine worship and to hold daily family worship (something that apparently caught on slowly in Cardiganshire, judging from Richard's repeated exhortations for elders to enforce the practice). The denomination's by-laws also established procedures for organizing a new *seiat* and chapels and for members to resolve their differences without resorting to government authorities.[35]

By the time Ebenezer Richard died in 1837, he had extended and solidified the network of chapels and Sunday schools across Mynydd Bach, adding at least eleven new chapels to the region's Calvinistic Methodist provision.[36] These institutions formed a sacred landscape rich with biblical allusions. Chapels named Hermon, Bethania, Elim, Tabernacl, Bethel, Bethesda, Tabor, Soar, and Moriah recalled biblical places, each one associated with a sacred story. Many chapels also had a *tŷ capel,* or chapel house, a small dwelling adjoining the sanctuary. Those in Cardiganshire typically consisted of two small rooms, one where an itinerant preacher could eat a meal and entertain visitors, another furnished with a bed where he could rest before setting out on his next engagement. Because the *tŷ capel* and its resident caretaker (often an impoverished single woman) added to the financial burden on chapel members, the little house next to the chapel signified members' seriousness about religion and their desire to attract a regular stream of visiting preachers.

Inside Welsh chapels, whether Calvinistic Methodist, Congregational, or Baptist, the lack of any ostentatious decoration was meant to humble the soul and concentrate the mind on the word

---

35. *The History, Constitution, Rules of Discipline, and Confessions of Faith, of the Calvinistic Methodists in Wales,* 3d ed. (Mold: H & O. Jones, 1840), 33–42; *Cylchgrawn Cymdeithas Hanes y Methodistiaid Calfinaidd.* vol. 27, no. 1 (March 1942): 78. Richard noted in October 1814, for example, "[t]hat the Elders are to make a particular enquiry in their different Societies respecting Family Worship and who amongst the members are found guilty of neglecting the same with the causes of neglect." Ibid.

36. Barnes, *People of Seion,* 156–69.

of God. Yet the severely simple architecture had its own lexicon of spiritual and social meaning. A Cardiganshire minister's description of the interior of Llangeitho chapel suggests the extent to which biblical imagery influenced popular imagination. John Evans recalled the building from his childhood in the 1840s as having two large chambers with massive columns that visually divided one room from the other. The two rooms were "looked upon as the courts of the ancient temple; the court of the Gentiles, and the court of the Israelites. When a believer was seen to be further away from the pulpit toward the columns, it was considered a sign of backsliding; and if an unconfessed [person] approached the columns in the direction of the pulpit, it would be a sign that he was becoming a believer."[37] Every Welsh chapel had a place near the pulpit for the *sedd fawr*, the big seat, where the elders sat facing the minister, setting an example for seemliness. Behind the *sedd fawr*, one's proximity to the pulpit indicated how comfortably one bore the preacher's gaze and, where the chapel charged pew rents, how comfortable one was in terms of "the things of this life."

Outside the chapel walls religion was a constant element in some people's lives, filling their speech with biblical allusions and preoccupying their conversations with fellow believers. John Evans remembered walking across Mynydd Bach as a boy in the company of adult believers, leaving the morning service at one chapel for the afternoon service at another. "The subject of conversation the whole way was the sermons, old and new, and chapters [memorized] for the Sunday school. We were coming through meadows of varied views, and along the shores of rivers, and many a beautiful place, but only spiritual things attracted the attention of the old pilgrims we were following."[38]

In the course of defining the sacred, Calvinistic Methodism also aggressively redefined certain traditional aspects of Welsh folk culture as profane. Lay leaders and preachers cultivated disapproval of all carnal entertainments, including outdoor recreation. Farm laborers had customarily come down to Aberaeron's beach to bathe and play on Sunday, the one day when they had respite from their work. In the wake of a Methodist revival in 1818, lay leaders in the village decided that their admonitions against this shameless desecration of the Sabbath needed the force of economic sanction. With the backing of local gentry, they instituted

37. Evans, *Hanes Methodistiaeth*, 94.
38. Ibid., 188–89.

a fine of five shillings for unruly behavior. This effectively silenced the beaches on Sunday, for five shillings was the equivalent of a week's wage. Llan-non was likewise a popular Sunday resort before the spread of Calvinistic Methodism. It was known for its public dancing, men's football, and a popular game for girls called "First to the Gap." As Welsh Calvinism took hold, such entertainments died out, and with them whole genres of folk culture that remained largely intact in Catholic Ireland, Brittany, and the Hebrides.[39]

Of course, not everyone on Mynydd Bach was a "Pilgrim" or "Israelite," as the Welsh referred to devout Calvinistic Methodists. The squatters village of Pen-uwch, located on the moors above Llangeitho, shared Trefenter's reputation for wildness. When a teetotaling Methodist forbade alcohol from being served at a livestock fair that was to be held on his farm in Llanrhystud, "the thieves of Penuwch . . . moved the fair" to their neighborhood, "where there was plenty of beer as thick as porridge, for sale to everyone."[40] A few neighborhoods had Congregational chapels, notably at Nebo in Llansanffraid parish. Other neighborhoods wished to support institutional religion but could not afford to build a chapel. The people of Blaenpennal did not manage to raise funds for a chapel until 1898, and only then thanks to financial help from friends in London.[41] Generally speaking, however, Mynydd Bach was a stronghold of well-developed Calvinistic Methodist chapels by 1835. Particularly strong congregations were located in two bands around Llangeitho, the first an inner circle of territory that drew members to the mother chapel at Llangeitho itself, the second an outer ring of places beyond easy commuting distance to Llangeitho, including Rhydlwyd chapel at Lledrod and Tabor chapel in Llangwyryfon.[42]

The real importance of Nonconformist religious culture lay not in its most extreme practice but in its pervasiveness throughout

39. Ibid., 158–59, 135.

40. David Evans, *Adgofion yr Hybarch David Evans, Archddiacon Llanelwy* (Memoirs of the Right Reverend David Evans, Archdeacon of Llanelwy) (Lampeter: Gwasg Eglwysig Gymreig, 1904), 15.

41. Evans, *Hanes Methodistiaeth*, 18–22.

42. Records from Llangeitho chapel show much higher Sunday school attendance at that chapel than at its branches in the 1820s; Book of accounts and memoranda, 1825–1836, Capel Gwynfil, Llangeitho, ms. no. 5824A, National Library of Wales. Tabor had 220 members circa 1830 and repeatedly regained members after new chapels temporarily decreased its membership in 1832–1834; Phillips, *Dyn a'i Wreiddiau*, 122.

rural Welsh society. It enriched the language and imposed a widely accepted moral code. It also structured the ways believers used their time outside work by calling them to honor the Sabbath, to attend religious meetings during the week, and to commit themselves to Bible study. These customs were deeply ingrained in the Cardiganshire milk sellers with whom Gwyneth Francis-Jones grew up in turn-of-the-century London. She remembered as a girl watching

> John Davies and Dai Jones walking home from chapel, with Annie and Beti deep in conversation behind. It is certain that the men would be discussing the price of eggs or of unsalted French butter that came in distinctive hampers. This was as it should be for these things were their common interest. It is equally certain that, during the coming week, the words of a powerful sermon would turn over in their minds as they pushed their milk barrows, humming the hymn tunes.[43]

That one of the warmest hearths of self-proclaimed puritanical Welsh Calvinism also had unruly neighborhoods such as Pen-uwch and Trefenter raises interesting questions about the psychology of this region. One could say that the extremes of orthodox Calvinistic Methodism and high-spirited independence both expressed a willful resistance to external authority. If religious morality was gaining dominance over the older tradition of *charivari*, both asserted the right of native Welsh people to control their own society. It should not surprise us that the emigrants who left Mynydd Bach for Ohio in the 1830s and 1840s included horse traders from Pen-uwch and puritanical elders from Lledrod and Llangwyryfon. Both types of people possessed a strong sense of local identity and experience in community organization, traits that certainly would help stabilize any fledgling frontier settlement in the United States.

The Precipitating Event

The year 1837 was a turning point for many people on Mynydd Bach. In March they lost their gifted religious leader, Ebenezer Richard, to a sudden illness. His death could well have been a serious blow to believers in the region, from Llangeitho in the south to Llanddeiniol in the north. Although community and

---

43. Gwyneth Francis-Jones, *Cows, Cardis, and Cockneys* (Borth, Dyfed: Privately published, 1984), 59–60.

Fig. 3.3 Edward Jones. In addition to being considered the father of Calvinistic Methodism in Ohio, Jones was a schoolteacher and a master of shorthand.

chapel histories do not mention any crisis of leadership at that time, the vacuum he left behind may have made it easier for religious people to contemplate leaving their home chapels. At the same time, local people had access to the first detailed, comprehensive guide for Welsh emigrants to the United States, a booklet that was published in Aberystwyth just about the time of Richard's death. Its author, the Rev. Edward Jones (see fig. 3.3), was born on a farm just outside Aberystwyth in 1793. After apprenticing as a tailor he migrated to Crickhowell, Breconshire. He began to preach in 1818 and worked as a schoolmaster in the industrial village of Hirwaun, Glamorganshire, his last home before emigrating to Cincinnati in 1831 with his wife, Mary, and their five children. After many years of preaching and organizing chapels in Welsh settlements up and down the Ohio Valley, Jones decided that it was his duty "to serve such of his nation whom the wheel of providence in its wisdom has turned against"; namely, Welsh farmers who were failing to find land or work for their children, who were "running out of money, and portending to be burdens on their parishes before the end of their days." He wrote Y Teithiwr Americanaidd (The American Traveller) "so that they may not go that way, but that they may have sufficient room for themselves and their children, and that the parishes may be saved from paying for those who cannot work, through acquainting them with places where many of their kind have had a comfortable living without support."[44]

Like many emigrant guides prepared for other nationalities, Jones's booklet provided basic facts about the United States and brief reports on the kind of work, land, and religious provision that were available in all Welsh American settlements of any size. He described the cost and procedures to follow for each stage of the journey, including detailed itineraries of the most efficient routes to each major destination. Unlike commercially produced emigrant guides in the second half of the century, *The American Traveller* did not indulge in boosterism or hyperbole. Jones was concerned to give would-be emigrants accurate information so that they could avoid costly delays and disappointment. In a few passages, however, he wrote more freely, conveying a wonder and excitement that must have kindled similar feelings in his readers. He saved most of his enthusiasm for Ohio, the state with which he was most familiar. He knew that Welsh folk accustomed to winding, hedge-bound lanes would marvel at the streets of Cincinnati, which "run from North to South, and from East to West; they are 30 feet wide, without the side-walks, which are 13 feet yet again." He told them that Ohio's natural transportation routes were rapidly being supplemented with canals and railroads that promised good connections to urban markets. He praised the landscape as one "composed of broad plains and very lovely hills, from which flow healthful waters, similar to the Water of Wales." Best of all, he wrote, the state was a cornucopia for farmers:

> In this country there is very good land for wheat like the wheat of Wales, Indian corn, barley, oats, clover, and potatoes. There is also an abundance of tobacco, soap, water-melons, mush-melons, pumpkins, apples (some of which sometimes get three pence a bushel), pears, peaches, cherries, and every sort of sweet plum, which are so easily gotten that many a one has re-

44. R. D. Thomas, *Hanes Cymry America*/A History of the Welsh in America, trans. Phillips G. Davies (Lanham, Md.: University Press of America, 1983), 129–30; Daniel Jenkins Williams, *One Hundred Years of Welsh Calvinistic Methodism in America* (Philadelphia: Westminster Press, 1937), 129–32; Edward Jones, *Y Teithiwr Americanaidd: Neu Gyfarwyddyd i Symudwyr o Gymru i'r America* (The American Traveler: Or Advice to Emigrants from Wales to America) (Aberystwyth: E. Williams, 1837), 2.

gretted being too liberal with them! Sugar and treacle are also available in this country; and the tea bush has been planted here recently, which is coming along well.[45]

This was nothing short of paradise to people raised on oatmeal, buttermilk, leeks, and salty bacon.

In sum, Jones described Ohio as "the best place for the Welsh." He particularly urged emigrants to consider a small Welsh settlement in Jackson and Gallia counties, where inexpensive farmland was still plentiful and the charcoal iron industry provided wage labor. Jones had visited the settlement in 1834 or 1835 to the joy of four Welsh families who had been living there since emigrating in 1818.[46] As it happened, these families came from the parishes of Cilcennin and Llanbadarn Trefeglwys on the western side of Mynydd Bach. A few friends and relatives on Mynydd Bach were preparing to join them at the time of Jones's visit to the settlement. Without the minister's persuasive support, however, it is unlikely that so many people would have left in so few years to settle in Jackson/Gallia. Jones stayed in Cardiganshire for some months while preparing his guidebook, during which time he doubtless discussed emigration and the Jackson/Gallia settlement with his friends and neighbors. In the summer of 1837 he accompanied thirty emigrants from his native district back to the United States. A letter posted from New York City in July reported their successful crossing on a merchant vessel that also carried emigrants from Neath, Brecon, Ireland, and England.[47] Thus began ten years of chain migration that established "little Cardiganshire" in Jackson and Gallia counties, Ohio.

Who Were the Emigrants?

The first clue for placing emigrants from Mynydd Bach within the context of their native society comes in the names of their home farms. Of all the labels rural Welsh folk traditionally used to iden-

---

45. Jones, *Teithiwr Americanaidd*, 13–21, quotations on pp. 17, 13, 15.

46. Rev. William R. Evans, *Sefydliadau Cymreig Jackson a Gallia, Ohio* (The Welsh Settlements of Jackson and Gallia, Ohio) (Utica, N.Y.: T. J. Griffiths, 1896), 12–13. Evans was translated by Phillips G. Davies as *History of Welsh Settlements in Jackson and Gallia Counties of Ohio*, ed. Lillian Thomas Brownfield (Columbus, Ohio: Chatham Communicators, 1988).

47. Letter published in *Yr Athraw* (The Teacher), vol. 2 (November 1837), reprinted and translated in Alan Conway, ed., *The Welsh in America: Letters from the Immigrants* (Minneapolis: University of Minnesota Press, 1961), 23–24.

tify one another, farm names were the most telling, for they located a person both geographically and genealogically. As in other deeply rooted rural societies, knowing someone's family and farm in Wales provided a host of information about them, including their wealth, social status, and religious affiliation.[48] It is not surprising, then, that Welsh immigrants habitually noted their home farms in family remembrances, letters, and obituaries. Those names make it possible today to trace immigrants back to the places where they lived as children and young adults. Knowing their home address also enables one to estimate their economic circumstances, because official records such as the British census and the Tithe Commission surveys listed households according to their place of residence. Thus farm names are the linchpin for reconstructing the biographies of emigrants from Mynydd Bach. They provide the distinctive common element that makes it possible to link official British sources, immigrant obituaries, and the family histories that formed the basis for community reconstruction in the United States.

Of the 968 Welsh who settled in Jackson/Gallia up to 1860 for whom I have biographical information, a total of 846 (87 percent) came from Mynydd Bach. Map 3.2 shows the location of farms on Mynydd Bach where one or more emigrants lived before leaving Wales. The densest distribution of homes covers the southern half of the mountain, from the source of the Aeron River in Blaenpennal across to Pennant in Llanbadarn Trefeglwys. Another cluster of farms was located on the northwestern side of the uplands between Trefenter and Llanddeiniol. Only a few families and individuals are known to have come from the coastal plain between Llanrhystud and Llan-non, fewer still from the gentle hills southeast of Llangeitho. Once one crosses eastward into the Teifi Valley, the distribution of emigrant residences becomes attenuated. The area around Pontrhydfendigaid lost several score of its farming population to emigration in the 1840s but their favored destination was Waukesha County, Wisconsin.[49]

Curiously enough, it was easier to locate emigrants' homes on

48. One striking parallel is the geographical orientation among Moroccans, explained by Clifford Geertz in "'From the Native's Point of View': On the Nature of Anthropological Understanding," in Local Knowledge: Further Essays in Interpretive Anthropology (London: Fontana Press, 1983), 64–68. D. J. Williams writes about the Welsh passion for genealogy and its important function in Welsh society in The Old Farmhouse, chap. 1.

49. Anne Kelly Knowles, "Welsh Settlement in Waukesha County, Wisconsin, 1840–1873" (M.S. thesis, University of Wisconsin–Madison, 1989), 44–45.

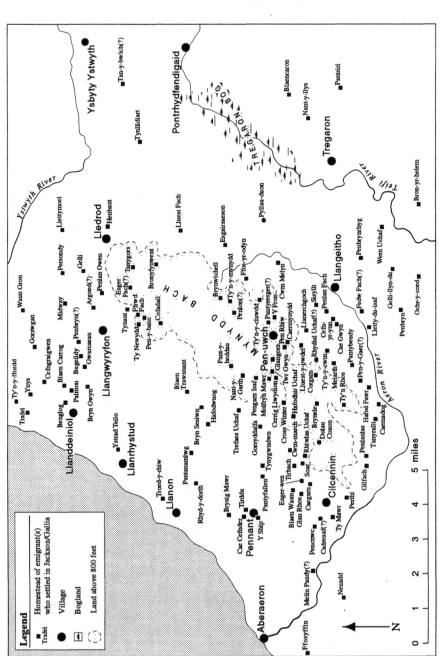

Map 3.2 Home farms of known emigrants in the Mynydd Bach area, 1818–1858

Table 3.3 Land tenure of emigrant holdings

Parish	Freehold		Tenancy	
	Number/ proportion	Average acres	Number/ proportion	Average acres
Cilcennin	4 (40.0%)	136.8	6 (60.0%)	47.0
Llanbadarn Odwyn	1 (14.3%)	72.0	6 (85.7%)	54.8
Llanbadarn Trefeglwys	1 (7.7%)	16.0	12 (92.3%)	108.6
Llanddeiniol	2 (40.4%)	42.5	3 (60.0%)	42.0
Llangeitho	3 (37.5%)	47.0	5 (62.5%)	40.2
Llangwyryfon	2 (22.2%)	3.0	7 (77.8%)	61.4
Llansanffraid	1 (33.3%)	84.0	2 (66.6%)	17.5
Llanychaearn	—	—	4 (100.0%)	46.5
Lledrod	1 (33.3%)	11.0	2 (66.6%)	114.5
Nancwnlle	2 (13.3%)	60.5	13 (86.7%)	65.1
Trefilan	—	—	2 (100%)	97.5
Totals	17 (21.5%)	63.7	62 (78.5%)	67.2

Sources: Tithe apportionment schedules for Cilcennin (1840), Llanbadarn Odwyn (1845), Llanbadarn Trefeglwys (1839), Llanddeiniol (1839), Llangeitho (1839), Llangwyryfon (1842), Llansanffraid (1844), Llanychaearn (1843), Lledrod (1843), Nancwnlle (1839), Trefilan (1838); immigrant biographies (see Appendix E and the Bibliography).

present-day Ordnance Survey maps than it was to find them in nineteenth-century documents.[50] Fewer than 30 percent of the holdings appear in the 1830 land tax assessments, and not all holdings appear in the 1841 manuscript census. The tithe schedules provide the best picture of the kinds of farms emigrants were leaving (see table 3.3, fig. 3.4). Over three-quarters of them were tenant farms (78.5 percent, compared to the overall proportion of 72.9 percent). The size of emigrant farms is more striking. In most parishes, both tenancies and freeholds where emigrants lived were significantly larger than the parish average. Except for two cottages with gardens in Llangwyryfon and two very small farms in Llanbadarn Trefeglwys and Lledrod, emigrant freeholds were among the largest owner-occupied holdings in their parishes. This general pattern shows that, like rural emigrants from Sweden and Norway later in the century, the farm families known to have left Mynydd Bach came predominantly from the upper-middle stratum of agricultural society.[51]

50. Ordnance Survey, Pathfinder series (scale 1:25,000), various dates.

51. This study is prey to biases inherent in the source material. Genealogies and local histories best represent families that remained rooted in a given settlement, whose progenitors tended to be among the early settlers because first-comers were able to buy more land and profited from rising land values as the settlement developed. They underrepresent people who arrived later or who had

It stands to reason that rural emigrants would generally come from families living above subsistence level, since emigration was a fairly expensive proposition. A Cardiganshire family of two parents and four children needed at least £30 to £40 to cover the costs of transportation if they sailed directly from Aberystwyth to a North American port and proceeded immediately to southern Ohio by the cheapest route.[52] If they had to purchase food and lodging along the way, the total could easily reach £50 or more, the equivalent of a year's profit from a large tenant farm's production during a good year.[53] Emigrants may also have received compensation from their landlords for unused manure and other improvements. Some Mynydd Bach families arrived with enough ready money to purchase improved farms at a cost of several hundred dollars.[54] Such families may in fact have been saving toward emigration while their neighbors were working their way

---

little money, whenever they came. Immigrant obituaries covering the early years of settlement help make up this gap. On Swedish and Norwegian emigrants, respectively, Robert C. Ostergren, *A Community Transplanted: The Trans-Atlantic Experience of a Swedish Immigrant Settlement in the Upper Middle West, 1835–1915* (Madison: University of Wisconsin Press, 1988), and Jon Gjerde, *From Peasants to Farmers: The Migration from Balestrand, Norway, to the Upper Middle West* (Cambridge: Cambridge University Press, 1985).

This general profile seems to be more true of areas without extensive cottage industry than regions where the rural economy was largely dependent upon cottage industry, such as hand-loom weaving. Emigrants from the Northern Brabant and Westfalia, two regions where linen weavers were being displaced by mechanized industry in the nineteenth century, appear to have come more predominantly from the lower strata of agricultural society. Yda Sauressig-Schreuder, "Dutch Catholic Emigration in the Mid-Nineteenth Century: Noord-Brabant, 1847–1871," *Journal of Historical Geography* 11 (1985): 48–69; Timothy G. Anderson, "Domestic Industry, Industrialization, and Overseas Migration in Eastern Westphalia, 1840–1880," paper delivered at the annual meeting of the Association of American Geographers, Atlanta, Georgia, April 1993.

52. Edward Jones set the cost of transport from New York City to Portsmouth, Ohio, at $13.33 per person and estimated the exchange rate at $4.44 1/2 per £1. *Teithiwr Americanaidd*, 29. A broadside advertising passage on the brig *Credo* from Aberystwyth to Quebec in 1848 listed passage rates at £3 per adult and £1 10s for each child, plus head money of 5s and 2s 6d, respectively. Passage to New York was more expensive.

53. A tenancy on the Nanteos estate with an annual rent of £60 in 1843 was expected to earn about £180 for its output, clearing £52 above and beyond the costs of operating the farm; Richard J. Moore-Colyer, "Landscape and Landscape Change," typescript, 1976, ms. pp. 22–23.

54. Abstracts of title, Gallia County, Perry and Raccoon townships, Gallia County Courthouse.

Fig. 3.4 Ty'n Rhos. This farmhouse, home of John and Elizabeth Jones, was typi-cal of larger tenant farms. It was built of local stone hewn into blocks that were fit-ted together with little mortar. Houses of this type in Cardiganshire typically had two rooms downstairs (parlor and kitchen) and up to four small bedrooms up-stairs. Servants slept together upstairs or in the hay barn. (Photo courtesy Rev. Stephen Morgan)

into the rentier class through investing in land and the local ship-building industry. Farmers, shopkeepers, and craftsmen of com-parable economic status to the wealthier emigrants dominate the lists of investors who financed ship construction in Aberystwyth and other nearby ports from 1828 through 1847, while not a sin-gle emigrant's name appeared on the lists during that period.[55]

The sequence of departures suggests that the time of a family's emigration roughly corresponded to their economic status. The families who first emigrated from the region, including those who founded the Jackson/Gallia settlement in 1818, included free-

55. Aberystwyth Borough Records, Acc. no. 278, AT/SHIP/1/1824–1832; Acc. no. 278, AT/SHIP/2/1832–1840; Acc. no. 278, AT/SHIP/3/1840–1853.

holders and tenants with exceptionally large lowland farms. Other substantial freeholders left between 1837 and 1841 along with a larger number of families from substantial tenant farms. Very few genuinely poor people left the smallholdings and tenancies on the upland moors and the roughest part of the mountain's back until 1845–1847. This pattern does not reflect the dissemination of an idea through space, as Ostergren suggested was the case with emigration from rural Dalarna, Sweden,[56] but rather the economics of emigration. Poorer families were probably more eager to go than their wealthier neighbors, but they were unable to leave until friends or relatives were established in Ohio and could loan them money for the passage. Local lore on Mynydd Bach today says that a man called "True John" traveled back and forth between Jackson/Gallia and Mynydd Bach in the 1840s, ferrying money and information from the new settlement to families waiting to emigrate. He was called "True John" because people on both sides trusted him to serve their needs faithfully.[57]

The economic standing of emigrant farmsteads should not be read too literally. Not all emigrants owned the freeholds or rented the tenancies where they lived. Biographical information makes it clear that in some cases a young man worked as a farm laborer on the holding that he later identified as his Welsh home. William J. Williams was known to have come from Ystrad Teilo, one of the largest farms in Llanrhystud parish, but that farm did not belong to his parents. As Williams's obituary explains, his parents "were compelled, because of straitened circumstances, to hire him out as a shepherd" to their wealthy neighbors when the boy was just seven years old, "as the poor were forced to do with their children."[58] Poverty did not prompt much assisted emigration from Mynydd Bach, however, at least among those who went to southern Ohio. I know of just one Welsh family in Jackson/Gallia who emigrated with financial assistance from their parish. Thomas and Margaret Davis and their five children re-

56. Ostergren, *Community Transplanted*, 115–23. Ostergren maps the diffusion of emigration over a period of twenty-five years (1864–1889) from Rättvik, a rural district slightly larger than Mynydd Bach, and from the larger region of Upper Dalarna from 1860 to 1875. Each is "a classic example of the way an innovation spreads over space and time." See his figures 4.1 and 4.2; quotation on p. 115.

57. Interview with Dafydd Jones, Bronyfynwent at Bronnant School, Dyfed, 11 April 1995.

58. *Y Cyfaill* (November 1882): 423–24.

ceived £8 from Llanbadarn Odwyn's poor-rate administrators to emigrate in 1847.[59]

Demographically, the emigrants from Mynydd Bach were very similar to other Europeans who traveled in family groups from rural areas during the mid–nineteenth century. They were predominantly mature families with two or more children and parents aged twenty-eight to forty years old. Several of the largest family groups consisted of networks of adult siblings who left in stages over several years' time, sometimes leaving the youngest brother behind to take over the parental farm.[60] Sibling networks commonly reestablished their former proximity by purchasing adjoining parcels of land in Ohio, creating neighborhoods that sometimes became known by particular families' names, such as Cooper Hollow, home of the extended family of Thomas J. Jones, Cooper.

More than any other category of rural emigrants, sibling networks make one pause before using the familiar metaphors that immigration writers so often employ to describe the pattern of emigration. We speak of people being struck by "emigration fever," a term that immigrants themselves often used,[61] and of departures coming in "waves." Both images appeal to the geographical imagination. One can easily visualize the departure of

59. Jones, *Mynydd Bach a Bro Eiddwen*, 38.

60. Freeholders in Cardiganshire usually refused to pass on their land to their children until one or both parents had died, resulting in the custom, unusual in European agriculture, of farms passing to the youngest son (where older siblings had lost patience, married, and moved away) or to a number of unmarried siblings. David Jenkins, *The Agricultural Community in South-West Wales at the Turn of the Twentieth Century* (Cardiff: University of Wales Press, 1971), 148–55.

Alwyn D. Rees documented a similar custom in the parish of Llanfihanel yng Ngwynfa in northern Montgomeryshire. He attributed the pattern of late inheritance to the medieval system of gavelkind in Wales, in which the male head of a household retained control of land until his death. Children who left home before the land passed on were entitled to equal shares of moveable property, a system that persisted in the nineteenth-century custom of paying adult children the money equivalent of equal portions of the land one of their siblings inherited, which the heir was responsible to pay. Rees noted that this manner of inheritance had psychological consequences: "The farmer's son has to serve a long apprenticeship, and it is my impression that the psychological effect of this prolonged boyhood may be observed in the reticent and subdued behaviour of farmers' sons as compared with labourers' sons as well as in an element of immaturity which seems to persist in the character of many an adult farmer." Alwyn D. Rees, *Life in a Welsh Countryside: A Social Study of Llanfihangel yng Ngwynfa* (Cardiff: University of Wales Press, 1971), 63–72, quotation on p. 63.

61. There are numerous examples in Conway, *Welsh in America*.

emigrants in wave-like patterns, particularly when large numbers of people were involved. The metaphor of a contagious fever gives the sense of an idea diffusing over space, and it conveys the excitement and fear that people must have felt when deciding to leave their home for an unknown world. Yet these images may distort the nature of emigration as mature adults experienced it, particularly siblings whose departures were coordinated over a fairly long period of time and whose considerations included the welfare of aged parents, many small children, and several households' worth of furniture. Although I estimate that 7–8 percent of Mynydd Bach residents emigrated from the region to Jackson and Gallia counties between 1837 and 1847—a high rate for rural Europe in this period[62]—it still seems grandiose to speak of "waves" when as few as six families were involved in a "crest" of migration activity. In actual space and time, emigration from Mynydd Bach was probably a slow, deliberate process for many people. Rather than give that process the anonymous compulsion of waves or fever, it seems more appropriate to describe it as a periodic gathering together of people, connected by kinship and other social relationships, who picked up their immediate community as they might a tent and set it down on the other side of the Atlantic.

Three examples of emigrant sibling networks came from the southern end of Mynydd Bach. The Alban siblings' youngest brother, John, took over their late father's 68-acre tenant farm in Cilcennin parish sometime before 1830, when John was about twenty years old. His brother Alban owned a 16-acre freehold just into the next parish, while Thomas, the eldest, occupied a 136-acre tenancy nearby. Like their sister, Catherine, the three brothers married locally in their mid-twenties. Alban and John

62. Precise calculation of emigration rates is unfortunately impossible. The information I have been able to gather shows that 689 confirmed individuals left between 1837 and 1847, which yields a percentage of 7.57 percent of the 1841 population in the thirteen parishes listed in table 1.2. Higher proportions left parishes with the greatest number of emigrants. For example, Nancwnlle lost at least 79 people during that decade, which would have been over 10 percent of the parish's 1841 population. Thus the rate of emigration from Mynydd Bach during this period may have exceeded the annual average rates of emigration from Great Britain, Sweden, and Germany from 1841 to 1850; Richard A. Easterlin, "Immigration: Economic and Social Characteristics," in *Harvard Encyclopedia of American Ethnic Groups*, ed. Stephan Thernstrom (Cambridge: Harvard University Press, 1980), 481, table 5. The annualized rate of emigration from Mynydd Bach was comparable to that from the regions of most intense emigration from Norway in 1856–1865; Gjerde, *From Peasants to Farmers*, 22, table 2.

were the first to emigrate with their families in 1834, including nine children. Thomas and Catherine's families followed in 1835, along with Thomas's teenage brother-in-law, David Morgan. The Albans were particularly close-knit because John's and Thomas's wives, Mary and Ann, were both Morgans from Gorsddalfa, another substantial tenant farm.[63] In other families, it appears that an aged parent or parents took the lead. Ann Richards was a widow of seventy when she relinquished her 87-acre tenant farm in Cilcennin parish in 1840. Her five adult children, their spouses and offspring all emigrated with her, a party of at least nineteen and perhaps as many as twenty-five persons.[64] David Evans, Y Wern, and his wife Margaret left their large tenant farm near Llangeitho at the same advanced age, in the company of their six adult children and several grandchildren. When entire sibling networks left in this way, a family disappeared from the neighborhood and often from the region's collective memory.[65]

Kinship was less important than friendship or the influence of a leading personality in forming other clusters of emigrants. I suggested earlier that the return of Edward Jones to his home district

63. Roberts and Evans Collection, Llanbadarn Trefeglwys and Cilcennin parishes, no. 58/27/1–32 and no. 56/12/1–12, respectively; immigrant obituaries; Alban family genealogy and correspondence with William R. Alban; "David Morgan's Account of Travel to America with John and Ann Alban," typescript courtesy of William R. Alban.

64. When a family uprooted itself in this way, they soon faded from the folk memory of their old parish. This is why American genealogists, returning to Europe in search of their family origins, often quicken interest in local history in the places they visit. Current residents of Mynydd Bach have learned much of what they know about the emigration to Oak Hill from visits by Evan E. Davis, a sixth-generation descendant of several families from the region, including Ann Richards.

65. Although local histories of Mynydd Bach mention the emigration generally or the departure of a few individuals, only Evan Jones, *Y Mynydd Bach a Bro Eiddwen*, acknowledges that the emigration was substantial and pins it accurately to the period 1835–1850. Aberystwyth geographer Emrys G. Bowen and the antiquarian Bob Owen, Croesor, both noted heavy emigration from Cardiganshire to Ohio during the mid–nineteenth century; see Emrys G. Bowen, "Welsh Emigration Overseas," *Advancement of Science* 17 (1960): 260–71; and Bob Owen, "Ymfudo o Sir Aberteifi i Unol Daleithiau America o 1654 hyd 1860" (Emigration from Cardiganshire to the United States of America from 1654 to 1860), *Ceredigion* (1952–1955): 160–69, 225–40; idem, "O Sir Aberteifi i Jackson a Gallia, Ohio" (From Cardiganshire to Jackson and Gallia, Ohio), *Cylchgrawn Cymdeithas Ceredigion Llundain* (Journal of the Cardigan Society of London) 11 (1955–1956): 17–21.

in the northwestern part of the region precipitated large-scale emigration in 1837. His influence might not have been so great had it not been for Edward Morris, an enthusiastic and charismatic young man who accompanied Jones on his return trip to Ohio in 1837. Morris was born in 1813, the eldest son of John and Mary Morris of Cefngraigwen farm, a tenancy of 109 acres on the border of Llanychaearn and Llanddeiniol parishes (see map 3.3). The farm was a good property with a large house and several outbuildings, as well as extensive arable, meadow, pasture, and bogland.[66] Edward's parents were well-respected farmers but were not "religiously inclined." Edward and his brother Morris, on the other hand, were ardent Calvinistic Methodists. By the time he was twenty, Edward was a ruling elder at Elim chapel in the village of Llanddeiniol. A few years later, Elim approved Morris as a preacher of the gospel.[67] If Morris Morris was a promising minister, Edward was a natural leader. Friends described him as "a deacon of great influence; he stood to the fore in mental ability and general knowledge." He was "a good scholar, a splendid writer, a poet of note, and much more amusing than was common."[68] Such a man could cajole and convince reluctant friends to do something daring, unprecedented. At least three families from the Llanddeiniol neighborhood went with Edward and his wife, Mary, when they left in 1837. The following year, at least twenty-nine people emigrated to Jackson/Gallia from Llanddeiniol, along with twenty-five others from adjoining parishes. Most of them traveled on the ship Oseola, which sailed from Liverpool to New York in the summer of 1838.[69]

Four miles to the southeast of Cefngraigwen and 100 to 150 meters higher in elevation, a cluster of holdings in Trefenter rep-

66. Tithe map and apportionment schedule, Llanychaearn parish (1845), National Library of Wales.

67. Y Cyfaill (April 1858): 129; Elim chapel, Llanddeiniol, in North Cardiganshire Presbytery Records 24(a), David Samuel Papers, ms. p. 3, National Library of Wales.

68. Evans, Sefydliadau Cymreig, 74, 73. These short pieces by Morris published in the Calvinistic Methodist monthly, Y Cyfaill, support his friend David Morgan's opinion of his writing. They are written in exceptionally graceful Welsh. His pen name was Elimson.

69. Port of New York, Ship Oseola manifest, State Historical Society of Wisconsin microfilm no. P77-898. The ship arrived from Liverpool on 2 July 1838. My thanks to John Evans of Llanddeiniol, Dyfed, and Lucille McFee of Madison, Wisconsin, for sharing their discovery of the Oseola manifest with me, and to John in particular for providing genealogical information confirming the identity of Oseola passengers.

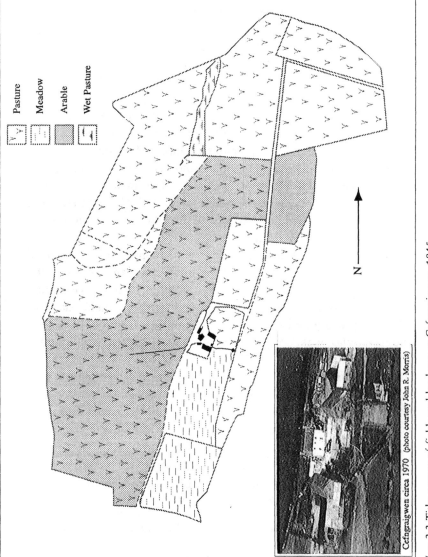

Map 3.3 Tithe survey of fields and land use at Cefngraigwen, 1845

Pasture

Meadow

Arable

Wet Pasture

N

Cefngraigwen circa 1970 (photo courtesy John R. Morris)

resented the range of homes that poorer emigrants left behind, from the 86-acre tenancy of Ty Nant to tiny Wain Gron and Ffrwd Fach[70] (see map 3.4). David Jenkins emigrated from Ty Nant at the age of twenty-one in 1836. His mother continued farming after he left, growing crops on the same amount of arable as Cefngraigwen but under less favorable conditions; the soils at Ty Nant are poorly drained, with many peaty areas suitable only for rough grazing. The Jenkins's house was a typical stone cottage with two rooms on the ground floor and a sleeping-hayloft above. Ty Newydd, a small freehold in the heart of the scattered Trefenter settlement, consisted of a cottage, garden, and three fields totaling just over five acres. The census of 1841 recorded Thomas and Mary Isaac, both in their fifties, as farmers at this small place, along with their adult children Margaret and Isaac, and fifteen-year-old John. The household also had two servants, a girl of fourteen and a boy of ten. In 1844 John left Ty Newydd with his wife, Mary, and their infant child. Unfortunately John had contracted tuberculosis before he left; he died of the disease in Ohio the following June.[71]

Like Thomas J. Jones, Cooper, who exemplified rural-rural emigration in chapter 1, most of the individuals and families who left Mynydd Bach had spent all their lives in their native region. Only a few are known to have lived and worked outside the area before they emigrated to Ohio. One of those exceptions was John Thomas, who was born in London but departed for America from Llangeitho. David J. Morgan also lived for some time in London. Nancwnlle native John Lot Davies converted to Calvinistic Methodism in Merthyr Tydfil and may have spent one or more long periods of time there, perhaps as an industrial worker.[72] Otherwise, the emigrants' obituaries and family histo-

70. Tithe map and apportionment schedule, Llangwyryfon parish (1843); site visit, 13 May 1992. The farmhouse ruins clearly show the typical layout of a two - room Cardiganshire cottage, which usually had a sleeping loft above; Martin Davies, *Traditional Qualities of the West Wales Cottage* (Llandysul: Crown Print, 1991), 9–10; Phillips, *Dyn a'i Wreiddiau*, 278–79. On the soils of the Mynydd Bach region, see "Llanilar" (scale 1: 63,360), Soil Survey of England and Wales, Sheet 178, 1969.

71. Obituary of John Isaac in *Y Cyfaill* (August 1845): 122.

72. Margaret Bartholomew and Martha Morgan, "The Evan Morgan Story," undated typescript, Oak Hill, Ohio, Public Library, unnumbered ms. p. 1; obituary of John Lot Davis, *Y Cyfaill* (December 1853): 473; E. O. Roberts, *Hanes Eglwys Gymreig Jackson, Ohio* (History of the Welsh Church in Jackson, Ohio) (Utica, N.Y.: T. J. Griffiths, 1908), 62–63.

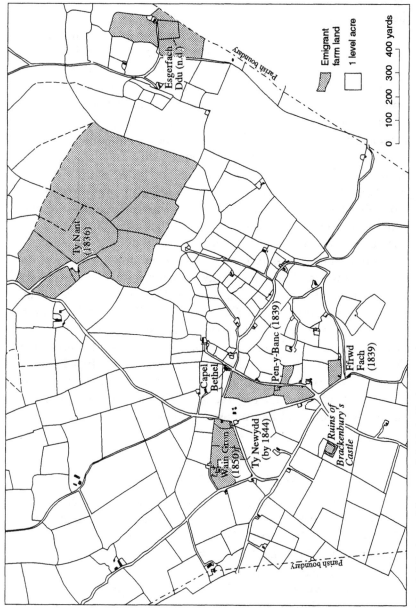

Map 3.4 Emigrants' farms and fields in Trefenter settlement, 1843

ries make no mention of their migrating within Wales or England.

Why were they prepared to take the revolutionary step of crossing the Atlantic ocean when they had not yet ventured outside their native region? Studies of other European emigrants have found that rural people who migrated within their own country were more inclined to emigrate than were people who had never before left home. This makes intuitive sense; internal migration could be temporary or seasonal, or in stepwise fashion the migrant's travel to increasingly distant destinations would gently loosen the bonds of home, whereas emigration as a first step was a sudden, violent severing of all familiar ties. Internal migration to higher-wage areas also provided money that enabled impoverished rural folk to make the move overseas. Most of the emigrants who left Mynydd Bach in 1837–1841, however, were probably able to save enough money to cover their passage and initial settlement from the proceeds of their own farms. My conclusion is that, in this case, emigration to a rural destination in the United States self-selected those families most determined to own their own land. The religiosity of many of the emigrants also suggests that they may well have been disturbed by news of the Sabbath controversy among Cardiganshire milk sellers in London and would have feared or scorned the unholy atmosphere of rough-and-tumble industrial towns like Merthyr Tydfil. From the choices with which they were most familiar, the Mynydd Bach emigrants selected the destination that best fulfilled desires to farm independently and to practice their religion free from the threats of commercial and industrial ungodliness.

Emigration and Settlement

Ironically, the Welsh families whom Edward Jones visited in Ohio in 1834 may have been partly motivated to emigrate by a desire to escape Calvinistic Methodist extremists. The six families who left Mynydd Bach for southern Ohio in 1818 were not known to be particularly religious people in Wales. Some of them may have been members of the Anglican church at Cilcennin, for those of the party who were religiously active in Ohio joined an American Methodist Episcopal church rather than form their own *seiat*. The leaders of the group, John and Eleanor Jones, farmed a small tenancy called Tirbach and owned the Ship tavern in Pennant, a hamlet on the road to Aberaeron.[73] By oral tradition, John and his sons-in-law and several neighbors reached their decision to emigrate while drinking pints of ale in the Ship's inglenook after church one Sunday.[74] One wonders whether the publican was worried that the growing influence of strict Calvinistic Methodism, symbolized by Aberaeron's new ordinance against unruly behavior on the Sabbath, would hurt business at the tap.

The "1818" Welsh, as they became known in later years, originally intended to join the prosperous Welsh farming settlement at Paddy's Run. They may have been part of a larger group, for at least three other Cardiganshire families settled in Paddy's Run in 1818, along with many more from Montgomeryshire.[75] The Mynydd Bach families, however, failed to reach Butler County. They stopped en route at the French settlement of Gallipolis, about two hundred miles downriver from Pittsburgh. One story says the Welsh were marooned there when a storm washed away their flatboat, another that discontented members of the party loosened the moorings. A third version credits the women in the group with halting the journey; having found a warm welcome among the French settlers at Gallipolis after months of uncertainty and hard travel, they refused to go any further. Their husbands and sons soon found work on a road being built through the Appalachian foothills from Gallipolis to Chilicothe. In the course of working their way north with the construction crew, the families bought land and set to farming in northeast Jackson County near the Gallia County border. Two of the six families moved on in 1822 to Radnor, Ohio, an established Welsh settlement that John Jones, Tirbach, had rejected as being too flat and malarial. He and the others stayed in Jackson County, immigrant exceptions on a slowly developing American frontier.[76]

73. Information about emigrants' home farms, families, and emigration comes from a great variety of sources, including published and manuscript obituaries; county, community, and chapel histories; and material provided by genealogists. For a complete listing of source material, see the Bibliography.

74. The tale has come back to Cilcennin from Ohio. The current proprietors of the Ship told me over a pint in May 1992 that they have learned everything they know about the 1818 emigrants from Welsh American tourists.

75. Rev. Benjamin W. Chidlaw, "An Historical Sketch of Paddy's Run, Butler County, Ohio," speech delivered on 30 July 1876, reprinted in Stephen Riggs Williams, *The Saga of Paddy's Run* (Oxford, Ohio: Miami University Alumni Association, 1972), 176.

76. Gwilym Jones, "The Saga of Cilcennin," *Cylchgrawn Cymdeithas Ceredigion Llundain* (Journal of the Cardigan Society of London) 22 (1966–1967):

In 1835, one year after Edward Jones's visit, the first group of new arrivals joined the Jones, Tirbach, clan. These settlers included members of the Alban family, two or three families from Llangwyryfon, and the first members of the large Edwards clan from Brynele, a tenancy in Nancwnlle parish. In 1836 the first resident minister arrived, thirty-five-year-old Robert Williams from Rhosybol, Anglesey, along with four other North Waleans and another eleven emigrants from Mynydd Bach. It was not until 1837 that the settlement received more than thirty Welsh settlers in a single year (see fig. 3.5). By 1842, sufficient numbers of emigrants were leaving Cardiganshire to fill ships sailing directly from Aberystwyth to New York City and Quebec.[77] In May 1847 a notice in the *Carnarvon and Denbigh Herald* informed readers:

> A greater proportion than the usual annual average of the agricultural population of the upper part of Cardiganshire, seem determined this year to improve their fortune by emigrating to America. Last week the new barque, the *Anne Jenkins*, sailed from Aberystwyth for New York with upwards of 80 emigrants; and in the beginning of June, the *Tamerlane*, of 700 tons . . . capable of accommodating 200 passengers, is expected to sail for Canada. These emigrants consist chiefly of small freeholders, farmers, and the more respectable of the rural labouring class.

In fact, the *Tamerlane* left Aberystwyth with 462 passengers and crew. The emigrants it carried "came chiefly from the eastern parts of Cardiganshire, from the neighbourhood of Lledrod, Mynydd-bach, and Tairhirion-y-rhos" (Tai-hirion, near Blaenpennal). Another paper, the *Welshman*, identified the male passengers as 75 farmers, 65 laborers, 13 carpenters, 17 tailors, 6 blacksmiths, 5 hatters, and 10 miners, the latter probably from the lead mining district northeast of Mynydd Bach.[78]

19–27; Virgil H. Evans, *The Family Tree of John Jones (Tirbach)* (Columbus, Ohio: Privately published, 1929; reprinted Oak Hill, Ohio: Cardiff Club, 1984), 39–41; Evan E. Davis, ed., *Our Heritage: Early History of Tyn Rhos Welsh Congregational Church and Its Neighborhood* (Oak Hill, Ohio: Privately published, 1979), 4.

77. Sailings 1842–1851, Aberystwyth Borough Records F11(a), National Library of Wales.

78. Ibid., 84, 85, quoting the *Herald* of May 8, 1847; *The Welshman*, June 4, 1847. Thanks to Rosemary Jones for sending me the item from *The Welshman*.

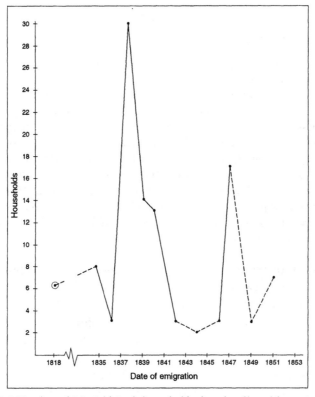

Fig. 3.5 Number of Mynydd Bach households directly affected by emigration

For people who had never before journeyed far from home, crossing the Atlantic was, as Benjamin Chidlaw wrote, "an important and sad experience."[79] It ruined some lives forever. Mary Davis never recovered from the loss of her youngest daughter, who died at sea after being splashed by scalding hot coffee.[80] Storms always inspired terror. Emigrants were locked below decks, left in darkness to imagine the worst while waves battered the ship. Such traumatic experiences deepened and strengthened bonds of friendship and mutual understanding between those who endured the passage together. Encountering other nationalities at close quarters also heightened Welsh emigrants' awareness of their own distinctive traits as a group, particularly what they saw as the sincerity of their religion. No group more sharply defined Welshness by contrast than the Irish. The 1837 group's

79. Rev. Benjamin W. Chidlaw, *The American*, trans. Rev. R. Gwilym Williams (Bala: County Press, 1978; originally published in Llanrwst by John Jones, 1840), 39.

80. Dan T. Davis, *Us Davises* (Oak Hill, Ohio: Privately published, 1950), 7.

letter is typical in painting Irish passengers as the antithesis of the pious, well-mannered Welsh:

> We advise every one who come here to take a liner as they are better prepared for rough weather. It is very dangerous to go to sea in an old ship with a small crew and many Irish crowded aboard. We were afraid many times that their ungodliness would move the Lord to sink us all in the sea not simply because they were papists but also because they were barbaric. They held family devotions towards the end of the journey praying to the saints like this: "Holy Virgin Mary, Mother of God, pray on Christ to have mercy on us etc." If you in Wales knew how pagan they were you would not bother to send your money to far countries [in missionary efforts] with so much need nearer to you.

By way of reassurance, the letter concluded, "Our captain and many of the crew supported temperance and we were able to hold family devotions quite often."[81]

The adventure of emigration continued for another week or two once the Welsh landed in New York, Philadelphia, or Baltimore. Many booked passage up the Hudson River to the Erie Canal, which took them to the Welsh settlement at Utica, New York. They then crossed Lake Erie by steamer to Cleveland, where canals and roads connected south to Jackson/Gallia. There was also the slow but fairly direct road over the Alleghenies to Pittsburgh, where many immigrants tarried to work for months or years to recoup the expenses of their journey and to save money for farmland. From Pittsburgh it was just a few days' travel by riverboat down the Ohio to Gallipolis, then a long day's walk to reach the Welsh settlement on the Jackson/Gallia border.[82] By the time Margaret Davis finally reached Gallipolis in the summer of 1847, she was so eager to see her friends that she insisted on setting off on foot immediately. She walked the whole sixteen miles dressed in heavy Welsh woolens. According to family legend, she "suffered from the heat ever afterward."[83]

Although the 1818 Welsh never fully reassimilated with the immigrants who followed them, their years of experience and willingness to help their kinspeople greatly facilitated the process of community formation. Timothy Jones, the most enterprising

---

81. Conway, *Welsh in America*, 24.
82. Jones, *Y Teithiwr Americanaidd*, 28–32.
83. Davis, *Us Davises*, 35, 25, quotation on p. 25.

child of John and Eleanor Jones, Tirbach, acted as a land agent and translator for the newcomers. In the mid-1830s he and an American named Reuben Rambo acquired considerable real estate in Madison and Raccoon townships along the boundary of Jackson and Gallia counties. They platted the village of Centerville midway between the county seats at Jackson and Gallipolis. As new Welsh settlers arrived, Timothy was ready to sell them village lots or unimproved land. He was also able to advise those who wished to buy land directly from the government. As justice of the peace, he was familiar with all the legalities of land purchase.[84]

The immigrants' purchases of land marked their first definitive break with the institutional traditions of Wales. Four of the six 1818 families left Mynydd Bach as tenant farmers. All of them owned at least eighty acres by 1822. One of their number, Evan Evans, had been a laborer for Cilcennin's wealthiest landlord. In Madison Township he eventually possessed 235 acres.[85] Those who came after 1835 continued the trend.[86] By 1837–1838, land in the immediate vicinity of Centerville was selling for up to $10.30 per acre, but large tracts of government land were still

84. Timothy Jones, alone and with partners, purchased at least 500 acres of land between 1830 and 1838, including 400 acres on the border of Raccoon and Madison townships where Centerville developed. Except for four town lots, all of his subsequent sales were to Welsh settlers. Abstract of land titles, Madison, Jefferson, and Raccoon townships, Jackson County Recorder's Office.

85. Throughout this section, sources for landownership and the physiography of the settlement area include immigrant obituaries; other biographical sources listed in the Bibliography; Abstracts of title, Perry and Raccoon townships, Gallia County, from the Recorder of Deeds Office, Gallia County Courthouse; U.S. Geological Survey 1:24,000 quadrangles for Ohio (Mulga [revised 1985], Oak Hill [revised 1985], Patriot [1961], and Rio Grande [revised 1975]); D. J. Lake, *Atlas of Jackson County* (Philadelphia: Titus, Simmons & Titus, 1875; reprinted Oak Hill, Ohio: Welsh-American Heritage Museum, 1975); William Griffith, Jr., *Illustrated Atlas of Gallia County, Ohio* (Cincinnati: Strobridge & Co., 1874; reprinted Athens, Ohio: Don F. Stout and Emmett A. Conway, 1976); and working maps of the settlement area compiled by Roland L. Edwards. I am grateful to Mr. Edwards for making copies of his maps available for my use.

86. A few men with Welsh surnames bought land in the Centerville area between 1822 and 1834. These were Thomas Lewis (first purchase in 1827, Raccoon Township, section 3; total purchases in Raccoon Township, 587.5 acres); David Jenkins (1832, 20 acres in section 24); William Hughes (1822, 80 acres in section 10); and William Lewis (first purchase in March 1834, section 3; total purchases in Raccoon Township, 336.5 acres). These may have been speculators; I have been unable to verify their identities or origins.

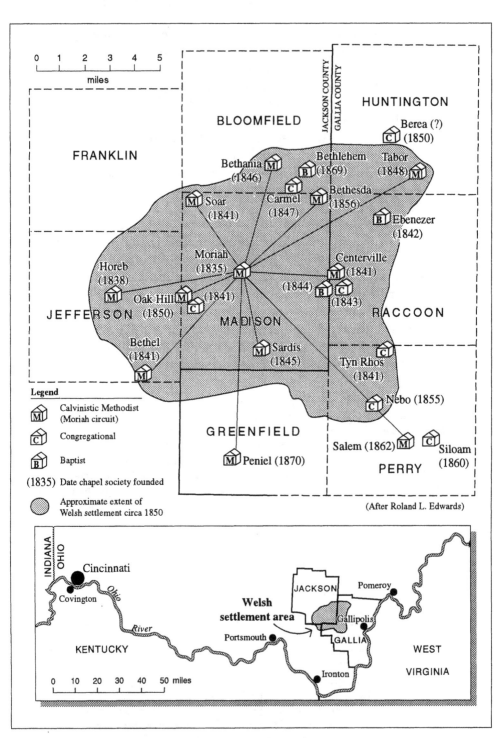

Map 3.5 Welsh settlement in Jackson and Gallia counties, Ohio

available in all directions and slightly improved land was selling for as little as $2.50 per acre. James Davies, a Welshman who settled in the village of Oak Hill (originally Portland) in Jefferson Township, assured immigrants in 1841 that the local real-estate market was still open to them. "There are many good farms here for sale by the English [that is, English-speaking Americans] for a low and reasonable price, and it is quite likely that the Welsh shall soon be their owners, and we shall be glad to see them come."[87]

As more and more Welsh came, the core of the settlement area shifted west to the center of Madison Township (see map 3.5). By 1850 the three townships with the greatest Welsh population (Madison, Jefferson, and Raccoon) had a total of 316 Welsh households, compared to 328 households headed by American-born men and women and 23 households of English, Irish, or German immigrants. The census for 1850 reveals a number of interesting things about the Welsh settlers vis-à-vis Americans in the area. In the core of the Welsh settlement area, Welsh households were significantly smaller than American households (see table 3.4). While this was partly due to Americans having more resident farm laborers, the difference also stemmed from Welsh families having fewer children. Welsh farms were on average one-third smaller than American farms and their land was only half as valuable. All of these differences reflect the fact that most Welsh immigrants arrived later than American settlers, who included notable clans such as the Cherrington family from Virginia. Their patriarch settled in Gallia County in 1805 and fathered sixteen children.[88] In 1850 his descendants' large farms included a 950-acre spread valued at $10,000. The smaller size of Welsh farms may also indicate that Welsh parents were already carving up their own land or buying starter farms for their children to a greater degree than were American parents.[89]

87. "Gair o Oak Hill" (A Word from Oak Hill), Y Cenhadwr (October 1841): 318.

88. William's first wife, Margaret, had eight children in Virginia; his second wife, Letita, had four children of her own and eight more with William. Gallia County Historical Society, Gallia County, Ohio: People in History to 1980 (Paoli, Pa.: Taylor Publishing Co., 1980), 68.

89. I found this to be true for the Welsh community in Waukesha County, Wisconsin, which was established a few years after the Jackson/Gallia settlement. Providing land for children resulted, in the long run, in higher rates of persistence. In Waukesha, 56 percent of Welsh households present in 1850 had at least one member still living in the three-township settlement area in 1870, compared to

Welsh immigrants who settled outside the core area lagged even further behind the Americans in 1850. In Greenfield and Perry townships, for example, Welsh farms averaged 82 acres, smaller than both the average American farm in those townships and the average Welsh farm in Madison and Jefferson. There are several explanations for the situation of Welsh settlers on the periphery. Most of them arrived during the mid-to-late 1840s, when the only inexpensive land left was the least desirable for farming, mainly steep, close-set hills (see fig. 3.6). Many of the late-comers from Mynydd Bach arrived with little or no financial reserves, which gave them no choice but to purchase mediocre land or rent from established farmers. Biographical information about Welsh settlers in peripheral townships is relatively scarce, which probably indicates that they were a more mobile population, had fewer personal contacts in the area when they arrived, and were less likely to have come from Mynydd Bach than were those who lived in the core of the settlement.

Although the Welsh did not match Americans in personal wealth or the size of their farms until after 1850, a greater proportion of Welsh than non-Welsh owned land and almost no Welsh were tenant farmers. New-world opportunities dissolved the old-world distinctions between cottager, tenant, freeholder, and landlord. In Jackson/Gallia, almost all Welsh farms were freehold, and even former cottagers and laborers could afford to buy twenty to forty acres as a first step toward becoming independent farmers. The immigrants' Ohio farms were both larger and more productive than their holdings had been in Wales. The Welsh may have been less wealthy than their American neighbors but most of them had significantly improved their economic circumstances and fundamentally changed their status in relation to land within a few years of emigrating.

Building a New Jerusalem

As in the immigrants' home district in Cardiganshire, the scattered farms of the Jackson/Gallia settlement did not cohere insti-

---

just 17 percent of American households. Knowles, "Welsh Settlement," 75–77. See also Kathleen Neils Conzen, "Peasant Pioneers: Generational Succession among German Farmers in Frontier Minnesota," in *The Countryside in the Age of Capitalist Transformation: Essays in the Social History of Rural America*, ed. Steven Hahn and Jonathan Prude (Chapel Hill: University of North Carolina Press, 1985), 259–92.

Table 3.4 Population and land relations in core Welsh area (Jefferson and Madison Townships, 1850)

	Welsh	Others
Households		
Number of households	236[a]	185[b]
Household population	1,347	1,204
Mean household size	5.7	6.5
Mean value of household property[c]	$620	$1,323
Landownership		
Number of landowners[d]	195	145
Farm owner-operators[e]	126	109
Tenants[f]	4	9
Total farm operators	130	118
Farmers without farms[g]	51	41
Farm value and size		
Most valuable farm	$3,000	$10,000
Mean value of farms	$859	$1,711
Mean acres per farm	104	170
Total acreage owned	13,526	20,076

[a] Welsh-born head of household.

[b] 168 U.S.-born heads of households; 8 English-born; 7 Irish-born; 2 German-born.

[c] The greater of values listed for real estate in the population and agricultural schedules for every household member.

[d] Individuals with real estate listed in the population schedule.

[e] Individuals with real estate listed in both the population and agricultural schedules and with entries in the latter for acreage and crop production.

[f] Individuals listed as farmers in the population schedule and with entries for acreage and crop production in the agricultural schedule but with no listing of real property in the population schedule.

[g] Individuals listed as farmers in the population schedule who have no acreage or crop production in the agricultural schedule. Typically, they possess a few horses and cows, sheep, and swine, not uncommonly enough animals to suggest that the sale of meat, butter, and fleece supplemented household income.

Sources: 1850 U.S. manuscript census for Ohio; Donghyu Yang, "Farm Tenancy in the Antebellum North," typescript dated July 1990, ms. p. 4, courtesy Allan G. Bogue.

tutionally around village or urban centers. If anything, the backwoods of southern Ohio were in some respects even more isolated in 1835–1850 than was Mynydd Bach. The area's rivers were unsuited to canals and no railroads reached Jackson County until 1850. Settlers' nearest connections to the outside world were the river ports of Gallipolis and Portsmouth, both about fifteen miles from the core of the settlement. The Welsh therefore

Fig. 3.6 The topography of Jackson/Gallia. David Jones left Penbryn, a parish in the lower Teifi valley, around 1820 and emigrated to Pittsburgh, where he lived for ten years. There he met and married Elizabeth Henry of Llandysul. In about 1830 they moved to Raccoon Township near the Jackson County border. In 1835 they bought their first 79 acres. By 1841 they had 157 acres and eight children. Their land was typical of the fairly steep, short hills and narrow valleys of much

had little traffic with outsiders during the early settlement period. They were left to their own devices to bring themselves together as a community. The organizational institution to which they naturally turned was neighborhood worship as they had learned to practice it in Wales under the tutelage of Ebenezer Richard. The first step was for an experienced chapel elder to organize a neighborhood *seiat* that would meet in his home or rotate between various members' homes week to week. The members of the *seiat* would continue to meet in this way to pray, read the Bible, sing, and discuss their religious experiences until their numbers outgrew domestic quarters and they had sufficient funds to finance construction of a chapel.[90]

The *seiat* was ideally suited to the American frontier, as American Methodists knew through their similar method of seeding congregations. Like American fellowship societies, the Welsh *seiat* required no clergy or church funds. The organization of lay worship created audiences for itinerant preachers and paved the way for institutional religion once denominations were ready to send ministers west. For the Welsh, the latter was no obstacle. There was never a lack of Welsh ministers eager to exchange

90. The *seiat* served the same purpose in every rural Welsh settlement during the nineteenth century. Williams gives a good summary of the operation of the *seiat* and prayer meeting in Calvinistic Methodist tradition in *One Hundred Years*, 8–13.

(Fig. 3.6, *continued*) of the Jackson/Gallia settlement area. Edwin F. Jones, a descendant of David and Elizabeth who now owns the farm, says that some farmers in these parts went into town so rarely that they did not cash the checks his father gave them for livestock from one year to another. Here as elsewhere in the two counties, scrub trees and undergrowth now grow on former pastureland where Welsh families grazed sheep and beef cattle. (Photos by the author)

their miserable pay in Wales for hopes of better remuneration in the United States. The Jackson/Gallia settlement had at least eight resident preachers by 1844, including one Congregationalist and a Wesleyan Methodist. None of them was "seated" in the sense of being called or assigned to a particular chapel; they all rode the Calvinistic Methodist or Congregational circuit, or both. Preachers from other settlements also visited, notably the well-known Congregationalists Jenkin Jenkins and Benjamin Chidlaw. Such men were continuing the Welsh tradition of itinerant preaching tours but on a much larger geographical scale.[91]

The transition from *seiat* to chapel was not quite as organic in Jackson/Gallia as it was in many other Welsh American settlements. The Calvinistic Methodists constructed chapels with striking regularity, both in time and space (see map 3.5). The first

91. Edward Jones came from Cincinnati to preach to settlers in the Moriah district in 1835. He preached the dedicatory sermon at the chapel's opening in 1836 and returned in 1838 to officiate at the first *Gymanfa* (Assembly) held at Moriah. Evans, *Sefydliadau Cymreig*, 12–13; on resident ministers, see pp. 99–128. Although Evans's book purports to be a history of the entire Jackson/Gallia settlement area, it says nothing about the Congregational chapels or their ministers. Davis, *Our Heritage*, p. 23, identifies John A. Davies as the preacher responsible for organizing Tyn Rhos and Oak Hill Congregational chapels. Jenkin Jenkins made a grand tour of Welsh American settlements, as did R. D. Thomas in 1851–1852 and at later points in his career. Benjamin Chidlaw went twice to Wales to brush up his Welsh on preaching tours. All three men wrote books about their travels.

chapel, Moriah, was built in the center of Madison Township in 1836, one year after a chapel society was organized in the neighborhood. Next came Horeb in 1838 in a recently populated territory west of Oak Hill, led by elders David Evans, Y Wern, of Llangeitho and William Jones, Cofadail, of Bethel chapel, Llangwyryfon. In 1841 three more chapels were built—Centerville, Soar, and Bethel—nearly equidistant from one another and standing like the legs of a tripod centered on Moriah. Sardis (1843) rounded the circle to the south, as Bethania (1846) did to the north. After that the Moriah circuit lost its symmetry as new neighborhoods pulled the circuit's itinerant preachers further afield and the growing village of Oak Hill demanded its own chapel. Eventually the circuit embraced congregations from the town of Jackson, north of the Jackson/Gallia settlement, and an arc of river towns from Portsmouth to Pomeroy along the Ohio River.[92]

The orderly placement of Calvinistic Methodist chapels on the landscape reflected both the logic of an outwardly expanding ethnic settlement and the organizational concerns of the denomination's local leader, Rev. Robert Williams (see fig. 3.7). More than anyone else, Williams sustained the vigor of Welsh Calvinism in Jackson/Gallia and reinforced its evangelical traditions. He was a handsome man, energetic, and a master of the extemporaneous style of Welsh preaching. "At times," his elegist wrote, "the power of his eloquence would descend upon the congregation like the falls of Niagara, invincible, sweeping away every obstacle that stood in its path." A witness to one of his sermons around 1845 recalled, "Before the end, many could not remain quiet, they gave vent to their feelings until they drowned out the preacher's voice, despite its being so clear and musical. Nor could they be still after leaving the chapel, but the 'sound of song and praise' was heard along the roads as they went home."[93]

92. Evans, *Sefydliadau Cymreig*, 9–40; Roland L. Edwards, "The Jackson and Gallia Circuit of Welsh Calvinistic Methodist Churches," undated manuscript map, courtesy the author; Rev. R. D. Thomas, *Hanes Cymry America/A History of the Welsh in America*, trans. Phillips G. Davies (Lanham, Md.: University Press of America, 1983; originally published Utica, N.Y.: T. J. Griffiths, 1872), 124–33.

93. Obituary of Robert Williams, *Y Cyfaill* (October 1876): 398; Mary Parry, *Cofiant y Parch. Robert Williams, Moriah, Ohio* (Biography of Rev. Robert Williams, Moriah, Ohio) (Utica, N.Y.: T. J. Griffiths, 1883), 114–15, quotation on p. 115.

Fig. 3.7 Robert Williams. Good looks and a piercing gaze gave extra power to a Welsh preacher's *hwyl* (charismatic style), and Robert Williams had both. (Photo courtesy of William R. Alban)

Robert Williams was born in 1802 and spent his teenage years with a religious family on Anglesey, where the Baptist evangelist Christmas Evans lived and preached. The family of Williams's first wife were close friends of John Elias, the dominant figure in upholding orthodox Calvinistic Methodism. Thus Williams's formative religious experiences in North Wales almost certainly included attending services by, and perhaps becoming personally acquainted with, two of Wales' most strict evangelical Calvinists. The connection is most clear in a letter that John Elias wrote to the Moriah chapel congregation on the occasion of Williams's ordination to the ministry in 1838. The Monthly Meeting of the Calvinistic Methodists in Anglesey had unanimously approved Williams as a candidate for ordination even though, technically speaking, neither he nor any other Welsh American minister needed approval from Wales because the denomination had established American associations with powers of ordination. Williams, for example, was ordained in Pittsburgh by the Association of Western Pennsylvania. In writing to a frontier settlement where his name was household currency, Elias was clearly trying to exercise his influence from afar just as he had tried to control Jewin chapel in London. "The Head [of the church] is as close to its members in America as it is to its members in Wales," Elias wrote. He urged Williams to recall the great Puritans of Massachusetts and to take them as his exemplar.

I have hopes for you, for you have proven [to have] the kind of taste and virtue in healthy doctrine such that you shall not change it; you have "drunk of old wine, nor shall you drink of the new in that place, but shall say, Better is the old." The Doctrine of the Gospel suits the sinner who knows himself— one who sees the greatness and purity of God—the great evil of sin—the depth of his fall —his immense wretchedness, etc. Nothing but the Doctrine of the Gospel shall content him. May God keep it in its purity amongst you.[94]

Although Williams came from far North Wales and so spoke a different dialect with a very different accent than the immigrants from Mynydd Bach, they would have found the vocabulary and rhythm of his "pulpit Welsh" perfectly familiar. Williams also suited the Jackson/Gallia community temperamentally, as he was a conservative Calvinistic Methodist well known throughout the Welsh American community as an exceptionally gifted preacher. Like Daniel Rowland, Williams rarely traveled outside his home district except to preside over meetings of the regional association. "He was king of the Jackson/Gallia settlement" and its overarching religious influence from 1836 until his death forty years later.[95]

It may have been Robert Williams who decided when and where a new chapel would be built in the settlement, or perhaps the example of Ebenezer Richard's planting of chapels provided the template. In any case, the chapels in Jackson/Gallia were constructed in a remarkably symmetrical pattern, none of them before its surrounding neighborhood could provide sufficient financial and membership support. Avoiding debt had practical advantages, of course, but among Welsh immigrants it also carried important symbolic connotations. Being debt-free implied that a chapel's members were responsible and industrious and that the community was prospering. Reports from rural settlements to Y Cyfaill and Y Cenhadwr throughout the 1840s and 1850s noted whether a new chapel was burdened with debt or "fully paid up." Debts on Jackson/Gallia chapels were cleared with exceptional speed, in a few cases in less than a year.

The gradual establishment of chapels in a ring around Moriah gave the community a strong central focus that helped prevent the estrangement of dispersed farm families. Moriah's location in the

---

94. Letter from John Elias to Moriah Chapel, Jackson County, dated 15 February 1838, published in Y Cyfaill (February 1842): 36, 37.

95. Parry, Cofiant Robert Williams, 22–23; Evans, Sefydliadau Cymreig, 101.

heart of the circuit and the settlement gave it a special status and function as *ein mam ni oll*, the mother of us all. It became the favored site for all community-wide religious activities, including Sunday school examinations where the *Gymanfa Bwnc* was ritually performed and the periodic hymn-singing assembly called the *Gymanfa Ganu*.[96] Keeping Moriah at the geographical center of the Calvinistic Methodist circuit made Williams's life easier as well, for it ensured that every chapel was within riding distance of his farm across the road from Moriah.

While the Calvinistic Methodist chapels were located mainly in Madison and Jefferson townships, the chapels built by Congregationalists and other denominations were concentrated along the periphery, particularly on the southeastern side of the settlement. John and Elizabeth Jones, Ty'n Rhos, former members of the Congregational chapel in Cilcennin, organized a *seiat* in their home shortly after settling in Raccoon Township in 1838. In 1841 they deeded a parcel of their land for the settlement's first Congregational chapel, appropriately named Tyn Rhos (today, pronounced *Tin Rohs*). The Congregationalists also established a chapel in Oak Hill in 1841. Centerville followed in 1843, then Carmel (1847), Berea (1850), Nebo (1855; see fig. 3.8), and Siloam (1860). Jackson/Gallia also had four small Welsh Baptist congregations—Ebenezer (1842), Centerville (1844), Oak Hill (1845), and Bethlehem (1869)—and a short-lived Wesleyan Methodist chapel.[97] The Baptists and Wesleyans do not figure prominently in the written histories of the settlement, perhaps because their members were among the poorer residents and may have included fewer Cardiganshire immigrants than the other two denominations. Rev. Abraham Edwards, an Episcopal priest from Llangeitho, founded a Welsh Episcopal church in Centerville in 1839. He was reputedly a popular man until he asked the Gallia Court commissioners to levy a tax in support of his church—in essence to reimpose the hated tithe on the new Welsh settlement. The church soon withered and it closed in 1845.[98]

The striking spatial segregation between Calvinistic Methodist chapels and those of other Welsh denominations is difficult to explain. Did the immigrants identify so strongly with their native

96. Parry, *Cofiant Robert Williams*, 69–70; Roland L. Edwards, ed. and comp., *Moriah, 1835–1985: 150 Years of Service* (Privately published, 1985); "The 'Pwngc' Sunday at Horeb, Jackson County, Ohio," *Cambrian* 6 (May 1886): 123–26.

97. Evans, *Sefydliadau Cymreig*, 26–81; Thomas, *Hanes Cymry*, 131–33.

98. Davis, *Our Heritage*, 6, 16–19, 7.

Fig. 3.8 Nebo chapel. Nebo is the finest chapel still standing in the Jackson/Gallia area. Its two bright green doors (traditionally, one for women, the other for men) face west, catching the late afternoon sun. It is kept in fine condition and is still occasionally used for community gatherings, including the annual *Gymanfa Ganu*. (Photo courtesy of Michael T. Struble)

denomination that they settled in religious clusters that were then manifested in chapel construction? The data I have been able to gather offer no clear answer. A few individuals switched their membership from one denomination to another whose chapel was closer to their home. The various denominations sometimes shared ministers, although Robert Williams usually preached in Calvinistic Methodist chapels while John A. Davies preached to the Congregationalists.[99] The very lack of comment about denominational relations in local histories, however (most striking in the Methodist history's failure to mention the existence of Congregational chapels), raises the suspicion that religious differences may have been an important part of individual and community identity. The situation in Jackson/Gallia appears to support the old, unproven saw that Calvinistic Methodists considered themselves superior to other Nonconformists because theirs was a heartfelt religion—and because they were a growing numerical majority by the middle of the century. The geographical pattern may also indicate that emigration was accepted at different times

99. Thomas, *Hanes Cymry*, 131.

in different chapel congregations on Mynydd Bach, although the data show a clear connection between chapel membership and date of emigration only in the case of the Elim congregation's loss of members in 1837–1838.

As was true of their economic circumstances, the immigrants' religious life changed in important ways in their new environment. One subtle but indicative change was the enhanced role of chapels in organizing social space, both functionally and imaginatively. In the absence of rural hamlets and parishes, Welsh settlers' sense of place and local identity became strongly associated with the chapel to which they belonged. Chapel names supplemented farm names as tags that the Welsh used to distinguish one another. Older people of Welsh descent in the area today still sometimes orient and identify themselves this way, saying they grew up "in the Nebo area," that someone lives "out by Horeb," and so forth.

The chapels in Jackson/Gallia were also repositories of Welsh culture, both architecturally and spiritually. Although wooden construction gave the structures an American texture, the earliest chapels reproduced styles of Welsh vernacular architecture. Horeb chapel's carpenter-builder Morgan Williams duplicated in wood the distinctive Welsh style known as the barn chapel, with two entrance doors on the broad side of the building and a tall, narrow window between (see fig. 3.9). The original Horeb was a smaller rendering in wood of Tabor chapel in Llangwyryfon, visible in the foreground of the view of Mynydd Bach in fig. 3.1. Men entered by the south door and sat in the southern pews, women entered by the north door and sat in the northern pews. Chapels with gable-end entrances also maintained the tradition of separate doors and seating for men and women, with men to the preacher's right and women to his left.[100] The Jackson/Gallia

100. Michael T. Struble, "Horeb Chapel: The Evolution of a Welsh Barn Chapel upon the American Landscape," *Material Culture* 25 (1993): 37–45; "Horeb, Jackson County, Ohio," *Cambrian* (1885), 46; Anthony Jones, *Welsh Chapels*, rev. ed. (Phoenix Mill: Alan Sutton Pub., in association with National Museums and Galleries of Wales, 1996); Dan T. Davis, *Early History of Horeb Church* (Oak Hill, Ohio: Privately published, 1938); site visits to Jackson/Gallia. Jim Lloyd's memories of Moriah chapel services in the 1930s show that these traditions seemed natural to community members. "Why men sat on the preacher's right and women on his left I do not know," Jim wrote me in 1992, "except it was the custom and only strangers did not follow the custom. Us boys used to dig each other with our elbows when someone would pull a stupid trick like sitting on the wrong side." The custom lingered in Wales well into the 1950s; Derec Llwyd Morgan, personal communication to the author, 3 April 1995.

Fig. 3.9 Horeb chapel, circa 1865–1870. The original Horeb, shown above, was built in 1838 in northwestern Jefferson Township. It was a fine example of the Welsh barn chapel, so named because the doors were located on the broad side of the building. Note the two doors (one for men, one for women) with two windows between—features that were also incorporated in Tabor chapel on Mynydd Bach. The interior design was also typical for this type of chapel: an elevated pulpit between the two doors with a bank of seats below (the *sedd fawr*) where the elders sat; rows of pews facing the pulpit and raked pews to either side. The seating gave everyone a good view of the preacher and of anyone who arrived late. (Photos courtesy of D. Merrill Davis and Mrs. Harriet Davis Walter)

settlers also replicated the architectural tradition of constructing a small building, the *tŷ capel* (chapel house), near the chapel as a hostelry for visiting preachers and a meeting place for elders and Sunday school classes. People in the area still call these structures by their Welsh name, pronounced "tee capel," although the meaning and spelling have evolved into *tea* house; no longer used to house circuit riders, the little frame buildings now host tea parties and other church socials as well as official meetings.[101]

The immigrants also endowed the space within chapels with social meanings derived from old-country practice. As in other Welsh American communities, many chapels in Jackson/Gallia maintained the tradition of charging pew rents, which meant that wealthier members of the congregation generally sat in the higher-rent seats closer to the pulpit. Backsliders and "listeners" who had not yet committed themselves to membership generally occupied pews in the rear of the sanctuary. The act of entering the sanctuary had ritual meaning as well. In Horeb chapel the pews were arranged in a semicircle facing the pulpit and the two doors. The congregation was audience to every entrance:

> As the congregation sat facing the doors either directly or obliquely, the late comer was obliged to make his way through a kind of *chevaux de frise* of gazes. To modest people this was a severe ordeal. But, on the other hand, it afforded vain and giddly people an excellent opportunity of showing their good clothes or pretty faces. I am glad to add, however, that tardiness in coming to the service was not a common thing at that church. Indeed, beginning the *"odfa"* (service) to the second was one of the points in the "letter of the law and testimony" which the good people of the congregation punctiliously observed.[102]

Religious practice remained virtually unchanged. The same liturgy of congregational hymn-singing, readings from the Bible, and a long sermon typified chapel services in Ohio as in Wales. As Edward Morris noted in his quarterly report as general secre-

101. Michael T. Struble and Hubert G. H. Wilhelm, "The Welsh in Ohio," in *To Build in a New Land: Ethnic Landscapes in North America*, ed. Allen G. Noble (Baltimore: Johns Hopkins University Press, 1992), 83–85; site visits with Michael Struble. Individual examples of the *tŷ capel* exist in other Welsh American settlements in the Midwest but I am not aware of any other community in which nearly every chapel built a *tŷ capel* as they did in Jackson/Gallia.

102. "Horeb," 46.

tary of the settlement's Methodist chapels, they faithfully employed Ebenezer Richard's rules for Sunday school examination. Every two months the Methodist Sunday schools convened in joint session for a long day of reading Scripture, singing, praying, and answering questions put to them by Robert Williams. The sessions also included addresses on temperance, a sermon, and a meeting where teachers received their assignments for the next two months' work.[103] Because the Welsh sent their children to English-language schools, however, Sunday schools' mission changed somewhat in Ohio. No longer the main vehicles for teaching literacy, they were able to concentrate their efforts on religious indoctrination and improving students' written Welsh. The latter change was reflected in the inclusion of written essays in Sunday school examinations, originally an oral tradition in Wales.[104]

The Llangeitho tradition was distilled to a new strength in Jackson/Gallia because of the number and character of chapel elders and devout believers who settled in the area. Among those immigrants for whom I have been able to develop biographies, sixteen were chapel elders in Wales. The thirteen who arrived during the formative years from 1835 to 1842 included several who had been converted during the last years of Daniel Rowland's ministry at Llangeitho. David Evans, Y Wern, became a Calvinistic Methodist after hearing Rowland preach in 1788. Evans served as an elder at Llangeitho chapel from 1815 until he and his extended family emigrated in 1837. By that time he was an old man of seventy. Friends marveled that he dared to make the arduous journey to Ohio, but Evans found renewed energy in the challenge of bringing religion to the wilderness. Religion became "the chief labor of his thoughts . . . He would lie in bed at night mulling over what needed to be done for the cause; and along the road, riding on his little mare, he would think about what needed to be considered at the meeting that night." He listened keenly to every sermon from his place "before the pulpit, having pulled his listening horn out of his pocket . . . and by the end of the sermon, he would always have an appropriate hymn stanza to suit the sermon, to sing at the conclusion."[105]

103. *Y Cyfaill* (January 1844): 10; "The 'Pwngc' Sunday," 123–26.

104. The Welsh in Waukesha County, Wisconsin, also added written work to their Sunday school examinations; see Daniel Jenkins Williams, *The Welsh Community of Waukesha County* (Columbus, Ohio: Hann & Adair, 1926) 134–39.

105. Obituary of David Evans by John W. Evans in *Y Cyfaill* (May 1849): 140–41. All I know of his wife Margaret is Ebenezer Richard's description of her: "[I]n

William Jones, Cofadail, was a boy during Rowland's last revivals and a middle-aged man when Augustus Brackenbury was expelled from Mynydd Bach. Jones joined the Calvinistic Methodists at thirteen but did not experience genuine conversion until he was twenty-one when, "at prayer by the side of the hedge, he had a vision quite bright and clear of his union with Jesus, and his claim in God as his covenanted God." He became an elder at Tabor and Bethel chapels in Llangwyryfon while farming at Cofadail, Brackenbury's last home. Jones, his wife Mary, and their four children emigrated in 1837. Later that year he became a founding elder at Horeb chapel. By several accounts, he was an exceptionally influential church elder who epitomized the ideal believer. "Discretion and intensity were strangely balanced in his expression, his appearance both zealous and genial, and authority and humility shone in his face." He "stood courageously for religion. He had fewer than the usual cares of this world; but no one exceeded him in godliness." He "lived in prayer with God, working and traveling, everywhere . . . He would come to the . . . society as if he were coming from heaven: there was a kind of heavenly quality to his counsel." He also possessed *hwyl*, being "exceptional in prayer: it had a kind of unyielding grip upon him; many a time it were as if he had left the earthly realm—having forgotten everything, in earnestness before the throne of grace."[106]

There were also a number of remarkably devout women in the settlement, the most eloquent of whom was Elizabeth Hugh Griffiths. As a girl in the 1810s, "Bety" had accompanied her father to night classes around Llangeitho, helping him teach farmers and laborers to read the Scriptures and to sing Welsh hymns. As an old woman in Ohio she could still recite whole chapters of the Bible from memory, weeping in sympathy for the suffering of Christ.[107]

Settlers such as William Jones, David Evans, and Bety Griffiths led by example. More domineering characters exercised stern control over particular chapels. One such man was John Evans of Bronnant, described as "[a] truly religious man, exceptionally

---

the words of Paul (Romans 16:7), 'She who is of note among the apostles'"; namely, she gave an excellent religious education to her children; obituary mentioning Margaret Evans, *Y Cyfaill* (August 1880): 313.

106. Obituary of William Jones by John W. Evans, *Y Cyfaill* (April 1849): 107–9; Evans, *Sefydliadau Cymreig*, 157, 33–34.

107. Obituary of Elizabeth Griffiths, *Y Cyfaill* (March 1870): 97.

zealous for the purity of doctrine . . . quite a judge of scriptural interpretation, very careful about church discipline." He was "Puritanical in his religious ideas" and "an excellent detective who hated any false heart."[108] Isaac T. Jones and John H. Jones exercised what Richard Tawney called "inquisitorial discipline"[109] as the leading elders at Bethel chapel for nearly fifty years (see fig. 3.10). As one of their neighbors from Lledrod delicately put it, Isaac Jones was "a little extreme. He was a decisive man, unbending, correct, unassuming, and serious. He was made to govern. He was able to keep control of his family without any difficulty. His children were afraid of him when they were fifty years old. He never had to punish or scold much. His gaze would be enough to secure obedience and to create fear." John H. Jones's special talent was convincing Bethel's members to contribute generously to chapel funds.[110]

Moriah chapel had a more diverse group of elders, including Edward Morris and the Albans' relative David Morgan, a cheerful man who had a special gift for teaching children.[111] But Moriah was also the home chapel of David Wynne, an imposing North Walean whose public behavior epitomized the stern Calvinist:

> He was very educated in the doctrines of the gospel, and a bit of a poet. He always wore a serious look in the *seiat*, and around the chapel, and in his appearance he carried quite an authority, and rarely did one hear him laugh; and when something unusually funny took place, all of us would look at Mr. Wynne, and if he was seen to smile, everyone would laugh. . . . No one was ever more zealous for Methodism and the Confession of Faith, and everything related to the [Calvinistic Methodist] Association. We think he was extreme, and perhaps not wholly free from prejudice toward other denominations. He had built his house upon the slopes of Mount Sinai, and there was always more of the law than the gospel about him.[112]

An incident recorded in the Methodist community's history sheds light on the extent of Wynne's influence over his chapel.

108. Evans, *Sefydliadau Cymreig*, 38–39.

109. Richard Henry Tawney, *Religion and the Rise of Capitalism* (Harmondsworth: Penguin Books, 1938; reprint, London: Penguin Books, 1969), 232.

110. Evans, *Sefydliadau Cymreig*, 56–58, quotation on p. 57.

111. Ibid., 35–36.

112. Ibid., 26, 44, 46–47, 73–74, quotation on pp. 46–47.

Fig. 3.10 Exemplary elders. Nineteenth-century photographs often make their subjects appear more stiff and serious than they were in life. Not so for these two portraits, which convey the rigidity and conviction contemporaries ascribed to Isaac T. Jones (*top*) and John H. Jones (*bottom*), the two senior elders at Bethel chapel for nearly fifty years. (Photos courtesy of William R. Alban)

One of his roles as an elder was to lead midweek prayer meetings, calling upon those in attendance to offer prayers and to speak of their religious experiences. Two men who attended these meetings at Moriah felt that Wynne was snubbing them because he always called on others to give the opening and closing prayers. When they took the matter to the Monthly Meeting,

Robert Williams and another elder ruled in Wynne's favor and ordered that the two men were not to be called on to pray in the church for one year. "The punishment was one of the strangest that was ever heard of," William Evans concluded, "but it appeared that Mr. Wynne stood so high in the minds of the leading men, that there was no point in anyone rising against him."[113]

Figures of authority could not exert such influence solely through force of personality. To some extent, their power came from the obedience of those who elected them and followed their lead. In other Welsh American settlements, old-world Puritans met some resistance from more progressive or less devout members of the community. The Welsh in Waukesha County, Wisconsin, were predominantly Calvinistic Methodists but did not all share the stern ethos of the community's most conservative members. When the elders of the settlement's leading congregation refused to bury an illegitimate child in the chapel cemetery, more liberal families broke off to form their own chapel with its own cemetery.[114]

The Puritans of Jackson/Gallia, however, followed their religious lay leaders as an exceptionally cohesive, committed, and well-trained religious community. In quarterly reports on Sunday school achievement that were published in Y Cyfaill in the 1840s, chapels in the core of the Jackson/Gallia settlement consistently topped the list for number of scholars and the number of Bible chapters they memorized (see table 3.5). Edward Morris assiduously noted the accuracy of the figures in a report published in 1844. They were in fact so carefully tabulated that they distinguished between "old work" (chapters recited more than once every two months) and chapters freshly committed to memory.[115] No other settlement took such pains in its religious accounting. To be fair, the low figures for the Welsh in older eastern settlements such as Oneida County, New York, reflect the extent to which the second and third generations had drifted away from Welsh religious tradition. Penycaerau chapel, for example, was founded in 1824 by immigrants from Aberdaron and was the first Welsh Calvinistic Methodist chapel in the United States. Of the Oneida community chapels listed in table 3.5, only one was

113. Ibid., 48.

114. Interview with Mildred Hughes Southcott at her home, Wales, Wisconsin, 24 June 1988.

115. Y Cyfaill (January 1844): 10.

Table 3.5 Feats of Bible memorization among leading Welsh American chapels, 1845

Settlement	Teachers	Students	Chapters memorized	Average per student
Oneida, N.Y.				
Remsen	7	44	745	16.9
Penycaerau	7	43	483	11.2
Penygraig	11	62	648	10.5
Enlli (2 branches)	13	63	538	8.5
"French-Road"	8	95	871	9.2
Ebensburgh, Pa.				
East branch	4	21	556	26.5
The town	5	40	1,026	25.7
Welsh Hills, Ohio				
Granville	7	32	997	31.2
Newark	12	55	1,045	19.0
Jackson/Gallia, Ohio				
Soar	10	43	1,644	38.2
Horeb	26	114	4,199	36.8
Centerville	9	38	1,288	33.9
Bethel	13	77	2,481	32.2
Moriah	16	66	1,708	25.9

Source: Y Cyfaill o'r Hen Wlad (February 1845), 27; (March 1845), 44.

established after 1835, a year before the Jackson/Gallia Welsh built their first chapel.[116]

One of the curious things about the Jackson/Gallia settlement is how rarely it surfaced in the Welsh American religious press, particularly given that it was one of the five largest rural Welsh settlements in the country by 1850. Aside from quarterly reports of Sunday school performance and chapel collections and the essays on Scriptural history that Thomas Llewelyn Hughes regularly contributed to Y Cyfaill, members of the community rarely sent news or commentary to the denominational magazines. Nor did Jackson/Gallia receive as many visitors from the outside world as did less remote settlements. In 1851, the peripatetic minister and writer R. D. Thomas visited all the Welsh settlements in Ohio ex-

116. Jay G. Williams III, Memory Stones: A History of Welsh-Americans in Central New York and Their Churches (Fleischmanns, N.Y.: Purple Mountain Press, 1993), 54–80. On the Utica community, see David M. Ellis, "The Assimilation of the Welsh in Central New York," Welsh History Review 6 (1973): 424–50; and Emrys Jones, "Some Aspects of Cultural Change in an American Welsh Community," Transactions of the Honourable Society of Cymmrodorion (1952): 15–41.

cept for Jackson/Gallia. When he finally called on the community during his third U.S. tour in 1870, he found it to be "a land of the Bible, of preaching, and of Sunday Schools, much like a more privileged Wales." This was a remarkable comment at a time when leaders in other Welsh American settlements were expressing growing concern about the loss of religious conviction in their communities.[117]

When Jenkin Jenkins visited Jackson/Gallia in 1844 he was shocked by what he saw as the settlers' timidity and their servile obedience to authority. After hearing him preach one service, the wife of a Calvinistic Methodist elder approached Jenkins to say that her chapel would like to invite him to preach that evening, but first they had to get the approval of the chapel trustees. Jenkins asked in astonishment, "were they under the necessity of speaking with the trustees every time they went to hold a religious meeting? No answer."[118] Writer Harrison Salisbury mentions in his memoirs that his mother was intensely unhappy as a child growing up in the oppressive Welsh Calvinism in Jackson County. Her father was Evan Evans "Straightback" (so called because he rode bolt upright on his horse), who had come to Jackson/Gallia as a child from Mynydd Bach. "She hated her Welsh father," Salisbury wrote, "the Welshiness of him, his hymn-singing, his Sabbath-keeping, prayer meetings, hellfire and damnation."[119]

How many young people of the second and third generations in Jackson/Gallia shared her dislike for Welsh religion, I do not know. Nor have other studies of localized immigrant culture in rural America focused to any great extent upon the attitudes or life courses of those who rejected such a culture, beyond noting classic intergenerational conflicts over issues such as language use, in part because of the difficulty of tracing a widely dispersed population of individuals who by definition tended not to follow predictable routes away from the home place. The loss of discon-

---

117. R. D. Thomas, *America: neu Amrywiaeth o Nodiadau am yr Unol Daleithiau*, translated as *America: or Miscellaneous Notes on the United States*, by Clare Thomas (1852; reprint, Aberystwyth: National Library of Wales, 1973); Thomas, *Hanes Cymry America*, 133.

118. Jenkin Jenkins, *Hanes Unwaith am Siencyn Ddwywaith* (The Singular History of Jenkin Jenkins) (Utica, N.Y.: T. J. Griffiths, 1872), 159.

119. Harrison E. Salisbury, *A Journey for Our Times: A Memoir* (New York: Harper & Row, 1983), 24, 51; telephone interview with James H. Lloyd, 27 February 1993.

tented members of a community was a part of the continuing process of cultural preservation, and may have reinforced characteristics that were already accentuated by self-selective emigration and settlement. In the case of Jackson/Gallia, it appears that a high proportion of the second generation did choose to stay, perhaps more because of the locality's improving economic situation after 1850 than out of any particular loyalty to Welsh traditions.

Agricultural Core, Industrial Periphery

By the early 1840s, Jackson/Gallia had a national reputation in the Welsh American community for being exceptionally religious and exceptionally poor. To some extent the latter reputation was undeserved, for outsiders who visited the area before 1850 were comparing a new frontier settlement to long-established agricultural communities such as Paddy's Run, the Welsh Hills in central Ohio, and Utica. It was true, nevertheless, that no other large Welsh American settlement had soils and slopes so ill suited to farming as those in Jackson/Gallia. Benjamin Chidlaw pointed to Jackson/Gallia as an example of the Welsh choosing mediocre land because it reminded them of Wales rather than braving the temporary isolation and lack of religion on the western frontier, where much better land was available. "Of all the land which the Welsh have chosen in Ohio," Chidlaw wrote, the Jackson/Gallia area "seems to have the poorest soil. In latter years hundreds have emigrated here from Cardiganshire; if they had proceeded a thousand miles further to the Mississippi valley they would have found much more valuable land for clearing. The hilly land contains plenty of stones and coal, but it is rather poor for pasture and corn-growing."[120]

Chidlaw was not alone in criticizing the settlement. When John Jones, Ty'n Rhos, passed through Pittsburgh on his way to Jackson County, he heard rumors "that the land was too poor to raise crops, and because of that, it was a place with little sustenance."[121] Jenkin Jenkins's critical account in 1844 of the area's religious orthodoxy also denigrated its physical attributes. "The

120. Rev. Benjamin W. Chidlaw, *The American*, trans. Rev. R. Gwilym Williams (Bala: County Press, 1978; originally published Llanrwst: John Jones, 1840), 30–31.
121. Letter from John Jones, Ty'n Rhos, to *Y Cenhadwr* (August 1845): 246.

roads were very muddy," he wrote, ". . . I do not recall ever in
my life seeing any so bad." He felt the same way about the
community's circumstances in general.

> In my opinion, because the land consists of yellow, infertile,
> weak soil, and because the residents generally had next to
> nothing when they began life there—because so many of them
> have come so recently to the same place, and they are at first
> so unfamiliar with the manner of marketing [goods] in this new
> country, they are people in the sorriest natural circumstances I
> have ever seen. Yet, considering that the times are reviving,
> that they are becoming more familiar with the country's ways,
> and that iron works are increasing in their area, perhaps our
> nation shall no more be seen in these circles in so low a condi-
> tion as they are at present.

In a final insult, Jenkins may have been responsible for the settlement being dubbed *gwlad yr asgwrn* (land of bones), a reference that compared Jackson/Gallia to the valley of dry bones and
death in the Book of Ezekiel: "and he brought me out by the
Spirit of the Lord, and set me down in the midst of the valley; it
was full of bones. . . . And he said to me, 'Son of man, can these
bones live?' And I answered, 'O Lord God, thou knowest.'"[122]
Jenkins's portrait of the settlement prompted an anonymous resident of Jackson/Gallia to write in its defense, "There are close to
3,000 Welsh here and they are comfortable in their temporal circumstances, although the Rev. Jenkin Jenkins, Dundaff, says that
these are the poorest people he ever saw in his life, and that the
soil is weak [and] yellow. We would like to have his explanation
of the word 'weak' in one of the future numbers."[123]

It was certainly true that the settlement's topography, soils, and
distance from markets disadvantaged its economic development.
In 1853, the state board of tax assessment ranked Jackson County
seventy-second out of eighty-eight Ohio counties in average land
value, at $7.48 per acre. Butler County, where Chidlaw lived,
ranked first at $36.08 per acre.[124] The villages of Centerville and
Oak Hill developed slowly and neither functioned as a trading

122. *Y Cenhadwr* (June 1844): 168–70; Roberts, *Hanes Eglwys Gymreig
Jackson*, 8; Ezek. 37: 1, 3.

123. Carwr Heddwch [Peace Lover], "Sefydliad y Cymry yn Swyddi Gallia a
Jackson" (The Welsh Settlement in Gallia and Jackson Counties), *Y Cenhadwr*
(July 1844): 217.

124. Ohio State Board of Equalization, *Proceedings of the State Board of
Equalization*, 7 November 1859 (Columbus, Ohio: 1860), 205–7.

center with outside markets until after 1850. Women who lived on the eastern side of the settlement rode or walked all the way to Gallipolis to market their eggs and butter, while people around Oak Hill traveled nearly as far to sell their produce in Portsmouth.[125]

Some families who could not afford to buy land when they first arrived did suffer long years of poverty. One such couple were Mary and John Lloyd, who emigrated with their three young children from Llan-non to Madison Township in 1840. As their grandson Virgil Evans relates in his family history, the Lloyds "settled on a hilly and rather poor tract of land" in Cooper Hollow, an established Welsh neighborhood on the north edge of Madison Township. They needed a cow to feed the children but had no money to buy one. John contracted with a neighbor to pay $7 for "a nice fresh cow" out of the wages he meant to earn working on the new canal in Logan County. But within a few days of reaching Logan, John caught dysentery. He died shortly after friends managed to bring him home in a borrowed two-wheel cart. Seven months later Mary delivered her fourth child, who did not long survive; then her two-year-old son was stricken with infantile paralysis. Her neighbor kindly never asked to be paid his $7. Although Mary escaped abject poverty in 1844 when she married Rev. Owen Jones, twenty-six years her senior, she never enjoyed an easy life (see fig. 3.11). Even as an old woman she would walk the fifteen miles to Gallipolis, balancing a basket of eggs on her head to sell in the market.[126]

In defense of the settlement, John Jones, Ty'n Rhos, argued that Jenkins and other critics did not appreciate the area's special advantages to Welsh immigrants. He pointed out that the problems posed by mediocre Appalachian soils were nothing new to Cardiganshire farmers. Jones himself had farmed a large tenancy on the moors of Mynydd Bach. In a letter to his compatriots in 1845, he reassured them "that if this land were manured and limed, in the same way that we tilled the land in Wales, there could be very abundant crops here."

> Some praise Illinois, others Wisconsin, and others Iowa . . . It is very likely that the earth here is not so deep as there; but I am very thankful to the Lord for leading me to this place.

125. Evans, *John Jones (Tirbach)*, 47; Evans, *History of Welsh Settlements*, 46.
126. Evans, *John Jones (Tirbach)*, 59; James H. Lloyd, personal correspondence.

Fig. 3.11 Mary Evans Lloyd Jones. In 1840, Mary emigrated from Llan-non to Madison Township with her husband John and their two young children. John died before their third child was born that same year. Even as an old woman, Mary would walk as far as Gallipolis, fifteen miles from her home, carrying a bas-ket of eggs balanced on her head to sell in the market. She lived to be ninety-one. This photograph was probably taken by the time she was blind, shortly before her death in 1893. (Photo courtesy of James H. Lloyd)

> Almost every kind of grain is raised here. . . . There are good oats, and the corn and the potatoes and beans look fine. There is a good place for every kind of fruit here, and a man can live here comfortably enough, if he makes a little effort with [the help of] providence.

Jones went on to emphasize that Jackson/Gallia offered immi-grants both inexpensive land and wage labor in the region's de-veloping charcoal iron industry. The furnaces "always have enough work for the Welsh, and at no small wages."[127] Chidlaw and Jenkins had both grudgingly acknowledged that rural indus-try might compensate for the area's poor land, but they failed to

127. Letter from John Jones, Ty'n Rhos, 246–47.

appreciate how significant that compensation could be or how the presence of coal mining and charcoal iron smelting would benefit farmers. Edward Jones, however—the man who recommended Jackson/Gallia in his guidebook for emigrants—noted that rural industry promised both wage labor and rising land values.[128]

For all its strict Calvinism and exceptional homogeneity, Jackson/Gallia was most unusual among Welsh American rural settlements in offering immigrants both pioneering agriculture and industrial employment. Although the settlement was predominantly agricultural in 1850, it lay within an extended band of rural, industrial, and urban Welsh communities that stretched along the Ohio River from Pittsburgh to Cincinnati. In the 1830s and 1840s, Welsh industrial workers formed a small but very important portion of the Ohio Valley's immigrant population. They filled positions as skilled laborers and managers at riverside rolling mills and forges that manufactured cast iron wares, kitchen stoves, and railroad wheels.[129] The various iron works at Portsmouth, located southwest of Oak Hill on the north bank of the Ohio River, included the Portsmouth Iron Works, built in 1831 and employing 150 hands; the Portsmouth Manufacturing Establishment, makers of steam engines and heavy machinery; the Scioto Rolling Mill, employing 120 hands; the Washington Foundry and Machine Shop; the Scioto Foundry; Washington Works, a machine shop and foundry; and People's Foundry. Several Welsh families from Cardiganshire settled in the town in 1837–1838 and were holding Sunday school meetings by the summer of 1840. By 1854 Portsmouth had a fine Welsh chapel and a long list of residents with distinctly Welsh names, many of them skilled industrial workers. There were also Welsh chapels in coal mining settlements at Pomeroy and Ironton, in Meigs and Lawrence counties, respectively, by the early 1850s.[130]

All of the iron works received their raw material—pig iron— from charcoal iron furnaces that dotted the surrounding country-

128. Jones, Y Teithiwr Americanaidd, 16–17.

129. J. P. Lesley, The Iron Manufacturers Guide to the Furnaces, Forges, and Rolling Mills of the United States (New York: John Wiley, 1859), 213–14, 254–58.

130. John J. Jones and John Edwards, "Byr Hanes y Cymry yn Portsmouth" (Short History of the Welsh in Portsmouth), Y Cyfaill (1840): 310; Portsmouth City Directory and Advertiser (Portsmouth, Ohio: printed in the Republican Office for sale by J. Stephenson and A. C. Post, July 1856); Thomas, Hanes Cymry America, 124–29.

side. When Welsh settlers arrived in the late 1830s, Jackson and Gallia counties were on the northern fringe of the expanding Hanging Rock iron district, which was on its way to becoming the leading charcoal iron–producing region west of the Alleghenies. The charcoal furnaces required labor and provision, both of which farm families could readily supply. A letter from Evan Evans in 1848 alerted prospective Welsh settlers that a new furnace was under construction just four miles from the Jackson/Gallia settlement, "where one can sell [cord-]wood, and also ore for use in the furnace, and that for ready money."[131]

The biography of Benjamin G. Williams illustrates how Welsh immigrants took advantage of the proximity of industry and agriculture. Williams was born in 1821, the fifth of six surviving children, on a large upland farm in Lledrod parish. Having lost a protracted court case against their landlord in April 1839, Benjamin's parents decided to follow the example of neighbors who had already emigrated to Jackson/Gallia. They arrived in southern Ohio in early August and soon bought an American's farm in Greenfield Township, Jackson County.

For the first two years Benjamin's work was confined to the farm, hoeing corn and shooting pheasant and wild boar in the woods. He took his first job at a charcoal iron furnace in 1841, working four months benching ore (a kind of shallow strip mining) at a wage of $16 per month, paid in food and supplies. "There I bought the 16-gallon kettle, coffee-grinder, skillets, and iron dogs to put under the firewood on the hearth," he wrote in his memoir. The next year he and three Welsh friends moved from one furnace to another, disappointed to find only goods for wages everywhere. They followed rumors of work for money wages on a new road project to Portsmouth, where one friend found work at a rolling mill. Work on the turnpike did not pan out and Benjamin found himself begging on the streets of Portsmouth, avoiding Welsh families there out of shame but also unwilling to go home. Eventually he found work at Mount Vernon Furnace, then on a canal, and finally a steady job as a coal miner in Pomeroy, where he earned as much as $75 a month, cash. Later that year, Benjamin's father gave him a deed for forty acres of land not far from the family homestead, adjoining his brother's new farm. He sold the land in 1846 and used the profit, along with his $100 in savings, to buy an eighty-acre

131. *Y Cenhadwr* (March 1848): 82–83.

farm next to his father's, with "a house, 30 acres cleared, and a fine orchard (which was valuable)." He returned one last time to Pomeroy to work up a grubstake mining, then sold his tools and came home to build a proper house for his future wife, Margaret Morgans. They were married in December 1847 and continued farming until 1877, when they moved into Oak Hill to live in genteel retirement.[132]

Jackson/Gallia may have been a particularly inviting settlement to Cardiganshire emigrants who initially settled in Pittsburgh. Among the immigrants I have specifically mentioned thus far, Isaac and John H. Jones of Bethel chapel both spent time in Pittsburgh before reaching Jackson County, as did John Lot Davis, who exemplified mixed rural-industrial migration in chapter 1. More emigrants from Mynydd Bach stopped in Pittsburgh than in any other location en route to Jackson/Gallia. They may have worked in the city's iron works, which employed a total of 658 hands in 1840. Or they may have found employment with the city's Welsh shopkeepers, who probably included D. T. Morgan, grocer and iron goods merchant; D. W. Davis, upholsterer and cabinet maker; and John Owens, steamboat joiner at the corner of Penn and Water Streets.[133]

Thus although Jackson/Gallia was a rural settlement where most families devoted their labor to agriculture, it was also part of a larger regional economy in which the iron industry played an increasingly important role. Work in rural and urban industries gave restless young men like Benjamin Williams an outlet for curiosity about their new country and various ways to earn money off the farm. The region's industries employed the skills that at least a few immigrants had learned in South Wales and taught industrial skills to those who came directly from rural areas. Americans were also employed in the furnaces, forges, and rolling mills, of course; numerically, they dominated the Ohio Valley's iron industry in this period. But Welsh workers were a distinctive immigrant element, particularly among the more skilled trades. Their experience in the charcoal iron business in

132. Benjamin G. Williams, "History of Benjamin G. Williams for His Son, Daniel Webster Williams," reprinted in *Jackson County, Ohio: History and Families 1816–1991*, comp. Jackson County Genealogical Society (Paducah, Ky.: Turner Publishing Co., 1991), 65–75, quotations on pp. 72, 74.

133. *Kimball & James' Business Directory, for the Mississippi Valley: 1844* (Cincinnati: Kendall & Bernard, 1844), State Historical Society of Wisconsin Microfiche no. 721, pp. 223–311.

particular would prove crucial to the next phase of community development after 1850, as would their possession of a growing portion of the area's land resources.

Emigrants from Mynydd Bach who settled in Jackson and Gallia counties reconstituted many aspects of the world they had known in Wales. They organized their community around chapel life and farming and vested a great deal of authority in male lay leaders who kept a strict watch over community practice and morals. But significant elements of their lives had changed. The hyperreligiosity of the Jackson/Gallia settlement is a fine illustration of Louis Hartz's thesis that ethnic settlements were composed of fragments of the immigrants' native society, and that the domination of a particular kind of people resulted in the heightened expression of certain cultural traits.[134] Economy changed more than culture for the Welsh in Jackson/Gallia, however. Up to 1850 most Welsh households were able to buy land in Ohio without the burdens or fears that accompanied freehold status in Wales. They had no financial obligations to a state church and owed no fealty, real or imagined, to English-speaking landlords. Although Jackson/Gallia was a poor settlement in its early years in comparison with older Welsh settlements, its residents' material circumstances and security were significantly better than they had been in Wales. The role of migratory labor in the Welsh household economy had also changed. Rather than migrate long distances to harvest other farmers' crops or work in heavy industry in order to pay the rent on a tenancy, Cardiganshire migrants in Ohio traveled short distances to earn money toward buying their own land. By 1850 they were poised to enter a new phase of development that would make full use of their earlier investments in land and in one another.

---

134. Louis Hartz, *The Founding of New Societies* (New York: Harcourt, Brace, & World, 1964). Other outstanding examples of this phenomenon were the Norwegian Lutheran community in Jackson and Trempealeau counties, Wisconsin and German Catholics in Stearns County, Minnesota; see Ann Marie Legreid, "The Exodus, Transplanting, and Religious Reorganization of a Group of Norwegian Lutheran Immigrants in Western Wisconsin, 1836–1900" (Ph.D. diss., University of Wisconsin–Madison, 1985); and Kathleen Neils Conzen, *Making Their Own America: Assimilation Theory and the German Peasant Pioneer*, German Historical Institute Lecture no. 3 (New York: Berg Publishers, 1990), 1–33.

Chapter Four

Charcoal Iron and the Welsh

Up until 1854, the Welsh community in Jackson and Gallia counties was much like other Midwestern ethnic farming settlements of its day. Most of the immigrants worked in agriculture, growing grain, potatoes, hay, and apples and raising livestock for home consumption and for sale. Although few Welsh farmers in the area had improved even half of their acreage by 1850, they were producing corn, oats, and other crops well in excess of what their families and livestock required. They took their surplus produce to several trading centers fifteen to twenty miles away, to Welsh-owned general stores in Centerville and Portland, or to any of a number of charcoal iron furnace company stores in the area. When they were not working on their farms or caring for their families, the settlers entertained, educated, and fortified themselves through religion, gathering as often as three times a week to worship, pray, sing, and discuss the word of God as they knew it, in Welsh.

Except for Timothy Evans's wool-carding factory, built in the early 1830s, and a steam-powered grain and lumber mill that Edward Morris and David Edwards built in Portland in about 1850, the Jackson/Gallia community showed no sign of entrepreneurial activity up to midcentury.[1] Proximity to the expanding charcoal iron industry, however, confronted the Welsh immigrants in Jackson/Gallia with opportunities and choices that gave their history an unusual trajectory for a rural Welsh farming community. Their relationship to the industry changed dramatically in 1854, when a large number of Welsh families banded together to build, and then attempted to operate, three charcoal iron furnaces in the heart of their own territory. The Welsh companies used a novel form of community-based venture capitalism to join a competitive industry. The consequences of their foray

1. The U.S. manufacturing schedule for Jackson County, 1850, lists Morris & Edwards as millers with $5,000 original capital, annual product worth $8,550, and seven employees who received a total of $182 in wages that year.

into rural industrial capitalism show that it created new tensions within the Welsh community even as it strengthened the immigrants' economic position in their locality.

The Nature and Organization of Charcoal Iron

Like the region around Merthyr Tydfil, the Hanging Rock iron district possessed all the natural resources necessary for making iron: abundant iron ore, limestone (for flux), forests that could be converted into charcoal, waterpower from streams, and easily mined seams of coal to fuel furnace engines where waterpower was not available.[2] The iron-making region extended from Greenup County in northern Kentucky to Logan County, Ohio (see map 4.1). The region's first charcoal iron furnace was built in 1818, the same year that the first six families from Mynydd Bach landed at Gallipolis. By 1852 there were forty-three furnaces in operation or under construction in the Hanging Rock district. The industry's last spurt of growth came in 1853–1856, when two railroad companies laid tracks connecting counties further north to existing rail and canal links and to ports on the Ohio River. Furnace investors seized on this development by constructing twenty-one new furnaces along the railroad corridor. Eight of them were located in Jackson County.[3]

Ohio's charcoal-fired furnaces employed essentially the same

2. The standard works on the Hanging Rock iron district are Eugene B. Willard, ed., *A Standard History of the Hanging Rock Iron Region of Ohio*, 2 vols. (N.p.: Lewis Publishing Company, 1916); Vernon D. Keeler, "An Economic History of the Jackson County Iron Industry," *Ohio Archaeological and Historical Quarterly* 42 (1933): 132–244; and Wilbur Stout, "The Charcoal Iron Industry of the Hanging Rock Iron District: Its Influence on the Early Development of the Ohio Valley," *Ohio Archaeological and Historical Quarterly* 42 (1933): 72–104. See also Christopher S. Duckworth, ed., "The Hanging Rock Charcoal Iron Industry," typescript, Ohio Historical Society, 1989. On coal mining, see Mark W. Long, "The Historic Coal Mining Industry of Jackson County," in *Jackson County, Ohio: History and Families 1816–1991*, comp. Jackson County Genealogical Society (Paducah, Ky.: Turning Publishing, 1991), 30–38.

3. Stout, "The Charcoal Iron Industry," 72–78; Willard, *Hanging Rock Iron Region*, vol. 1, pp. 441–42. Stout was state geologist of Ohio for many years but his passion was for the history of charcoal iron. His notes, along with several volumes of photographs and maps documenting the charcoal furnaces, are gathered in the Wilbur Stout Collection, vol. 408, Ohio Historical Society.

Brush Creek Furnace, built in Adams County in 1811, was the first charcoal iron furnace in southern Ohio. It was also the first in the United States to acquire a steam engine (in 1826) to run its bellows. Frank C. Morrow, comp. and ed., *A History of Industry in Jackson County, Ohio* (Wellston, Ohio, 1956), 25.

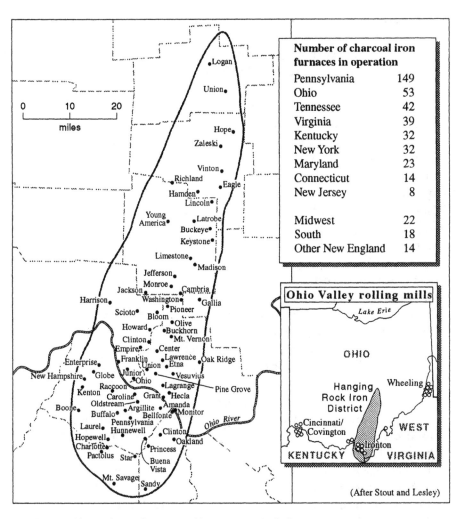

Number of charcoal iron furnaces in operation	
Pennsylvania	149
Ohio	53
Tennessee	42
Virginia	39
Kentucky	32
New York	32
Maryland	23
Connecticut	14
New Jersey	8
Midwest	22
South	18
Other New England	14

Ohio Valley rolling mills

(After Stout and Lesley)

Map 4.1 Charcoal iron furnaces in the Hanging Rock district, circa 1859

technology used to produce iron in the colonial period.[4] Although some nineteenth-century charcoal iron furnaces could

4. E. N. Hartley, *Iron Works on the Saugus: The Lynn and Braintree Ventures of the Company of Undertakers of the Ironworks in New England* (Norman: University of Oklahoma Press, 1957), esp. 165–76; Paul F. Paskoff, *Industrial Evolution: Organization, Structure, and Growth of the Pennsylvania Iron Industry, 1750–1860* (Baltimore: Johns Hopkins University Press, 1983), 102, 111; Keeler, "Jackson County Iron Industry," 147; Joseph E. Walker, *Hopewell Village: The Dynamics of a Nineteenth-Century Iron-Making Community* (Philadelphia: University of Pennsylvania Press, 1966), 139–64; Alfred Philip Muntz, "Forests and Iron: The Charcoal Iron Industry of the New Jersey Highlands," *Geografiska Annaler* 42 (1960): 315–23.

produce up to twenty tons of pig iron per day, their annual production averaged between 1,000 and 1,500 tons, a rate already eclipsed by the nearly 5,000-ton capacity of eastern Pennsylvania's anthracite furnaces in 1850. The physical properties of charcoal as a fuel imposed strict limitations on the technology's productive capacity. Because charcoal is lightweight and friable, it cannot sustain fires sufficiently hot to smelt iron in furnaces beyond a certain size. The friability of charcoal also meant that it turned to coal dust on long journeys, so that furnaces had to be built near their fuel supply, in the woods. Each charcoal iron operation in the Hanging Rock district consisted of a single "stack"—a massive, blunt pyramid of stone containing a crucible and chimney (see fig. 4.1)—surrounded by thousands of acres of timberland from which colliers could make charcoal to fire the furnace.[5]

The fact that charcoal iron resisted economies of scale did not mean that the industry was antiquated or its late proliferation in Ohio peculiar. As Jeremy Atack and others have observed, small-scale, dispersed iron production remained important in rural areas and as a source of supply for high-quality pig iron throughout the nineteenth century.[6] Charcoal's almost pure carbon content produced superior iron that was both malleable and strong. Charcoal iron was ideal for cast-iron holloware, farm implements, machine castings, and railroad car wheels. In heavily wooded regions such as southern Ohio, deforestation for making charcoal had the secondary benefit of clearing land for agricultural settlement. The Hanging Rock furnaces were essential to the mechanization and industrialization of the Ohio Valley. They supplied pig iron to forges and rolling mills from Wheeling, West Virginia, to Cincinnati. The furnaces that survived longest were niche producers who sold high-quality iron to specialty markets, such as the machine shops and iron goods manufacturers in canal towns in central Ohio (see map 4.2). Conversion to coal-fired

5. Keeler estimated that 325–350 acres of timber were required to fuel a furnace annually, a little higher than Williams's estimate of 300 acres; Keeler, "Jackson County Iron Industry," 153; Michael Williams, *Americans and Their Forests: A Historical Geography* (Cambridge: Cambridge University Press, 1989), 106, 147–52. On the process of making charcoal, see Eric Sloane, *Eric Sloane's Sketches of America Past* (1962; reprint, New York: Promontory Press, 1986), 283–86.

6. Jeremy Atack, "Firm Size and Industrial Structure in the United States during the Nineteenth Century," *Journal of Economic History* 46 (1986): 463–75.

A) The filler dumps raw materials into the stack mouth
B) Blasts of pressurized air from the blowing engine aid combustion
C) Molten iron collects at the bottom of the crucible
D) "Tapping" releases the molten metal into the main channel or "sow"
E) Side channels direct the metal into rows of molds, forming "pigs"
F) Once hardened, the pigs are broken out and loaded into wagons

Fig. 4.1 Reconstruction of Jefferson Furnace. The operation of Jefferson Furnace, here reconstructed from historical evidence, was typical for charcoal iron furnaces of its era.

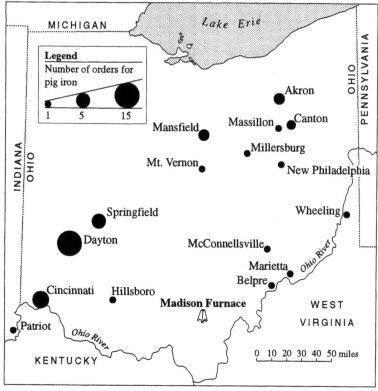

Map 4.2 Madison Furnace customers, circa 1869

technology in southern Ohio sputtered through several decades of experimentation as ironmasters struggled with the region's high-sulphur coal, and coal mine operators searched for better-grade deposits.[7] The first successful coal-fired furnace in Jackson County was built in 1872. As coal-fired technology improved, charcoal iron's share of the American pig iron market declined, from 47 percent in 1854 to 10 percent in 1884 and just 1 percent in 1909. The last charcoal furnace in Ohio finally went out of blast in 1916.[8]

7. Robert C. Allen, "The Shift to Mineral Fuel: Ohio Valley Blast Furnaces," working paper from Cliometrics Conference, Madison, Wisconsin (26–28 April 1973), typescript pp. 39, 43. See also J. P. Lesley, *The Iron Manufacturer's Guide to the Furnaces, Forges, and Rolling Mills of the United States* (New York: John Wiley, 1859), esp. 113–22, 213–14, 254–57.

8. Peter Temin, *Iron and Steel in Nineteenth-Century America: An Economic Enquiry* (Cambridge: M.I.T. Press, 1964), table C.3, pp. 268–69; John E. Jones, "Romance of the Old Charcoal Furnace Days of the Hanging Rock Iron District," paper presented at the Globe Iron Co. sales representatives meeting, Jackson, Ohio, 27–28 July 1934, unnumbered p. 2; Keeler, "Jackson County Iron

In addition to natural resources and capital, a furnace needed a labor force of skilled and unskilled workers (see table 4.1 and figs. 4.2 to 4.4).[9] Constructing furnace stacks became a speciality of several men in the Hanging Rock iron district. Whether carved directly from a sandstone cliff or built block upon massive block, the stack had to possess certain refractory qualities and withstand decades of use. The "furnaceman" or "blower" needed years of experience to judge the qualities of each batch of charcoal, iron ore, and limestone that constituted the charge loaded into the furnace at the beginning of the blast. Competent engineers were needed to run the blast engine that forced cool or hot air into the burning charge (hence "cold-blast" or "hot-blast" charcoal iron[10]). The man who tapped the molten ore and directed its flow into the oblong molds of sand on the casting floor could also be considered a skilled worker. The skills necessary to make charcoal, mine iron ore, and quarry limestone were perhaps easier to learn; certainly those workers earned lower wages than the workers who actually produced the pig iron. Making charcoal required as much patience as skill, for colliers had to tend the smoldering mounds of charcoal for weeks at a time, keeping watch all hours of the day and night to make sure that the mounds maintained a steady heat in order to char the wood properly. Mining and quarrying were less technically sophisticated in the Hanging Rock region than was hard-rock mining in South Wales and eastern Pennsylvania, since most coal in southern Ohio was worked from shallow drift mines that did not require elaborate tunneling, pumping, or ventilation. Limestone was quarried directly from outcroppings or hewed below ground as an adjunct to coal mining where limestone and coal strata lay

Industry," 192–231.

9. In addition to the sources cited for table 4.1, the following discussion is based upon the Madison Furnace Company Collection, vol. 161, Ohio Historical Society (hereafter Madison Collection, vol. 161); Morrow, *Industry in Jackson County*; Stout, "The Charcoal Iron Industry"; Long, "Coal Mining Industry of Jackson County," 30–31; W. N. Davis, "Out of the Past," installment no. 84, "Charcoal Burning," *Oak Hill Press*, 26 February 1969, p. 5; telephone interview with James H. Lloyd, Oak Hill, Ohio, 29 May 1993; and Charles Tomlinson, ed., *Cyclopaedia of Useful Arts & Manufactures* (London: George Virtue, 1853), 76–82, 281–82, 285–87.

10. In a cold-blast furnace, bellows forced air at normal temperature into the crucible. The hot blast preheated air to a temperature of 300–400 degrees Fahrenheit. Cold blast produced iron of superior quality; hot blast was more efficient and reduced charcoal consumption by as much as 35 percent. Morrow, *Industry in Jackson County*, 37.

Table 4.1   Charcoal iron furnace labor

On-site labor (furnace in blast)	
Skilled	*Low skill or unskilled*
1 manager	5–9 chargers or fillers (weighed and loaded charge into stack)
1 foundryman or blower (sometimes also manager)	2 helpers
2 engineers (day and night shifts)	3–5 cast-house workers (formed molds, broke pigs out of molds
2 keepers (discharged iron and slag, regulated blast air)	4–6 slag removers, loaders, cleaners
1 store manager/bookkeeper	1–2 store clerks
1 blacksmith	
Off-site labor (seasonal and part-time)	
Skilled	*Low skill or unskilled*
2–10 colliers (made charcoal)	50 wood cutters
15–20 ore miners and limestone quarriers	2–5 ore burners (roasted ore to remove impurities)
	5–10 haulers

	Totals:		
		Skilled workers	5–37
		Low skill or unskilled workers	72–89
		Approximate furnace workforce	100–125

Sources: Duckworth, "Hanging Rock Charcoal Iron Industry," 28; Madison Furnace Company Collection, Ohio Historical Society mss. 161, box 51 (time books), box 29 (returnables book), and box 2, no. 21 (journal of deliveries, 1869–1871); Jefferson Furnace Company, Ohio Historical Society, vol. 489.

in close proximity. The most common method of obtaining iron ore was called scraping, or benching, a kind of strip mining in which two men, working with a rectangular, horse-drawn metal scoop, dug ore directly from the hillsides. (Scraping left shallow, stepped banks that are still visible in the landscape today.) Each furnace also had its bookkeeper, who often doubled as manager of the company store, and one or two young clerks.

Hauling, wood chopping, and general manual labor were the least skilled kinds of furnace work and the most plentiful. Local farmers and their children hauled charcoal and iron ore and delivered animal feed and provisions to the general store. Local people also chopped wood for charcoal, although furnace records and the U.S. census indicate that chopping and other kinds of manual labor, such as roasting ore to remove impurities, were more commonly done by landless people than by farmers.

Fig. 4.2 Breaking pigs. Olive Furnace was one of John Campbell's operations and was located in Lawrence County. In this late-nineteenth-century photo a workman holds a sledgehammer overhead, poised to break the slender rod of iron that connected each pig to the feeder line from the sow. The furnace crucible glows through the gate behind him. (Ohio Historical Society)

All told, a charcoal furnace in blast employed about 25 workers on site and another 75 to 100 in various part-time or seasonal occupations at the furnace or in the woods. Ordinarily, a furnace remained in blast for about nine months. It had to be shut down for three months each year for workers to clean and reline the stack interior and to restock fuel and ore for the next year's blast.

Generally, charcoal iron and agriculture were complementary economic activities. The annual winter lull in iron making at Jackson County's Madison Furnace coincided with the slowest time of the agricultural year, giving both furnace workers and farmers time to supplement their income by chopping wood, making charcoal, or mining. The slight drop in man-hours at Madison Furnace during the month of September does suggest, however, that harvesting still took priority over furnace labor in this rural-industrial region during the antebellum period. Furnaces also provided a local market for agricultural produce. When new furnaces were built in Jackson County in the mid-1850s, for example, the price of wheat rose from 65¢ to $1.65 a

Fig. 4.3 Shoeing oxen. Oxen were the preferred beasts of burden for furnace work because of their strength and endurance. Teams of oxen hauled ore, limestone, and charcoal to the furnace site and took away the finished iron. Wilbur Stout estimated that each furnace needed up to two hundred oxen each year; providing feed for the animals became a major by-industry for local farms. (Ohio Historical Society)

bushel.[11] Furnaces in turn were able to satisfy some of their labor needs with local men.

All the charcoal iron furnaces in the Hanging Rock iron district shared these characteristics. Those owned by Americans also shared a common corporate structure, management, and levels and methods of capitalization that reflected both the customs of small-scale, mid-nineteenth-century business in the United States and certain attitudes toward risk and profit. Like charcoal iron firms elsewhere in the country, those in the Hanging Rock district were organized as small partnerships.[12] In contrast to large-scale ventures such as railroads and canals, charcoal furnaces generally did not attract small investors. A few wealthy individuals, each

11. Madison Collection, vol. 161; Willard, *Hanging Rock Iron Region*, vol. 1, p. 456.

12. Paskoff, *Industrial Evolution*. The following discussion is based upon credit reports from the R. G. Dun & Company Collection, Baker Library, Harvard University Graduate School of Business Administration; along with Keeler, "Jackson County Iron Industry"; and Stout, "The Charcoal Iron Industry."

Fig. 4.4 Hauling wood for charcoal. Charcoaling devastated the hardwood forests of southern Ohio and opened the way for subsequent land use, whether farming or strip mining. In this photo one team of five yoke of oxen begins to haul away a wagon loaded with charcoal from the pit just visible to the wagon's left, while another team descends the steep hill with an empty wagon ready for more. (Ohio Historical Society)

worth from $10,000 to $100,000, usually bought all of the shares in a new furnace, forming a company whose members were liable under Ohio law for double the value of their stock.[13] In some cases only two or three men provided all the financing for a furnace's construction, the purchase of timber and mineral land, and initial operating expenses, which together reached $60,000 to $100,000 by the end of the first year of production. More often, four to eight investors bought shares to get a company started. Certain names crop up time and again in credit reports on Hanging Rock charcoal iron furnaces, indicating a degree of specialization among capitalists who chose to invest in the industry. Most of them lived in the Hanging Rock region, although individuals from as far away as Cincinnati also "became interested." In almost every case, at least one investor lived in the

13. "At the present time," wrote Cora M. Thompson in 1984, "statutes making stockholders liable to the extent of stock held, which were interpreted as imposing double liability are no longer in force as to business corporations in any jurisdiction." In some states, double liability survived until the 1950s. *Fletcher Cyclopedia of the Law of Private Corporations* (Wilmette, Ill.: Callaghan & Co., 1984), rev. vol. 13A, sec. 6224, p. 80. Regarding the Ohio statute, see *Irvine v. Elliott,* 203 F. 82 (D.C. Cir. 1913).

county where the furnace was located and took responsibility for overseeing daily operations. That person's knowledge of charcoal iron could prove critical to the company's success.

The premier example of the owner-manager in southern Ohio was John Campbell. Between 1833 and 1856 Campbell invested in at least ten furnaces in five counties. He had a special knack for understanding the fickle nature of charcoal iron, whose quality could be affected by weather and atmospheric moisture as well as the chemical content of the iron ore. Campbell amassed a personal fortune of over $250,000 as a charcoal iron investor but he was most famous as an ironmaster. All of his furnaces did well and several were among the most profitable and long-lived in the Hanging Rock district. His last new venture in charcoal iron, Jackson County's Monroe Furnace (built in 1855–1856), was the largest charcoal furnace in the Hanging Rock district, with a daily capacity of twenty tons. Campbell was also involved in the post–Civil War growth of Ironton, an industrial town dominated by early coal-fired iron furnaces.

The wealthiest man in Ohio charcoal iron was probably H. S. Bundy. He began as financial agent of Latrobe Furnace; went on to buy up nearly all of the firm's stock as well as the stock of Keystone Furnace Company, considered a model operation in its day; and he became a leader in the development of coal mining in Jackson County. A fine orator in a rather old-fashioned way, Bundy won a state senate seat in 1855 and later served in the U.S. Congress, retiring at last in 1895.[14]

The manager's skills in handling furnace chemistry and day-to-day operations were important to its success, but the critical ingredient in guaranteeing any firm's long-term survival was capital. A company could easily go bankrupt if a leading stockholder pulled out his investment or died in debt. When iron markets slowed, firms whose partners lacked capital reserves were the first to fail. This proved to be a crippling problem for some of the firms that built new furnaces between 1853 and 1856. Partners normally expected to recoup their initial debt from sales of iron in the first two to three years of operation. In the financial panic of 1857 and the ensuing national depression, however, many

14. Jackson, Lawrence, and Scioto counties, Ohio, vols. 103, 110, and 166, R. G. Dun & Company Collection, Baker Library, Harvard University Graduate School of Business Administration; Stout, "The Charcoal Iron Industry," 75–78; Willard, *Hanging Rock Iron Region*, vol. 2, pp. 1129–31; and vol. 1, p. 458; Long, "Coal Mining Industry of Jackson County," 34.

new companies foundered, unable to sell their pig iron in a sluggish and uncertain market.

The pattern of such companies' failure is revealed in reports on the creditworthiness of charcoal iron firms prepared by the roving investigators employed by R. G. Dun & Company. In December 1857 the Young America Furnace was just beginning to produce iron. "I suppose they have a tolerably large debt to carry," the R. G. Dun reporter noted, "but they have a good property and if the furnace works well will be able to carry the indebtedness. I consider them responsible but understand that they do not pay promptly and probably will not be able to do so for some time." 13 September 1858: "Creditors had best be wide awake." 2 October 1858: "In great difficulty.... We learn they owe a great deal in Cincinnati and there are now large claims against them." The entry for January 1860 notes that the firm was "Broken up but all debts prior to May 1857 can probably be made; about that time all the responsible partners left the concern."[15] When "responsible" parties remained involved, their deep pockets could save imperiled furnaces. John Campbell was a major investor in four of the Jackson County furnaces built between 1853 and 1856. In the wake of the 1857 economic crash, Campbell's furnaces struggled to pay their debts. Early in 1862, Campbell mortgaged all of his property "to secure his creditors." Not a month later, confidence was restored. "The pecuniary difficulties of John Campbell has [sic] not affected the standing of the firm," read the March credit report. "No one need fear trusting them."[16] All of John Campbell's furnaces survived the depression and remained productive for many more years.

Reluctant Entrepreneurs

The first sign of entrepreneurial response among the Welsh to the region's developing industry came in 1851, when Thomas T.

15. Jackson County, Ohio, vol. 103, pp. E, F, in the R. G. Dun & Company Collection. In these and other quotations from the R. G. Dun & Company Collection, I am spelling out in full the many words that the credit reporters abbreviated, such as "co.," "resp.," and "K" for capital.

16. Lawrence County, Ohio, vol. 110, p. 86, R. G. Dun & Company Collection. The failure of a furnace company did not necessarily spell financial ruin for investors, because Ohio law limited stockholder liability. As one reporter noted, "the owners of a furnace therefore may be wealthy and the company 'hard up.'" Jackson County, Ohio, vol. 103, p. 22.

Jones, a former horse breeder and farmer from near Lampeter, Cardiganshire, contracted to build a section of the Scioto and Hocking Valley Railroad through southern Jackson County. Jones had settled in Jefferson Township in 1839 or 1840 after spending six months in Pittsburgh and about a year in the Welsh settlement at Palmyra, Ohio. By 1850 he had sold his family's first farm in Jefferson Township, bought a better one, and improved 50 of its 120 acres. His new log house was "considered one of the best farmhouses in the county." Two other Welshmen of Jefferson Township, Thomas Llewelyn Hughes and William Evans, were among the citizens who organized the public celebration that greeted the first train to the town of Jackson on 18 August 1853. Jones, Hughes, and Evans helped make sure that the railroad line was built along the western side of Oak Hill, through the core of the Welsh settlement. They were also among the Welshmen who attended meetings at the home of farmer John Hughes in late 1853 or early 1854, when members of the Horeb neighborhood decided to build a charcoal iron furnace about a mile west of the new Oak Hill railroad station.[17]

Meanwhile, Welshmen and women in other parts of the settlement were discussing similar plans. Families living southeast of Horeb, as well as settlers along the border of Bloomfield and Madison townships, also decided to build charcoal furnaces. All three neighborhoods hatched essentially the same scheme. Lacking wealthy individuals who could personally bankroll a new venture, the Welsh community struck on a way to secure necessary resources using the one capital asset they had in abundance, namely land. Welsh farmers deeded their land to one of the furnace companies in exchange for shares of company stock. (They could also purchase shares outright for cash, an option exercised by a number of important investors.) The land-for-stock scheme gave each of the new Welsh furnaces timber rights and probably mineral rights for more than enough land to provide a base for long-term productivity. In deeding their land to a furnace company, most families reserved ownership of their homes and farm buildings as well as the right to continue farming the acres they had already improved.[18] The Horeb community named its ven-

17. Willard, *Hanging Rock Iron Region*, vol. 2, pp. 1070–71 and vol. 1, pp. 444–45, quotation on p. 1071; U.S. manuscript census for Jackson County, Ohio, 1850; Evan E. Davis, *Industrial History, Oak Hill, Ohio*, 2d ed. (Portsmouth: Compton Printing, 1980), 19; Dan T. Davis, comp. and ed., *Early History of Horeb Church* (Oak Hill, Ohio: Privately published, 1938), 15.

18. Jackson and Gallia county deed books (see Appendix B for a typical deed).

ture Jefferson Furnace Company. The neighborhood to the south-east called its furnace Cambria. The third furnace, called Lime-stone, was located to the north of Madison Furnace (see map 4.3).

Thomas Ll. Hughes explained the Welsh community's ratio-nale for building these furnaces in an open letter to readers of *Y Cyfaill*, written on 20 February 1854 and published in the April number. As his letter makes clear, the Welsh in Jackson/Gallia did not take the lead in industrial development in their locality; far from it. They were reluctant entrepreneurs who were com-pelled to act only when American capitalists brought charcoal iron to the very doorstep of the Welsh community:

> The neighborhood was, until recently, dependent for work, and a market for crops, on the iron works to the south of here, between us and the Ohio River, namely Bloom, Washington, Gallia, Olive, Vernon, and others. But about a month ago an-other was begun, namely the Madison [Furnace], two miles to the north of Oak Hill. All of them belong to Americans. Seeing them sweeping all before them, it came to mind among some of the Welsh to take a stab at what they could do, before all of the [ore] mines were claimed; and the result was the incorpo-ration of two strong companies, which are now in full swing building two new furnaces, namely the Jefferson . . . and the Cambria . . . [Limestone was started in the autumn.] Each one's capital is $60,000; and all of it has been taken up by the Welsh; and it is also expected that yellow iron will be raised in the re-gion during the coming summer. This has raised wages very high in the area; laborers are paid $1.25, and carpenters and stone masons from $1.75 to $2.00 a day; and there aren't half enough men at those high prices. So, Welsh boys of the poor regions of Newark, Steuben, and Wisconsin, if you want to earn a pretty penny, get yourselves to this place.
>
> This is no boastful tale, but words of truth and sobriety.[19]

True and sober, yes, but one can sense how Hughes relished his community's ability, finally, to exercise a bit of one-upsman-

---

Minutes from the Jefferson stockholders' meeting on 22 May 1855 note that the company agreed to allow a stockholder to exchange the land he had deeded to the company for another parcel on condition that he find 1,000 cords of wood and that the company "retain ore privilege on said land." If this means that the Jefferson Furnace Company held mineral rights to all the land it purchased, some parcels may have been significantly undervalued at $12 per acre.

19. *Y Cyfaill* (April 1854): 153.

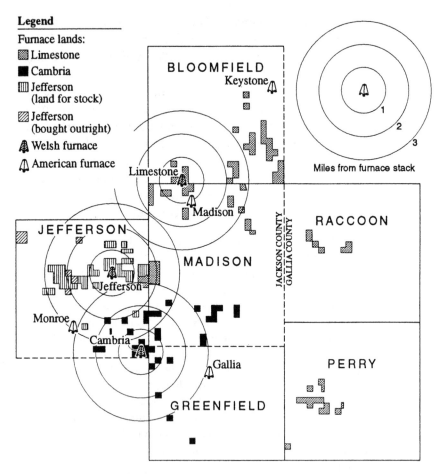

Map 4.3 Location of lands purchased by Welsh charcoal iron firms, 1854–1857

ship over other rural Welsh settlements to which Jackson/Gallia had been so unfavorably compared.

The timing, means, and consequences of Welsh involvement in charcoal iron say a great deal about the character and aspirations of the Jackson/Gallia Welsh community. More significantly, this part of their story reveals the ways in which cultural constructs influenced economic behavior at a critical juncture in a locality's economic development. The case of the Jefferson Furnace Company in particular offers an exceptionally clear window through which to see whether immigrants who became entrepreneurially involved in rural industry were acting as individuals to maximize profits from their investments or as a cooperative community engaged in strategies to preserve long-term family security.

ORGANIZATION OF JEFFERSON FURNACE COMPANY

Evidence of the stock-for-land scheme survives for all three companies in the deed records of Jackson and Gallia counties. The organizers of Jefferson Furnace, however, left a more extensive paper trail than did the other two companies, both in the deeds and in the one extant volume of Jefferson Company records, which covers the period of the furnace's construction and operation from 1854 through 1857 and stockholders' meetings through 1882. The Jefferson accounts thus make it possible to reconstruct the origins and initial operations of what was to prove the most successful of the three Welsh furnaces.

In June 1857, Jefferson stockholders entered the articles of agreement for the firm with the Jackson County recorder[20] (see Appendix B), detailing the method and intent of the company's initial financing. The agreement begins,

> Evry Member of the Company owning land is to deed his land to the company at twelve dollars per acre reserving one acre where the Building stands on and also reserving the privelege of cultivating what land he has already cleared for his own personally benefit but not use any green Timber nor to hinder the Company at any time enter the land . . .

A share of company stock was valued at $500. Each full share gave its owner or owners one vote at stockholders' meetings, whose business included the election of the furnace manager and the clerk or secretary. These officers were to be elected annually and were subject to ejection by a two-thirds vote. Investors purchasing shares in cash were allowed to pay in three installments during 1854, but if they failed to make their quarterly payments the company could reclaim the stock by refunding the amount invested to that date. The company reserved the right of first refusal on the sale of any shares and prohibited use of the company name "to raise money or goods except under direction of the Manager." Furthermore, the company had the right to compel quarrelsome members to sell their shares if they failed to settle their differences amicably through third-party mediation. The agreement called for an annual accounting of the company balance sheet, and company books were to be open and available to all stockholders at all times. Once the timber on company lands

20. Jackson County Deed Book Q, pp. 461–62.

was exhausted, the company would sell the land "to the highest bidders for the mutual benefit of all the different Members of the Company." The company was also empowered to sell land by a majority vote of the stockholders present at a meeting called for that purpose.

Although Welsh syntax, mispellings, and awkward literal translations mar the agreement's English, there is nothing naive or unsophisticated about the document. It outlines a system of democratic business management in which stockholders retained control over most decisions while giving company officers responsibility for daily operations and the obtaining of credit (use of the company name "to raise money or goods"). Annual elections kept officers on a fairly short leash; anyone whose actions displeased a voting majority of the stockholders could lose his position and the salary that went with it.

Each of the Welsh furnaces had from thirty to sixty shareholders at its inception.[21] Between 1854 and 1857, Jefferson Furnace acquired land from fifty-one Welsh individuals, most of them married couples. The purchase of these Welsh holdings gave the company 1,785 acres of timber and mineral land, most of which was located within two and a half miles of the furnace. Land purchased from American settlers added another 613 acres, for a total of 2,370 acres. Twenty-six Welsh families and individuals received shares of Jefferson stock in exchange for their land, while none of the Americans did. The company accounts make no mention of women, but the fact that wives and husbands are named jointly in the deeds of transfer to all three companies suggests that women were considered joint shareholders with their husbands.[22] Some of the farmers who exchanged land for shares also paid cash for stock, while eight paid only cash for stock. A

21. The first entries for Limestone and Cambria in the R. G. Dun & Company credit reports estimate company membership at "about 30 persons" and "30 or 40 persons," respectively. The first entry for Jefferson vaguely refers to "quite a number of members." R. G. Dun & Company collection, Jackson County, Ohio, vol. 103, pp. D, 17, 22. Not until many years later, when ownership of Jefferson had become somewhat concentrated in fewer hands, did the reporter attempt to list the names of shareholders or company officers. In contrast, investors' names figure prominently in early reports for American-owned firms.

22. Jackson County deed book Q, pp. 489–520. Jefferson Furnace accounts record the purchase of 633 acres "for furnace use" on 9 February 1854, distinguishing those parcels from those that were "received on stock." Company records list land-for-stock transfers totaling 1,880.5 acres in 1854, all in the months of January and February. Jefferson Furnace Company records, vol. 489, Ohio Historical Society (hereafter cited as JFC records, vol. 489).

total of nearly eighty Welsh men and women invested capital to get Jefferson up and running. Although the corporate charter does not explicitly state that only persons of Welsh birth or Welsh descent could own stock, this appears to have been an unwritten rule, implicitly understood and enforced by provision number six in the Jefferson charter: "No member of the Company shall sell any Shares without first giving the Company the refusal of the same." According to extant company records, this rule was neither bent nor broken between 1854 and 1882, except on one occasion in 1858 when a meeting of the shareholders voted to permit Thomas J. Jones to transfer three shares of stock to a John Kendle, who, if he was a Welshman, was not a resident of the Jackson/Gallia community.[23]

No company records survive for Cambria or Limestone Furnace. Deeds record the sale of land to Cambria Furnace by thirty-four individuals (including sixteen couples) between 1854 and 1857, and by seventy individuals (thirty-four couples) to Limestone Furnace during the same period. All of Cambria's initial 1,239 acres came from Welsh farms. The company's first R. G. Dun & Company credit report, dated 23 January 1856, notes that its members were "mostly Welsh," while a report in 1858 describes Cambria as being "composed of . . . Welsh farmers" and makes no mention of non-Welsh involvement. Limestone bought more of its land from non-Welsh settlers than did the other two furnaces. Nearly 23 percent of its 3,079 acres had belonged to American or German families. Although at least one American owned Limestone shares, the great majority of its stockholders were almost certainly Welsh.[24] Altogether, about one-third of the Welsh in the settlement invested in one or another of the three charcoal iron furnaces in 1854–1855.

Acquiring land gave companies the raw materials necessary to make iron, but it also burdened them with considerable debt.

23. JFC records, vol. 489. The author of "A Brief History of Jefferson Furnace" (anonymous typescript [with material by Wilbur Stout] submitted to the Ohio State Archaeological and Historical Society in support of a proposal to restore Jefferson Furnace, November 1934), claimed that the first constitution of the company decreed that "only Welshmen could hold stock in the company and the furnace should never operate on the Sabbath day" (ms. p. 3). If these strictures were written down, the document containing them is not a part of the extant company records.

24. Jackson County deed books O, P, U, V, Z; Gallia County deed books, vols. 27, 32, 33; Jackson County, Ohio, vol. 103, p. 17, R. G. Dun & Company Collection.

Credit reporters in the 1850s expected new furnaces to incur about $60,000 of debt at the outset, much of it from purchasing raw materials. Debt in itself would not lower a firm's credit rating, for "a good running furnace in ordinary times with proper management would carry [$60,000] without serious embarrassment," because earnings from the sale of iron would meet all obligations within a few years.[25] In extraordinary times such as the depression of 1857–1862, however, some young companies buckled under their initial load of debt. By the end of 1857, Jefferson had signed deeds for land valued at a total of $27,319. Cambria's land cost $18,980 and Limestone's $47,700. The most ingenious feature of the stock-for-land investment scheme was that it obviated this paper debt to the extent that sellers accepted stock as payment for their land. Jefferson's actual out-of-pocket expenses for land in the first three years were only $4,715, paid in cash and long-term notes.[26] As we shall see, the other two furnaces did not minimize their debt to the same degree, in part because they both accepted land for stock at the rate of $15 per acre compared to Jefferson's $12, but also because they purchased more land outright from Americans.[27]

CAPITAL FROM COMMUNITY

Land was not the only heavy drain upon a young furnace company's finances. The expense of building the furnace complex exceeded the capital stock of some companies. A furnace also had to pay workers, stock the general store, and cover railroad fees and taxes. American-owned firms typically took out loans to cover these start-up costs. If the Welsh firms had borrowed heavily, they would have had only their land for collateral, and the deed records show no trace of mortgages on Welsh furnace lands

25. Jackson County, Ohio, vol. 103, pp. 50, 22, R. G. Dun & Company Collection.

26. There are slight discrepancies between the Jackson County deeds and Jefferson Furnace Company accounts. The former yield an initial investment in land totaling $24,329. The latter list a total investment in land of $27,319.20, of which $4,715 was paid, in cash and notes, to American grantors. The Jefferson Company agreement states that the company's capital was $60,000—the same figure that Thomas Ll. Hughes cited in his report to *Y Cyfaill* on 20 February 1854—but the extant company accounts do not confirm that high amount.

27. Willard, *Hanging Rock Iron Region*, vol. 1, p. 455; land deeds for Limestone Furnace.

through the 1850s and 1860s. How did the Welsh meet demands for operating capital?

Again, the evidence is best for Jefferson Furnace. The furnace clerk and bookkeeper was the same Thomas Llewelyn Hughes who stood on the railroad platform to welcome the first train to Jackson in 1853 and who reported the birth of the Welsh charcoal iron companies to the Welsh American press. Hughes was a meticulous if self-taught accountant. His daily ledger of Jefferson Furnace accounts records deliveries of raw materials, building supplies, and provisions; iron sales; stock purchases; loans the company received; money it advanced on credit to workers; notes it issued; and detailed information about the kind of labor workers performed and the wages they received, from the furnace manager to wood choppers and boys who helped their fathers haul corn. The accounts suggest that Jefferson survived the tough years before the war mainly through continued community support and avoidance of debt. In addition to minimizing its expenses for land, the company received steady infusions of cash from Welsh investors between April and October 1854, reaching a total of almost $10,300. In exchange, investors' stock accounts accumulated shares. The cash came mainly from shareholders who had bought shares outright rather than from those who exchanged their land for stock. A total of $3,698 came from four men who invested only cash: Thomas Ll. Hughes; John D. Davies, who became manager of the furnace in 1857; William M. Jones, the furnace storekeeper;[28] and Edward Morris. Although these men's investments gave them more shares than most other investors, they did not dominate to the same extent as the partners in American firms. The two key differences between the ownership of Jefferson and ownership of American furnaces were that Jefferson stock was widely dispersed among a large number of shareholders and that no one owned shares in more than one Welsh furnace. In the first round of stock purchases in 1854–1855, no Jefferson investor bought more than four shares of stock. On the list of stockholders appended to the company agreement in 1857 (which excludes some of the early investors), ownership ranges from one-half share to ten shares, with six of twenty-three members holding six or more shares (see table 4.2).

I know of no precedent for this kind of broad-based community ownership of an industrial venture in other Welsh American

28. "A Brief History of Jefferson Furnace," ms. p. 6.

Table 4.2 Shareholders in the Jefferson Furnace Company, circa 1857

Name	Shares	Company office	Chapel (elder)	Home in Wales
David Edwards	10	trustee	Oak Hill C.M.	Llangwyryfon (?)
Thomas T. Jones	9	financial agent	Horeb	Lampeter area
William S. Williams	8			[born in Utica]
Thomas S. Jones	7		Horeb	Nancwnlle
John J. Jones	7			Nancwnlle
John Hughes, Sr.	6		Horeb (E)	Llansanffraid
Thomas Ll. Hughes	5	clerk	Oak Hill C.M. (E)	Denbighshire
Thomas Jones, North	5		Nebo	North Wales
Morgan Williams	5		Horeb	Lledrod
John D. Davis	4	manager	Tyn Rhos	Nancwnlle
Thomas J. Jones	4		Bethania (E)	Nancwnlle
Thomas Miles Jones	3	furnace mason		North Wales
William Jones	3		Horeb (?)	Llangwyryfon (?)
Robert Edwards	2		unknown	unknown
John H. Jones	2		Bethel (E)	Lledrod
John T. Jones	2		Oak Hill C.M.	Lledrod
John Jenkins	2		Centerville C.M. (E)	Llangeitho
John D. Jones	2		Horeb	Llangywryfon
Lot Davis	1		Tyn Rhos	Nancwnlle
Thomas G. Davis	1		[unsure]	Llanychaearn
Joshua Evans	1		Horeb (E)	Llanddewibrefi
John Hughes, Jr.	1		Horeb	Llansanffraid
James R. Jones	1/2		unknown	unknown

Sources: Jackson County deed book Q, p. 462; immigrant biographies.

settlements or in Wales, except perhaps for small coal mining companies in Glamorganshire and Carmarthenshire that were financed by Welsh landowners, merchants, and professionals in the late eighteenth century.[29] It is possible, however, that a few attempts at worker-ownership elsewhere in the Hanging Rock iron district may have inspired the Welsh charcoal iron companies' form. In about 1850 a group "composed almost exclusively of Welsh mechanics" organized the Ironton Rolling Mill in Lawrence County. An R. G. Dun & Company report filed in August 1852 describes the mill and its general store as "an association of practical workers" who had "an actual capital sufficient to do business" valued at $60,000 or $70,000. The firm failed in 1858 as the national depression took hold. Another outfit called Williams & Company owned the Hanging Rock Rolling Mill and general store. They were a firm "composed principally of operatives, [who] are good workmen but bad financiers," with

29. Arthur H. John, *The Industrial Development of South Wales, 1750–1850* (Cardiff: University of Wales Press, 1950), 27.

property including machinery worth $50,000. They failed in 1854.[30] The farmers in Jackson-Gallia were probably aware of these attempts by Welsh iron workers to capitalize on their skill and could well have known the parties involved.

Because Jefferson Furnace met its obligations through a complex mix of cash payment, provisions, merchandise, notes, and room and board for workers, it would be difficult to say with certainty whether the $10,300 it received on stock up to November 1854 was sufficient to meet the company's cash needs. It appears that cash began to run short that summer. The company first borrowed cash in June, on a variety of terms. Rev. Robert Williams (who did not invest in any of the Welsh furnaces) demanded interest of 10 percent per day on his note for $150, a rate so usuriously high as to strain credulity. John Williams, a mason, was more generous; he required no interest on the twelve-month note for his loan of $100. A few loans were clearly taken out to cover specific bills. The $221 borrowed from Thomas Jones, North, was immediately used to pay Damarin & Company, a rolling mill in Portsmouth. Similarly, the company paid off part of its debt to the provisioners Ward, Murray & Company with the $700 cash it received toward stock from Thomas T. Jones.

Thomas Ll. Hughes recorded nine cash loans worth a total of $582 from June through September 1854. In November and December of that year loans became larger and more numerous. In April 1855 an American farmer named Noah Dever loaned the furnace $2,903, with $500 payable upon demand and the balance on a twelve-month note held by Dugan & Company, merchants in Portsmouth. It appears that the Horeb community had exhausted, or decided to withhold, its disposable funds after fifteen months of close financial involvement with Jefferson's affairs. Of the loans recorded through July 1855, the majority came from Welshmen, but with Dever's loan and a few others the furnace's indebtedness to non-Welsh creditors was beginning to grow. While this may have worried Welsh shareholders it did not concern the R. G. Dun & Company reporter, who issued a mild warning to creditors in January 1856 that the company's owners were "rather tight" (i.e., hard up for cash).[31]

In early 1855 the company began to find customers for its iron.

---

30. J. L. Abrams, "The Welsh People of Ironton, Lawrence Co., O[hio]," *Cambrian* (1880), 86–87; Jackson County, Ohio, vol. 110, pp. 108, 103, R. G. Dun & Company Collection.

31. Scioto County, Ohio, vol. 166, p. 49, R. G. Dun & Company Collection.

The first sale, ten tons to Dew & Company of Wheeling at $28 per ton, came on 3 February 1855. By the end of that year the firm had sold pig iron worth $47,764 to a number of small manufacturers along the Ohio River as well as one large order to the Pomeroy Rolling Mill. More large orders followed in early 1856, notably from the Scioto Rolling Mill. The price of Jefferson iron increased markedly during that period, from a low price of $23 per ton to a high of $35 per ton in November 1855, perhaps reflecting an improvement in the product's quality.[32] As Jefferson cashed in purchasers' notes it moved toward profitability and made an increasingly good impression on R. G. Dun & Company credit reporters. The first report, dated November 1855, describes Jefferson as "A new furnace, perfectly good, quite a number of members. It is doing well." Reports in 1856 and 1857 were brief and optimistic: "Succeeding well"; "Doing well"; "Good"; "No change." As the postpanic depression began to bite, the tone of the commentary changed. On 8 February 1858 the field reporter wrote, "Good furnace and doing well as any of the new furnaces. They have all had a hard time of late. The business sustained herself as well as any of them." July 1858: "One of the best furnaces in Jackson Co." In 1859: "This is one of the best companies in the county. It is abundantly good for all its engagements." July 1860: "They have not been sued for more than a year and have at no time been much troubled with their debts. If any furnace weather the storm, this one will. Is owned by Welshmen who are economical and honest, should not be afraid to trust them as prudent and experienced." In October and December of 1862, as the economy was righting itself and the Civil War was driving up demand for iron, the reporter summarized the key to Jefferson's survival: "Regarded here as good, all the people living in its vicinity are willing to trust it. . . . Have always had confidence in this company, even in the great iron crisis of the last four years."[33]

The most trusting people were the Welsh themselves. The construction and initial operation of Jefferson Furnace was overwhelmingly a Welsh concern. Welshmen and their sons came from as far away as the Tyn Rhos neighborhood in eastern Madison Township to work at Jefferson. During the company's first

32. Company accounts list thirty-four purchases for a total of 2,195 tons of iron, on notes worth $64,984.39, between 3 February 1855 and 17 June 1856.

33. Jackson County, Ohio, vol. 103, p. D, R. G. Dun & Company Collection.

eighteen months, the Welsh put in 4.2 times more man-hours building and operating the stack than did non-Welsh workers. Most of the non-Welsh labor entered in the company ledger was for chopping wood, hauling supplies, and other work off site. It was Welsh crews who built the furnace stack, supervised by Thomas Miles Jones, the son of Thomas Jones, North. Welsh masons and carpenters constructed the other buildings that completed the furnace complex. Welsh women opened their homes to workers, setting up impromptu boardinghouses that lodged mainly Welsh boarders. The James family, for example, provided meals for several workers in March 1854:

> David Edwards, 18 meals
> Rees Williams, 13 meals
> Thomas Rees, 41 meals
> Strangers, 11 meals[34]

The amount of work done by Welsh residents of Jackson/ Gallia in part reflects their eagerness to work for relatively good wages. Throughout the 1840s and early 1850s Cincinnati had been a magnet for poor young Welsh men and women from Jackson/Gallia who migrated to the city in search of work as laborers, clerks, and domestic servants.[35] The furnaces brought local wages closer to par with other rural areas in the Midwest. Thomas Ll. Hughes's boast that furnace laborers earned $1.25 a day was a mild exaggeration; the typical rate of pay for all but the most skilled workers remained $1.00 for men and 50¢ for boys throughout the 1850s and 1860s. Still, $1.00 a day was more than Benjamin Williams had earned as a laborer in the late 1840s. Better wages, however, were not the main motivation behind the Welsh community's outpouring of effort in constructing their furnaces, particularly for those who invested sweat equity in hopes of long-term profit.

Deferred gratification is clearest in the evidence that Jefferson workers were willing to accept deferred wages. Nearly half of Jefferson's Welsh workers waited for one or more months to receive their wages and a few waited more than a year. For example, John Walters and his son, John, Jr., worked in many capaci-

34. JFC records, vol. 489.

35. Rev. Daniel Jenkins Williams, *The Welsh of Columbus, Ohio: A Study in Adaptation and Assimilation* (Oshkosh, Wis.: Privately published, 1913), 51 and note 1, same page.

ties at the furnace throughout 1854, but only John, Jr., received any cash wages during the year, totaling just $15.25.[36] The company officers, all Welsh, deferred payment of their considerable salaries throughout 1854 and into 1855.[37] It may be, as local historians recall, that the company offered stock in exchange for labor.[38] The records explicitly mention three minor examples of this kind of sweat equity, and the stock accounts for company officers Thomas Ll. Hughes, John D. Davies, and William M. Jones grew substantially during the later months of 1854, although John Walters's stock account did not. Whether or not labor purchased stock, the cooperation of Welsh workers and management appears to have bought the company time by allowing it to operate on a minimum of loans.

This kind of cooperation exacted a small price from Welsh workers and company officers, given that most of them owned farms that provided a more than adequate subsistence for their families. The same could be said of Americans who worked for Jefferson Furnace in those early months, yet all of them were paid within thirty days of completing a given task. The fact that Welsh workers' wages were deferred while Americans were paid promptly and in cash reflects the differing moralities of exchange that the Welsh applied within their ethnic group and toward outsiders. As anthropologists have emphasized, a society that customarily demands immediate cash payment by outsiders may condone many other kinds of exchange between the members of that society. Mutual trust and mutual obligations within the group provide mechanisms to ensure fairness that cannot be applied to strangers.[39] To the James family and to Thomas Ll. Hughes,

36. The accounts list a number of entries in which Welshmen, including one furnace officer, paid John Sr. a total of $48.60, but do not specify the reason for payment, which could as easily have been for work Walters did for them outside the furnace as their payment of his furnace wages.

37. Only two non-Welshmen appear in management positions in the Jefferson accounts: a Mr. G. W. Baker, who was brought in to manage the furnace briefly in February 1857, when the firm was trying to decide between several Welshmen for the job; and a T. Stokes, who was hired in 1858 to examine the company books.

38. Davis, *Industrial History*, 27; "A Brief History of Jefferson Furnace," ms. pp. 5–6. The entries for wage and salaried labor do not correspond neatly with entries for disbursement of funds in the one extant account book. The accounts appear to be incomplete, for the amount of money due to laborers and management far exceeds the amount recorded as paid out in cash or other forms through 1855. Perhaps another ledger, now lost, was the final record of furnace labor.

39. Jonathan Parry and Maurice Bloch, "Introduction: Money and the Morality

American and Irish workers were strangers who should be treated fairly and kept at a suitable distance. Hughes recorded entries for non-Welsh labor punctually and precisely, noting in most cases the worker's full name, kind of labor, rate of pay, and the total amount payable. Entries were similar where they recorded the labor of Welshmen who worked only occasionally, completed a specific task (such as cleaning the boilers), or who did not own stock. The entries for stockholders' labor, in contrast, were sporadic and far less specific. Some shareholders' work was recorded several months after the fact with no reference to the kind of labor performed, just so many days of work at a given rate per day.

Thomas Ll. Hughes did not need to keep detailed records of shareholders' labor because he trusted and knew them all, and they him. Their common ethnic identity, as well as their shared experiences in building first an agricultural community and then an iron company gave them the kind of basis for trust that was evident in the economic relationships of many rural immigrant communities.[40] The constancy of Welsh shareholders' wages over time, and their apparent relationship to the individual's skill and his family's investment in the furnace, may indicate that shareholders reached their own agreements with the furnace officers about the kinds of work they would undertake at certain rates of compensation. But the outpouring of effort evident in the company accounts also shows a communal spirit of enterprise, as Welsh men and women were willing to perform whatever work was required to get their furnace built and operating.

Figure 4.5 summarizes the differences between the community corporations formed to finance and organize Jefferson and the other Welsh furnaces and the typical American partnership. In the American model, a limited number of investors contributed large sums of capital to purchase the necessary land, mineral resources, fuel, and labor. The Welsh model drew a smaller sum of capital from a much larger pool of investors, then spent significantly less than American firms to purchase resources and labor through the various strategies discussed above. Perhaps the most

---

of Exchange," in *Money and the Morality of Exchange*, ed. Jonathan Parry and Maurice Block (Cambridge: Cambridge University Press, 1989), 1–32.

40. Arnold Strickon emphasized the importance of ethnic identity to trust in economic relationships in "Ethnicity and Entrepreneurship in Rural Wisconsin," in *Entrepreneurs in Cultural Context*, ed. Sidney M. Greenfield et al. (Albuquerque: University of New Mexico Press, 1979), 176–77, 184–87.

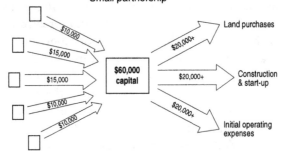

American model of charcoal-iron operation:
Small partnership

Welsh model of charcoal-iron operation:
Community corporation

Fig. 4.5 American and Welsh models of furnace capitalization

important result of the Welsh model was the minimization of
financial risk by dispersing that risk among a greater number of
investors and by reducing cash outlays in two of the three main
categories of expenditure.

Assessing the Risk and Consequences of Charcoal Iron for the Welsh

Two series of events indicate that charcoal iron had an unsettling
effect upon certain elements of the Welsh community. The first
involved Limestone Furnace. Limestone was organized as Evans,
Waterhouse & Company in the autumn of 1854, nearly nine
months later than Cambria and Jefferson. When the R. G. Dun &
Company reporter first inquired about the firm in November, he
found a group of investors who were "prepared to go to work
but had some disillusion in ranks and it is thought [they] will
abandon the enterprise." The company managed to put its furnace in blast one year later, but in January 1857 the reporter
wrote that the costs of "construction of [the] furnace stack I think
have as is usual exceeded their capital stock and thereby occa-

sioned them some embarrassment." An American-born share-holder had sold his interest in the firm by that time but about forty investors were still committed. In February 1858, the death knell came: "They have good property but have let their debts get ahead of them and are just now having trouble with them. A number of their company have brought suit. . . . Their present trouble I think is for want of proper management." By June 1858 the company was "very much embarrassed" and the property was assigned to a receiver.[41]

"Disillusion in ranks" is a suggestive phrase. Had Welsh farmers on the northeastern side of the settlement let themselves be talked into a scheme of which they did not approve or whose risks made them increasingly uneasy? The company may have had difficulty gaining investors' confidence because it lacked the concentrated geographical base of the other two furnaces. The land that Limestone was able to secure was scattered across four townships, adding time and expense to the gathering of resources (see map 4.3, above). Judging by 1875 county plat maps, Limestone's land included fewer mineral deposits than Jefferson's, although Limestone Furnace itself was situated near an ore bed.[42] Buying ore from outside suppliers could have further weakened the company's financial position.

Lack of confidence or disillusionment may also have arisen from the financial insecurity and inexperience of investors at Limestone and, to a lesser degree, Cambria. The age of investors did not differ much between the Welsh furnaces; in all three ventures, the male head of most investing households was between forty-three and forty-seven years old and the family owned between sixty and eighty acres of land. However, Limestone and Cambria investors were significantly less wealthy on average than Jefferson investors, and more of them deeded *all* of their land to the furnace of their choice, thereby risking greater loss than those who deeded a portion of their land in exchange for stock. The relative prosperity of Jefferson investors reflected both their earlier arrival in Jackson/Gallia and the quality of their land. Among Jefferson investors for whom I have a certain date of emigration,

41. Jackson County, Ohio, vol. 103, pp. 22, 50, R. G. Dun & Company Collection. The first land transfers to Limestone Furnace were dated October 1854, while the first deeds to Jefferson were dated January 1854 and to Cambria in February 1854.

42. D. J. Lake, *Atlas of Jackson County* (Philadelphia: Titus, Simmons & Titus, 1875, reprinted Oak Hill, Ohio: Welsh-American Heritage Museum, 1975), 31, 39, 43; Keeler, "Jackson County Iron Industry," 173.

66 percent arrived in the United States before 1840, compared to 40 percent of Limestone investors and 20 percent of Cambria investors.[43] Those who settled in the area before 1840 had access to better land and also had more time to improve their farms before becoming investors. The differences in investors' prior exposure to industry is even more striking. Jefferson's investors included no fewer than ten families who had spent some amount of time in industrial locations in Britain and/or the United States before they settled in Jackson County. Only four Limestone families and two at Cambria are known to have migrated via industrial locations. These numbers may be misleading, for the data are incomplete. Nevertheless, Jefferson appears to have benefited most from the confluence of industrial and rural Welsh migrants in the Ohio Valley.

A general familiarity with industrial places and the work culture of industry may have been more important in making Welsh migrants comfortable with the new charcoal iron furnaces than whether they possessed specific knowledge of iron-making technology before they arrived. One of the curious things about charcoal iron is that experience with advanced coal-fired technology, like that used in the South Wales iron industry, did not prepare one for making charcoal iron. David Lewis, organizer and manager of Cambria Furnace, emigrated from the iron district of South Wales. He first settled in the industrial town of Tallmadge in northeastern Ohio, where he and several partners attempted to duplicate South Wales coal-fired iron technology in a furnace they dubbed Cambria Union. The furnace was poorly sited on wet ground, which prevented the blast from firing properly. Technical problems also afflicted the second Cambria Furnace in Jackson County, and Lewis failed to make necessary repairs during the early 1860s when the furnace could have earned high profits. Cambria also suffered a serious loss in early days when its first manager, William Evans, was killed in an accident at the furnace site. Cambria Furnace never achieved the levels of production that were routine at Jefferson and other successful furnaces. The company had sold almost all of its land by 1874 and it ceased production in 1878.[44]

43. N for Jefferson = 24; N for Limestone = 15; N for Cambria = 10.

44. Wilbur Stout, typescript history of Cambria Union Furnace, Tallmadge, Ohio (undated); Keeler, "Jackson County Iron Industry," 183; obituary of William Evans, *Y Cyfaill* (September 1854): 357; *Atlas of Jackson County*, 39, 43; William Griffith, Jr., *Illustrated Atlas of Gallia County, Ohio* (Cincinnati: Strobridge & Co., 1874; reprinted Athens, Ohio: Don F. Stout and Emmett A.

Jefferson's long-time manager, John D. Davies, also came to Jackson/Gallia after experiencing life in a region of heavy industry. His family stayed in Pittsburgh from 1841 until 1848, by which time John was twenty-six years old. Pittsburgh's rolling mills, forges, and foundries used charcoal iron in that period, so it is possible that John may have gained some knowledge of the technology before he and his family moved on to Jackson/Gallia. What is certain is that he worked for several years as founder at Gallia Furnace in Gallia County, perfecting charcoal iron-making techniques under the tutelage of ironmaster John Campbell, before joining the Jefferson Furnace Company as an investor and then as manager.[45] Jefferson also benefited from the business experience of Thomas Ll. Hughes (see fig. 4.6), who served for many years as the company clerk and secretary. Originally trained as a saddler, Hughes emigrated with his wife to Cincinnati in 1840. He worked there as a salesman in a shop for some years, then ran his own store across the Ohio River in Covington, Kentucky, in partnership with Abel Wynne, the brother of Moriah elder David Wynne. They sold the shop and moved to Jackson County in about 1846. Hughes bought a farm in the heart of the Welsh settlement and opened a dry-goods store in Oak Hill in partnership with another Welshman.[46] Thus by the time he took part in organizing Jefferson Furnace, Hughes had considerable experience in keeping accounts and running a small business. He was also fully bilingual and a highly literate man, familiar to the national Welsh American community as the author of a long-running series on biblical history in *Y Cyfaill*.

The most forceful personality among Jefferson's leaders was doubtless Thomas T. Jones, a handsome man from southern Cardiganshire. Jones wore many hats at Jefferson but worked longest as the company's financial agent, selling iron and arranging business transactions. Local stories say that he was the talented younger son of one of Cardiganshire's wealthiest families, the Joneses of Derry Ormond (I have been unable to verify any connection), and that his family's banking connections may have helped save Jefferson from bankruptcy during the prewar depres-

---

Conway, 1976), 30; Willard, *Hanging Rock Iron Region*, vol. 1, p. 455.

45. Leland D. Baldwin, *Pittsburgh: The Story of a City, 1750–1865* (1937; reprint, Pittsburgh: University of Pittsburgh Press, 1981), 149, 221; Davis, *Industrial History, Oak Hill*, 10.

46. "Hon. T. L. Hughes, Oak Hill, O.," *Cambrian* (1888), 225–26; Evans, *Hanes Sefydliad*, 77.

Fig. 4.6 Jefferson Furnace Company
officers. David Edwards (*above, left*)
acted as trustee for the land that Welsh
immigrants mortgaged to Jefferson and
was himself an investor in the company.
His family emigrated from a farm near
Llangeitho called Gelli-hir in 1837, perhaps in the company of Thomas T. Jones,
"Agent" (*left*) and his wife, Mary
Edwards, who may have been David's
sister. Thomas Llewelyn Hughes (*above*)
was one of the few North Wales immigrants in the Jackson/Gallia settlement.
He served as cashier and secretary for
Jefferson Furnace for twenty-six years.
(Photo of Edwards courtesy of William
R. Alban; photos of Jones and Hughes
courtesy of Evan E. Davis)

sion.[47] Even without that kind of financial leverage, the combination of technical skills, management experience, and business acumen that Davies, Hughes, and Jones brought to the company made them more capable of running a successful charcoal iron operation than were the officers at the other two Welsh furnaces.

The Exodus to Minnesota

Even Jefferson, however, experienced troubles among the ranks of investors in its early years. Between autumn 1855 and summer 1857, one-third of the furnace's initial investors left Jackson/Gallia to resettle in Blue Earth and LeSueur counties, Minnesota. They were among the approximately 150 Welsh from the locality who formed the nucleus of what became known as the Jackson colony.[48] This "exodus," as local histories call it, included families of all ages and from all parts of the Ohio settlement, from the Bethania chapel neighborhood in Bloomfield Township to the Cambria neighborhood in northeast Greenfield Township. A number of Welsh families and individuals from the coal mining community in Pomeroy also went with the Jackson group. In several respects, the Minnesota migration bore an uncanny resemblance to the first major departure from Mynydd Bach in 1837. Once again, the recommendations of a trusted Calvinistic Methodist preacher precipitated the move and localized the resettlement on a distant frontier; the main goal for most of the migrants was to find better, less expensive land; and once again the lay leader of the migration was Edward Morris.

The promotion agent this time was Rev. Richard Davies, a Montgomeryshire native who emigrated in 1837 and preached in the Jackson/Gallia settlement from about 1840 to 1847. He then lived in Pomeroy before moving west to explore settlement sites in hopes of creating a new Welsh colony. His enthusiastic letters

47. Immigrant biographies; Rev. William R. Evans, *Sefydliadau Cymreig Jackson a Gallia, Ohio* (The Welsh Settlements of Jackson and Gallia, Ohio) (Utica, N.Y.: T. J. Griffiths, 1896), 77; *History of the Lower Scioto Valley* (Chicago: Inter States Publishing, 1884), 562–63; obituary of Thomas T. Jones, *Y Cyfaill* (June 1889): 233–34; interviews with Evan E. Davis at his home in Oak Hill, Ohio, 8 and 28 July 1990.

48. Revs. Thomas E. Hughes and David Edwards, and Messrs. Hugh G. Roberts and Thomas Hughes, eds., *History of the Welsh in Minnesota, [and in] Foreston and Lime Springs, Iowa* (Privately published, in Welsh and English, 1895), 38–41; immigrant biographies. All citations to Hughes et al. are to the English portion of the book unless otherwise noted.

to *Y Cyfaill* first urged Welsh immigrants to settle in western
Wisconsin, but from early 1855 he devoted his promotional efforts to the prairies of southern Minnesota. Given Davies's residence in Jackson/Gallia and Pomeroy, it is no surprise that the
first large group of Welsh to respond to his campaign came from
those two settlements. He was not the first Welshman to admire
the new territory. In 1844 another minister named Peter Lloyd
had urged the Welsh to give up their poor farms in New York,
Pennsylvania, and Ohio to resettle on the rich lands of western
Wisconsin, where the black earth was "ready for the plow." As
in 1837, however, it took the urging of a friend at an opportune
time to convince the Cardiganshire immigrants to move on to
greener pastures.[49]

Rural immigrant settlements in the United States commonly experienced cycles of overcrowding and periodic loss of population
to daughter settlements, which developed like archipelagoes trail-
ing in the wake of the advancing frontier.[50] Overcrowding played
some part in the Jackson colonists' departure for Minnesota, for
land values had risen sharply since the early 1840s as the local
population increased and the railroad and charcoal iron began to
transform the local economy. The Minnesota group included ten
or more families whose parents were over forty years of age and
whose children were coming to maturity and so needing their
own land.[51] Demographic explanations, however, are insufficient
in this case. A closer look at who left suggests that through the
variety of individual reasons for migrating west ran a thread of
economic opportunism and cultural calculation which focused
on migrants' appraisal of the relative merits of staying in a mixed

49. Evans, *Sefydliadau Cymreig*, 107; Margaret Williams Carr, *The Descendants and Ancestors of the Williams, Crane, Herbert Families* (Privately published, 1992), 304; *Y Cyfaill* (February 1855): 75–76; "Henry Hughes Autobiography," trans. Albert Barnes Hughes, typescript, 1947, in collection of the Southern Minnesota Historical Center; *Y Cyfaill* (November 1844): 181–82.

50. Michael P. Conzen, "Ethnicity on the Land," in *The Making of the American Landscape*, ed. Michael P. Conzen (London: HarperCollins, 1990), 242–45. See also Jon Gjerde, *From Peasants to Farmers: The Migration from Balestrand, Norway, to the Upper Middle West* (Cambridge: Cambridge Univer-sity Press, 1985), 138, 153.

51. Immigrant biographies; 1857 Minnesota state manuscript census for Blue Earth, LeSueur, and Nicollet counties; research notes of Mary T. Dooley, Professor Emerita of Geography, Mankato State University, extracted from General Land Office records on file at the National Archives Records Center at Suitland, Maryland. I am grateful to Mary Dooley for kindly sharing her research with me.

rural-industrial location versus devoting their energies and their way of life to agriculture.

The first inkling that some Welsh families viewed charcoal iron as a short-term investment came on 12 January 1854, when Richard and Elizabeth Morgan sold eighty acres of their land to Jefferson Furnace, including the acre encompassing their homestead and outbuildings. This was highly unusual among the first round of investors, as most reserved at least the one acre of land including the homestead and outbuildings in order to continue farming. By 9 February the Morgans had sold the remainder of their 165 acres to Jefferson.[52] In October 1855 Richard Morgan and several other Jefferson Furnace investors traveled to Minnesota to verify Rev. Davies's optimistic reports about the prairie country along the Minnesota River. By December the scouts had purchased a number of lots in the new town of South Bend and staked a claim on farmland nearby.[53] In the meantime Jefferson Furnace shareholders had agreed to buy back stock from nine families, including the Morgans, at the remarkable price of $900 per share—an 80 percent markup over the original purchase price—plus interest on any late payment. Richard and Elizabeth Morgan thus realized a profit of $1,584 on their initial investment in less than two years' time. Altogether, Jefferson investors who migrated to the Minnesota frontier in spring 1856 left with $20,894 in cash and promissory notes.[54] Investors in the other two Welsh furnaces also found buyers for their stock. A number of Cambria investors sold out their interest to the rest of the shareholders early in 1856 and a wealthy American farmer named Riley Corn bought out several Limestone investors.[55]

It is remarkable that the R. G. Dun & Company reporter missed or chose not to report this series of events, particularly in regard to Jefferson Furnace. Jefferson's good press throughout the late 1850s may have reflected a closing of ranks in the Welsh community that prevented news of the situation from leaking out. Although nothing in the company records suggests discord among the stockholders or resentment against those who wanted to leave, their departure saddled the company with unprece-

52. Jackson County deed book Q; JFC records, entries for land received on stock dated 9 February 1854.

53. Hughes et al., *Welsh in Minnesota*, 37; *Y Cyfaill* (December 1855): 467.

54. Minutes of Jefferson Furnace shareholders meeting, 8 October 1855, JFC records, vol. 489; Hughes et al., *Welsh in Minnesota*, 37, 39–40.

55. Willard, *Hanging Rock Iron Region*, vol. 1, pp. 455–56; Jackson County, Ohio, vol. 103, p. 17, R. G. Dun & Company Collection.

dented debts that could have resulted in bankruptcy. When iron prices plummeted in 1857 not even Jefferson could find buyers for its iron. According to oral histories gathered by Evan E. Davis, the company was offered for sale in 1858 but found no takers, perhaps because the Welsh refused to lower their price to match the bargains available from bankrupt American firms during the depression.[56]

The standard history of the Welsh in Minnesota, written in 1895, states that the Jackson County migrants cashed in their furnace investments out of fear: "Many of them having risked their all in the enterprise, began to be really scared, and determined to sell out their shares at once before the crash came, and move in a colony to some western country." Was this incident another example of the fabled Cardiganshire conservatism and tightfistedness? It may be that those who chose to leave were in fact nervous about risking their farms for the sake of investing in a volatile, unfamiliar industry, particularly if they were persuaded to commit family assets against their better judgment. Limestone Furnace's early difficulties certainly could have undermined confidence throughout the settlement. The credit reports indicate, however, that Jefferson and Cambria looked as promising as any charcoal iron furnaces in the region in 1855–1856. At a time when the iron industry was buoyant and expanding, Cardiganshire farmers could hardly have predicted the national economic collapse of 1857.

It seems more likely that those who left were taking advantage of exceptionally favorable economic opportunities which allowed them to realize profits on their land and purchase better land elsewhere. In the first instance they sold their land for somewhat inflated prices, thanks to the region's speculatory fever over new charcoal iron ventures;[57] then they took quick, hefty profits by selling back their shares to other investors who expected charcoal iron to do very well in the near future. Thus for some Welsh families, investment in a blast furnace was a short-term strategy to

56. Davis, *Industrial History*, 27.

57. Using the valuation of land given in the census, Jefferson shareholders' farmland was worth from $6.25 to $10.83 per acre in 1850. The coming of railroads into the region in 1853 undoubtedly increased land values, yet Jefferson managed to purchase land from non-Welsh farmers in 1854 for rates as low as $4.38 per acre. Minutes of stockholders meetings, 18 January 1854 and 9 February 1854. Some of the property deeded to Cambria and particularly Limestone was such poor farmland, and so meagerly endowed with mineral resources, that it was almost certainly overvalued at $15 per acre.

generate funds for reinvestment on the agricultural frontier. It was a plan wholly consistent with those particular migrants' past behavior, for, so far as I know, none of the furnace investors who went to Minnesota had lived in an industrial location before settling in Jackson-Gallia. All of their prior migration choices in Wales and in the United States had expressed a desire to farm and to own land.[58] This was not true for all the Welsh immigrants who moved from southern Ohio to Minnesota during the exodus. The Pomeroy contingent included a number of young men like Henry Hughes, a coal miner from the age of nine who emigrated from the South Wales iron district to Minersville, Ohio, in 1851. His migration to Minnesota exemplified a first-time "knight's move" into agriculture; until 1855 he had never laid hand on a plow. Having lost both parents in childhood, he may have made the move mainly in order to stay with his sister's family as they migrated west.[59]

Up to this point I have argued that economic gain was the prime motivation behind the exodus to Minnesota. The more one knows about an individual migrant's life, however, the more difficult it becomes to ascribe his or her actions to a single cause. Two of the leading families in the Jackson colony illustrate how untidy the circumstances and thoughts behind migration could be.

John and Ursula Walters' lives were transformed in many ways by Jefferson Furnace. They had emigrated with their three children from a tenancy on the western flank of Mynydd Bach in 1838 or 1839. Upon reaching Jackson County they bought eighty acres of rolling land along Black Fork Creek, less than one mile from Horeb chapel. John was a quiet man. He and Ursula were leading members of the Horeb congregation. In 1850 their farm was typical for the area: thirty-five improved acres produced corn, oats, wheat, and hay for the family's two horses, three milk cows, and one steer. Their sheep and swine foraged among the trees on the hillside. By 1850, the family had grown to include six children, two girls and four boys. In January 1854 the Walters were among the first to sell their land to Jefferson Furnace in exchange for company stock, reserving the one acre where their house and farm buildings stood. In February the firm com-

58. Local histories of the Oak Hill community speak of the 1856–1857 departures as a case of "migration fever" prompted by the desire for more and better land.

59. "Henry Hughes."

menced construction of the furnace stack in the middle of the Walters' former land. Although the stack itself was fairly small, standing thirty-seven feet tall and perhaps twenty feet wide at the base[60] (see fig. 4.1, above), the entire furnace complex covered an acre or more of ground, and roads leading to the site cut wide swaths through the landscape. John and his eldest son, John, Jr., worked a total of 305 days at the furnace over the next eighteen months, doing general labor as well as digging ore, hauling supplies, and filling the furnace stack. The family also sold hay to feed company livestock and boarded workers in their home. All told, the family earned about $540 from their labor, most of which remained unpaid on the company books.

The Walters' relations with Jefferson Furnace went sour when accidents at the furnace damaged the family's property. In October 1854, the furnace company and three individual Welshmen contributed $18.32 in credit to John's account for no identified reason. Later that month the accounts noted that the furnace paid John $13.50 "for damage on his wheat." Shortly after that a more formal entry stated, "Rec'd of J. Walters a due bill given him by the company . . . for damage done to his lands, $150." The notes in the company ledger do not explain what happened, nor do they say whether John ever received the money that was owed him. In December, an entry recorded that John Walters still owed the company $40 "to make up his land into 2 shares, his land being 81 acres, so the acre reserved is free to him." One can imagine that the company's insistence that he pay up his stock account may have rankled. In addition to the physical damage to crops and perhaps farm buildings, the Walters endured the noise and filth of living on the furnace grounds. Once the furnace went into blast in October 1854, it ran twenty-four hours a day, six days a week, for at least six or seven months. Its lurid red-orange glow, the sulphur fumes, the chuffing steam engine in the boiler room, the constant traffic and shouts of workmen day and night, would have made life hellish for the entire family. It is no wonder that the Walters migrated to Minnesota in 1856, as did the Evan Griffiths family, upon whose land Cambria Furnace was built.[61]

Edward Morris's motivations for leaving Jackson/Gallia are not nearly so obvious. Morris was called "the Moses of this Jackson

60. "A Brief History of Jefferson Furnace," ms. p. 7.

61. JFC records, vol. 489; "A Brief History of Jefferson Furnace," ms. pp. 1, 10. Biographical information conflicts about just when Evan Griffiths went to Minnesota; he and his family left in either 1856 or 1870.

exodus."[62] As a mature, experienced community leader of forty-three, he was just the sort of person to give shape and purpose to discontent and desire within the community. Thomas Ll. Hughes witnessed Morris's influence over his fellow settlers on many occasions in the *seiat* at Moriah:

> He was possessed of beautiful cheerfulness and depth of feeling at the same time. . . . his ruling bent was for treating of the serious, substantial matters of the eternal world . . . There he is, rising up in the *seiat;* the faces of the assembly show that they have serious expectations; he goes on to speak, half smiling, but it is the smile of a serious man. He begins to talk and takes hold of the matter immediately, and is in his element discussing it, and often his serious speech would follow us for days afterwards, and continue to sound in our ears like the crashing of the deluge.[63]

Rev. R. H. Evans called Morris "a deacon of great influence" who "hated hypocrisy and prejudice," a man of few words who "knew when to speak, and to speak to a purpose, and therein lay the secret of his strength. When feeling the importance of any matter or movement, he spoke as one with authority."[64] He was a founding elder at Moriah chapel in 1838 and filled the same role for the new Calvinistic Methodist chapel in Oak Hill in 1850. He worked for years as the reporting secretary for all the Jackson-Gallia Calvinistic Methodist chapels and occasionally wrote religious items for *Y Cyfaill*, always sounding a note for orthodoxy and discipline in church affairs.[65]

Sure as he was in spiritual matters, Morris's actions in relation to Jefferson Furnace suggest that he had an ambivalent attitude toward investment. He was the wealthiest individual in the Jackson/Gallia Welsh community in 1850, with a farm worth $1,800, a partnership in a grain and lumber mill, and personal property worth $3,500. When Jefferson Furnace was organized he purchased stock with $850 cash. In March 1854 he worked briefly as company clerk, filling in for Thomas Ll. Hughes. But in May he withdrew $130 of his investment and had the balance transferred to the credit of his business partner, David Edwards,

---

62. Hughes et al., *Welsh in Minnesota*, 40.

63. Obituary of Edward Morris by Thomas Ll. Hughes, *Y Cyfaill* (April 1858): 132.

64. Evans, *Sefydliadau Cymreig*, 74–75.

65. Ibid., 25–27, 71, 73. Morris's reports appeared regularly in *Y Cyfaill* in the 1840s and 1850s.

who was also the trustee in charge of all land transfers for Jefferson Furnace. It appears that Edward and Mary sold their farm in 1856, fully intending, like the other migrants, to resettle permanently in Minnesota.[66] Yet the Morrises stayed in Blue Earth County for only a few weeks before beating a hasty return to Oak Hill. "The cause of his sudden departure," noted the editors of the history of the Welsh in Minnesota almost forty years later, ". . . were the mosquitos [sic], which, though, they belonged not to the sons of Anak, were to the early settler fully as formidable." This was a reference to a warlike tribe mentioned in the Old Testament book of Deuteronomy: "They are great and tall people, the descendants of Anakim, of whom you know, for you have heard it said, 'Who can withstand the sons of Anak?'"[67] The image of a middle-aged Welshman fleeing a swarm of mosquitoes will seem ludicrous only to those who have not camped outdoors during mosquito season in Minnesota (see fig. 4.7). The Jackson colony arrived during the hatching season of several varieties of mosquito, including *Culex communis* DeGeer, a swarming species with an "exceedingly painful" bite, and *Culex excrucians* Walker, a "very annoying species which feeds in the shade at all times," according to William Owen Bert.[68] Both species are commonly found along woodland/prairie borders like the area where Morris and his fellow migrants chose to settle.

The question remains, why did Mary and Edward Morris elect to leave their flourishing farm and investments to start over on an inhospitable frontier? As a well-to-do couple with only two children, they faced none of the constraints that made Jackson/Gallia problematic for less wealthy families. Unfortunately, no accounts survive of their thoughts on the matter. Thomas Ll. Hughes dismissed Morris's leadership of the Minnesota migration as a decision reached "at some uneasy hour" which his friend soon regretted. This accords well with a local minister's description of Edward Morris's temperament. "At times he would speak excit-

---

66. U.S. manuscript census for Jackson and Gallia Counties, Ohio, 1850, 1860; Jefferson company records. The 1860 census for Madison Township lists Mary Morris, widow, with $4,000 in personal property and just $400 in real estate, compared to the family's $1,800 in real estate in Jefferson Township 1850. This suggests that Mary and Edward sold their farm before moving west but held onto other assets, perhaps including their Jefferson stock.

67. Hughes et al., *Welsh in Minnesota*, 40; Deut. 9:2.

68. William Owen Bert, "The Mosquitoes of Minnesota, with Special Reference to Their Biologies" (Ph.D. diss., University of Minnesota, 1936 [published with no publication information]), 35, 37.

Fig. 4.7 Minnesota's revenge. A frontier artist penned this cartoon of a giant Minnesota mosquito in 1862, several years after the beasts reputedly drove the Morris family back to Ohio. The woods and lake included in the sketch are not just background; most mosquito species breed in lakes or damp areas and many species found in Minnesota occur thickly along the prairie/woodland border, just the kind of land Edward and Mary Morris intended to settle. (Artist: Albert Colgrave, Minnesota Historical Society)

edly," Rev. R. H. Evans wrote, "although he had perfect control over himself. There was nothing conservative in him, rather he moved along with the age in every measure of reform."[69] Perhaps Edward and Mary were both eager to retaste the excitement of pioneering new land. Maybe Edward was hankering to lead more than a *seiat*. If so, one wonders how mosquitoes could have driven them away. Sadly, Edward Morris died of typhoid fever in Oak Hill in November 1857, aged forty-five. He never knew that the *seiat* in LeSueur County, which he probably had organized,

69. Obituary of Edward Morris, 130; Evans, *Sefydliadau Cymreig*, 75.

eventually built a chapel and named it Elim in remembrance of the chapel in Llanddeiniol, Cardiganshire, where he had first served as an elder.[70]

The move to Minnesota was easy for no one. John Walters hated the mosquitoes in Minnesota; he declared they were "the size of geese." Prairie weather posed a more serious threat. Richard Davies had told prospective Welsh settlers to expect fairly mild winters in southern Minnesota. The region's blizzards and subzero temperatures caught them completely unprepared. The winter of 1856–1857 was in fact one of the coldest ever recorded in Minnesota, with an average temperature in January of 4 degrees below zero. All through that awful winter, "The mud-plastered cabin of the settler afforded but slight protection against the wintry blast, and the small old-fashioned cook-stove gave but little heat to the shivering family huddled close around it." They had no furs or heavy flannel, "and the thin low-cut shoes of southern Ohio were ill-designed for the cold and deep snow of Minnesota." The nearest town of any size was St. Paul, located one hundred miles to the northeast, a three- or four-week journey through snow drifts. Two Welshmen froze to death that winter. The settlers faced new fears just as the snow was melting, when panicked reports reached them of a Sioux uprising to the south. The white settlers in South Bend built a palisade around a Welsh family's house, while the settlers at Judson and Eureka built a small fort. None of the Jackson County Welsh were hurt or even engaged in the fighting, but it was a terrifying episode.[71]

The Jackson migrants doubtless saw the mosquitoes, the snow, and the Sioux as trials sent to test their resolve to make a fresh start as farmers on the rich Minnesota prairie. They set to work breaking ground and reorganizing their religious life as soon as they arrived (see fig. 4.8). The largest number bought government

70. Obituary of Edward Morris, 132; Hughes et al., *Welsh in Minnesota*, 53–55 (Welsh section).

71. Hughes et al., *Welsh in Minnesota*, 302, 47–48, 50–53, 305. The estimated mean monthly temperatures for Minneapolis–St. Paul show December 1856 with an average temperature of 8.6 degrees Fahrenheit; in January 1857, –4.1; in February, 15.1. January and February reached lows estimated at –37 and –35, respectively. April recorded a low of 1 degree and had an estimated average temperature just below freezing. As of 1984, January and April 1857 were the coldest of their respective months in state history. Charles John Fisk, "Reconstruction of Daily 1820–1872 Minneapolis–St. Paul, Minnesota, Temperature Observations" (M.S. thesis: University of Wisconsin–Madison, 1984), tables 27 and 29, and p. 92.

Fig. 4.8 John Walters in Cambria, Minnesota. The hills and difficult, shallow soils of Jackson County posed familiar challenges to Cardiganshire farmers, but Minnesota's prairie, with its heavy soils, extreme weather, and uninterrupted horizon, confronted them with an entirely new environment. According to family history, moving to Minnesota brought out the best in John Walters. He lost some of his shyness and became a leading elder at the new Horeb chapel at Cambria, Minnesota, whose congregation is shown below.

land in what they called the Big Woods (*Coed Mawr*) area of northern Cambria and Judson townships in Blue Earth County. Another band established a smaller enclave in Cleveland and Ottawa townships in LeSueur County.[72] The Jackson colony maintained a distinctive and influential identity in this corner of Minnesota for several generations in spite of intermarriage with settlers from North Wales who had migrated from settlements in central Wisconsin and, eventually, intermarriage with non-Welsh residents in the area. Their Calvinistic Methodist chapels continued to teach the strict morals and Bible learning and recitation drawn from Llangeitho tradition. The largest of their early chapels was named Horeb.[73]

Success and Change in Welsh Involvement in Charcoal Iron

Back in Jackson County, Jefferson continued to produce iron as the national depression dragged on but was able to sell little of it, even at the low price of $14 per ton.[74] The saving grace for Jefferson and Cambria, as well as the rest of industry in the Hanging Rock iron district, was the Civil War. The Union army's escalating needs for military ordnance and railroad car wheels created a powerful surge in demand for charcoal iron. Inflation drove the price of top-grade charcoal iron as high as $90 a ton during the war. Companies could scarcely make iron fast enough. One story tells of Jefferson Furnace workers hurriedly loading iron still hot from the blast and the teamsters "pouring water on . . . [the] iron enroute to the railroad yard at Oak Hill, for fear of causing the wagon to take fire."[75] In 1861 Jefferson Furnace returned its first dividend to shareholders, a modest 10 percent. They received 20 percent in 1862, 30 percent in 1863, 100 percent in 1864. Annual returns on investment ranged from 20 to

72. Dooley research notes; 1857 Minnesota state manuscript census, Blue Earth County; "Ethnic Background: 1880, Resident Rural Landowners, Blue Earth County, Minnesota," sheet map (1.35 mm to the mile), Mary T. Dooley, Phil Kelley, and Perry Wood, project directors (Bureau of Planning and Cartographic Services, Geography Department, Mankato State University, no date).

73. Hughes et al., *Welsh in Minnesota*; Hughes (Thomas and Family) Papers, Southern Minnesota Historical Center collection S101, box 10, "Stories of Old Settlers."

74. "A Brief History of Jefferson Furnace," ms. p. 8.

75. Ibid.; Stout ms. 408, box 4, notes on Jefferson Furnace, unnumbered p. 5.

120 percent from 1867 through 1874.[76] Although these figures reflect wartime inflation, profits from charcoal iron did contribute significantly to individual families' wealth and the overall prosperity of the Welsh community, as we shall see. Jefferson's promise bore fruit as the company attained exceptional success during its first twenty years of operation. It also proved remarkably durable over the long run. Jefferson was the last charcoal iron furnace to produce pig iron in Ohio, going out of blast for the last time in 1916.[77]

The Civil War inspired scores of Jackson/Gallia Welshmen to join the Union army, echoing the overwhelmingly Republican, antislavery politics of Welsh Americans across the country. Fifty-seven members of Horeb chapel signed up for military service with the Union army; many of them mustered to fight in Tennessee during 1864 under the leadership of Captain David J. Jenkins.[78] The loss of young men to the war did not significantly affect the supply of labor to the charcoal iron furnaces in the Welsh settlement, however. Welsh labor had begun to withdraw from the Welsh furnaces long before war called them away. The reader will recall that Welsh workers did the lion's share of on-

76. Keeler, "Jackson County Iron Industry," 181; minutes from Jefferson stockholder meetings, JFC records, vol. 489. The company optimistically declared its first dividend—$100 per share—at a special meeting on 16 March 1859, contingent upon the sale of $7,650 worth of metal, but later minutes do not record that the dividend was paid. Minutes from 26 February 1862 called for the sale of 400 tons of iron as soon as possible "to pay up" the dividend already on the books and to "make $100/share more," perhaps a reference to the first, unpaid dividend. The minutes confirm agreements to disburse dividends of 100 percent ($500) per share in February 1864, 120 percent in May 1865, 60 percent in March 1866 and again in March 1867, 20 percent in April 1868 and April 1869, 80 percent in May 1871, 120 percent in 1873, and 80 percent in 1874. The depression of the mid-1870s dried up profits; dividends did not reappear until March 1879, when the firm declared $100 for each share and another $100 "to be made abouth [sic] the end of August next if it can be done."

77. Davis, Industrial History, 29; "A Brief History of Jefferson Furnace," ms. p. 12.

78. Alan Conway, "Welshmen in the Union Armies," Civil War History 4 (1958): 143–74; Maldwyn Jones, "Welsh-Americans and the Anti-Slavery Movement in the United States," Transactions of the Honourable Society of Cymmrodorion (1985): 105–29; Davis, Early History of Horeb Church, 40; Official Roster of the Soldiers of the State of Ohio in the War of the Rebellion, 1861–1866, compiled under the direction of the Roster Commission, vol. 9 (Cincinnati: Ohio Valley Press, 1889), 603–4. Other Welshmen enlisted in companies mustered at Portsmouth, Ohio, in 1861; see Official Roster, vol. 5 (1887), 97–102, 108–10, 717.

site work at Jefferson in 1854–1855. In 1857, a majority of the Jefferson Furnace workers who boarded with the Evan Pugh family were still Welsh. By 1860, however, non-Welsh laborers were doing most of the rough work of making iron, digging ore, and preparing charcoal (see table 4.3). Industrial jobs were the primary occupation of 59 percent of the non-Welsh workforce in 1860, compared to 27 percent of the Welsh workforce. Recent Irish immigrants made up a large share of the miners in Jefferson Township, while trans-Appalachian migrants accounted for most of the colliers and many furnace laborers. The only categories of industrial labor with nearly equal numbers of Welsh and non-Welsh workers were teamsters and skilled iron workers.

The ethnic bifurcation of the workforce was even greater in 1870 (see table 4.4), when only one in six industrial workers was Welsh and only one in ten non-Welsh workers owned his own farm. The industrial workforce grew significantly from 1860 to 1870, with the biggest increase, ironically, coming in the number of non-Welsh miners, reflecting the growth of coal mining in a county where the Welsh were predominantly engaged in agriculture.[79] Retracing the sequence of census entries as a surrogate for household location[80] suggests that Welsh workers' residences were concentrated around Cambria and Jefferson furnaces. Few if any Welshmen lived near American-owned Monroe Furnace, where the census taker began his route. Of the first 144 heads of household listed in the 1870 census for Jefferson Township, none was Welsh. Those heads of household included 76 blast furnace workers (69 American-born, 7 German, Irish, or Scottish); 38 miners (22 Americans); 5 colliers; 1 quarrier; and 6 skilled furnacemen (all Americans). Because furnace workers usually lived in company housing located near the works that employed them, one can reasonably conclude that most of the non-Welsh furnace workers in Jefferson Township were employed at John Campbell's Monroe Furnace, while the Welsh worked at Cambria or Jefferson, the furnaces closest to their

79. According to Long, coal was first mined commercially to fuel the boilers at Jackson Furnace (the first charcoal iron furnace in the county) in 1836, and the first shaft mine was sunk in 1861 in the town of Jackson. Long, "Coal Mining Industry of Jackson County," 33.

80. Michael P. Conzen, "Spatial Data from Nineteenth-Century Manuscript Censuses: A Technique for Rural Settlement and Land Use Analysis," *Professional Geographer* 25 (1969): 337–43.

Table 4.3 Occupations in Jefferson Township, 1860

	Welsh (% of Welsh)		Others (% of Others)	
Agriculture				
Farmers	113		80	
Farm laborers and tenants	26		38	
Totals	139	(57.2%)	118	(31.4%)
Rural crafts[a]	20	(8.2%)	20	(5.3%)
Industry				
Miners	4		51	
Colliers	2		28	
Furnace laborers	26		104	
Teamsters	12		16	
Skilled or managerial labor[b]	17		16	
Unskilled or other labor[c]	4		6	
Totals	65	(26.7%)	221	(58.8%)
Village and professional jobs[d]	19	(7.8%)	17	(4.5%)
Total in work force	243		376	

[a] Smith, mason, carder, cooper, carpenter, joiner, miller, saddler, sawyer, shoemaker, tailor, weaver, tanner, wagon maker, and harness maker.

[b] Engineer, filler, blower, keeper, agent, company clerk, and furnace manager.

[c] Furnace store keeper, store clerk, brickmaker, crib tender, coal stocker, switch tender, and boardinghouse mistress.

[d] Grocer, butcher, clerk, domestic servant, mailman, merchant, milliner, plasterer, teacher, silversmith, student, and tinsmith.

Source: 1860 U.S. manuscript census for Ohio.

homes. Thus a high degree of spatial segregation by residence and employment reflected cultural divisions between Welsh and non-Welsh residents of the area. In the township overall, the Welsh dominated the ranks of skilled and managerial labor in 1870. From 1850 to 1870, they also accounted for an increasing proportion of merchants, teachers, and domestic servants as the sons and daughters of Welsh farmers set up small businesses in the village.

Why did the Welsh withdraw from furnace labor? The simplest answer is that they did not need or want work that was physically demanding, unpleasant, and often dangerous. In addition to the injuries common to any industrial site, furnace workers were exposed to extreme heat near the crucible and cold drafts in winter. Smelting iron produced large amounts of carbon monoxide and dioxide, as well as fumes containing sulphur and cyanide compounds. Men who worked as fillers (dumping the charge into the

Table 4.4 Occupations in Jefferson Township, 1870

	Welsh (% of Welsh)		Others (% of Others)	
Agriculture				
Farmers	84		71	
Farm laborers and tenants	72		62	
Totals	156	(48.3%)	133	(18.7%)
Rural crafts	22	(6.8%)	26	(3.7%)
Industry				
Miners	36		249	
Colliers	1		14	
Quarriers	0		5	
Furnace laborers	39		217	
Skilled or managerial labor[a]	20		7	
Unskilled or other labor[b]	1		10	
Totals	97	(30.0%)	502	(70.6%)
Village and professional jobs				
Merchants	6		0	
Grocers and butchers	0		6	
Ministers	3		0	
Lawyers and physicians	2		2	
Teachers	8		4	
Domestic servants	11		19	
Milliners	4		5	
Other[c]	14		14	
Totals	48	(14.9%)	50	(7.0%)
Total in work force	323		711	

[a] Engineer, agent, bookkeeper, financier, furnaceman (manager), and molder.

[b] General laborer and railway worker.

[c] Artist, painter, plasterer, jeweler, seamstress, soldier, student, tinner, loafer, pauper.

Source: 1870 U. S. manuscript census for Ohio.

top of the open furnace stack) suffered disfigured noses and lips, to say nothing of damage to their respiratory systems, through exposure to these toxins. Gas poisoning and bronchial disease were probably less common among charcoal iron workers than steel workers because of better ventilation at the exposed rural furnaces, but they were still significant health hazards.[81] For enduring these problems through twelve-hour shifts workers received from 50 cents to $1.50 a day, with no other benefits ex-

81. Interview with Don Craig, manager of the historical museum at Buckeye Furnace, Ohio, 7 January 1990; George M. Kober, "Iron, Steel and Allied Industries," in *Industrial Health*, ed. Kober and Emery R. Hayhurst (Philadelphia: P. Blakiston's Son & Co., 1924): 176–83.

cept, for some, access to low-rent housing. By 1860 the standard of living of most Welsh families was well above this level. Most owned their own homes if not also a sizeable farm. Furnace work was for them one of many options for employment. Many of the Welsh who did work at the furnaces in 1860 were young men who were accumulating a nest egg toward a future outside industry. The difference between their situation and that of landless, impoverished laborers is starkly evident in the census, where one entry after another for non-Welsh workers shows $100 or less in net worth compared to the $500 to $1,000 typical of Welsh workers.

The increasing numbers of Welsh professionals and merchants between 1850 and 1860 paralleled the growth of Oak Hill as a hub of local trade. By 1870 the village represented the ascendancy of a Welsh middle class whose wealth was largely derived from immigrants' investments in charcoal iron (see table 4.5). When Oak Hill published its first business directory in the 1875 *Atlas of Jackson County*, thirty-six of the fifty-four business concerns and prominent individuals listed were Welsh. Several of them were Jefferson investors, and shareholder profits may have helped establish immigrants' children in genteel occupations. (Unfortunately, because of the abbreviation of many names in the Oak Hill listings, one cannot be sure which businesses belonged to investors and which to the children of investors.)[82] Farm families who had not invested in charcoal iron also benefited from the sustained prosperity based on rising land values and the local demand that furnaces created for provisions and labor. Overall, the Welsh living in the core of the settlement benefited disproportionately from the golden decade of 1863–1873. In 1870, three-quarters of the Jefferson Township families worth $10,000 or more were Welsh, although the Welsh population (immigrant and offspring) accounted for less than one-third of all households. The economic position of most non-Welsh residents was the mirror image of Welsh prosperity. Almost 90 percent of households worth less than $200 were American or belonged to another ethnic group, notably German or Irish (see fig. 4.9).[83]

Poor people in Jefferson Township in 1870 were predominantly male furnace workers, miners, colliers, and their families.

82. Lake, *Atlas of Jackson County*, 41.

83. U.S. manuscript census for Ohio, Jackson County population and agricultural schedules.

Table 4.5 Economic status and ethnicity in Jefferson Township, 1870

Ethnicity of Household head	N	Mean net worth	Most wealthy quartile (mean)	Least wealthy quartile (mean)
Welsh	171	$4,703	$14,215	156
American	323	910	3,337	0
German	28	667	1,953	86
Irish	25	180	583	0
Other[a]	6	3,635	10,155	50

[a] English, Scottish, French, Spanish. These figures are skewed upward by the high net worth of one immigrant, John Hamer, an Englishman who owned $19,110 of real and personal property.

While some of them migrated into the area in the early 1850s and became settled in their work, as a whole they were a transient population. Of the 206 American heads of household in the township whose net worth was $200 or less, only 15 percent can be found in both the 1860 and 1870 censuses. The Irish were the least persistent ethnic group. Only two of twenty-five Irish households (12.5 percent) are present in both the 1860 and 1870 censuses for Jefferson Township. This compares to 65 percent of Welsh households in the township over the same period.

Two families who worked at Madison Furnace typify the transient and stable members of the area's non-Welsh laboring class. Michael Hollin and two of his young sons appeared for a fleeting eleven days in the Madison Furnace time book for 1870 at an unspecified rate of pay. The census for that year listed Hollin, Sr., as a miner aged forty-three. Mary Hollin and her husband had emigrated from Ireland with their first son around 1850. Six more children were born in Ohio. The family owned no land and possessed only $100 in personal property. Not all furnace workers were as poor as the Hollins. Alexander Kinneer, his wife, Mary, and their seven children came to Madison Furnace from Kentucky shortly after the Civil War. Kinneer supervised loading the charge for each blast at Madison for many years. He worked every month of the year, sometimes seven days a week. (Madison, like most charcoal iron furnaces in the Hanging Rock district, normally shut down on Sundays to "rest" the furnace and to observe the Sabbath.) He was paid $1.73 per day, considerably higher than the common wage of $1.00 a day for manual labor. The additional furnace labor of four sons helped give the Kinneer household a substantial income. They owned no land in 1870 yet

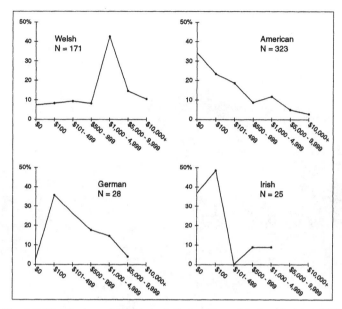

Fig. 4.9 Distribution of wealth in Jefferson Township by ethnicity, 1870

had personal property worth $2,500, an amount equal to the wealth of many middling farmers in the area.

The Hollins and Kinneers belonged to a rural industrial proletariat of landless laborers. The more lucky members of this class found steady work at a furnace and rented one of the log cabins built for workers on company property (see fig. 4.10). Others moved from one short-term employment to another. Transient laborers found it difficult to save enough money to pay back debts, let alone to buy land, particularly if they relied upon the furnace company store for their provisions. Each furnace had a store where workers could purchase goods against their wages with no money changing hands. During hard economic times a furnace might pay only in scrip—as Benjamin Williams found in the late 1840s and as happened again after the panic of 1857— most readily redeemed at the company store.[84] The Madison

84. Neither Madison nor Jefferson company accounts distinguish between payment in scrip and payment in cash, so one cannot determine which form of payment prevailed when. In another remote area, the Maramec Iron Works in central Missouri issued scrip in denominations of $1 to $5: "although this scrip circulated as currency in the Maramec area, and therefore did increase his working capital, it really represented an additional indebtedness on James's [the owner's] part." James D. Norris, *Frontier Iron: The Maramec Iron Works, 1826–1876* (Madison: State Historical Society of Wisconsin, 1964), 159.

Fig. 4.10 Furnace worker's cabin. This cabin and shed, located in Jackson County near Buckeye Furnace, were typical of the housing provided for furnace workers. Workers' cabins were clustered around the work site and strung out in haphazard ribbons among the woods nearby, forming furnace communities that are clearly marked in county atlases from the 1870s. Few cabins remain standing today. (Ohio Historical Society)

Furnace store was typical in adding a substantial markup to the goods it sold: 54 percent on molasses, 78 percent on calico, 100 percent on coffee.[85] John P. Jones, a Welsh immigrant, worked full-time for Gallia Furnace in the early 1860s, earning a steady wage of $1.00 a day. Between March 1862 and May 1863, Jones regularly bought flour, sugar, cornmeal, potatoes, salt, molasses, tea, coffee, and soda from the store—all the basics of a backcountry diet except for bacon, which he bought in small amounts just twice. He also frequently bought material for clothing, tobacco, candy, soap, candles, paper, and postage. Shoes and iron cost him dearly. In the spring, grass and garden seed were cheap. The store also served as a bank for Jones, keeping account of his wages and the purchases made against them as well as paying his creditors. Of the $353 that Jones earned during this period, all but $34.19 went back into the coffers of the company store.[86]

85. Inventory of merchandise, 19 February 1869, box 2, no. 19, compared to records of company store, 1870, box 2, no. 20, Madison Collection, vol. 161.

86. Company store records, 1862–1863, Gallia Furnace Company records, vol.

While this could represent an annual savings rate of nearly 10 percent (assuming the family did not spend the money elsewhere), it would have bought just three acres of poor land in Gallia County at the time.

Land was the basis of wealth in Jackson-Gallia. Welsh and non-Welsh landowners alike benefited from the area's greater integration with the regional and national economy in the years leading up to the 1857 crash. As Martha James of Raccoon Township wrote to her relatives in Llanina, Cardiganshire, in the autumn of 1855,

> There is a great difference now from when we came here [circa 1837]. The land has risen such that one cannot get land near these parts short of 15 to 20 dollars per acre if houses and water and everything are convenient . . . The [iron] works are coming along well throughout the land, new furnaces are being built, two of them within five miles or less from us, and a rail road runs through the country from New York to Cincinaty and from there to the State of Virginia, to Pittsburgh and Baltimore [and there are] branches of them coming within six miles of us. This has helped prices here and the awful war in the east has raised the price of labor . . . This is a good place for workers; the whole country from New Orleans to New York is full of stirring. [87]

Westward expansion of communications and developing rural industries were good for workers but even better for landowners like Martha James and her family. Rising land values provided the means for Welsh farmers to create furnace companies, the profits of which in turn gave some of them additional capital and experience that they put to use in other enterprises. In 1863 John M. Jones and Jefferson builder and investor Thomas Miles Jones opened the third coal shaft in the town of Jackson. Two years later John M. Jones and four Americans organized Star Furnace to smelt iron using the mine's coal.[88] A group of Welshmen from the managerial ranks of Jefferson Furnace bought out the failing

---

125, Ohio Historical Society.

87. Marth [Martha] James to David Thomas, Velin Wern, Parish of Llanina, Cardiganshire, dated 20 September 1855, National Library of Wales ms. 11614E, Album of John Lloyd Jones. The 1850 manuscript lists Martha and John James in Perry Township; their land may have stradled the Perry-Raccoon Township border.

88. Wilbur Stout Collection, vol. 408, Ohio Historical Society, typescript history of Star Furnace, unnumbered p. 1.

partners of Buckeye Furnace in 1865. Four years later the company was deemed "very safe . . . composed of a number of honest, thrifty Welshmen . . . They made a good deal of money running Jefferson Furnace and they bought Buckeye with it."[89] Welsh capitalists made their biggest investment in the emerging coal-fired technology in Jackson when Thomas T. Jones, Jefferson's financial agent, led a group of Welsh and American stockholders in organizing the Globe Furnace Company in 1872. Jones and his fellow Jefferson officers also founded Triumph Iron and Coal Company in Jackson, although that company soon closed down because its coal was of inadequate quality to make iron. Welshmen associated with Jefferson created two other coal-fired furnaces in Jackson in 1873. Tropic Furnace was organized by five Welshmen who chose Thomas Miles Jones as the plant's superintendent. He was also chosen as secretary for the other firm, Huron Furnace, whose chief organizer was Lot Davies, the brother of Jefferson's manager, John D. Davies.[90]

The Welsh who participated in this second phase of larger-scale entrepreneurial capitalism organized their new firms along the lines of the earlier American model, in which a handful of wealthy stockholders with multiple industrial interests pooled their resources. Several of the new Welsh firms in Jackson opened stock ownership to American investors. Yet the Welsh coal-fired plants were run according to the familiar philosophy of avoiding debt in order to maximize long-term profitability. According to Thomas T. Jones's grandson, who inherited the top post at Globe Furnace, the company modeled itself on Jefferson Furnace. "Beginning in 1901 we have never passed a dividend and since that time have returned in cash to the stockholders many times their investment, and in addition they own a new modern blast furnace plant, coal acreage owned in fee that will last 35 to 50 years, and iron, securities and other assets upon which there are no bonds or mortgages or liens of any nature. Of course at times we pay the very minimum in dividends in order to conserve our resources. Such is 'Old Globe.'"[91]

The notion of ethnically restricted, community-based venture

89. Jackson County, Ohio, vol. 103, pp. 7, 11, R. G. Dun & Company Collection.

90. Stout Collection, undated typescript histories of Globe, Triumph, Tropic, and Huron furnaces, Jackson County, Ohio.

91. Jones, "Romance of the Old Charcoal Iron Days," unnumbered p. 7.

capital also re-emerged in the 1870s. Jefferson shareholders combined with other Welsh families in 1873 to create two fire-brick manufacturing plants in Oak Hill. Both firms were located near rich veins of subterranean clay ideal for producing refractory bricks to line coal-fired blast furnaces. Lest one be tempted to attribute a noncompetitive ethos to the Welsh community, it is worth noting that the two firebrick firms were incorporated within twelve days of each other and were direct competitors in a specialized market. Among the fourteen original shareholders of the Aetna Fire Brick & Coal Company were John D. Davies and David Edwards, both officers at Jefferson Furnace, as well as John J. Jones, son of John Jones, Ty'n Rhos. (At last leading Congregationalists were ready to participate in a business venture with Calvinistic Methodists.) The Oak Hill Fire Brick & Coal Company followed the model of community-wide investment even more closely with forty-five shareholders. All but two of the original stockholders in these companies, and all of the original managers, were Welsh or of Welsh descent. Oak Hill Fire Brick issued its first sixty shares of stock at the price of $500 per share, just as Jefferson Furnace had done. The Oak Hill and Aetna companies formed the base of a local clay products industry that continued to provide jobs and wealth to the Welsh community up through World War II.[92]

The Making of Welsh Capitalists

The dominant impression one gets of European immigrants' involvement with nineteenth-century American industry is that they provided the cheap labor that made rapid industrialization possible. Irish families replaced young Yankee women as low-wage labor in the mill towns of New England. German and Irish craftsmen assumed positions as operatives at a growing number of Connecticut Valley factories after 1840. Welsh coal miners

92. Jackson County, Ohio, vol. 103, pp. 2, 12, R. G. Dun & Company Collection; Davis, *Industrial History*, 11, 13, 33–42; G. E. Carlyle and D. D. Davis, eds., *History of the Pioneer Men and Plants in Southern Ohio, Kentucky, and Oak Hill Fire Brick Districts* (Privately published, 1948), 36–37, 40. Along with coal mining, the firebrick industry supplanted charcoal iron as the industrial base of the Hanging Rock iron district after the Civil War. The first firebrick plant was built by Reese Paul Thomas (a Welshman) at Sciotoville in 1861. He also constructed the Oak Hill Fire Brick plant. Carlyle and Davis, *Fire Brick Districts*, 18.

brought skills that unlocked the wealth of Pennsylvania's anthracite mines and then supervised the work of unskilled immigrants from southern and eastern Europe. Italians and East European Jews filled the sweatshops of New York City's lower East Side. Whether they brought specific industrial skills or were peasant farmers encountering industry for the first time, immigrants are familiarly depicted (and rightly so) as exploited newcomers to the working class of American cities and factory towns.[93] Studies of rural European immigrant communities, on the other hand, rarely discuss industry. They focus on the richer agricultural areas of the Midwestern and Plains states, where immigrants participated in industry only to the extent that they sold farm produce to urban consumers and adopted mechanized farming and other improvements to increase their farms' productivity. Jon Gjerde captured the essence of this view of rural immigrants in describing Norwegian immigrants' transition from peasants to farmers.[94]

The Welsh in Jackson/Gallia straddled the worlds of agriculture and industry as well as the definitions that scholars have developed to classify them. They worked as skilled and unskilled industrial laborers at American-owned charcoal iron furnaces along the fringes of the Jackson-Gallia settlement for many years. They also built a conservative agricultural community based on private landownership and Welsh custom. In any given year, members of the same family could exemplify a mobile, landless proletariat and a sturdy, territorially stable class of yeoman farm-

93. John Bodnar, *The Transplanted: A History of Immigrants in Urban America* (Bloomington: Indiana University Press, 1985), quotation on p. 216; Christopher Clark, *The Roots of Rural Capitalism: Western Massachusetts, 1780–1860* (Ithaca: Cornell University Press, 1990); William D. Jones, *Wales in America: Scranton and the Welsh, 1860–1920* (Cardiff: University of Wales Press, 1993); Ewa Morawska, *For Bread with Butter: The Life-Worlds of East Central Europeans in Johnstown, Pennsylvania, 1890–1940* (Cambridge: Cambridge University Press, 1985); Oscar Handlin, *The Uprooted*, 2d ed. (Boston: Atlantic Monthly Press, 1973).

94. Robert C. Ostergren, *A Community Transplanted: The Trans-Atlantic Experience of a Swedish Immigrant Settlement in the Upper Middle West, 1835–1915* (Madison: University of Wisconsin Press, 1988); Terry G. Jordan, *German Seed in Texas Soil* (Austin: University of Texas Press, 1966); D. Aiden McQuillan, *Prevailing over Time: Ethnic Adjustment on the Kansas Prairies, 1875–1925* (Lincoln: University of Nebraska Press, 1990); and Jon Gjerde, *From Peasants to Farmers: The Migration from Balestrand, Norway, to the Upper Middle West* (Cambridge: Cambridge University Press, 1985).

ers. With the coming of the railroad after 1850, however, these two strands were plaited together with a third element that drew the Welsh into a new relationship with industry and land, with one another, and with the non-Welsh population, namely the deployment of their capital and skills in community-owned enterprise.

Local reinvestment of capital by Welsh business people and farmers strengthened the area's economy while keeping Welsh hands on the reins of local industrial development. Jefferson's investors and managers headed a new Welsh middle class whose diverse economic activities and personal wealth resembled the profiles of American investors in charcoal iron back in the 1840s and 1850s. Thomas T. Jones was worth $78,482 in 1870. David Edwards, Jefferson's trustee, was the second wealthiest man in Jefferson Township, with $51,300 in land and other assets. The township's nine richest families in 1870 were all Jefferson investors (see figs. 4.11–4.12).[95]

Even as their wealth increased, the first generation of Oak Hill's Welsh elite and many of their children remained in the area and continued to live on their farms. From 1850 onward, the Welsh in Jackson County became more involved in politics than was typical in other rural Welsh settlements, perhaps reflecting the extent of their involvement in the local economy. Thomas Ll. Hughes and William J. Evans served in the Ohio state house, and other Welshmen were elected to lower levels of government.[96] Seated close behind the honorable and the wealthy in chapel were farmers and merchants who had achieved a comfortable living that was bolstered by small investments in charcoal iron and other industrial concerns. The Welsh middle class in Jackson-Gallia continued to support their chapels and to worship in Welsh as long or longer than other rural Welsh communities. The members of Horeb chapel held out against regular English-language worship services until 1901 and heard the last Welsh sermon preached at a Sunday service sometime between 1918

---

95. U.S. manuscript census for Jackson County, Ohio, 1870; JFC records, vol. 489.

96. Willard, *Hanging Rock Iron Region*, vol. 1, pp. 447–48. The *Carnarvonshire and Denbigh Herald* (24 January 1874) noted in its summary of Americans' high opinion of the Welsh that not only were there "no Welsh paupers and no Welsh criminals" in the United States but, "what it suggested as being equally creditable, no Welsh office-seekers." First-generation Welsh immigrants were rare in public office beyond the local level.

Fig. 4.11 The home of Jefferson Furnace investors John T. and Rachel Jones. John and Rachel sold seventy-nine of their eighty acres to Jefferson Furnace in January 1854 and paid cash for a fractional share later that year. This engraving from the 1875 *Atlas of Jackson County* is a somewhat fanciful picture because the Marietta and Cincinnati Railroad did not run past their original place. The image does beautifully capture the elements of Welsh prosperity: a well-established farm with cropland, livestock, poultry, and an apple orchard; strip mining on the hillside above the apple trees; and contact with external markets and the outside world represented by the train. (Used by permission of the Welsh-American Heritage Museum, Oak Hill, Ohio)

Fig. 4.12 Manager Lot Davies and crew at "Old Jefferson." By the late 1880s or early 1890s, when this photograph was taken, Jefferson Furnace was one of the last charcoal iron furnaces still in production in the United States. The works had not been modernized since their construction in 1854, although regular maintenance kept the stack and engines in good working order. The white-bearded gentleman standing in the center of the group is Lot Davies, brother of Jefferson's long-time manager John D. Davies. Lot may have been the model for a character named Lloyd Davis in the novel *Owen Glen* by Ben Ames Williams. Lloyd was an old Welshman, manager of a local furnace, who viciously opposed unions while his company voted handsome dividends to stockholders. Charcoal iron labor in Ohio was never unionized and wages remained as low as 75¢ a day into the twentieth century. (Photo courtesy of the Welsh-American Heritage Museum, Oak Hill, Ohio)

and 1922, by which time Welsh Calvinistic Methodists across the United States were preparing to merge with the English-speaking Presbyterian Church of the U.S.A.[97] Ethnic distinctions survived as the Welsh language faded from use. Dan T. Davis, a third-generation, bilingual resident of Oak Hill, distinguished between Welsh and non-Welsh members of Horeb chapel in terms of language even when English was the common language of religious and social discourse. "Today we are glad to announce," he wrote in 1938, "that many original English speaking families are members, listeners and supporters of the church"—families such

97. E. Edwin Jones papers related to his activity in bringing about the union between Welsh Calvinistic Methodist churches and the Presbyterian Church of the U.S.A., consulted with kind permission of D. Clair Davis.

as the Crabtrees, Leedys, Snyders, Simes, Leonards, and John-sons.[98] The last generation to grow up speaking only Welsh before attending school was born on farms in the 1920s.

While the immigrant generation maintained insular religious traditions, they sent their children to college in unprecedented numbers. Nearly 80 percent of the Welsh students who matriculated at Ohio University at Athens between 1851 and 1883 came from the Jackson-Gallia community.[99] As in other rural ethnic communities, education and travel away from home hastened the processes of language loss and cultural assimilation among the Welsh. Yet if geography is any indication of persistence, then the continued presence of a concentrated Welsh population in southern Ohio testifies to the legacy of Welsh involvement in charcoal iron in the middle of the nineteenth century.[100] It is also no accident that Oak Hill is home to the country's only Welsh American Heritage Museum or that the annual summertime *Gymanfa Ganu* at Tyn Rhos chapel draws hundreds of singers, many of whom can sing the old hymns in Welsh. An intensely localized Welsh culture flourished here, not only because the initial settlement was dominated by immigrants from one particular part of Wales, but because the immigrants and their descendants took part in the local economy's growth and diversification during a critical period of capitalist transformation.

98. Davis, *Early History of Horeb Church*, 36. The language has effectively died out in Jackson and Gallia Counties. Some local residents attend beginning Welsh classes taught by a first-generation immigrant, mainly in order to learn pronunciation, a highly valued skill among those Welsh Americans who continue to sing traditional nineteenth- and early twentieth-century hymns in the vernacular at hymn-singing festivals.

99. D. J. Evans, "Welsh Students in the Ohio University," *Cambrian* (April 1887): 105–6.

100. Jackson County registered as a county in which the Welsh ethnic population "is a relatively high proportion of the total county population" in the 1980 census. See "Welsh Ancestry," map in James Paul Allen and Eugene James Turner, *We the People: An Atlas of America's Ethnic Diversity* (New York: Macmillan, 1988), 46–47.

Chapter Five

The Moral Context of Migration

In literary accounts of Welsh Calvinist emigration, the motivations for leaving the homeland figure as an important leitmotif running through the drama of departure, the perilous journey, and arrival in a strange new world. The most revealing moment in several of these narratives comes during a raging storm on the North Atlantic. Those who are sure that emigration is a part of God's plan endure the tempest with equanimity, while those who know in their hearts that they left Wales in search of riches and an easy life interpret the storm as God's wrath raining down upon them, demanding that they repent. The crash of heavy seas against the ship's hull and the agony of seasickness convince these terrified emigrants that they will never again set foot on solid ground. In one fictional account of a Welsh ship's journey to New York the passengers cry out to their Maker, desperately regretting their fateful decision. One character moans, "We could have lived at home alright, were it not for the lust for cheap lands and the splendid life in America; and here I am, ruined . . . Oh! what shall I do?" Another passenger comments bitterly, "This is the fruit of our greed, this the recompense for our uneasiness . . ."[1]

Most Welsh emigrants' explanations for leaving their homeland came down to a desire to make a better life for themselves and their children, which meant finding higher wages or cheaper, more fertile, more abundant land in a country that afforded tremendous opportunity. In short, they left for economic reasons, as did most European emigrants during the nineteenth century. The ability of relatively poor people to make such a dramatic move in pursuit of economic opportunity was unprecedented in

1. Llywelyn Davies [?], *Hanes Môr-Daith y Brig Albion, Aberteifi, (Llywelyn Davies, Llywydd), gyda Mudolion (Emigrants) &c. o Gaernarfon, i Ogledd America* (Story of the Sea-Voyage of the Brig Albion, Cardigan [Llywelyn Davies, Captain], with Emigrants & etc., from Carnarvon, to North America) (Carnarvon: Peter Evans, 1820), 15, 20–21.

European history. For many Europeans, emigration was a grand leap that they had reason to believe would land them significantly higher up the social and economic ladder. For migrants of strong religious beliefs, however, that leap could pose serious questions touching on doctrine, obedience to God, and the morality of deserting one's native community. As Stephen Innes points out in his assessment of the economic culture of Puritan New England, social mobility was a core issue in the "Protestant dilemma" because it tempted the individual "to get out of his place, to strive to grow richer, and eventually seek profit for himself and not for God and community." A dangerously thin line separated industrious devotion from devotion to industry.[2] If people were so keen to advance in the world that they were willing to leave their homeland forever, surely they had crossed that line and forsaken their obligations to community and God in pursuit of base economic interest.

Looking at emigration in this context, it is no wonder that rural people in conservative, tradition-bound regions such as central Cardiganshire might construe voluntary emigration as a violation of deep-seated values and norms of social behavior. Emigrants were turning their backs on their *bro*, their native region, and embracing a new world in implicit judgment of the old. Leaving the home place was a decisive break from all that was customary and traditional, which meant, in a word, all that was moral.[3] They threw aside their obligations to the community in favor of pursuing their own dreams and economic interest. To borrow Fernand Braudel's summary of individualistic, capitalist *mentalité*, emigrants were "awake to profits" and were prepared to calculate their future prospects "in terms of return on investment"— more land for the money, higher wages for the same employment, a better standard of living for equivalent effort.[4]

The problem of justifying emigration may have been particularly difficult for orthodox Calvinists. How could they square predestination with emigration, a blatant assertion of individual will? A graver question for many mid-nineteenth-century Calvinists was how they could resist the manifold temptations of the

2. Stephen Innes, *Creating the Commonwealth: The Economic Culture of Puritan New England* (New York: W. W. Norton, 1995), 25–26.

3. Yi-Fu Tuan suggests this dichotomy in general terms in *Morality and Imagination: Paradoxes of Progress* (Madison: University of Wisconsin Press, 1989).

4. Fernand Braudel, *The Wheels of Commerce*, vol. 2 of *Civilization and Capitalism, Fifteenth–Eighteenth Century*, trans. Sian Reynolds (New York: Harper & Row, Perennial Library edition, 1986), 291.

United States, a country famous for its inhabitants' loose morals and economic excess. For Welsh Calvinists, the answer to the latter issue, if not the former, was to impose constraints upon their own economic behavior in keeping with the dictates of their religious faith. Their efforts to resolve what Simon Schama called "the moral ambiguity of materialism"[5] were also intrinsic to the formation of Welsh ethnicity, for the social mores and institutions that constituted their localized moral economy became a cornerstone of their ethnic identity.

"Where would you rather be, in America or in Heaven?"

The Welsh were one of several kinds of Calvinist immigrant groups to found rural settlements in the United States. Among the most prominent of the other groups in voicing concern about the morality of emigration were Dutch Calvinists, whose commentaries show how harshly orthodox Calvinists could judge emigration. According to Piethein Burmanje, "To orthodox observers, it was a scandalous and sinful act, since God had put his people on earth as his sentry guards, not allowing them to leave their place without an obvious sign from heaven." Anthonie Brummelkamp, outspoken editor of the Calvinist weekly *De Bazuin*, campaigned vigorously against emigration. In 1857 he wrote, "At one point the immigrant has to leave everything behind and he has to stand trial before God, in order to explain why he went to America. Therefore, I would like to ask all emigrants: 'Where would you rather be, in America or in Heaven?'" Dutch folk may imagine that America is the land of milk and honey, these critics warned, but where wealth came easily, moral corruption followed close behind. Immigrants themselves wrote to *De Bazuin* to warn innocent newcomers of the many temptations that awaited them in America, such as "[c]ursing, drinking, mail on Sundays, dancing and the temptations of the theatre." Brummelkamp's editorial on the assassination of President Lincoln declared "that the saddest part of the death was the fact that he was killed 'while visiting a theatre, and has to appear before God in that manner.'"[6]

5. Simon Schama, *The Embarrassment of Riches: An Interpretation of Dutch Culture in the Golden Age* (New York: Knopf, 1987), 49.

6. Piethein Burmanje, "Trouble in Paradise: The Dutch Reformed Press and Its Views of Calvinist Emigration," in *The Dutch in North-America: Their Immigration and Cultural Continuity*, ed. Rob Kroes and Henk-Otto Neuschafer (Amster-

Brummelkamp's brother-in-law, Albertus Van Raalte, was one of the most important leaders of midcentury Dutch emigration. He tried to justify emigration as a "God-given opportunity" for "freedom of conscience and a good livelihood for the next generation," but he also acknowledged that it threatened believers' morality. Like Brummelkamp, he urged Dutch migrants to avoid American cities, where "material things will become too important to them." Both men anticipated an enduring theme in evangelistic Dutch-American theology when they asserted that highly disciplined Dutch colonies could spread the true Calvinist faith and serve as models of moral achievement in American society. Van Raalte hoped that immigrants would be able to preserve their moral and religious standards in rural settlements, but over the years he became increasingly disillusioned with his craven followers. "They know, indeed, how to acquire good farms, earn money, etc.," he wrote, "but they are not motivated, either by love for the Fatherland, nor by religious commitments, to dedicate themselves to more noble pursuits, such as the establishment and developments of a Christian community." He was sadly discouraged by their "worldly-mindedness, pride, and unbelief."[7]

Many orthodox Welsh Calvinists may have similarly regarded emigration as a sinful act, particularly as predestinarian theology came to dominate religious discourse in Wales in the early nineteenth century. Two Welsh narratives from this period present a range of judgments against emigration. The first, a ballad entitled Cân Newydd (A New Song), emphasized the predestinarian view that emigrants were fooling themselves if they thought they could improve their state simply by moving to America. Thomas Francis of Nevern, Pembrokeshire, wrote Cân Newydd around the turn of the nineteenth century, during a spate of Baptist emigration from southwest Wales.[8] The piece is constructed as a dia-

dam: VU University Press, 1991), 25, 27.

7. "Voices from North America" (two letters by Albertus c. Van Raalte, dated 27 November and 16 December 1846), trans. John Dahm, Heritage Hall Publications, no. 3 (Grand Rapids, Mich.: Calvin College and Calvin Theological Seminary Archives, 1992), 14, 17; Jacob Van Hinte, Netherlanders in America: A Study of Emigration and Settlement in the Nineteenth and Twentieth Centuries in the United States of America, trans. Adriaan de Wit, ed. Robert P. Swierenga (Grand Rapids, Mich.: Baker Brook House, 1985; originally published in Holland, 1928), 123–28, 259, 283.

8. Hywel M. Davies located Francis's poem in the papers of the William Richards Legacy, John Hay Library pamphlet PB2287, vol. 3, at Brown University. It was bound with other papers into a volume that also contained another piece

logue in verse between two characters, "Anesmwyth" (Uneasy) and "Esmwyth" (Comfortable), representing, respectively, "those who intend to take their Journey to America, and those who are satisfied with the Land of their Birth." Uneasy justifies emigration as a way to escape famine, war, scarcity, and dependency:

> Instead of failing to have barley, we'll eat the white wheat;
> For they have broad lands, and of money more and more,
> Who here were in necessity, needing help from our parish.

Comfortable replies,

> Yes, yes, some went away from their native land
> To search for the profit that never lasts long;
> And perhaps they got some wealth and enjoyed it for a while,
> If living and dying unclean, all despite their woe.

The debate moves back and forth from stanza to stanza. Uneasy argues that people must have some choice in life and should take the chance to escape misery while they may; Comfortable responds that misery follows sin and that good things will come to those who have faith in God. The crux of the argument is the author's conviction that emigration was primarily motivated by greed and that it denied the Calvinist notion of predestination. "He orders all," Comfortable says; "why is your faith so weak?"

During the late eighteenth and early nineteenth centuries, predestination gained strength as a central tenet of faith in all the main Welsh Nonconformist denominations. The notion that God chose the elect for salvation took root most strongly among the Calvinistic Methodists, but Congregationalists and Baptists also referred to devout believers as "saints" whom God had chosen. All three denominations embraced the belief that God had preordained human affairs, a belief that made thoughtful Nonconformists distinctly uncomfortable with emigration. Some Calvinistic Welsh preachers went further, branding emigration as an assertion of individual will in opposition to God's plan. The Baptist "Bishop of Anglesey," Christmas Evans (1766–1838), regarded emigration as an act of worldliness and ingratitude. He disapproved of those who went to America without good cause for

---

by Francis dated 1797. Davies, "'Very Different Springs of Uneasiness': Emigration from Wales to the United States of America during the 1790s," *Welsh History Review* 15 (1991): 389–91; letter from Jean Rainwater, Reader Services Librarian, John Hay Library, Brown University, Providence, Rhode Island, dated 10 February 1993.

much the same reason that he criticized those who meddled in politics; namely, that they were putting their own selfish interests above obedience to God. "I had occasion to see those two well-spoken, amusing men," he wrote sarcastically, "namely Mr. Politician and Mr. Going to America, *alias* Mr. Lover-of-Wealth, chilling the zeal of religion and driving professors to abandon prayer and to backslide." Evans particularly criticized preachers who wore the mantle of preaching in the wilderness as a disguise for their real intention—to get rich—and he declared that anyone who emigrated to America was lost to religion forever. Rev. Benjamin Evans of Trewen, Cardiganshire, argued that "emigration to America was an abnegation of responsibility to the church at home."[9] This was a real issue for Welsh Nonconformist denominations, for the loss of a few talented preachers or experienced lay elders could have serious consequences for the development of the cause in a given locality. As Christmas Evans's biographer D. Densil Morgan points out, Evans himself considered emigrating to New York City in 1799–1800, when crop failures were making life very difficult in Wales. Had he left then, he might not have become a preacher, and the history of the Calvinistic Baptists in Wales might have been very different.[10]

The second piece, a prose narrative called *Hanes Môr-Daith y Brig Albion* (History of the Sea-Voyage of the Brig Albion), is a deeper exploration of the immorality of taking fate into one's own hands by emigrating. It was written by, or in honor of, Llywelyn Davies, a native of Cardigan town and captain of the brig *Albion*. The account survives in several ballads and as a long prose version published in 1820 that was probably the first rendering of the story.[11] *Y Brig Albion* combines realistic entries from the captain's log with moralistic and comical set-piece conversations between passengers and shipmates. These characters

9. Davies, "Springs of Uneasiness," 387–88; D. Densil Morgan, *Christmas Evans a'r Ymneilltuaeth Newydd* (Christmas Evans and the New Nonconformity) (Llandysul: Gwasg Gomer, 1991), 62, quoting from William Morgan, *Cofiant, neu Hanes Bywyd y diweddar Barch. Christmas Evans* (Cardiff, 1839), 39.

10. Morgan, *Christmas Evans*, 61–62.

11. The National Library of Wales holds several versions of the tale. The earliest prose version was published as Captain Llywelyn Davies, *Hanes Môr-Daith y Brig Albion* (see note 1, above). For a lengthy discussion of the tale's discovery and thorough treatment of the various versions, prose and verse, see Peter Thomas, *Strangers from a Secret Land: The Voyages of the Brig "Albion" and the Founding of the First Welsh Settlements in Canada* (Toronto: University of Toronto Press, 1986), esp. 6–28.

were modeled after the allegorical figures in John Bunyan's *Pilgrim's Progress*, which was translated into Welsh and was a popular text among Welsh Nonconformists.

Like Christian in Bunyan's classic moral tale, the emigrants aboard the *Brig Albion* are setting off into the wicked world armed only with their faith. Each of the central characters represents a particular position on emigration. The chief mouthpiece for the desire to emigrate is a young man named *Credadwy* (Credible or Gullible), who has swallowed all of the wonderful things he has heard about the good life in America. Throughout the voyage he is mercilessly quizzed by *Cyfaill* (Friend), a sharp-tongued critic who considers emigration a sin of ambition. (Friend's own reasons for being aboard the ship are not entirely clear, but he functions in the narrative as an alter ego for the Captain.) In one of the most closely reasoned exchanges between them, Gullible challenges Friend to explain why it is a sin to emigrate to America when it is not a sin to leave Carnarvonshire for Shrewsbury or any other place within Britain.

> FRIEND: The Apostle says, "Everything is allowed me, but not everything profits me; everything is allowed me, but not everything is constructive." You are turning your back upon your country, where you could live (you say); you are likely to lose the means of grace [religious worship in Welsh] . . . and are going to a land to try to increase in the things of this world; and there is room to fear that that will be of no advantage or benefit to you in things eternal; and you are exchanging the greatest of things for the least of things.
>
> GULLIBLE: But doesn't God say, "Be fruitful, and multiply, and fill the earth"? There is much space in America with no people in it.
>
> FRIEND: Yes, and to those who have received that talent, and are willingly obeying God's Command, the Lord gives virtue for doing that; and I do not blame you for going to America, if you have failed to find *any* place in Wales that will do for you to multiply; but why would you increase America rather than Botany Bay, or one of the lands in the east that are scarce of inhabitants?[12]

Friend's argument expresses a point of view consistent with early Calvinism's approach to the moral and religious governance of economic appetites. According to Calvin's teachings, there was nothing sinful in striving to fulfill one's duty to God, nor anything

---

12. Davies, *Hanes Môr-Daith y Brig Albion*, 29–30.

inherently sinful in a modicum of success that might follow as the fruit of such labor. What offended Calvin and those who embraced his teachings in their purest form was seeking economic gain for individual satisfaction. Defining the boundaries of acceptable profit and the amount of interest one could permissibly charge on loans were moral issues that bedeviled Calvinism for centuries.[13] It was a simpler matter to distinguish pure from impure motives for emigration. Emigrants who left their homeland in order to get rich were obviously sinning against the economic morality that required subordination of one's own desires to God's will. Only those who were persecuted, or were told by God to emigrate, could claim religious justification.

The Captain's point of view in the debate remains ambivalent. Transporting emigrants to America is a mainstay of his maritime business, but he is deeply suspicious of the passengers' motives and of their professed religiosity. He more than anyone appreciates the irony and hypocrisy of Calvinists taking fate into their own hands by choosing to emigrate. During storms they moan that God is punishing them for asserting their will against his; as soon as the sea grows calm, they go back to planning how much land they will own in the new world. The Captain's observations dwell on an important point. Why did these people suddenly decide they could not tolerate conditions that previous generations had endured? As Friend puts it to Gullible, "Look you, I understand that you were poor at the start of your life; but through industry and care, the Lord has blessed your labor, and you are ready to trust in him as for yourself; but now . . . you want to see what *you yourself* can do for your children, and fail to trust in Him regarding them."[14] Wanting a secure future for one's children could not mask impure motives or a lack of faith.

Calvinistic Methodist ministers were acutely aware of the moral dilemma that emigration posed for their faith. Rev. John Jones of Talsarn, Carnarvonshire, was a high Calvinist who struggled for years to find some moral justification for emigrating to the United States. He mastered his first eagerness to go to America after hearing John Elias sternly counsel against emigration in a sermon at Bangor in 1831. The desire to go kept returning, however. In the 1840s Jones wrote several letters to members of his family who had emigrated to Wisconsin, in which he dwelt upon how much

13. Richard Henry Tawney, *Religion and the Rise of Capitalism* (Harmondsworth: Penguin Books, 1938; reprint, London: Penguin Books, 1969).

14. Ibid., 23–24.

he would like to join them. On preaching tours through North Wales he reportedly mulled over the pros and cons of emigration and took any opportunity to talk with people he met about the excellent farms in America. Eventually, Jones's religious convictions brought his adventurous spirit to heel, and he concluded that he must abide by the argument he had used to persuade his own brother, David Jones, to stay in Wales. "He stood strongly against my moving from here on one account," David wrote to a friend in the States in 1850. "Only when Providence has freed us" would their emigration be justified. Until God sent a clear signal, "there is nothing to do but wait quietly for that time."[15]

How did the Calvinists of Mynydd Bach overcome the moral obstacles to emigration? Although none of them left epistles documenting their process of decision, the facts surrounding their departure suggest that they thought about the question in much the way that John Jones, Talsarn, advised for his brother. They waited quietly for the time when Providence signaled them to go. The signal came in the personal assurances of Edward Jones, a sober and trusted Calvinistic Methodist minister. Once settled in Ohio, they could answer the objections of critics such as Thomas Francis and Llewelyn Davies by pointing to their continued willingness to live under self-imposed restraints that kept their social and economic behavior within the guidelines established in the *Rules of Discipline*. Far from repudiating their Calvinistic faith and its values, they structured their lives in Jackson/Gallia according to those traditions, even when pressures for change from the outside world compelled them to take the radical step of forming their own industrial enterprises.

Followers and Leaders

Until plans were announced to extend the Scioto and Hocking Valley Railroad through Jackson County, the Welsh community showed little interest in economic development beyond the establishment of general stores and small mills. The railroad's approach galvanized a few Welsh farmers to make sure that the railroad came through Oak Hill, guaranteeing that progress would

15. Material relating to John Jones, Talsarn, National Library of Wales, Aberystwyth, ms. 12788C, letters in files no. 6–9, 11, 12, 14, 15, 17, 20, 21, 24, 28, quotation from David Jones letter, in file no. 24(a); Owen Thomas, *Cofiant y Parchedig John Jones, Talsarn* (Biography of Rev. John Jones, Talsarn) (Wrexham: Hughes & Son, 1874), 618–21.

not pass the village by.[16] If these men anticipated that the railroad would also bring charcoal iron furnaces to their community, however, they did not hasten to develop the industry on their own. Not until three years later, when an American-owned furnace was under construction within their own territory, did the Welsh organize themselves "to take a stab at what they could do."[17] They were followers in the development of industrial capitalism in southern Ohio, not leaders.

The Welsh in Jackson/Gallia were also followers in the sense of taking their lead from chapel elders in whom they had vested authority over religious matters and many aspects of secular life. Chapel elders' authority over their fellow believers best explains why so many Welsh families took the risk of exchanging their land for shares in a charcoal iron furnace despite having no prior experience of industry or entrepreneurial investment other than buying and selling land. Ten of the founding investors at Jefferson were chapel elders, including Thomas Ll. Hughes and Edward Morris (elders at Oak Hill's Calvinistic Methodist chapel); John Hughes, Joshua Evans, and William Jones, Cofadail (Horeb); Thomas J. Jones, Cooper (Bethania); John Jenkins (Centerville); and John H. Jones, Bethel's outstanding fundraiser. According to Horeb's chapel history, "Before actually starting on the venture [of organizing Jefferson Furnace], many meetings were held in the home of John Hughes, Penbank."[18] The men who attended those meetings were accustomed to making policy decisions for their community. They also enjoyed high regard as relatively wealthy farmers. The combined weight of ten elders' opinions could well have persuaded reluctant families to invest in Jefferson Furnace.

Striking parallels between the organizational structure and governance of Jefferson Furnace and the settlement's Calvinistic Methodist chapels mark the furnace as the brainchild of chapel elders. Under the *Rules of Discipline*, none were to "take the lead" in a church or *seiat* "but those who are chosen by it," that is, by a majority vote of the congregation. No church member was to take another to court, "but that they place the matter in

16. Willard, *Hanging Rock Iron Region*, vol. 2, pp. 1070–71; and vol. 1, pp. 444–45; Evan E. Davis, *Industrial History, Oak Hill, Ohio*, 2d ed. (Portsmouth: Compton Printing, 1980), 19.

17. *Y Cyfaill* (April 1854): 153.

18. Jefferson Furnace Company records, vol. 489, Ohio Historical Society (hereafter cited as JFC records, vol. 489); Dan T. Davis, *Early History of Horeb Church* (Oak Hill, Ohio: Privately published, 1938), unnumbered p. 13.

dispute before the Church, and that they be submissive to the judgment of the Church in every such affair," which meant following an orderly procedure that began with hearings before chapel elders and continued through third-party mediation and on up through the layers of denominational hierarchy. Members who refused to abide by the final decision rendered by this process could be excommunicated.[19] Jefferson's operations were to be governed by similar rules. The company's charter stated that officers would be elected annually by a majority vote of the shareholders. Shareholder disputes that could not be settled amicably by the disputants would be decided by third-party mediation. If the parties still could not reach an agreement, the company would exercise its right to buy out the shares of anyone who was "disposed to quarrel and interrupt the Business of the Company," a form of corporate excommunication.[20]

Thus the incorporation of Jefferson Furnace shows the creative adaptation of a familiar mode of social organization to a new need in the community. The original impetus to organize furnaces, however, may well have come from outside the core of the tight-knit community of immigrants from Mynydd Bach. Most of the men who assumed leadership positions at Jefferson Furnace were not natives of Mynydd Bach, and most of them had some kind of previous experience in industry or commerce that distinguished them from the majority of the Cardiganshire-born settlers. Jefferson's first manager was Thomas Jones, North, so-called because he was one of the few settlers from North Wales. He and his family came to Jefferson Township after living a number of years in Pittsburgh and Pomeroy. The company's secretary, Thomas Ll. Hughes, was also from North Wales. After emigrating from Denbighshire, Hughes and his family lived in Cincinnati and Covington, Kentucky, before coming to Jackson/Gallia. Thomas T. Jones, the company's financial agent and sometime manager, came from near Lampeter, some ten miles south of Mynydd Bach. The only natives of Mynydd Bach who held positions of responsibility at Jefferson Furnace were Edward Morris, who served briefly as secretary, and David Edwards, who acted as trustee for all land exchanged for company stock. Organizers of Cambria and Limestone similarly included men

19. *The History, Constitution, Rules of Discipline, and Confession of Faith, of the Calvinistic Methodists in Wales,* 3d ed. (Mold: H. & O. Jones, 1840), 40–41, 37.

20. Jackson County Deed Book Q, pp. 461–62.

who were born or who had traveled outside the locality of Mynydd Bach.

In chapter 3 I described Jackson/Gallia as the agricultural core of an extended rural-industrial Welsh settlement region. It was also a place where a confluence of migrations came together. The largest stream consisted of Cardiganshire farm families. A smaller, contributory stream of families and individuals came to the settlement via industry and commerce in southeast Wales, Pennsylvania, the iron works and coal mines along the upper Ohio River, and developing industrial and marketing centers such as Cincinnati and Covington. The latter settlers became catalysts for change in the community once opportunity and necessity were ripe, both because they possessed useful knowledge and skills and because they did not view industry as a foreign, unknown entity. The resources of the first group combined with the resourcefulness of the second to make Jefferson, Cambria, and Limestone furnaces possible.

What of those who did not invest in one of the Welsh-owned furnaces? Noninvestors fell into three social categories, each situated in a particular geographical context. The first category were economically well-off families living in the center of the Jackson/Gallia settlement, most notably virtually the entire Moriah neighborhood. No families in the immediate vicinity of Moriah, mother chapel of the settlement and the seat of Rev. Robert Williams, chose to invest in any of the furnaces, including none of Moriah's elders. (Edward Morris and Thomas Ll. Hughes were founding elders at Moriah but had moved their membership to the chapel in Oak Hill before 1854.) The farms in the Moriah neighborhood were among the most prosperous in the settlement, having been established as early as 1835 and with some of the best land in the area. In the early 1850s the chapel's elders included Abel Gwynne, the fiercely orthodox disciplinarian from North Wales. According to the Jefferson Company records he contributed neither labor nor capital investment during the company's first three years of operation. Robert Williams appears only once in the company records, when he loaned the firm $150 at punitively high interest. His biography is strangely silent about Jefferson Furnace and says nothing about the impact of charcoal iron on the community. If these two men strongly opposed involvement in the charcoal iron ventures, the other elders and members at Moriah would have found it difficult to contravene them. There may also have been geographical reasons for Moriah families' abstention from iron investment. A higher proportion of their land was arable than on the farms of most investors, while investors' land included most of the coal and iron reserves within the Welsh settlement area. Those who invested in iron stood to gain most from supplying resources for iron production; families with relatively good land could perhaps more profitably invest in improving their farms' productivity.

The second category of noninvestors were those who were not Calvinistic Methodists. Congregationalists and Baptists accounted for approximately 40 percent of the local Welsh population in the 1850s but only 17 percent of investors of known chapel affiliation. Although most Congregationalists lived some miles away from the proposed furnace sites and did not have significant iron ore or coal deposits on their land, their lack of participation can best be attributed to the social distance and differences between them and the Calvinistic Methodists. Not a single Congregational elder invested in a Welsh furnace. They may have lacked the organizational skills necessary to organize their own furnace. In Wales as in America, each Congregational chapel governed its own operations without the hierarchy of authority that made Calvinistic Methodism's presbyterian system a training ground for democratic self-government.[21] Welsh Americans in Oak Hill today say that their ancestors were a factious, competitive lot and that the Congregationalists and Calvinistic Methodists scarcely acknowledged one another as Christians.[22] If so, mutual distrust may have prevented them from becoming business partners.

The third category of noninvestors were families who arrived after 1842 and who settled on the periphery of the Welsh territory. Many of these immigrants were just getting themselves established by the early 1850s. They were in the least secure position financially to risk investment; their land was at the greatest distance from Jefferson and Cambria furnaces; and the poor quality of their land may have made it unacceptable at the agreed rates of exchange ($12 or $15 per acre). The failure of Limestone

21. Ieuan Gwynedd Jones, "Religion and Society in the First Half of the Nineteenth Century," in *Explorations and Explanations: Essays in the Social History of Victorian Wales* (Llandysul: Gwasg Gomer, 1981), 217–35; David Williams, *A History of Modern Wales* (1950; reprint, London: John Murray, 1969), 154–57, 167–68.

22. Interview with Evan E. Davis in his home in Oak Hill, Ohio, 7 January 1990.

Furnace, the furnace with the greatest number of relatively late-arriving, peripherally located investors, indicates the vulnerability of would-be investors in this category.

Risk, Moral Economy, and Immigrant Mentalité

The financial risks of investing in charcoal iron were significant for all of the Welsh who "became interested," as the R. G. Dun & Company reporters put it. Chapter 4 explained that investors were liable for double the value of their investment, and that some Welsh investors who exchanged their farmland for stock risked losing everything they owned if their company went bankrupt. The issue of risk needs closer examination, for the level of risk assumed by Welsh iron investors seems to contradict the pattern of conservative, risk-averse behavior that scholars have documented among both immigrant and native-born rural Americans. Neither coercion by Calvinistic Methodist elders nor the trust they inspired completely explains why one-third or more of Welsh families in the Jackson/Gallia settlement changed their investment strategy from a classic "safety-first" position, investing in land and the improvement of land mainly for secure family subsistence,[23] to highly risky entrepreneurial ventures in rural industry. To understand their decision more fully, it will be helpful to assess it in light of the concepts of moral economy and *mentalité*, both of which bring together elements of economy and culture that were crucial to the way in which immigrant Welsh Calvinists evaluated their relationship to American society.

A moral economy is generally understood to mean an economy whose operation satisfies conceptions of a just price, social justice, and the proper fulfillment of rights and obligations.[24] Scholars have interpreted popular protests against unfair prices and the failure of powerful individuals and organizations to meet

23. James A. Henretta, "Families and Farms: *Mentalité* in Pre-Industrial America," *William and Mary Quarterly*, 3d ser., 35 (1978): 3–32. Contrasting studies that document safety-first behavior among Midwestern Germans and German-Americans are Sonya Salamon, "Ethnic Communities and the Structure of Agriculture," *Rural Sociology* 50 (1985): 323–40; and Kathleen Neils Conzen, "Peasant Pioneers: Generational Succession among German Farmers in Frontier Minnesota," in *The Countryside in the Age of Capitalist Transformation: Essays in the Social History of Rural America*, ed. Steven Hahn and Jonathan Prude (Chapel Hill: University of North Carolina Press, 1985), 259–92.

24. E. P. Thompson, "The Moral Economy Reviewed," in *Customs in Common* (New York: New Press, 1991), 259–351.

their obligations or to honor the rights of ordinary people as protests against a kind of economic immorality, often as part of a breakdown in traditional economic order in favor of advancing forms of capitalist enterprise that robbed ordinary people of control over the means of production. In late-eighteenth-century England and Wales, for example, townspeople rioted during a period of famine when officials refused to distribute grain that was being stored for sale at inflated prices. In the uplands of rural Georgia, subsistence farmers resisted the change to commercially oriented cotton production because it undermined their independence by giving greater control to creditors and merchants. In both instances, "the logic and relations of commodity production" disrupted what producers recognized as the normal, just, fair operation of the agricultural economy.[25] To their distress, neither group had the power to do more than deflect or slightly delay changes that lessened their control over their local economies.

The Welsh immigrant community in Jackson and Gallia counties found itself in an analogous situation to that which confronted Georgia yeomen and many other rural Americans during the nineteenth century, as commercial, market-driven agriculture and rural industry transformed the rural economy. The transformations caused by the charcoal iron industry were graphic in southern Ohio: charcoal iron furnaces devoured forests; they created islands of heavy, if small-scale, industry in the midst of farming communities; they were owned and run by entrepreneurial capitalists who often did not live locally; and they attracted an itinerant labor force of mostly low-skilled, poorly educated, impoverished workers. For the Welsh the confrontation with this form of industrial capitalism was all the more threatening because the capitalists and their workforce were not Welsh. When Madison Furnace began construction on the doorstep of the Welsh settlement's territory, the invasion had begun.

From this perspective, the Welsh response to charcoal iron in 1854 takes on a historical resonance that I believe was part of the thinking of immigrants, particularly those like William Jones,

25. E. P. Thompson, "The Moral Economy of the English Crowd in the Eighteenth Century," in *Customs in Common* (New York: New Press, 1991), 185–258; Steven Hahn, "The 'Unmaking' of the Southern Yeomanry: The Transformation of the Georgia Upcountry, 1860–1890," in Steven Hahn and Jonathan Prude, eds., *The Countryside in the Age of Capitalist Transformation: Essays in the Social History of Rural America* (Chapel Hill, N.C.: University of North Carolina Press, 1985), 179–204, quotation on p. 180.

Cofadail, who came from upland neighborhoods on Mynydd Bach. Jones had witnessed the "war of the little Englishman" thirty years before, when established farmers, craftspeople, and squatters drove away the peremptory English landlord who threatened to deny them access to their traditional summer pastures and fuel. Like the resistance mounted against Augustus Brackenbury, the decision to form Welsh corporations to produce charcoal iron was an essentially defensive act to maintain control of the land and resources upon which the immigrants depended and which they considered theirs by right. If they did not build their own furnaces they ran the risk of perhaps forever remaining second in wealth and status to Americans and having little say about the economic development of their locality. American companies might try to buy land from Welsh farmers, diminishing the community's territorial base and social cohesiveness. There was also the intangible element of community pride, which shone clearly in Thomas Ll. Hughes's letter to Y Cyfaill: "Seeing them [Americans] sweeping all before them, it came to mind among some of the Welsh to take a stab at what they could do." Family security, independence, and community pride demanded swift response on both occasions. The differences between the two events highlight the structural changes that had transformed the immigrants' society in the fifteen to twenty years since they left Mynydd Bach. Former squatters and tenant farmers had become landowners who possessed valuable farms and mineral resources. Where the people of Mynydd Bach organized violent mass protests, the Jackson/Gallia settlers held formal meetings, drafted corporate charters, organized an elaborate and creative scheme for pooling community capital, and set to work building companies the likes of which they never could have owned in Wales.

In this case, I would argue, immigrant farmers chose to participate in entrepreneurial industrial investment in order to defend and strengthen what they considered to be a moral economy. Their creative adaptation of existing institutional forms and cultural attitudes further supports this conclusion and offers an illuminating example of immigrant *mentalité*, that is, of the ways in which immigrants' culture influenced their economic behavior. Creating furnace companies on their own land, to retain profits within their own community and compete for local economic power against outsiders, was not sufficient to satisfy the Welsh Calvinists' conception of a moral economy. The Jefferson Furnace also had to be run according to principles congruent with the *Rules of Discipline*, including the scrupulous avoidance of debt. Rule 19 of the Calvinistic Methodist code ordered that members of the faith should "not borrow or get any thing upon trust, without conscientiously endeavouring to repay, and having at the time some hopeful prospect of being able to fulfil their engagements. It is the character of the wicked man, that 'he borroweth and payeth not again.'" Any church member who owed money to another and refused to repay as much of the debt as possible was to be excommunicated, as was anyone who left business debts unpaid through "living wastefully and prodigally above his income" or failing to keep proper accounts.[26]

The Calvinistic Methodists who invested in Jefferson Furnace took these rules seriously. The contract for construction of the second Horeb chapel, built in 1845, specified that the congregation "will not enter into any debt whose payment is not reasonably foreseen before it is contracted." It also spelled out a schedule for the payment of pledges intended to clear the debt within eighteen months.[27] This accounting *mentalité*—an example of what James Cassedy called "the beginnings of the statistical mind"[28]—is evident in nineteenth-century Nonconformist chapel records in Wales and the United States. Chapels did not always record births, deaths, or baptisms (life events that were traditionally the responsibility of the Established Church) but they did scrupulously document quarterly contributions to the ministry and the number of Bible verses that each person memorized and recited at Sunday school. The chapels whose members were most active in Jefferson Furnace led the league among all Welsh Calvinistic Methodist chapels for feats of Bible memorization at midcentury, exceeding the diligence of larger and wealthier rural settlements as well as the rates achieved by chapels on Mynydd Bach itself.

It would therefore not be accurate to characterize the Welsh charcoal iron ventures as the manifestation of an American capitalistic *mentalité*. The events of 1854–1856 manifest a cluster of attitudes that allowed change in the direction of prevailing American economic values while limiting the potentially destabi-

26. *Rules of Discipline*, rules 19–21, pp. 37–38.
27. Davis, *Early History of Horeb Church*, unnumbered p. 18.
28. Quoted in Winifred Barr Rothenberg, *From Market-Places to a Market Economy: The Transformation of Rural Massachusetts, 1750–1850* (Chicago: University of Chicago Press, 1992), xi.

lizing effects of change. The template for a Welsh Calvinist way of doing business eventually proved so successful that it was employed repeatedly in later decades as the Welsh of Jackson/Gallia cautiously diversified their industrial portfolio with coal-fired furnaces and firebrick companies. A similarly restrained Welsh business style was evident among entrepreneurial Welsh cattlemen in Kansas during the late nineteenth century. According to anthropologist Joseph V. Hickey, Welsh ranchers in Bala, Kansas (many of them originally from Bala, Merionethshire) placed a high value on landownership, which prompted them to reinvest more of their profits in land than did American, English, and Scottish settlers in their locality. Welsh cattlemen employed family labor more extensively than did non-Welsh cattle companies; they rarely bought cattle on credit; and they formed loose alliances with one another to buy and sell livestock in order to avoid paying fees to non-Welsh middlemen. The Kansas Welsh also avoided conspicuous consumption. "English and Scottish ranch managers sometimes spent lavishly on ranch buildings and furnishings, and on fine cattle and horses," Hickey wrote. "Even after they had made their fortunes, there are relatively few examples where Welsh stockraisers did the same." Like rural Welsh iron makers in Ohio, the Kansas stockraisers used conservative business strategies to achieve long-term success in the capitalist system. "We took the slow and steady way," one Welsh American told Hickey; "we rarely made big profits, but, at the same time, we rarely experienced major losses."[29]

Welsh Calvinists' Responses to Economic Success

The example of Jefferson Furnace illustrates how an immigrant community could respond creatively to the perceived need to become engaged in the process of rural industrialization. That process continued to pose problems for orthodox Calvinists, however. I suggested in chapter 4 that some conservative Welsh Calvinists may have been so distressed by the changes that charcoal iron brought to their community that they decided to resettle on the agricultural frontier in Minnesota. Those who stayed in Jackson/Gallia faced another problem as economic success finally came to their community. How could they maintain orthodox

29. Joseph V. Hickey, "Welsh Cattlemen on the Kansas Flint Hills: Social and Ideological Dimensions of Cattle Entrepreneurship," *Agricultural History* 63 (1989): 56–71; quotations on pp. 67, 70.

morality when prosperity threatened to undermine key aspects of their ethnic identity?

This question moves us into territory familiar to scholars of trans-Atlantic immigration, for one of the basic dynamics of change common to virtually all European immigrant groups during the nineteenth century was the gradual loss of community cohesion and distinctiveness as economic prosperity lessened the need for close group cooperation and changed many aspects of the groups' material life. Prosperity dissolved the structural bonds that made the immigrant generation appear clannish, including use of a common foreign language, occupation of a spatially concentrated ethnic territory, and intense identification with particular religious practices and values. It did so through a complex process of substitution in which loyalty to and identification with the immigrant group was replaced with new loyalties, new identities, and an ever wider scope for individual action. These changes are usually measured and discussed in terms of cultural assimilation, that is, the loss of traits from the old-world culture and their replacement with corresponding traits from American culture. Rarely, however, have studies of immigrants' cultural assimilation specifically addressed the ways in which economic prosperity influenced that process.

For many of the Welsh of Jackson/Gallia and other rural Calvinist settlements, economic success posed a direct threat to important religious values, including obedience to authority and humility before God. Conservatives responded to this threat in essentially two ways: by maintaining the appearance of modesty and humility and by following the letter of religious law. According to Max Weber, the central paradox of Calvinistic faith was that personal salvation could never be confirmed through experience. Calvinists therefore lived in a constant state of anxiety, unsure of whether they were indeed saved. They found relief from what philosopher Gillian Rose called "the incessant anxiety of autonomy" mainly through devotion to their calling and the practice of ascetic discipline, which kept sin at bay so long as one followed the rules.[30] For Welsh Calvinists, these rules prescribed simple attire and the lack of any bodily adornment. "Outward signs portrayed the inner man," as Thomas Ll. Hughes wrote in his obituary of a leading Calvinistic Methodist elder. Daniel

---

30. Max Weber, *The Protestant Ethic and the Spirit of Capitalism* (New York: Charles Scribner's Sons, 1958); quotation from Gillian Rose, *Love's Work* (London: Chatto & Windus, 1995), 35.

Jenkins Williams wrote that even in the late nineteenth century, the Jackson/Gallia Welsh viewed "[p]arting the hair . . . as a sign of too much pride. The men combed their hair straight down over their foreheads."[31] Social amusements were also severely restricted and all popular entertainments were banned, from card playing and dancing to lawn croquet. People who conscientiously practiced this kind of asceticism were praised as "saints," "Israelites," and "pilgrims." The latter was no accidental allusion. John Elias commended the Pilgrim Fathers to the Jackson/Gallia Welsh as role models of ideal behavior. Like John Winthrop, Welsh immigrants should found their city on a hill and remain above worldly temptation.[32]

As the Puritans of Massachusetts Bay had discovered two hundred years before, it was extremely difficult to maintain exacting standards of ascetic behavior when a community began to prosper economically. The best defense against the corruption of moral standards was a combination of strong internal mechanisms of social control and geographic isolation. The Welsh in Jackson/Gallia had both, the first based in the authority conferred upon elected lay leaders and the second in the remote location of their settlement in the Appalachian foothills. Although no group of immigrant Welsh Calvinists established a true theocracy like those created by Dutch Calvinist immigrants and the English Puritans in Massachusetts Bay Colony, there was such a close interweaving of religious and civic government within some rural Welsh settlements that one could consider them quasi-theocracies. An anonymous contributor to an early-twentieth-century history of the Hanging Rock iron district wrote that the Welsh in Jackson County "were at first almost a state by themselves. They established their own churches, in which only the Welsh language was used. They cared for their own poor, and they settled their disputes in their churches." The Calvinistic Methodist minister Daniel Jenkins Williams spent many years among descendants of the Jackson/Gallia immigrants in Columbus, Ohio, in the years leading up to World War I. He also traveled to Welsh American communities across the United States as a guest preacher and in the course of doing research for his definitive history of Welsh Calvinistic Methodism in America. Williams con-

31. Daniel Jenkins Williams, *The Welsh of Columbus, Ohio: A Study in Adaptation and Assimilation* (Oshkosh, Wis.: Privately published, 1913), 107.

32. Letter from John Elias to Moriah Chapel, Jackson County, dated 15 February 1838, published in *Y Cyfaill* (February 1842): 36.

sidered Jackson/Gallia "the strongest and best organized Welsh settlement in America in her balmy days, and the best fortified by natural environment against extraneous influences." "There were no public conveniences to disturb . . . [their] peace and custom," he concluded. "They had but little contact with the outside world and what contact they had was forced upon them by circumstances."[33]

Judging by local histories and conversations with descendants of the early Welsh settlers, the most potent symbol of the Welsh community's fidelity to its immigrant values was that the community strictly observed the biblical injunction to cease all labor on the Sabbath. Even Jefferson Furnace never operated on Sunday. Two local stories have elevated this distinction to popular myth. In one story, Jefferson's financial agent Thomas T. Jones discovered the furnace blacksmith chopping kindling wood for his forge on a Sunday morning. "William," Jones said, "don't you know that such work is against the rules of the furnace?" Outdoor labor on the Sabbath was unthinkable in a community where women peeled potatoes on Saturday night for Sunday dinner. The other story concerns a trip that Thomas Ll. Hughes made to Cincinnati to testify as a witness in a court trial. The prosecuting attorney happened to ask Hughes how many tons of iron Jefferson Furnace produced. "Ten tons per day," Hughes answered.

> How much per month was the question. And he [the attorney] began to count 30 days in a month, when the witness interrupted him and said, "Count only 26 days sir, the Jefferson never runs on Sunday." Judge Swing was on the bench and, being a religious man, was very much moved by this statement . . . and, on adjournment of the court, [he] stepped to the witness and congratulated him and the Jefferson Furnace Company through him, and made many friendly remarks in regard to the company and the Welsh settlement in general.[34]

Keeping the Sabbath was considered an important manifestation of Christian values in immigrant and American communities throughout the nineteenth century. According to Ohio State geol-

33. Eugene B. Willard, ed., *A Standard History of the Hanging Rock Iron Region of Ohio*, vol. 1 (N.p.: Lewis Publishing Company, 1916), 448; Williams, *The Welsh of Columbus*, 109, 105–6.

34. "A Brief History of Jefferson Furnace," anonymous typescript submitted to the Ohio State Archaeological and Historical Society in support of a proposal to restore Jefferson Furnace (November 1934), unnumbered pp. 4, 5.

ogist Wilbur Stout, the first charcoal iron furnace manager in the Hanging Rock district to suspend operations on Sunday was an American named Robert Hamilton, who initiated the practice in 1844 at Pine Grove Furnace. "The results were so satisfactory," Stout noted, "that other furnaces followed the practice."[35] To the Welsh, however, honoring the Sabbath became a badge of ethnic identity and religious purity in contrast to more worldly Americans. In their eyes, the fact that Jefferson Furnace shut down on Sundays honored a specifically Welsh tradition, which Jackson/Gallia settlers could date back to at least 1839, when representatives of their community supported the declaration, passed by the Pennsylvania Association of Calvinistic Methodists meeting in Pittsburgh, that "no one (whomsoever) would be suffered to be church members, who were guilty of working on the holy day in [industrial] works or on boats of any kind."[36] By 1888 the Sabbath rule had become the stuff of myth. An article about Thomas Ll. Hughes published in the Welsh American monthly *The Cambrian* in that year claimed that the articles of agreement for Jefferson Furnace "contained the provision that the furnace should not, under any circumstances, be run on the Sabbath." (The only surviving articles of agreement, written in a volume of Jackson County deeds, include no such provision.) "And this rule has been carefully observed without a single exception up to the present time," the article continued. "Very few smelting furnaces in the world have ever done this, because stopping of the fires on the Sabbath involves a risk of great loss to the owners. The Jefferson Furnace Company, however, proved very successful in their enterprise, having paid to its shareholders larger dividends than any other Iron Company in Ohio."[37] The connection between godliness and worldly success was clear.

The Welsh claim on the Sabbath stemmed both from historical associations and from cultural developments that were ongoing in Wales during and after the period of heavy emigration from Mynydd Bach. In the wake of High Calvinism's victory over more liberal forms of theology after 1830, Nonconformity in Wales produced a culture that "emphasized the new puritanical Sunday as 'The Welsh Sunday,' the new 'Welsh way of life' being that of

35. Wilbur Stout, "The Charcoal Iron Industry of the Hanging Rock Iron District: Its Influence on the Early Development of the Ohio Valley," *Ohio Archaeological and Historical Quarterly* 42 (1933): 79.

36. *Y Cyfaill* (July 1839): 210–11.

37. "Hon. T. L. Hughes, Oak Hill, O.," *Cambrian* (1888), 226; Jackson County Deed Book Q, pp. 461–62.

the chapel, the singing school (for hymns not ballads), the temperance assemblies, the *[G]ymanfa Ganu* . . . and much else which is familiar to the twentieth century as the typical Wales."[38] Rural Welsh American settlements across the country strictly observed the Sabbath, regardless of the immigrants' denominational affiliation. Congregationalists in Waukesha County, Wisconsin, for example, also peeled their potatoes on Saturday night.[39] In Jackson/Gallia, keeping the Sabbath holy may have brought special satisfaction to those who remembered "the milk war" among the Calvinists of Jewin chapel in London. Neither farming nor the iron furnaces required them to work seven days a week. In fact, honoring the Sabbath made business sense for iron furnaces. In 1884 a furnace manager wrote in the *Journal of the U.S. Association of Charcoal Iron Workers*, "We do not claim to make as much iron in six days as we could in seven, but in the long run, Sabbath-keeping furnaces make more in a year than those which do not rest." Oak Hill resident Evan E. Davis also pointed out to me that it did no one any good to have men hungover from Saturday night trying to produce iron on Sunday, especially when all the managers were in church.[40]

Strict observation of the Sabbath was one way to stay on the right side of the line that separated industrious devotion from devotion to industry. The other was to cultivate modesty, inoffensiveness, and religious piety, personal characteristics that had developed in impoverished circumstances in Wales but continued to represent religious purity in the minds of conservative Welsh Calvinists in the United States.[41] Like American Mennonites in the mid–nineteenth century, devout Welsh Calvinists regarded humility as a personal ideal, as "a way of life, shaping everything

38. Prys Morgan, "From Death to a View: The Hunt for the Welsh Past in the Romantic Period," in *The Invention of Tradition*, ed. Eric Hobsbawm and Terence Ranger (Cambridge: Cambridge University Press, 1983), 95.

39. Interview with Gwen Davies (b. 1899), conducted by Edward Wicklein, 26 December 1978, Presbyterian Historical Association, Philadelphia; interview with Mildred Hughes Southcott at her home, Wales, Wisconsin, 24 June 1988.

40. *Journal of the U.S. Association of Charcoal Iron Workers* (October 1884), quoted in Keeler, "An Economic History of the Jackson County Iron Industry," *Ohio Archaeological and Historical Quarterly* 42 (1933): 160; interview with Evan E. Davis at his home in Oak Hill, Ohio, 7 January 1990.

41. See, for example, Rev. William W. Rowlands's address to a Welsh audience, quoted in Y *Cyfaill* (February 1846): 46, in which he expresses his *"earnest wishes"* that the Welsh sustain "their present high standing in this country for integrity, inoffensiveness, and obedience to the established laws of the United States."

from economics to culture to personal relationships," and as the key to spiritual salvation. Members of Calvinistic Methodist chapels were told by the denomination's rules that they should not be "contentious, proud disputers, . . . but humble, meek, peaceable, gentle, easy to be entreated, and willing to be taught." Their leaders should be "not only men of gifts, but men of grace, of a humble temper, spirituality of mind, and such as love Christ. They must . . . be temperate in all things, liberal and not covetous, or greedy of filthy lucre; given to hospitality; not brawlers, but meek and patient."[42]

No one in the Jackson/Gallia community better personified these qualities than Thomas Llewelyn Hughes. In addition to running his own small businesses and serving as accountant for the Jefferson Furnace Company, Hughes was a biblical scholar and man of letters. William R. Evans, a second-generation Calvinistic Methodist minister in Jackson/Gallia who knew Hughes as an old man, described him as being tireless in his quest for spiritual knowledge and understanding. Evans wrote in his history of the settlement that Hughes "would rise . . . very early and spend a great deal of time before his neighbors were out of their beds[,] holding communion with his God in secret, and it showed that He who sees in secret evidently paid him, in his long life [Hughes lived to be ninety years old] and the plentiful blessings of this earth." Hughes told his readers that he wrote "only at night, because I never spent so much as five minutes of daylight at it [the Scriptural histories], nor any other writing of mine, and that because of the very sensible reason, I dare say, that daylight is to be used entirely for winning bread for myself and those who depend upon me day after day; and if I were to lose one day of work there would be a scarcity in their comforts, if not in the necessities of life, likely to be felt at once."[43] The voice that comes through in Hughes's writing is practical and righteous. He did not let his genuine concern for the spiritual welfare of his local and national communities interfere with his business obligations, nor did he see any contradiction between them. Industriousness and diligence—two of the words most commonly used to praise

42. Joseph C. Liechty, "Humility: The Foundation of Mennonite Religious Outlook in the 1860s," *Mennonite Quarterly Review* 54 (1980): 12; *Rules of Discipline*, rules 5 and 33, pp. 33, 41–42.

43. Rev. William R. Evans, *Sefydliadau Cymreig Jackson a Gallia, Ohio* (The Welsh Settlements of Jackson and Gallia, Ohio) (Utica, N.Y.: T. J. Griffiths, 1897), 76; Thomas Ll. Hughes, *Y Cyfaill* (February 1860): 75.

Welsh immigrants in their obituaries—were signs of spiritual well-being.

Thomas T. Jones was a very different sort of Welshman. His love of horses began in Cardiganshire, where he was reputed to breed Welsh cobs. He continued to enjoy fine horses in Ohio. By 1870 he was the richest Welshman in Jackson County and he conspicuously played the part of the local squire, putting on the attire and manners of an English gentleman. As an old man he always went out "dressed in broadcloth, Prince Albert coat, very shiny boots, immaculate linen and a silk hat." Jones fittingly met his Maker at the age of eighty-two when his spirited horse turned a corner too sharply and toppled the carriage in which he was riding.[44]

The evident pleasure that Jones took in his affluence might have seemed normal in less strict immigrant communities, such as the Norwegian settlement in southern Wisconsin where immigrant farmers enjoyed their improved economic status in the style to which bourgeois ladies and gentlemen in Norway were accustomed.[45] In Jackson/Gallia, however, Jones was a chanticleer. He regularly attended Horeb chapel and its Sunday school but lived above the law that elders such as Hughes tried, by example and sanction, to enforce. Jones's sharp eye for business won him enemies in the community. According to local historian Evan E. Davis, Jones and his son Ebenezer, who succeeded him at Globe Furnace, were not well liked by their fellow immigrants. In one telling incident, which goes unrecorded in the community's written histories, Jones bought up a large amount of Jefferson's unsold pig iron during the prewar depression and had it shipped to warehouses in Portsmouth and Cincinnati. When iron prices rose dramatically during the war, he sold the iron for nails which he then traded at an even higher price. Company stockholders demanded that he share his profits with them, but Jones refused.[46] Given his wealth and prominence in the community, the fact that local histories scarcely mention Thomas T. Jones seems either an implicit indictment of his character or a sign that he was far less involved in community life than men who were both religious and business leaders.

44. Obituary of Thomas T. Jones, Y Cyfaill (June 1887): 233–34; Jones, "Romance of the Old Charcoal Furnace Days," unnumbered pp. 2, 5.

45. Gjerde, Peasants to Farmers, 220–31.

46. Interviews with Evan E. Davis at his home, Oak Hill, Ohio, 7 January 1990, 8 July 1990.

Welshness and the Sin of Pride

"Industriousness and frugality brought wealth, which in turn brought temptation and worldliness," Stephen Innes wrote of the English Puritans in Massachusetts; it was a paradox, he suggested, "we might dub the 'Protestant dilemma.'"[47] In rural Wales, most chapel members lacked both the means and the free time to indulge in games or ostentation. In the United States, ready money created a host of temptations. During the late 1840s and early 1850s, public concern in the Calvinistic Welsh American community about the cultural consequences of prosperity was often expressed in terms of one of the cardinal sins, namely, the sin of pride (*y pechod o falchder*). One early commentary on this theme, published in the Calvinistic Methodist monthly, *Y Cyfaill*, in 1848, drew explicit connections between the corruption of Welsh youth who migrated to London and the threat to immigrants' morality in the United States. Its author, John Williams, explained how one could recognize the signs of pride:

> 1. Some pride themselves in their bodies and their dress. Many of the youth of our nation, in the land of our birth, were seen to leave Wales for London; and having returned, the sign of being possessed by the beast was clear enough on their foreheads: when they were dressed in silks and English broadcloth, they were as proud as Lucifers; and it would be a great feat to get them to speak their mother tongue, even though they managed the other language [English] but imperfectly. I dare say, that the attitude of many of our nation in this country is similar to theirs. . . .
> 2. Others take pride in their worldly riches. . . . Many of the Welsh nation in America possess something of this "unjust mammon"; and their hearts swell as their wealth may grow (as the ships you have in New York City rise higher with the incoming tide); thus did Haman, Nebuchadnezzar, and the wealthy in the Gospel.[48]

The sin of pride threatened Welsh identity in two respects. It marked the proud as having disowned their peasant roots and it showed that they had turned against God. To immigrants such as John Williams, the moral ambiguity of materialism went hand-in-hand with the moral implications of assimilation into non-Welsh

---

47. Innes, *Economic Culture*, 25.

48. John S. Williams of Trenton [N.Y.], "Y Pechod o Falchder," *Y Cyfaill* (November 1848): 324–26.

culture. Becoming wealthy, proud, and vain meant losing one's Welsh identity. The enduring dilemma of Welsh identity, whether in the context of Wales or the United States, has been the association between poverty and Welshness on the one hand and prosperity and English-speaking culture on the other. In the last century as today, remaining true to one's Welsh identity meant retaining a modest demeanor, in contrast to the stereotypical haughtiness of the English. The highest praise a "great man" can receive in Wales today is that he has not let his greatness go to his head.[49] The historic lack of strong class distinctions in Welsh-speaking communities in Wales and the powerful working-class solidarity among Welsh industrial workers reinforced the notion that Welshness meant de-emphasizing differences of wealth and status.[50]

Thomas Ll. Hughes indirectly addressed the sin of pride in one of his rare expressions of personal opinion in his scriptural commentaries. From the early 1840s, Hughes wrote regularly for *Y Cyfaill*, beginning with transcribed sermons from his home chapel in Wales and culminating in a comprehensive history of the Scriptures and the Holy Land published in monthly installments over a period of twenty years. His purpose in writing the commentaries was to make Bible stories more real and comprehensible to Welsh immigrants by explaining their geographical, historical, and moral context. Ordinarily he confined himself to the subject at hand, but on a few occasions he allowed himself scope to write as a cultural arbiter for the Welsh American community. For example, in his 1852 piece on the parting of the Red Sea, he acknowledged that the Israelites' joyful celebrations upon safely crossing the sea might trouble orthodox readers who disapproved of dancing and the use of musical instruments in worship. "It is obvious from the history," he wrote, "that the whole

49. In all my discussions with Welsh people, I have never heard this cliché applied to a Welsh woman. The most striking example of cultivated humility that I have encountered is the operatic bass-baritone Bryn Terfel, a self-described farm boy from northwest Wales, who at twenty-eight was already in great demand for leading operatic roles. When I interviewed him before his debut at Chicago's Lyric Opera as Donner in *Das Rheingold*, he told me, "My ego hasn't grown at all since the beginning of my career because people [at home] would say, 'Oh, he has a big head.' But if you have this kind of character [easy-going and modest] people don't keep you at a distance." Anne Knowles, "The Thunder God Is Smiling," *Y Drych* (The Mirror) (April 1993): 18.

50. Carol Trosset, *Welshness Performed: Welsh Concepts of Person and Society* (Tucson: University of Arizona Press, 1993), 77–89.

great crowd, men and women singing together, were using dance and musical instruments in an orderly and regular fashion, to demonstrate their love and thankfulness to their savior and their God."[51] In a commentary published in February 1854, when the Welsh of Oak Hill and Horeb chapel were organizing Jefferson Furnace, Hughes specifically addressed the sin of pride in an unusual editorial aside.

> Oppression and poverty always brought Israel to her senses . . . But as . . . one after the other of them followed each other throughout the world, and a new nation grew up in the midst of success and luxury, some of them held that the pure, faithful worship of God's word was too miserable a thing for their taste, and they swarmed along with the pagan nations around them, to their feasts and to the vulgar, wanton worship of idols, which was more compatible with corrupt nature.
>
> It was foretold to them many times that this would be the consequence of leaving the Canaanites without completely uprooting them from the land. Not much better is the Christian world, although its privileges are much greater, than was the world of the Jews. There is the man of Israel facing great temptation, his desires boiling in his breast, directing his steps toward the idolizing feast, with food and drink and every excitement for his appetite. He went this way even though he knew that disgrace and times of tribulation would soon follow. There is the man of Wales living in an age and under a government one hundred times more enlightened, following his companions and his pleasures, although his conscience testifies within him that disgrace and eternal wretchedness will be the result.[52]

To Hughes's readers, "the man of Wales living in an age and under a government one hundred times more enlightened" applied even more to Welsh migrants than to natives of Wales who remained in the old country. His warning to avoid corruption applied to both populations, for by the mid-1850s growing numbers of rural Welsh people were migrating from the "oppression and poverty" of the countryside to industrial South Wales, London, and other destinations where they lived "in the midst of success and luxury." Only the "pure, faithful worship of

51. Thomas Ll. Hughes, "Yr Hanesyddiaeth Ysgrythyrol, Pennod 19: Yr Exodus (Ex. 13: 20–22)" (The Scriptural History, Chapter 19: Exodus . . .), Y Cyfaill (February 1852): 42.

52. Thomas Ll. Hughes, Y Cyfaill (February 1854): 51.

God's word" could prevent Welsh migrants at home and abroad from falling into "disgrace and eternal wretchedness."

There were acceptable forms of pride. One was embodied in the image of the Welsh miser, a popular stereotype which developed in many rural Welsh American communities during the middle of the nineteenth century and still survives today. In Wales, Wisconsin, for example, I have heard stories of farmers who hid hundreds of thousands of dollars in mattresses while refusing to pay for indoor plumbing or electricity.[53] Similar stories persist in the Jackson/Gallia community, where the prejudice against conspicuous consumption remains strong. An extreme example of the Welsh miser in the mid–nineteenth century comes from Utica, New York. In 1847, neighbors discovered that a peculiar old woman named Elinor Jones had hoarded over $2,000 during a lifetime of conspicuous penury and hard work. According to her obituary, it was said that she allowed herself a weekly living allowance of just two shillings. People said that when a young man offered to marry her, Elinor refused, declaring crossly, "You won't get any of my money." She left $1,200 of her savings to found the Utica Charitable Society.[54]

Like far wealthier Dutch Calvinists in seventeenth-century Holland,[55] Welsh Calvinists in nineteenth-century America found it most acceptable to display their wealth in charitable works and contributions to the church. When families in Jackson/Gallia finally achieved middle-class status, they bragged openly in the Welsh American press not of their personal wealth but of generous contributions to the community's religious organizations. Contributions were public knowledge in Welsh American congregations, for it was common practice to read out the names of contributors and the amount of their gifts during chapel services. Bethel elder John H. Jones reported to the national weekly newspaper Y Drych (The Mirror) in 1863, "There was strong emotion in the congregation on the Sabbath, upon hearing the list of names read and the contributions, and upon realizing that the youths who had gone to the war, all except one or two, had remembered the Bible Society, every one sending his dollar to contribute to the collection." Mindful of his community's reputation

53. Interview with Mildred Hughes Southcott, 8 July 1988.

54. J. C. Roberts, *Hanes Cymdeithas Elusengar Utica a'r Cylchoedd, o'i Sefydliad yn 1849 hyd Ionawr 1, 1882* (The History of the Charitable Society of Utica and Its Region, from Its Establishment in 1849 to January 1, 1882) (Utica, N.Y.: Ellis H. Roberts, 1882), 46–48, quotation on p. 47.

55. Schama, *Embarrassment of Riches*, 330ff.

for poverty, he added, "I am sending this to be mentioned in *Y Drych* as an example to others."[56] Accumulating wealth was perfectly acceptable if it was balanced with generosity toward religion. As Thomas Ll. Hughes wrote in his obituary of Edward Morris, "Although he like many Welshmen liked well enough to earn a penny, and to hold it tight to keep it for a rainy day, as we say, yet when the cause of the Mediator would come to the table in financial need, it would be let go freely and cheerfully. No one was more ready or generous in his offerings than he; he contributed like a gentleman unstintingly and uncomplainingly."[57]

A third form of acceptable pride was a community's celebrating its triumph over adversity. This theme was so fundamental to the hagiography of European immigrant groups in the United States that I need not elaborate upon it here. For the Welsh in Jackson/Gallia, the greatest moment of community pride came with their decision to incorporate their own charcoal iron furnaces. At last the community could boast of an unprecedented achievement to the rest of Welsh America through their spokesman, Thomas Ll. Hughes: "So, Welsh boys of the poor regions of Newark, Steuben, and Wisconsin, if you want to earn a pretty penny, get yourselves to this place. This is no boastful tale, but words of truth and sobriety."[58]

Welsh historian Arthur H. Dodd summarized the culmination of first- and second-generation Welsh immigrants' attitudes toward economic success as the "worship of respectability."[59] Although Dodd was referring to Welsh American settlements in general, the trait he identified was particularly evident in Welsh Calvinistic Methodist communities. One could trace it throughout the history of Calvinistic Methodism, from Daniel Rowland's refusal to leave the Anglican Church and Ebenezer Richard's emphasis upon family discipline to the many provisions of the *Rules of Discipline* that aimed to inculcate respect for authority and proper behavior in all spheres of life. Historians of other branches of British and American Methodism have argued that the same emphasis on respect for authority and the worship of respectability followed quickly on the heels of religious conversion in industrial communities and so made religion an indispensable

56. "Efell Las" [John H. Jones] to the editor, *Y Drych* (25 April 1863): 126.

57. Obituary of Edward Morris by Thomas Ll. Hughes, *Y Cyfaill* (April 1858), 131.

58. *Y Cyfaill* (April 1854): 153.

59. Arthur H. Dodd, *The Character of Early Welsh Emigration to the United States*, 2d ed. (Cardiff: University of Wales Press, 1956), 39.

tool for controlling industrial labor during the nineteenth century.[60] For the Welsh in the Jackson/Gallia settlement, respectability had been an essential part of their self-image since their first encounters with heathen Irish immigrants on their passage across the Atlantic. Many Welsh letter-writers, like Edward and Mary Morris and Edward Jones, expressed this new self-awareness in terms of the exceptionally righteous, proper, restrained behavior of the Welsh as it compared with the "barbaric" Irish.[61] Respectability not only made the Welsh equals of the English and their surrogates, the Americans, it was also an acceptable form of pride. Achieving middle-class status through hard work and self-discipline was, of course, a staple of American social mythology dating back to Puritan New England. Immigrant Welsh Calvinists cultivated yet another "culture of discipline" within American society, renewing in their particular localities the conviction that "striving, sobriety, and self-denial" were essential characteristics of Christian communities.[62]

Calvinists Incorporated

In our efforts to assess the ways in which persistent, localized immigrant cultures influenced American social and economic history,[63] we should remain alert to historical parallels as well as historical discontinuities. While new streams of immigrants brought fresh infusions of European culture to established ethnic settlements, some immigrant groups reinforced or gave a new impetus to cultural norms already well developed in American society.

The Welsh of Jackson/Gallia are best understood as a local example of the latter phenomenon. They created a local variant of puritanical Protestant culture which they understood to be consanguine with the foundations of American society but which also distinguished them as an ethnic group with particular values.

60. Edward P. Thompson, *The Making of the English Working Class* (New York: Vintage, 1963), esp. chap. 9; Paul E. Johnson, *A Shopkeeper's Millennium: Society and Revivals in Rochester, New York, 1815–1837* (New York: Hill & Wang, 1978).

61. Alan Conway, ed., *The Welsh in America: Letters from the Immigrants* (Minneapolis: University of Minnesota Press, 1961), chap. 1.

62. Innes, *Economic Culture*, 38.

63. See Kathleen Neils Conzen, "Mainstream and Side Channels: The Localization of Immigrant Cultures," *Journal of American Ethnic History* 11, no. 1 (1991): 5–20.

Their involvement with rural industrial capitalism demonstrates the extent to which culture could shape a community's response to economic change and the emerging forms of capitalism in their locality. In essence, their story is a study of transition and incorporation in three acts. Each of the three major points of transition for the Welsh Calvinists of Jackson/Gallia involved a confrontation between religious values and a choice for change. The first such confrontation was the decision to emigrate; the second, the decision to become engaged with charcoal iron; the third, the prolonged negotiation with the meaning and consequences of prosperity. Each transition produced a new social formation. The self-selecting process of emigration produced a community in Ohio of exceptional religiosity and social cohesiveness. The decision to organize Welsh charcoal iron furnaces created a new form of community corporation which became a model for a Welsh way of doing business, as well as internal tensions and perhaps schism within the community. The prosperity that followed influenced the formation of Welsh American ethnic identity. At each stage, change both incorporated values from the group's existing social and moral lexicon and brought the Welsh into a closer relationship with American society. To borrow Kathleen Neils Conzen's words, these steps were part of the long process of creating a localized, "immigrant-constructed culture" which embedded and reproduced itself "not only in the family, small group, and organizational relationships internal to the immigrant group," but also in economic relations conducted through particular kinds of business.[64]

Welsh Calvinists' strict moral code, with its emphasis on hard work, deferred gratification, and spiritual asceticism, predisposed them to do well in the American capitalist system, perhaps even to profit by it more quickly than immigrant groups with a less disciplined ethos. The knowledge of industry that some Welsh immigrants brought with them also contributed directly to the rapid development of industrial capitalism in the United States. If the immigrants from Mynydd Bach were latent capitalists, however, what prevented them from blossoming as investors, business people, and commercial farmers in Wales? Lack of capital is the main answer, for it was the immigrants' accumulation of capital resources in Ohio which made it possible for them to craft their community corporations. The structural and physical limitations of the rural Welsh economy were not solely responsible for the

64. Ibid., 6–7.

lack of economic initiative among Cardiganshire farmers, however. To the extent that Welsh Calvinism curbed individualism and reinforced the deeper, older conservatism of Welsh folk culture, it may have retarded both emigration from and economic development in rural Wales, in contrast to the effect of Calvinism on economic development in Holland and in Puritan England. The Welsh remind us that, historically, there was more than one kind of Protestant ethic, just as there was more than one spirit of capitalism.[65]

The debate over rural economic transformation has tended to analyze social structure and conflict in terms that set economy and culture in opposition to one another. We might find more examples of ways in which culture and economy reinforced one another if we look at places where capitalism developed in the absence of overt conflict, as indeed Christopher Clark demonstrated in his detailed study of economic development in western Massachusetts. It is also time to examine the influence of American capitalism upon rural immigrant culture and the extent to which immigrant culture imposed its own stamp upon the encounter. Many nineteenth-century immigrants came from deeply conservative, localized folk cultures in Europe and encountered a radically expanded range of economic opportunities in the United States. Processes of economic and cultural transformation were often dramatic and readily visible in their American settlements. This is not to say that the farming and industrial frontiers were a crucible in which immigrant cultures were destroyed, but rather that immigrants faced choices, whether of their own making or forced upon them, that accelerated decisions they might have been able to postpone in their home countries. They also may have reached quite different compromises with capitalism than those formed by American communities.

Rural Europeans' encounters with capitalism often began decades before they decided to emigrate to the United States. Internal migration to industrial and urban centers in their home country gave many Welsh people a taste of city life, wage labor, and undeniably capitalist economic relations. The decision to emigrate was itself a decisive first step toward a fundamentally new relationship with the capitalist system for Welsh people who had never before ventured outside their native region or owned their

---

65. The classic argument for Calvinism as a spur to economic activity is Weber, *The Protestant Ethic and the Spirit of Capitalism*. Tawney explains the rise of individualism in English Puritanism in *Rise of Capitalism*, chap. 4.

own land. In many respects, the whole range of Welsh migrants' experience was a prolonged encounter with capitalism, which registered in their economic behavior, in their attitudes toward their native and adopted countries, and in their ethnic identity. Simon Schama observed in his study of Dutch Calvinist culture that many societies have struggled with "the moral ambiguity of materialism" in their efforts "to patrol manners in the best interest of the safety of the community. But while the tensions of a capitalism that endeavored to make itself moral were the same whether in sixteenth-century Venice, seventeenth-century Amsterdam or eighteenth-century London, the social forms and vocabularies generated by them were particular to each community."[66] The same was true for immigrant communities in the nineteenth-century United States. The more we learn about the connections between economy and culture in those communities, the better we will understand the genealogies and cultures of American capitalism.[67]

---

66. Schama, *Embarrassment of Riches*, 49.

67. Keith Tribe, *Genealogies of Capitalism* (London: Macmillan, 1981); Alan Macfarlane, *The Culture of Capitalism* (London: Blackwell, 1987).

Appendix A
Occupations of Cardiganshire Natives in the Merthyr Tydfil Area, 1851
(as recorded in the British manuscript census)

Industrial, skilled

agent
archer
boilermaker
coal miner
coker
collier
contractor
drawing out in
  forge
engineer
finer
fireman
iron baller
iron filer

iron founder
iron heater
iron manufacturer
iron miner
iron roller
iron rougher
iron shearer
iron straightener
machine man
mill supervisor
miner
moulder
nail straightener
pattern maker

pit sinker
puddler
quarryman
rail dresser
rail filer
rail passer
rail presser
rail shearer
rail straightener
railman
shearer
smith in iron
  works

Industrial, unskilled

blocklayer
breaker of stone
brickfiller/brick-
  woman
burner of mine
carrier
cleaner of blast
  engine
cleaner of mine
coal discharger

coal layer
coal unloader
engine tender
filler
haulier
hitcher
hooker
iron keeper
iron layer
iron weigher

laborer
lander
limestone woman
metal breaker
mine worker
patchman/patcher
piler of iron
roadman
tipper

Nonindustrial crafts

blacksmith
boat construction
butcher

cabinetmaker
carpenter
cobbler/shoemaker

cooper
cordwainer
currier

Note: The chief reference for allocating census occupations to the categories here was Charles Tomlinson, ed., *Cyclopaedia of Useful Arts & Manufactures* (London: George Virtue, 1853), especially the entries on iron (pp. 67–95) and mining (pp. 271–88). Occupations are listed as they appear in the census.

horse farrier
hosier
hostler
joiner
knitter of
  stockings

mason
master craftsman
painter & glazier
plasterer
sadler
sawyer

smith
stone engraver
stone mason
tailor
wheelright

Service and retail

barber
bonnet maker
bookseller
brewer
charwoman
cleaner of chapel
coacher
cook
curate
doctor
draper
dressmaker
grocer

hawker
housekeeper (with
  lodgers)
innkeeper
laundress/washer-
  woman
milliner
minister
plumber
police
porter
publican

rector
rubbish tipper
school teacher/
  mistress
seamstress/sewing
servant
shop keeper
shop assistant
tallow melter
tea dealer
tinker/sells small
  things

Miscellaneous

agricultural laborer
domestic duties
  [housemaker]
door keeper
errand boy
farmer

housekeeper
house proprietor
hunter
navigator
pauper

rag dealer
scholar
shorewoman
visitor
working out

Appendix B
Jefferson Furnace Company Land Agreements

Sample deed between Welsh investors and the Jefferson Furnace Company

David P. Davis and Jane Davies
To Deed Jefferson Furnace Co

Know all men by these presents that we David P Davies and Jane Davies his wife of the County of Jackson and State of Ohio in consideration of the sum of Nine hundred and sixty dollars in hand paid by the Jefferson Furnace company of the same place have bargained and sold and do hereby grant bargain sell and convey unto David Edwards in trust for said Jefferson company their heirs and assigns forever the following premises situated in the County of Jackson in the State of Ohio and bounded and described as follows the west half of the north west quarter of section twenty two Township five (5) Range Eighteen (18) containing Eighty acres reserving one acre where the building stands on to have and to hold said premises with the appurtenances unto the said David Edwards in trust for the said Jefferson Furnace Company their heirs and assigns forever and the said David P Davies for himself and heirs doth hereby covenant with said David Edwards he is lawfully seized of the premises aforesaid that the premises are free and clear of all incumbrances whatsoever and that he will forever warrant and defend the same with the appurtenances unto the said David Edward in trust for said Jefferson Furnace Company their heirs and assigns against the lawful claims of all persons whomsoever In testimony whereof the said David P Davies and Jane Davies have hereunto set their hands and seals this 16th day of Jany in the year of our Lord one thousand and Eight hundred and fifty four

Executed in the presence of us

Isaac Jones	David T. Davies
T. L. Hughes	
John D. Davies	Jane ✕ Davies

State of Ohio Jackson County S.S.
Before said Thomas L. Hughes a Justice of the peace in and for
said County personally appear the above named David P. Davies
and acknowledged the signing and sealing of the above
conveyance to be his voluntary act and deed this 16th day of Jany

> Thomas L Hughes
> Justice of the peace

State of Ohio Jackson County S.S.
Before said Thomas T. Jones a Justice of the peace in and for said
County personally appeared the above named Jane Davies wife of
David P Davies and acknowledged the signing and sealing of the
above conveyance to be her voluntary act and deed and the said
Jane being examined by me separate and apart from her said
Husband and the contents of said Instrument made known to her
by me and she then declared that she did voluntarily sign seal and
acknowledge the same and that she is still satisfied therewith this
19th day of March AD 1855

Recd for record June 18th 1857   Thomas T. Jones
and recorded June 23rd 1857   Justice of the peace

[Jackson County deed book Q, p. 490]

Company agreement

Jefferson Furnace Co   Articles of agreement of Jefferson
    Agreement   Furnace Company we the subscribers
To members of   agree to abide by the following rules the
    said Furnace   Jefferson Furnace shall be named

I   the Jefferson Furnace Company and the firm the Jefferson
      Company

II   Evry Member of the Company owning land is to deed his
      land to the company at twelve dollars per acre reserving
      one acre where the Building stands on and also reserving
      the privelege of cultivating what land he has already
      cleared for his own personally benefit but not use any
      green Timber nor to hinder the Company at any time enter

III   the land that five hundred dollars is to be share of the
      Furnace and each 500 dollars subscribed and paid is to
      entitle the subscriber to one vote in the Election of officers

IV   and other affairs of the Company the majority vote of all
      the members of the Company present after due notice by
      the manager shall always rule in all the transactions of the
      Company the manager and Clerk to be Elected by Majority
V   vote to hold their office for one year but subject to be
      removed at any time by two thirds of the vote of the
      members present; no member of the said Company shall
      under no pretence make use of the Company name to raise
      money or goods except under direction of the Manager.
VI   No member of the Company shall sell any Shares without
      first giving the Company the refusal of the same
VII   Should any Member or Members of the Company be
      disposed to quarrel and interrupt the Business of the
      Company the Company shall have the privelege to compell
      such Member to sell his share or shares said shares to be
      valued by two disinterrested Men one to be chosen by the
      Company and one by the Members selling out and if said
      two Men fail to agree they shall chose a third person
VIII whose decision shall be final the books of the co shall be
      open for inspection for all the partners at any and all
      reasonable time and a balance sheet shall be made out at
      the expiration of each year showing the condition of said
IX   Company the Furnace shall be kept in operation by
      making iron year after year until all the Timber on lands
      deeded to the Company is exhausted then said lands shall
      be sold to the highest bidders for the mutual benefit of all
X   the different Members of the Company the Capital Stock of
      the Company shall be Sixty thousand dollars and to be
      paid in proportion to the Member [number] of Shares held
      by Each individual as follows one third the first of March
      1854 one third the first of June 1854 and the last third the
      first of September 1854 and in case of failure to pay within
      thirty days of said times the balance of the Company shall
      take the Stock of said delinquent by refunding to him the
      amount he shall have paid into said co up to that time the
      Latter parts of this clause refers to money Shares only that
XI   all lands purchased by the said Company shall be deeded
      or conveyed to David Edwards in trust for the Jefferson
      Furnace Company and it is further agreed that if at any
      time it shall become necessary for said Company to convey
      by deed or otherwise any parts of said Lands that the said
      David Edwards is hereby authorized and empowered with

the written concurrence of the Managers and Clerks of said co to convey by deed of general warrantee or otherwise

XII   any or all of said partnership lands the Manager and Clerk shall be empowered to give their written concurrence to convey by deed of general warranty or otherwise any or all of said partnership Ship lands by a Majority vote of all the Stockholders presents at the meeting after being duly notified by the Manager ten days previous to the time of

XIII   holding such meeting and it is further agreed that if at any time the said David Edwards shall sell his interest in said Company or if at any time the Majority of said Company shall desire it necessary to remove said David Edwards shall convey all the partnership lands belonging to said Company to such person as a Majority of said co may

XIV   designate for that purpose and it is further agreed that if the person holding the legal title of the lands belonging to the Jefferson Furnace Company shall die his place shall be immediately supplied by a Majority of said Company selecting some one of their own of members to fill such

XV   vacancy it shall be the duty of the Manager to preside at all meeting of the Company and it shall be the duty of Clerk to keep a book and record the transaction of each meeting therein which book shall at all times be open for inspection of the Stockholders the foregoing Rules may be altered or amended by a two thirds vote of the Company after due notice being given by the Manager of a meeting

XVI   for that purpose in case that the Company would deem it expedient to sell or trade of any part or parts of the lands deeded to the said Company the value of the improvements thereon must be appraised as directed in Article No. seven and the amount paid over to the late owner of the land

[Jackson County deed book Q, pp. 461-62]

Appendix C

Cân Newydd,
Ar Ddull o Ymddiddan rhwng yr ANESMWYTH a'r ESMWYTH;
sef y rhai sydd yn bwriadu cymmeryd eu Taith tu ag *America*, ag
eraill sydd yn boddloni Gwlad eu Genedigaeth.
—gan Thomas Francis, Vachongle [plwyf Nevern].

ANESMWYTH.

Ein ffryns, pa beth yw'r achos, na ddowch chwi bant ymhell
Oddi yma, lle mae'r prinder, i 'mofyn gwlad sy well?
Sef morio tu ag *America*, yr unig le sy'n llawn,
'Does yno ddim newynu, ein llwyr ddigoni a gawn.

ESMWYTH.

'Ry'm ni'n *resolfo* aros yn y gym'dogaeth hon,
Er dioddeu ambell 'storom, a'n taflu o donn i donn,
Ni brof'som yma ddaioni yn helaeth amser mawr,
Os yw hi'n awr yn dywyll, pwy wyr na thor y wawr?

ANESMWYTH.

Wlad hon sy'n cael ei bygwth a barn er's llawer dydd,
Trwy ryfel a thrwy newyn, mae pawb a'u bronnau'n brudd,
Os barn a ddaw trwy'r cleddeu, neu starfio yn ddistwr,
Bydd braf bod ni'n ddiangol yr ochr draw i'r dwr.

ESMWYTH.

Eich pechod chwi a ninnau yw'r achos yn ddiau,
O fod y fath galedi, nid ar y wlad mae'r bai;
Os ydych chwithau'n haeddu, er myn'd ymhell i fyw,
Y farn a'ch dilyn yno, nid ewch chwi o wyddfod Duw.

ANESMWYTH.

Onid aeth pechaduriaid i bant o'r parthau hyn?
Oe'n methu cael y barlys, 'nawr bwytta'r gwenith gwynn;
A chanddynt diroedd llydain, ac arian fwy na mwy,
Oedd yma mewn angenrhaid gael, *help* oddi wrth en plwy'.

ESMWYTH.

Do, do, fe aeth rhai ymaith o'u genedigaeth wlad,
I hela am yr elw sy heb iddo fawr barhad;
A fallai cael rhyw gyfoeth, dros 'chydig i'w fwynhau,
Os byw a marw'n aflan, mae'r cyfan er eu gwae.

ANESMWYTH.

O ddynion, dyn ddwli, mewn geiriau roesoch maes,
Oes dim i ddyn i ddewis, na cheisio dim ond gras,
Tra b'o ni ar y ddaear, mae'n rhaid cael pethau'r byd,
Ag onite ni starfwn, ni drengwn oll ynghyd.

ESMWYTH.

Nid y'm ni'n ammeu hynny, mae chwant ar bob dyn byw,
Ond trachwant sydd yn nafu a nychu dynol ryw,
'Nol iddynt gael eu digon, am ragor maent heb ffael,
A mentrant eu bywydau, mi goela am ei gael.

ANESMWYTH.

Yr oe'm ni'n dirgel ddirnad, mae ofn oedd arnoch chwi,
I fentro'r cefnfor garw, yn hoyw gyd â ni;
Pa ham mae'ch ffydd mor waned? 'run Gwr a all yn wir,
Eich cadw ar y tonnau yn fyw fel ar y tir.

ESMWYTH.

'Run Gwr sy'n cynnal pobl, yr ochr draw y donn,
Gall roddi prinder yno, 'run modd a'r ochr hon;
Am hynny gallwch aros yn llonydd yn eich man,
Efe sy'n trefnu'r cwbl, pa ham mae'ch ffydd mor wan?

ANESMWYTH.

Y farn sy'n ddigon amlwg yn nesu nos a dydd,
A chwant sydd ar ein calon, rhag iddi fyn'd yn rhydd;
Dihangodd *Lot* i *Zoar*, a'i ferched ganddo'n lân,
Cadd holl drigolion *Sodom* eu difa fawr a man.

ESMWYTH.

Da sydd i'r cyfiawn etto, gall beidio bod mewn braw,
Caiff yr hyn fo oreu iddo y byd hwn a'r byd a ddaw;
Ond chwi sy'n caru'r golud a byw mewn bywyd llawn,
Am gyfoeth ac anrhydedd, 'rhyn sydd niweidiol iawn.

ANESMWYTH.

Pwy ddrwg i Job wnaeth cyfoeth, ac amryw gyd ag ef?
Fu'n berchen golud lawer, sydd heddyw yn y Nef;
Pe caem ni ond yr hanner o dda a gafodd e',
Ni fyddem yn foddlongar, yn lân ym mhob rhyw le.

ESMWYTH.

I Job nid y'ch chwi debyg, a chredu hynny a wna,
'Roedd ef yn foddlon derbyn y drwg yr un modd a'r da;
A chwithau sydd yn grwgnach am brinder 'chydig bach,
Heb brofi fawr o eisiau, a chael eich cyrph yn iach.

ANESMWYTH.

Chwi ellwch siglo dwylo yn gryno â ni gyd,
Mae pawb am gael y goreu tra bo nhwy byw yn y byd;
Am hynny, 'rym ni'n 'madael, yn dawel ac yn dde',
'Nol i ni fyned ymaith, cewch chwithau fwy o le.

ESMWYTH.

Eich lle nid y'm ni am dano, chwi ellwch goelo'r gwir,
Gwell gennym i chwi aros yn y rhan hyn o'r tir;
Nid er ein mwyn 'rych chwithau'n ro'ch lle a myn'd i bant,
Ond am gael gwell bywioliaeth mwy helaeth, dyna'r chwant.

ANESMWYTH.

'Does i ni ond ffarwelo, rwi'n blino ar fath ble,
Ni hwyliwn i'r Gorllewin, yn llawen, dyna'r lle;
Mae yno bob rhinweddau, a ffrwythau afalau per,
Ni chlywsom well hanesion am wlad o dan y ser.

ESMWYTH.

Wel, rhwydd deb i chwi bellach, fyn'd i'ch bwriadol daith,
Ni cheisiwn mwy eich rhwystro fyn'd dros y moroedd maith;
Am f'allai draw mae'ch beddau, lle rhaid i'ch fyn'd ryw bryd,
I orwedd hyd yr alw ddaw godu'r meirw gyd.

Ac ni ddymunwn lwyddiant i chwi gael meddiant mawr,
Fel byddoch byw'n gysurus tra bo chwi ar ddaear lawr;
Ni roddwn hyn o gyngor yn rhagor i chwi heb gel,
Am geisio gras a'ch cadwo yn nydd y farn a ddel.

Mae brenin dychryniadau a'i gleddau ym mhob gwlad,
Yn symmud pob rhyw ddynion i'r byd sy o hir barhad;
O! am gael cwrdd ag angeu a'i golyn gwedi myn'd,
Pryd hynny gellwch alw ei enw ef yn ffrynd.

Os na chawn gwrdd ond hynny, yr ochr hon i'r bedd,
Gobeithio cyfarfyddwn yn hyfryd wlad yr hedd;
Le na bydd ofni 'madael, fel 'rym ni yma o hyd,
Ond caru a chlodfori Iachawdwr mawr y byd.

ANESMWYTH.

'Ry'm ninnau yn ddiolchgar, a dweud y gwir ar go'dd,
Dymunwn yr un daioni i chwithau yn ur modd;
Yn awr yr y'm ni'n 'madael, yn ddigon gwael ein gwedd,
A Duw a drugarhao, ffarwelwch bawb mewn hedd.

I. Evans, Argraphydd, Caerfyrddin
[Cyhoeddwyd *circa* 1800]

A New Song
In the form of a conversation between the Uneasy and
Comfortable; namely those who intend to take their Journey to
America, and those who are satisfied with the Land of their Birth.
—by Thomas Francis, Vachongle [Nevern parish]

UNEASY.

Our friends, what is the cause, that you won't come far away
From here, where there's scarcity, to seek a better land?
Namely, sail to America, the only bountiful place;
There is no starving there, we shall have our fill.

COMFORTABLE.

We are resolved to stay in this neighborhood,
Though suffering storms that toss us wave to wave,
We have experienced goodness for a long time here,
If it is dark now, who knows but that dawn won't break?

UNEASY.

This country's been threatened with judgment a long time now
By war and famine, everyone is sick at heart.
If judgment comes by the sword, or silent starvation,
It will be good that we've escaped to the other side of the sea.

COMFORTABLE.

Your sin and ours doubtless is the cause
For this kind of hardship, it is not the country's fault;
If you deserve it, though you go far away to live,
Judgment shall follow, you cannot escape all-knowing God.

UNEASY.

Have not sinners gone away from these parts?
Those who failed to get barley, now eat the white wheat,
And have extensive lands, and more and more money,
Who here were in need, getting help from our parish.

COMFORTABLE.

Yes, yes, some left their native land,
To chase after the profit that never lasts long,
And perhaps got some wealth, to enjoy for a while,
If living and dying unclean, all to their grief.

UNEASY.

O men, foolish man, in the words you have uttered
There is nothing for man to choose or try for but grace;

n this earth, we must have the things of this world,
we shall starve, we will all perish.

COMFORTABLE.

e do not doubt that all men want to live,
But greed wounds and vexes humankind;
Once they get enough, they want more without fail,
And venture their lives, you better believe it, to get it.

UNEASY.

We secretly knew that you were afraid
To venture onto the rough sea, gaily with us;
Why is your faith so weak? The same Man, it's true,
Can keep you alive on the waves as on the land.

COMFORTABLE.

The same Man who sustains folk this side of the wave
Can give scarcity there, in the same way as here;
Therefore you can stay contented where you are;
It is He who orders all, why is your faith so weak?

UNEASY.

It's clear enough the judgment is nearing night and day,
And desire is in our hearts, lest it should get loose;
Lot escaped to Zoar, his daughters pure with him,
All the inhabitants of Sodom destroyed, great and small.

COMFORTABLE.

Yet good comes to the just, he need have no fear,
The best in this world and in the world to come he will get;
But your love is for wealth and living a happy life,
You want riches and honor, which are very harmful.

UNEASY.

What evil did riches do Job, and many a one with him?
He owned great wealth, and is today in Heaven;
If we had only half the goods that he possessed,
We would be contented, pure in every way.

COMFORTABLE.

You are not like Job, and that I do believe;
He was willing to receive the bad with the good;
You are grumbling about a little bit of scarcity
Without tasting much of want, and having bodily health.

UNEASY.

You can shake hands with all of us together;
Everyone wants the best while they live in the world;
For that, we are leaving, quietly and rightly,
After we've gone away, you will have more room.

COMFORTABLE.

It's not your place we want, you can believe it's true.
We would rather you stayed in this part of the world;
Not for our sake are you making room and going away,
But to get a better, abundant living, that's your desire.

UNEASY.

Naught remains us but farewell; I'm tired of this plea;
We will sail to the West joyfully, that's the place;
All virtues are there, and the fruit of apples sweet;
We've not heard better of any country 'neath the stars.

COMFORTABLE.

Well, good luck to you, to go on your intended journey.
We'll try no more to stop you from crossing the mighty seas;
For perhaps your graves are yonder, where you must go sometime,
To lie until the call comes to raise all the dead.

And we wish you success in getting great possessions,
That you may live in comfort while on the earth below;
We give you this piece of advice freely,
To seek grace that may keep you in the judgment day to come.

The king of terrors and his swords are in every land,
Moving every kind of man to the world that is everlasting;
O! to meet with death, its sting already gone,
That you may then be able to call his name as friend.

If we do not meet 'till then, this side of the grave,
I hope we shall meet in the lovely land of peace,
Where we needn't fear parting, as we do here,
But love and praise the great Savior of the world.

UNEASY.

We are grateful, to tell you truthfully,
We wish the same good to you in the same way.
Now we are departing, our faces wan;
May God be merciful, farewell to all in peace.

I. Evans, Printer, Carmarthen
[Published circa 1800]   [translated by the author]

Appendix D
Welsh Immigrants to the Jackson/Gallia Settlement

The following table includes all Welsh settlers in the Jackson/
Gallia community for whom I was able to verify a place of origin
in Wales. Origins outside the Mynydd Bach study area are identified by county as well as locality, where possible. Most listings
also include the date of emigration ("E-date") and information
about other family members who migrated with the named individual or couple ("Family"). The table is organized by stem family, consisting of the head of household, spouse, and children,
and any other immediate family members who left Wales together. Relatives who followed later are listed separately. Where
parents and children parted ways after reaching the United States
and only one offspring settled in Jackson/Gallia, that individual is
listed under the "Immigrants" heading and his or her parents are
listed as family immigrants. Married couples are listed under the
husband's surname unless the wife remarried in the United States
and was known in Jackson/Gallia by her second married name.
The places listed under "Welsh home, parish, or county" apply
to the husband or the married couple; women's premarriage residences, where known, follow their names in parentheses.

While this table omits many details about individual migrants
and their families, it does indicate the importance of kinship and
geographical proximity to the processes of emigration and settlement which connected Mynydd Bach to Jackson and Gallia counties, Ohio, during the mid-nineteenth century. (Readers may find
it useful to consult maps 3.1 and 3.2 in the text to locate parishes
in the Mynydd Bach region and individual farms.) I hope this
appendix may also be of some assistance to family researchers
wishing to verify the origins of their ancestors in Wales and to locate them in British records.

Welsh Immigrants to the Jackson/Gallia Settlement

Immigrants	Family	E-date	Welsh home, parish, or county	Stops in United States
Alban, Alban & Mary Ann (nee Davies)	4 children incl. Thomas	1834	Tynygwndwn, Llanbadarn Trefeglwys; Gors-lwyd, Cilcennin	Welsh Hills, OH; Alban died 1846
Alban, Catherine	Siblings	1834–35	Pennant (?), Llanbadarn Trefeglwys (?)	Granville, OH
Alban, John & Mary (nee Morgan [Gors-ddalfa])	Siblings	1834	Tynygwndwn, Llanbadarn Trefeglwys	Newark, OH
Alban, Thomas & Ann (nee Morgan [Gors-ddalfa]	5 children, brother-in-law David Morgan (Tirddu, Llanbadarn Trefeglwys)	1835	Tynygwndwn and Pant-y-fallen, Llanbadarn Trefeglwys	David Morgan in Newark, OH
Alban, Thomas A.	Son Isaac (?)	1858	Perthi, Cilcennin	To Van Wert Co., OH in 1866
Bowen, William		by 1838	Llansamlet, Carmarthenshire	
Daniel, David & Elizabeth	Child Ann	1847	Blaenpennal	
David ("Deio'r Gof" [Dave the blacksmith])				
Davies, Daniel & Sarah (nee Davies [Ty'n-y-clawdd, Llangeitho])		1864	Pen-uwch, Nancwnlle or Llangeitho	
Davies, David	4 daughters (?)	1840	Llangwyryfon	
Davies, David & Sarah	Children Evan D., Mary	1847	Pengarn Uchaf and Nant-y-garth, Llanbadarn Trefeglwys	
Davies, David L.		1838	Nancwnlle	Cincinnati, OH, and Pittsburgh, PA

Name	Family/children	Date	Place	Destination
Davies, David T.		1839	Gilfach, Trefilan	
Davies, Evan O. & Mary (nee Jenkins)	Children David, Ann, Elizabeth, Thomas E.; Mary, Jenkin, Margaret born in USA	1841 or 1838	Ty'n-y-ffordd, Llanychaearn	Blossburg, PA; Paddy's Run, OH
Davies, Evan (Rev.) & Mary (nee Pugh)		1855	Ceinewydd (New Quay), Cardiganshire	
Davies, Hannah & Isaac		1837	Llan-non, Llansantffraid	
Davies, Jenkin		1838	Llangeitho	Died 1843
Davies, Joel		1851	Cardigan town, Cardiganshire	
Davies, John & Margaret S.	3 children incl. Mary S.	1840	Llanilar	
Davies, John & Mary (?)			Cae Cefnder, Llanbadarn Trefeglwys	
Davies, John		by 1837	Esgairsaeson, Blaenpennal	
Davies, John B. "Gof" (blacksmith) & Catherine	4 children	1838	Llangeitho	
Davies, John C. & Mary C.	Child John J.	1837–38	Cardiganshire	Pittsburgh, PA
Davies, John C. (Cooper) & Mary	Children Elizabeth, Evan, Jane	by 1817	Cardiganshire	Pittsburgh, PA; Delaware Co, OH
Davies, John D. & Mary (?)		1846	Llanychaearn	
Davies, John K.	His family	1842	Cae Cefnder, Llanbadarn Trefeglwys	

(Continued on next page)

(Appendix D—*Continued*) Immigrants	Family	E-date	Welsh home, parish, or county	Stops in United States
Davies, John Lot & Ann (Cwm-march or Gwrthgwynt Uchaf, Cilcennin)	Children John D., Lot	1841	Abermeurig, Gartheli; Merthyr Tydfil; Tan-yr-allt, Nancwnlle	Abermeurig, Gartheli; Merthyr Tydfil; Tan-yr-allt, Nancwnlle
Davies, John W. & Mary	Children Stephen J., David, Daniel	1849	Cardiganshire	
Davies, Lewis & Mariah (nee Evans [Esger-wen])	Children John, David	1818	Rhiwlas Uchaf, Cilcennin	
Davies, Morgan			Esgerfach, Llangwyryfon	
Davies, Owen & Eliza	4 children	1849	Llangwyryfon	
Davies, David (Rev.) & Mary (nee Jenkins)	6 children incl. Evan Ll., Peter S., David S., John S., Mary S.	1837	Tirgwyn and Brynawen, Llandysiliogogo (?)	Family to MN in 1856
Davies, Richard (Rev.)		1840–41 or 1837	Newtown, Montgomeryshire	Pomeroy, OH, ca. 1847; promoted emigration to MN; settled there in 1855
Davies, Thomas & Jane	Child John	1831	Licswm, Ysgeifiog, Denbighshire	John to Nebo, Scioto Co., in 1864
Davies, Thomas G.		1837	Llanychaearn	Pittsburgh, PA (Ledley Coal Co.); to Oak Hill with wife Gaynor in 1847
Davies, Thomas (Gareg Lwyd) & Mary	6 (?) children incl. Mary, David T.	1846	Brynwichell, Blaenpennal	
Davies, William & Margaret	Child Elizabeth D.	1849	Llanrhystud	

Name	Details	Date	Location	Destination
Davis, Ann	Father David Davis, 2 others	1849	Llansantffraid	Pittsburgh, PA
Davis, David	Followed parents, brother John David (Y Fron)	1858	Pyllau Duon, Llanbadarn Odwyn	Returned to Wales in 1860
Davis, David & Margaret	Children John, Jenkin	1841	Glan Rhos, Cilcennin	Pittsburgh, PA (coal mining)
Davis, Evan T. (Y Gweydd [weaver]) & Margaret (nee Davis [Pant-yr-esger])	Children Jane, Thomas	1847	Lletty-du-isaf, Betws Lleucu or Capel Betws	
Davis, Jenkin		1847	Moelfryn Mawr (?), Llanbadarn Trefeglwys	
Davis, John & Mary (nee Davis [Lluest-y-gors, Nancwnlle])	Children Stephen, David J. B., Thomas, Daniel J., Jane	1847	Y Fron, Llangeitho	
Davis, John & wife	Child John Davis, Saer (carpenter)	1847 (?)	Pant-yr-esger, Llangeitho	
Davis, John (G. or J.)			Ty'n-y-clawdd, Llangeitho	
Davis, Morgan		1847	Hafod Hir Uchaf, Llanbadarn Trefeglwys	
Davis, Stephen & Mary (nee Albans)	4 children	1836	Brysig Mawr, Llanbadarn Trefeglwys	
Davis, Thomas & Margaret (nee Evans [Penlan Fach])	5 children	1847	Pyllau Duon, Llanbadarn Odwyn	
Davis, Thomas P.	Parents John & Elizabeth Phillips	1840	Cardiganshire	
Edwards, Abraham (Sr.) & Ann	Soon joined by Abraham Jr., Y Ffeiriad (the priest)	by 1836	Llangeitho	

(Continued on next page)

Immigrants	Family	E-date	Welsh home, parish, or county	Stops in United States
Edwards, Daniel & Mary (nee Hughes [Glanbran])	Children Susan, Elizabeth, John D., Mary, Catherine, Jenkin, Daniel born in USA	1834–35	Brynele, Nancwnlle	Beulah, Cambria Co., PA
Edwards, David & Catherine	Children Evan, Edward, Mary; joined brother Abraham and parents, Abraham & Ann	1838	Blaen Trawsnant, Llanrhystud; Llangeitho	
Edwards, David & Margaret	Child Elizabeth	1837	Gelli-hir, Llangeitho (?)	
Edwards, David	Brother Thomas (?)	1835 (?)	Argoed, Llangwyryfon	
Edwards, David N. & Eleanor (nee Jones [Benglog] Evans)	6 children incl. Avarina	1835	Brynele, Nancwnlle	
Edwards, Edward & Mary (nee Lewis)	1 child; Richard born in USA	1838 or 1843–50	Cardiganshire	
Edwards, Edward & Gaynor	Child Thomas E. (?)		Blaenpennal	
Edwards, Elizabeth ("Aunt Betty")	Children Nathaniel, Daniel, Reese N., David C., Elizabeth, Margaret, Edward (?)	1865	Cross Winter, Llanbadarn Trefeglwys	
Edwards, Evan T. & Margaret (Deitws)		1838	Blaenplwyf, Llanychaearn (?)	
Edwards, Evan W. & Susan (nee Hughes)	Children Evan, Sarah, Nathaniel, Mary, Elizabeth, Margaret, Edward, John, Jane	1838	Brynele, Nancwnlle	

Edwards, Jenkin & Mary	Child Deborah (?)	by 1844	Pennant, Llanbadarn Trefeglwys	
Edwards, Lewis & Ann (?)	3 children	by 1849	Llanrhystud	
Edwards, Reese & Letitia	Children	1841	Meiarth, Nancwnlle	
Edwards, Thomas & Catherine	Child Margaret	1837	Grinle, Denbighshire	
Edwards, Thomas		1837	Cardiganshire	
Elias, Elizabeth & John (?)		1836	Penrhyndeudreath, Merionethshire	South Newcastle, Gallia Co., OH
Evans, Benjamin & Mary (nee Davies [Brynwichelll])		1846	Blaenpennal	
Evans, Dafydd "Teiliwr" (tailor) & Mary	Child Jane	1844	Tan-y-ffordd, Gartheli; Court Newydd, Capel Betws, Gwynfil	Newark, OH
Evans, David & Ann	Children Jenkin, David, Richard D.	1839	Blaen Waun, Cilcennin	
Evans, David & Hannah (nee Williams)	Children Ann G., Mary	1847–50	Lochtyn, Llangrannog, Cardiganshire	
Evans, David & Margaret	Children	1839	Ty Nant, Caron; Hafodwnog, Llansantffraid	
Evans, David		1847 (?)	Penlan Fach, Llanbadarn Odwyn	
Evans, David G. & Jane	Children Francis, Evan	1840	Llanddeiniol	
Evans, David J. & Margaret (Pensarn, Llansantffraid)	3 children	1841	Llansantffraid	
Evans, David (Y Wern) & Margaret (nee Davies [Bwlch-gwernen-fawr, Llanddewibrefi])	Children David, Joshua, Evan, Margaret Thomas, Daniel, Mary, Eleanor Morgan & families	1837	Caerllugest, Llangeitho; Gelli-llyn-du, Llanddewibrefi	

(Continued on next page)

Immigrants	Family	E-date	Welsh home, parish, or county	Stops in United States
Evans, Edward D. & Rachel (nee Phillips)	Children Rachel, Kate, Mary; Elizabeth born in USA	ca. 1849	Hafod Fawr, Nancwnlle	
Evans, Evan & Margaret	Child Margaret	by 1840	Soar, Cilcennin	
Evans, Evan & Mary	6 (?) children	1842	Y Banc (Pengarn Isaf), Llanbadarn Trefeglwys	Sugar Creek, PA
Evans, Evan E.		by 1853	Cardiganshire	
Evans, Evan J. & Mary	Children Elizabeth, Mary, John E., Evan, Edward, Ann, Jane, Margaret, James	1840	Gwarcaeau, Llangwyryfon	John E. in Cincinnati, OH
Evans, Evan "Settler" & Susanna (nee Jones [Tirbach])	Children Evan, David (?), sister Elizabeth	1818	Ty Mawr, Cilcennin	David settled in Apollo, PA, Elizabeth in Ebensburg, PA, and Dayton, OH
Evans, Evan "Soar" & Margaret (nee Richards)	Children	1840	Cwrt Newydd, Nancwnlle (?)	
Evans, Isaac & Mary	5 children incl. David	1850 or later	Ochr-y-coed, Betws Lleucu; Gorswgan, Llanilar	
Evans, Jane Morgan	Children	1849	Gors-ddalfa, Llanbadarn Trefeglwys	Died ca. 1850
Evans, John & Elizabeth		1839	Pen-y-banc, Llangwyryfon	
Evans, John		1838 or 1841–42	Bronnant, Lledrod	
Evans, John D. & Mary (nee Jones [Maenelyn])	Child Elizabeth	1850	Blaencarrog, Llanddeiniol	Pittsburgh, PA

Evans, John E. & Mary		1834–35	Rhydiol Uchaf (?), Nancwnlle	
Evans, John J.	Parents John & Mary	1849	Ty'n-y-cwm, Nancwnlle	
Evans, John R. & Elenor (Gwarcwm/Troed-y-rhiw)	Child Rowland H., in-laws (?)	1838	Rowland to Columbus, OH, in 1860; Johnstown, PA, in 1869; Hyde Park, PA, in 1874; Waukesha, WI, in 1878	Newark, OH
Evans, John ("Rock John") & Mary (nee Jones [Tirbach])	Children John J., Eleanor, William, Mary	1818	Penlanlas, Trefilan	
Evans, John W. (Rev.) & Mary (nee Williams [Bronyfrynwent])	Brother Morgan, parents (?)	1841	Tan——, Bronnant, Lledrod	Morgan drowned 1843
Evans, Joshua & Margaret (nee Evans [Y Wern, Llanddewi])	Child Mary	1837	Wern Uchaf, Llanddewibrefi or Llanio	
Evans, Lewis L. & Sarah (nee Jenkins)	Children John L. W., Owen L., Catherine (died at sea); sister Ann & husband David Jones, 2 children	1839	Rhyd-y-dorth (also Troed-yr-aur?), Llansantffraid	
Evans, Mary P. & Evan P.	(Blaenglaswood, Mynachlog-ddu, Pemb.)	ca. 1840	Merthyr Tydfil	Pittsburgh, PA
Evans, Moses & Mary		ca. 1850	Pantsiri, Caron	
Evans, Owen & Eleanor (nee James)	Children David O., William, Jane	1839–42	Llansantffraid	
Evans, Rebecca & husband (?)		by 1843	Llangwyryfon	
Evans, Richard & Rachel (Lluest-y-gors, Nancwnlle)		by 1846	Corgam Bach, Nancwnlle	

(Continued on next page)

Immigrants	Family	E-date	Welsh home, parish, or county	Stops in United States
Evans, Thomas & Margaret (?)	Children John, David, Margaret, Madalaine	1818	Cilcennin (?)	To Delaware Co., OH, in 1822
Evans, Thomas & Margaret		1833–34	Llansantffraid	
Evans, William & Ann	Children	1814–15	Cardiganshire	To Jackson/Gallia in 1834
Evans, William & Margaret (Midway, Llangwyryfon)			Blaenant-y-cadno, Carmarthenshire	PA; Coalport & Pomeroy, OH, for 10 years
Fowley, John & Anne (nee Daniel)		1832	Llansamlet, Glamorganshire	Carbondale, PA, 4.5 years; Salisbury, PA, 5 years
Griffiths, David & Elizabeth Hugh (Bety G.)	Child Jane	1838	Bron-yr-helem, Llanddewibrefi	Jane to Ironton, OH, in 1855–65; then to New Cambria, MO
Griffiths, Evan (Davies in Wales) & Jane (Bremelyn, Llangeitho)	Children Margaret, Mary	1837	Talfan, Trefilan; Corgam Mawr, Nancwnlle	To Ottawa, MN, in 1856
Herbert, John & Jane (Llwyngwyn/Tan-y-bwlch)	5 children	1838	Ynys Morgan; Llwyngwyn; Tan-y-bwlch (Tyn-y-bwlch?), Lledrod; Gwnnws Isaf	
Hopkins, Owen		1832	Ystradgynlais, Glamorganshire	Carbondale, PA, 4 years; Coalport, OH, 3 years
Hughes, Evan & Elizabeth	Child Anne	1839	Neuadd, Henfynyw	
Hughes, John & Anne (nee Williams or Phillips)	Children Lewis, David, John, Winnie (and Thomas J.?)	1838	Banc-yr-eithin, Bethania, Llanbadarn Trefeglwys; Pantybeddau, Llansantffraid	Sons David & John to MN in 1856–57

Name	Family	Date	Place	US Location
Hughes, Mary & Thomas		1846	Tan-yr-allt, Nancwnlle	
Hughes, Robert H.		by 1839	Chwilog Fawr, Eifionydd, Carnarvonshire	
Hughes, Thomas Llewelyn		1840	Ffynon Tudor, Llanelidan, Denbighshire	Cincinnati, OH; Covington, KY
Hughes, William & Anne	Children Mary, Anne, John, Evan; parents David & Margaret	1838	Pobty and Bryngwyn, Llanddeiniol	
Isaac, Evan & Ann	Children Thomas, Morgan, Margaret, Ann, Elizabeth & husband John Williams "Mason," children Evan, Sarah	1838	Gwarcaeau, Llangwyryfon	
Isaac, John & Mary	1 child	by 1844	Ty Newydd, Llangwyryfon	
Jenkins, David & Mary	Child Ann	1846	Ceinewydd (New Quay), Cardiganshire	Pittsburgh, PA
Jenkins, David T.		1836	Ty Nant, Llangwyryfon	Pittsburgh, PA
Jenkins, Elizabeth & Moses (?)	Children David, Thomas, Stephen, Hannah, Margaret (?)	by 1839	Llangeitho	
Jenkins, Evan & Elizabeth (Park-yr-ynn)	Children D. J., Edward J., John (?)	1837	Lluest-y-pwdel (?), Llanbadarn Odwyn (?)	
Jenkins, James & Jane	Children Catherine, David J.	1837	Pen-bryn-rhyg, Gwynfil	
Jenkins, John & wife	Children, incl. Margaret (?)	1849 (?)	Llangeitho (?)	Newark, OH
Jones, Catherine T. Jenkins	Parents James & Jane	1847	Pen-bryn-rhyg, Llanddewibrefi	

(Continued on next page)

Immigrants	Family	E-date	Welsh home, parish, or county	Stops in United States
Jones, Daniel & 1st wife Ann (nee Evans [Hafodwnog or Ty Nant])	Children	1839	Bryn Sesiwn, Llanrhystud	
Jones, Daniel W. & Jane (nee Roderick [Ffos-ddu])	Children incl. Thomas D.	1847	Ty Llwyd, Llangeitho	Pittsburgh, PA
Jones, David & Anne (Rhyd-y-dorth)	Children Mary, John D. W., David, Margaret; sister Ann	1838	Benglog, Llanddeiniol	
Jones, David & Mary		1842	Melin Pandy, Aberaeron	Pittsburgh, PA
Jones, David	Children Ann, David (?)	1839	Cwm-march, Cilcennin	
Jones, David D.		by 1820	Penbryn, Betws Lleucu	
Jones, David E. & Ann	Children incl. David D. (?)	1852	Penlanlas, Trefilan	
Jones, David E. & Ann (nee Thomas)	Children Mary, Ann	1847	Llangeitho.	Newark, OH
Jones, David E. & Elizabeth	Children David D., William E.	1841	Trallwng (Welshpool), Montgomeryshire	Newark, OH, ca. 1841–46; William E. to Ottawa, LeSueur Co., MN, in 1856; David D. to Big Woods, MN, in 1870
Jones, David (Palmon) & Margaret	Children Mary, Elizabeth, Sarah	1838	Palmon, Llanddeiniol	
Jones, David (Ship) & Ann (Llan-non)	Children Daniel, Eleanor, John, Mary	1836–37	Y Ship and/or Tirbach, Cilcennin	

Name	Children	Year	Place in Wales	Destination
Jones, Ebenezer E.	3 children incl. Jane	1844	Llandyrnog, Llangollen, Denbighshire	Cincinnati, OH
Jones, Elizabeth & Isaac T.	Children	1840	Llansantffraid	Pittsburgh, PA; Pomeroy, OH
Jones, Elizabeth & Richard (?)	Child Anne	1847	Troed-y-rhiw, Llansantffraid	Coalport, OH
Jones, Evan & Jane	Children Ann, Elizabeth	1840	Persondy, Rhostie	
Jones, Evan		1839	Caerdorth (Cadreuaf), Cilcennin	
Jones, Evan C. & Elizabeth		1838	Llanddeiniol	
Jones, Evan S. (Rev.) & Mary (nee Davies)	Child Mary	1839	Ffrwd Fach, Llangwyryfon	
Jones, Evan T. & Elizabeth (nee Ellis [Hendref])		1846	Tan-yr-allt, Blaenpennal	To MN in May 1856; settled in Sharon Twp., LeSueur Co., MN
Jones, Evan (Teiliwr [tailor]) & Jane	Child John	1840	Celynin, Towyn; Manchester; Capel Prion, Wrexham, Denbighshire	Cincinnati, OH
Jones, Hugh & Mary (nee Jones [Blaenperis, Llanrhystud])		1838	Capel Rhiwbwys, Llanrhystud	
Jones, Isaac (brother of John Jones, Ty'n Rhos) & Gwenllian (Cilfachreda, Llanarth)	Children David G. ("Cardy") John, William, Thomas I., Edward, Daniel (?)	1839	Cwm-march, Cilcennin; Gwrthgwynt Uchaf, Trefilan; Caegarn; Esger-wen; Drefach; Caegarn	
Jones, Isaac T. & Elizabeth (?) (Llansantffraid)		ca. 1840	Llansantffraid (?)	Pittsburgh, PA; Pomeroy, OH (?)

(Continued on next page)

Immigrants	Family	E-date	Welsh home, parish, or county	Stops in United States
Jones, J. Edward	Parents Edward E. & Elizabeth (Cerrigceinwen, Anglesey), sibling(s)	1831	Llanbadrig, Anglesey	Remsen (NY or OH?)
Jones, Jenkin & Catherine (nee Richards)		1840	Cilcennin (?)	
Jones, John D.	Parents Daniel & (?)	1846	Ty'n Rhos, Nancwnlle	
Jones, John E.		by 1837	Glangors, Nancwnlle	
Jones, John H.		1837, 1847	Tan-y-gors, Lledrod	Pittsburgh, PA; returned to Lledrod 1842; 1847 returned with wife Mary (nee Edwards) & sons; Mary died in 1848 (?)
Jones, John I. (J.?)		1836–37	Llwyn-bedw, Cardiganshire	Scout to MN in 1855; to Minneopa Creek, MN, in 1856 with wife Esther Jones, Cofadail
Jones, John P. & Ann (nee Lewis [Y Banc, Lledrod])	Child Jane A.	1850	Maesgwyn and Wain Gron, Llanilar	
Jones, John (saddler) & wife		1847	Pen-uwch (?), Nancwnlle or Llangeitho (?)	To Big Woods, MN, settlement
Jones, John Sisyllt & Margaret (nee Morgan)		1879	Sisyllt, Llangeitho	
Jones, John T.		by 1841	Bryn Garw, Lledrod	

Name	Children's families	Date	Place	Location/Notes
Jones, John & Eleanor (Tirbach/Ship)	Children's families (Mary [Jones] & John Evans, Susanna [Jones] & Evan Evans, Timothy & Jane	1818	Tirbach & Y Ship, Cilcennin	
Jones, John (Ty'n Rhos) & Elizabeth (nee Samuel [Bryngalem])	Children John J., Isaac (?)	1838	Cwm-march, Cilcennin; Ty'n Rhos, Nancwnlle	John J. to MN (and back?)
Jones, Joseph			Caermynydd, Nancwnlle	
Jones, Margaret E. & 1st husband Wm. Rees (Rice)	Children Mary, Elizabeth	1838	Elim, Llanddeiniol	
Jones, Margaret (nee Price) & 1st husband Evan Evans		1835	Llan-non, Llansantffraid	Columbus, OH
Jones, Margaret (nee Williams) & Thomas S.		ca. 1838	Bethania (?), Nancwnlle	Newark, OH
Jones, Morgan & Winifred	4 children incl. Evan	1847	Lluest Fach, Blaenpennal	
Jones, Rachel		by 1854	Pen-y-cae and Nant-y-glo, Monmouthshire	PA; married John T. Jones (see above)
Jones, Thomas J. (Cooper) & Elinor	3 children incl. Thomas J.	1847–48	Fron Felin, Llangeitho; Brynamlwg, Llangwyryfon; Llwynpiod; Pontbrencareg, Llangeitho or Caron; Cerrig Llwydion, Nancwnlle	Scout to MN, 1855; to Minneopa Creek, MN, in 1856; Thomas J., Jr., to Big Woods, MN
Jones, Thomas L. & Jane (nee Isaac [Gelli, Llangwyryfon])		1847–48	Elim (Gelli), Llanychaearn (?)	
Jones, Thomas M. & Jane			North Wales	Sandusky, OH

(Continued on next page)

Immigrants	Family	E-date	Welsh home, parish, or county	Stops in United States
Jones, Thomas M. & Jemima (Llanycrwys, Carmarthen)		1852	Penlanlas, Trefilan	
Jones, Thomas O. & Margaret	Children Daniel O., Mary (or Elizabeth?)	1840	Dolau Couon (Dolen Corris in obit.), Trefilan	
Jones, Thomas S. & Margaret		ca. 1838	Bethania, Nancwnlle (?)	Newark, OH
Jones, Thomas T. ("Agent") & Mary (or Jane) (nee Edwards [Tanlan; Fedw Fawr])	Children Ann, Thomas, David T., Ebenezer, Margaret	1837–38	Maesfelin Fach, Betws Bledrus; Fedw Fach, Betws Lleucu (?)	Pittsburgh, PA; Palmyra, OH; David T. to Van Wert Co., OH, in 1860
Jones, Thomas Y. (Yr Ynys) & 2d wife (nee Anne Jones [Penlon, Llansantffraid])	6 children (5 died at sea)	1840	Y Goitre, Llanrhystud; Sgrygos, Lledrod; Yr Ynys, Llanychaearn	Pittsburgh, PA
Jones, William & Ann	Child Mary	1849	Nant-y-llys, Caron	
Jones, William (Cofadail) & Mary	Children John D., Esther, Jane, William D.	1837	Ffos-y-bontbren, Llanilar; Cilfach cwd (Gilfachgoed?) and Cofadail, Llangwyryfon	
Lewis, David (Rev.)			Neuadd, Henfynyw; Llanidloes, Montgomeryshire	
Lewis, John R. & 1st wife Ann	4 children incl. Zillah	1829	Y Waen, Denbighshire	Pittsburgh, PA
Lewis, Morgan & Elizabeth (nee Hughes [Moelceris, Llanfihangel Genau'r Glyn])	Children incl. David M.		Penpompren, Llanddeiniol; Brynllys, Llangwyryfon (?); Tai Gwynion, Llansantffraid	
Lewis, Thomas & Margaret	Child John	1834–37	Llangwyryfon	John to Pomeroy, OH

Name	Family	Year	Location	Destination
Lewis, William & Sarah (nee Lewis [Llanilar])	Child Margaret D.	1835	Llanddeiniol; Bugeildy, Llangwyryfon	Granville, OH
Lloyd, Einion		1845–50	Llanarth, Cardiganshire	
Lloyd, James H. & Esther	Children incl. Elizabeth H.	1841	Llanarch, Cardiganshire	
Lloyd, Jane		1847	Pen-uwch (?), Nancwnlle or Llangeitho (?)	
Lloyd, John A. & Mary (nee Evans)	Children Mary, David A., John	1840	Llan-non, Llansantffraid	
Lloyd, Lewis & Jane	1 child (?)	1847	Llanddewibrefi	
Lloyd, Mary & Daniel	Children incl. Margaret D.	1847	Penbwlch Bach, Llansantffraid	
Lloyd, Mary & husband Evan (?)		1849	Llanbryn-mair, Montgomeryshire	Pittsburgh, PA
Lloyd, Mrs. (nee Richards) & husband	Children incl. John; siblings (?)	1840	Cilcennin	
Morgan, Catherine Isaac	Parents Isaac & Margaret Isaac		Tre'r Ddol, Cardiganshire	To California
Morgan, Daniel E. & Elinor (nee Morgan [Caegwyn])		1838	Caegwyn, Llanbadarn Odwyn	Coalport, OH
Morgan, David & Margaret	Children Margaret, John, Elizabeth	1841	Llangeitho; Tynllidiart (and Penderlwyn Goch) and Rhosmihirin, Gwnnws Isaf	
Morgan, David & Margaret (Lledrod)	Children	1850	Pen-y-gaer (?), Nancwnlle	
Morgan, David J.		1836	London; Cardiganshire (?)	

(Continued on next page)

Immigrants	Family	E-date	Welsh home, parish, or county	Stops in United States
Morgan, Evan	Parents George & Eleanor, siblings	1837	Cefn-yr-ynn, Llanbadarn Odwyn	To MN (?)
Morgan, Hugh & Mary	Child Jane		Penlan Owen, Llangwyryfon	Pittsburgh, PA
Morgan, Jenkin		after 1841	Esger-wen, Cilcennin	
Morgan, John D. & Margaret	Children Evan J., Catherine, Eleanor, David E., John F., Morgan J.; Margaret born in USA	1847–48	Gors-ddalfa, Llanbadarn Trefeglwys	
Morgan, John E. & Mary		by 1844	Cardiganshire (?)	
Morgan, Moses	Children David, Margaret	1840–41	Caegwyn, Llanbadarn Odwyn	
Morgan, Richard & Elizabeth (nee Jones [Cofadail])	3 children incl. David Ll.	1837 or 1829	Llangwyryfon (?)	Scout to MN in 1855; family to Cottonwood, MN; Richard & Elizabeth returned to Oak Hill
Morgan, Stephen D.		1840	Caemadog, Nancwnlle	Pomeroy, OH
Morgans, Elizabeth Davies		1840	Llan-non, Llansantffraid	Cincinnati, OH
Morgans, George & Eleanor (nee Evans [Y Wern])	Eleanor's father David Evans, children Margaret, Anne, Evan	1837	Cefn-yr-ynn, Llanbadarn Odwyn	
Morgans, Morgan & Jane (nee Edwards [Pant-y-rhew, Llangeitho])	Children Mary, Margaret, Daniel, John, Jane	1840	Ffos-yr-odyn, Blaenpennal	

Name		Year	Place of origin	Destination
Morris, Edward & Mary (nee Morris [Llanilar])		1837–38	Cefngraigwen, Llanychaearn	To MN in 1856; returned to Oak Hill
Morris, Evan & Hannah (Breconshire) (?)		1849	Tredegar, Monmouthshire	Pittsburgh, PA
Morris, Morris & Sarah (?)		1844	Cefngraigwen, Llanychaearn	
Owens, Evan	Children Daniel, Owen, Margaret, Diana, Jane	1840	Midway/Tycwrdd Wesley, border of Llanilar/Llangwyryfon/Rhostie	Margaret in Coalport, OH
Owens, Martha	Parents Evan & Mary, siblings	1842	Llwyn-y-gog; Ty Newydd, Llanbadarn Trefeglwys	
Parry, David & Mary (nee Jones)		ca. 1820		Pittsburgh, PA
Parry, Griffith & Jane (nee Evans [Caecwtta, Rhosybol])		1841	Gorslwyd, Rhosybol, Anglesey	
Parry, Thomas		by 1836	Denbighshire (?)	
Phillips, David & Margaret (nee Williams [Lluest Fach, Blaenpennal])		1838	Penlon, Blaenpennal	Pittsburgh, PA
Phillips, Lewis		1840	Llanerchgoch, Llanbadarn Odwyn	
Powell, William		1851	Twr Gwyn, Nancwnlle; Liverpool	Cincinnati, OH
Price, James & wife	3 children incl. Lewis	1840	Ffosyffin, Llanarth, Cardiganshire	
Price, John & wife	Children		Tredegar, Monmouthshire	
Price, John		by 1839	Hendre, Cardiganshire	Granville, OH

(Continued on next page)

Immigrants	Family	E-date	Welsh home, parish, or county	Stops in United States
Pugh, Evan & 2d wife Mary Williams		1854	Blaenplwyf, Llanychaearn; Aberaeron	
Rees, Charles & Elizabeth (nee Parry)	Children Charles, David, John, George, Elizabeth born in USA	by 1850		Pittsburgh, PA
Rees, Evan & Ann (nee Richards) (Nannie)	Children	1840	Pencnwc, Cilcennin	
Rees, William (Rice) & Margaret (nee Edwards)	Children Elizabeth, Mary	1838	Llanrhystud	
Rhydderch, John (Rev.)		1844	Llanelli, Carmarthenshire; Penycae (Ebbw Vale), Monmouthshire	To Pomeroy, OH, in 1851
Richard, David & Mary		1839	Penbryn, Betws Lleucu	
Richards, Ann (widow of John)	Children Thomas, Margaret Evans, Catherine Jones, Ann Rees & families	1840	Pencnwc, Cilcennin	
Richards, Daniel & Eleanor	Children Hannah, David, Margaret, Daniel, Gwinifred	1847	Penbryn, Betws Lleucu	
Richards, David & Jane	1 child	1847	Moelfryn Mawr, Llanbadarn Trefeglwys	
Richards, David D.		1847	Penbryn, Betws Lleucu	To Columbus, OH, to retire
Richards, Jacob			Merthyr Tydfil	Died 1863
Richards, Jane & Thomas	Children (?)	1839	Llansantffraid	

Name	Family	Date	Place	Notes
Richards, Thomas & Eleanor (nee Jones)	Child Daniel D.	by 1830	Cardiganshire	
Roderick, Thomas & Margaret (nee Thomas [Bryncroes])	Children William W., Mary, John, David, Thomas, Evan, Hannah	1837	Ty'n-y-mynydd, Lledrod	
Rosser, Elizabeth Jones	Parents John & Mary Jones	1818	Trefaes Uchaf, Llanbadarn Trefeglwys	Cincinnati, OH; Covington, KY (?)
Rowlands, John	Parents John R. & Magdalen	1880	Llangeitho	
Sam ——		1840	Blaencaron, Caron	
Shadrach, Evan & Jemima (nee Thomas [Godreudewi, Trelech])	Children	1840	Tewdraeth, Pembrokeshire; Pantgwyn; Nantyrafon, Trelech, Carmarthenshire	
Thomas, David & Jessedinah	3 children incl. Abraham, Elizabeth	1837–38	Pen-uwch, Nancwnlle or Blaenpennal, Lledrod (?)	
Thomas, David		1829	Cilcennin	
Thomas, Edward "Centerville"		by 1839	Llanidloes, Montgomeryshire	To MN in 1855
Thomas, Enoch & Margaret (Llangwyryfon)		by 1841	Carmarthenshire (?)	Cincinnati, OH; to MN (?)
Thomas, Evan D.	Mother Ellen (?)	1844	Newcastle Emlyn, Cardiganshire	
Thomas, John & Margaret (nee Evans [Y Wern])		1837	London; Llangeitho	
Thomas, John		1830–31	Cilcennin (?)	
Thomas, Margaret & Enoch (?)		by 1842	Llangwyryfon	
Thomas, Margaret (Mrs. Robert Williams)		1857	Cefnrhydcoed, Llanymddyfri, Carmarthenshire	

(Continued on next page)

Immigrants	Family	E-date	Welsh home, parish, or county	Stops in United States
Thomas, B. F. (Rev.)	Parents	1847	Llangeitho	Newark, OH
Thomas, Thomas & Ann	3 or 4 children	1841 or later	Trafel, Llanddeiniol	
Thomas, Thomas & Sarah (nee Rees [Rhaiadr, Lledrod])	Children Sarah, Margaret, Mary S., John, Thomas, Sophia, Rees	1838	Llettymoel, Rhostie, Cardiganshire	
Thomas, Thomas	Family	1843	Llanarth, Cardiganshire	
Thomas, William	Children incl. Catherine	by 1847	Carnarvon town, Carnarvonshire	
Thomas, William	None—stowaway			Pomeroy, OH
Thomas, William E. & Mary (Abergwili)		by 1855	Penycae and Rhymney, Monmouthshire	
Walters, John & Ursula	Children Margaret, John, Mary	1838–39	Pant-amlwg, Llanrhystud	To MN in 1856
Williams, David D.	Parents David & (?)	1838	Pantybeudy, Nancwnlle	
Williams, David Sr. & Catherine	Children David D., others?	1838	Cilerth, Llangeitho; Pantybeudy, Nancwnlle	
Williams, George D. & Hannah D. (Corgam, Llangrannog)	Children David, George, Benjamin G., William	1839	Henbant, Lledrod	
Williams, Mary		by 1855	Penyrheol, Glamorgan or Monmouthshire	
Williams, Morgan & Ann (nee Jones [Tanygors, Lledrod])		1838	Bronyfynwent, Lledrod	Pittsburgh, PA

Name	Origin	Year	Destination
Williams, Rees & wife	Llanwennog, Cardiganshire	1853	
Williams, Robert (Rev.) & Mary (nee Jones [Neuadd Cemmaes, Llanbadrig]) Cousins William & Parry Griffiths, David G. Williams (?)	Liverpool; Llandwrog, Carnarvonshire; Gorslwyd (Fawr?), Rhosybol and Amlwch, Anglesey; Dublin	1836	Cincinnati, OH
Williams, Thomas & Ann	Cardiganshire	1837	
Williams, Thomas & Sarah (nee Jones [Pen-yr-allt, Llangeitho])	Bwlch-y-ddwyallt, Llanbadarn Odwyn; Cwm-melyn, Llangeitho	1866 (?)	California ca. 1850
Williams, Thomas	Castell, Llanllywel, Breconshire; Nant-yr-arian, Maes Mynys, Breconshire	1832	Port Carbon, PA; Pittsburgh, PA
Williams, Thomas J. & Ann Children Daniel, Thomas J.	Carmarthenshire	1841	Pittsburgh, PA
Williams, William & Catherine Children Evan, Elenor Evans & family (?)	Penybont, Llanychaearn	1837 or 1840	Evan scout to MN in 1855; moved 1856 with 2d wife Mary Williams (Soar) to Minneopa Creek, MN
Williams, William & Margaret Children Morgan, Eleanor, Hannah, David, Ebenezer, Ann, Mary, Margaret, Thomas B.	Pantyfallen, Llanbadarn Trefeglwys	1818	To Delaware Co, OH in 1822

(Continued on next page)

(Appendix D—*Continued*)

Immigrants	Family	E-date	Welsh home, parish, or county	Stops in United States
Williams, William J. & Mary	5 children	1841	Ystrad Teilo, Llanrhystud	Pittsburgh, PA; Ebensburgh, PA; Johnstown, OH
Wynne, Abel		1837–40 (?)	Calch Hill (?), Denbighshire	Cincinnati, OH; Covington, KY
Wynne, David		1837 (?)	Calch Hill, Denbighshire	

Bibliography

Primary Documents and Government Records

Abstracts of title. Recorder of Deeds, Gallia County Courthouse, Gallipolis, Ohio.

Abstracts of title. Recorder of Deeds, Jackson County Courthouse, Jackson, Ohio.

Aberystwyth Borough Records. Aberystwyth Town Hall and National Library of Wales.

Calvinistic Methodist Archives. National Library of Wales.

Census of Great Britain. 1841, 1851, 1861, 1871, Enumerators' Returns. Public Record Office, London.

Census of Great Britain. 1851, *Population Tables*, pt. 1, vols. 1 & 2; pt. 2, vols. 1 & 2. London: Her Majesty's Printing Office, 1852 and 1854, respectively.

Gallia Furnace Company records. Vol. 125. Ohio Historical Society.

Hughes (Thomas and Family) Papers. 1855–1946. Ms. S101. Southern Minnesota Historical Center, Mankato State University.

Jefferson Furnace Company records. Vol. 489. Ohio Historical Society.

Kimball & James' Business Directory, for the Mississippi Valley: 1844. Cincinnati: Kendall & Bernard, 1844. State Historical Society of Wisconsin microfiche no. 721, pp. 223–311.

Material relating to John Jones, Talsarn. Ms. 12788C. National Library of Wales.

Madison Furnace Company Collection. Vol. 161. Ohio Historical Society.

Minnesota State manuscript census. 1857. Minnesota Historical Society.

North Cardiganshire Presbytery Records. National Library of Wales.

Official Roster of the Soldiers of the State of Ohio in the War of the Rebellion, 1861–1866, compiled under the direction of the Roster Commission. Vol. 9. Cincinnati: Ohio Valley Press, 1889.

Ohio State Board of Equalization. *Proceedings of the State Board of Equalization*, 7 November 1859. Columbus, Ohio: 1860.

Portsmouth City Directory and Advertiser. Portsmouth, Ohio: Printed in the Republican Office for sale by J. Stephenson and A. C. Post, 1856.

Post Office London Directory. Vol. 2 (1841).

Post Office London Directory 1851. Vol. 3 (1851).

R. G. Dun & Company Collection. Baker Library, Harvard University Graduate School of Business Administration.

Roberts and Evans Collection/Cardiganshire Land Tax Assessments. 1830. National Library of Wales.

Ship manifests for the *Orpheus* (1840) and *Oseola* (1838). State Historical Society of Wisconsin microfilm, reels P77–903 *(Orpheus)*, P77–898 *(Oseola)*.

Wilbur Stout Collection. Vol. 408. Ohio Historical Society.

Tithe apportionment schedules and maps of Cardiganshire parishes. National Library of Wales.

Tithe files. Mss. IR/18. Public Record Office, Kew.

U.S. Bureau of the Census. *Historical Statistics of the United States from Colonial Times to 1957*. Washington, 1960.

U.S. Bureau of the Census. *The Seventh Census of the United States: 1850*. Washington: Robert Armstrong, Public Printer, 1853.

U.S. Bureau of the Census. *Twelfth Census of the United States, 1900*. Washington: U.S. Government Printing Office, 1900.

U.S. manuscript census. 1840, 1850, 1860, 1870, 1880. State Historical Society of Wisconsin and Ohio Historical Society.

Atlases and Maps

British Geological Survey. "Llanilar: Solid and Drift" (scale 1:50,000). England and Wales Sheet 178, 1994.

Carter, Harold C., ed. *National Atlas of Wales*. Cardiff: University of Wales Press, 1988.

Clout, Hugh, ed. *The Times London History Atlas*. New York: Harper Collins, 1991.

Edwards, Roland L. "The Jackson and Gallia Circuit of Welsh Calvinistic Methodist Churches." Undated manuscript map, courtesy the author.

"Ethnic Background: 1880, Resident Rural Landowners, Blue Earth County, Minnesota." Sheet map (1.35 mm to the mile). Mary T. Dooley, Phil Kelley, and Perry Wood, project directors. Bureau of Planning and Cartographic Services, Geography Department, Mankato State University, n.d.

Griffith, William, Jr. *Illustrated Atlas of Gallia County, Ohio*. Cincinnati: Strobridge & Co., 1874. Reprint, Athens, Ohio: Don F. Stout and Emmett A. Conway, 1976.

Lake, D. J. *Atlas of Jackson County*. Philadelphia: Titus, Simmons & Titus, 1875. Reprint, Oak Hill, Ohio: Welsh-American Heritage Museum, 1975.

Lewis, W. J. *Ceredigion: Atlas Hanesyddol* (Cardiganshire: An Historical Atlas). Aberystwyth: Cyngor Sir Ceredigion, 1955.

Ministry of Town and Country Planning for the Ordnance Survey, comp. "Rainfall, Annual Average, 1881–1915" (scale 1:625,000). Great Britain Sheet 2, 1949.

Ordnance Survey, Pathfinder series (scale 1:25,000), various dates.

Soil Survey of England and Wales. "Llanilar," sheet 178 (scale 1:63,360), 1969.

Soil Survey of England and Wales. "Soils of Wales" (scale 1:250,000), 1983.

U.S. Geological Survey, quadrangles for Ohio (scale 1:24,000), various dates.

Books

Allen, James Paul, and Eugene James Turner. *We the People: An Atlas of America's Ethnic Diversity*. New York: Macmillan, 1988.

Anderson, Michael. *Family Structure in Nineteenth-Century Lancashire*. Cambridge: Cambridge University Press, 1971.

Avery, B. W. *Soil Classification for England and Wales*. Harpenden: Soil Survey, 1980.

Bailyn, Bernard. *Voyagers to the West: A Passage in the Peopling of America on the Eve of the Revolution*. New York: Vintage Books, 1986.

Baines, Dudley. *Migration in a Mature Economy: Emigration and Internal Migration in England and Wales, 1861–1900*. Cambridge: Cambridge University Press, 1985.

Baldwin, Leland D. *Pittsburgh: The Story of a City, 1750–1865*. 1937. Reprint, Pittsburgh: University of Pittsburgh Press, 1981.

Bassett, T. M. *The Welsh Baptists*. Swansea: Ilston House, 1977.

Bebb, W. Ambrose. *Dial y Tir* (The Land's Revenge). Llandybïe: Llyfrau'r Dryw, 1945.

Bick, David, and Philip Wyn Davies. *Lewis Morris and the Cardiganshire Mines*. Aberystwyth: National Library of Wales, 1994.

Bodnar, John. *The Transplanted: A History of Immigrants in Urban America*. Bloomington: Indiana University Press, 1985.

Boon, George C. *Cardiganshire Silver and the Aberystwyth Mint in Peace and War*. Cardiff: National Museum of Wales, 1981.

Borrow, George. *Wild Wales: The People, Language, and Scenery*. London: J. M. Dent & Sons, 1906.

Bowen, Ivor. *The Great Enclosures of Common Lands in Wales*. London: Chiswich Press, 1914.

Braudel, Fernand. *The Wheels of Commerce*. Vol. 2 of *Civilization and Capitalism, Fifteenth–Eighteenth Century*, trans. Sian Reynolds. New York: Harper & Row, Perennial Library edition, 1986.

Carlyle, G. E., and D. D. Davis, eds. *History of the Pioneer Men and Plants in Southern Ohio, Kentucky, and Oak Hill Fire Brick Districts*. Privately published, 1948.

Carr, Margaret Williams. *The Descendants and Ancestors of the Williams, Crane, Herbert Families*. Privately published, 1992.

Carter, Harold, and Sandra Wheatley. *Merthyr Tydfil in 1851: A Study in the Spatial Structure of a Welsh Industrial Town*. University of Wales Board of Celtic Studies, Social Science Monograph no. 7. Cardiff: University of Wales Press, 1982.

Carter, Kate B., comp. *The Welsh in Utah*. N.p.: Daughters of Utah Pioneers, Central Company, Lessons for October 1949.

Chapman, John. *A Guide to Parliamentary Enclosures*. Cardiff: University of Wales Press, 1992.

Chidlaw, Rev. Benjamin W. *The Story of My Life*. Privately published by the author, 1890.

Clark, Christopher. *The Roots of Rural Capitalism: Western Massachusetts, 1780–1860*. Ithaca: Cornell University Press, 1990.

Conway, Alan, ed. *The Welsh in America: Letters from the Immigrants*. Minneapolis: University of Minnesota Press, 1961.

Conzen, Kathleen Neils. *Making Their Own America: Assimilation Theory and the German Peasant Farmer*. German Historical Institute Lecture no. 3. New York: Berg Publishers, 1990.

Coombes, B. L. *These Poor Hands: The Autobiography of a Miner Working in South Wales*. London: Victor Gollancz, 1939.

Curtis, L. F., F. M. Courtney, and S. T. Trudgill, *Soils in the British Isles*. London: Longman, 1976.

Cymry Llundain Ddoe a Heddiw (The Welsh of London Yesterday and Today). London: Undeb Cymdeithasau Diwylliannol Cymraeg, 1956.

Davies, Hywel M. *Transatlantic Brethren: Rev. Samuel Jones (1735–1814) and His Friends, Baptists in Wales, Pennsylvania, and Beyond*. Lehigh: Lehigh University Press, 1995.

Davies, John. *A History of Wales*. London: Allen Lane/Penguin, 1993. Welsh original: *Hanes Cymru*. London: Penguin, 1990.

Davies, Llywelyn [?]. *Hanes Môr-Daith y Brig Albion, Aberteifi, (Llywelyn Davies, Llywydd), gyda Mudolion (Emigrants) &c. o Gaernarfon, i Ogledd America* (Story of the Sea-Voyage of the Brig Albion, Cardigan [Llywelyn Davies, Captain], with Emigrants & etc., from Carnarvon, to North America). Carnarvon: Peter Evans, 1820.

Davies, Martin. *Traditional Qualities of the West Wales Cottage*. Llandysul: Crown Print, 1991.

Davis, Evan E. *Industrial History, Oak Hill, Ohio*. 2d ed. Portsmouth: Compton Printing, 1980.

Davis, Evan E., ed. *Our Heritage: Early History of Tyn Rhos Welsh Congregational Church and Its Neighborhood*. Oak Hill, Ohio: Privately published, 1979.

Dennis, Ronald D. *The Call of Zion: The Story of the First Welsh Mormon Emigration*. Provo, Utah: Brigham Young University Press, 1987.

Dodd, Arthur H. *The Character of Early Welsh Emigration to the United States*, 2d ed. Cardiff: University of Wales Press, 1956.

Dodd, Arthur H. *The Industrial Revolution in North Wales*, 3d ed. Cardiff: University of Wales Press, 1971.

Eames, Aled. *Ships and Seamen of Anglesey, 1558–1918*. London: National Maritime Museum, Modern Maritime Classics reprint no. 4, 1981.

Edwards, Hywel Teifi. *Arwr Glew Erwau'r Glo: Delwedd y Glowr yn Llenyddiaeth y Gymraeg, 1850–1950* (Brave Hero of the Coal Fields:

The Image of the Miner in Welsh Literature, 1850–1950). Llandysul: Gwasg Gomer, 1994.

Edwards, Rev. E. *Byr Hanes am Blwyf Nantcwnlle* (A Brief History of Nantcwnlle Parish). Privately published, 1930.

Edwards, Roland L., ed. and comp. *Moriah, 1835–1985: 150 Years of Service.* Privately published, 1985.

Elsas, Madeleine, ed. *Iron in the Making: Dowlais Iron Company Letters, 1782–1860.* Cardiff: Glamorgan County Council, 1960.

Evans, Chris. *"The Labyrinth of Flames": Work and Social Conflict in Early Industrial Merthyr Tydfil.* Cardiff: University of Wales Press, 1993.

Evans, David. *Adgofion yr Hybarch David Evans, Archddiacon Llanelwy* (Memoirs of the Right Reverend David Evans, Archdeacon of Llanelwy). Lampeter: Gwasg Eglwysig Gymreig, 1904.

Evans, Rev. John. *Hanes Methodistiaeth Rhan Ddeheuol Sir Aberteifi o Ddechreuad y "Diwygiad Methodistaidd" yn 1735 hyd 1900* (The History of Methodism in Southern Cardiganshire from the Beginning of the "Methodist Revival" in 1735 to 1900). Dolgellau: E. W. Evans, 1904.

Evans, Rev. Joseph. *Biographical Dictionary of Ministers and Preachers of the Welsh Calvinistic Methodist Body.* Carnarvon: D. O'Brien Owen, 1907.

Evans, Rev. William R. *Sefydliadau Cymreig Jackson a Gallia, Ohio.* Utica, N.Y.: T. J. Griffiths, 1896. Translated by Phillips G. Davies as *History of Welsh Settlements in Jackson and Gallia Counties of Ohio,* ed. Lillian Thomas Brownfield. Columbus, Ohio: Chatham Communicators, 1988.

Evans, Silas, ed. *The Memoirs of the Rev. R. H. Evans.* Kansas City, Mo., 1908.

Francis-Jones, Gwyneth. *Cows, Cardis, and Cockneys.* Borth, Dyfed: Privately published, 1984.

Gallia County Historical Society. *Gallia County, Ohio: People in History to 1980.* Paoli, Pa.: Taylor Publishing Co., 1980.

Gjerde, Jon. *From Peasants to Farmers: The Migration from Balestrand, Norway, to the Upper Middle West.* Cambridge: Cambridge University Press, 1985.

Gomme, George Laurence. *London in the Reign of Victoria.* Chicago: Herbert S. Stone, 1898.

Gould, Peter, and Rodney White. *Mental Maps.* 2d ed. Boston: Allen & Unwin, 1986.

Grinberg, Leon, and Rebeca Grinberg. *Psychoanalytic Perspectives on Migration and Exile.* Trans. Nancy Festinger. New Haven: Yale University Press, 1989.

Hahn, Steven, and Jonathan Prude, eds. *The Countryside in the Age of Capitalist Transformation: Essays in the Social History of Rural America.* Chapel Hill: University of North Carolina Press, 1985.

Handlin, Oscar. *The Uprooted.* 2d ed. Boston: Atlantic Monthly Press, 1973. Orig. ed., Boston: Little, Brown, 1951.

Hartley, E. N. *Iron Works on the Saugus: The Lynn and Braintree Ventures of the Company of Undertakers of the Ironworks in New England*. Norman: University of Oklahoma Press, 1957.

Hartmann, Edward G. *Americans from Wales*. New York: Octagon Books, 1983.

Hartz, Louis. *The Founding of New Societies*. New York: Harcourt, Brace, & World, 1964.

Hatch, Nathan O. *The Democratization of American Christianity*. New Haven: Yale University Press, 1989.

The History, Constitution, Rules of Discipline, and Confession of Faith, of the Calvinistic Methodists, in Wales. 3d ed. Mold: H. & O. Jones, 1840.

History of Gallia County. Chicago: H. H. Hardesty & Co., 1882.

History of the Lower Scioto Valley, Ohio. Chicago: Inter State Publishing Co., 1884. Reproduced by the Scioto County Genealogical Society, Portsmouth, Ohio. Mt. Vernon, Ind.: Windmill Pubs., 1990.

Hoppe, Göran, and John Langton. *Flows of Labour in the Early Phase of Capitalist Development: The Time-Geography of Longitudinal Migration Paths in Nineteenth-Century Sweden*. Historical Geography Research Series no. 29. London: Institute of British Geographers, 1992.

Hoppe, Göran, and John Langton. *Peasantry to Capitalism: Western Ostergotland in the Nineteenth Century*. Cambridge: Cambridge University Press, 1994.

Howell, David. *Land and People in Nineteenth-Century Wales*. London: Routledge & Kegan Paul, 1978.

Howell, David W. *Patriarchs and Parasites: The Gentry of South-West Wales in the Eighteenth Century*. Cardiff: University of Wales Press, 1986.

Hughes, Philip Gwyn. *Wales and the Drovers*. 1943. Reprint, Carmarthen: Golden Grove Editions, 1988.

Hughes, Rev. Thomas E., et al., eds. *History of the Welsh in Minnesota, [and in] Foreston and Lime Springs, Iowa*. Privately published, in Welsh and English, 1895.

Innes, Stephen. *Creating the Commonwealth: The Economic Culture of Puritan New England*. New York: W. W. Norton, 1995.

Jackson County Genealogical Society. *Jackson County, Ohio, History and Families, 1816–1991*. Paducah, Ky.: Turner Publishing Co., 1991.

Jenkins, Dan, ed. *Cerddi Ysgol Llanycrwys* (Poems of Llanycrwys School). Llandysul: Gwasg Gomer, 1934.

Jenkins, David. *The Agricultural Community in South-West Wales at the Turn of the Twentieth Century*. Cardiff: University of Wales Press, 1971.

Jenkins, Evan. *Cerddi Ffair Rhos* (Poems of Ffair Rhos). Aberystwyth: Gwasg Aberystwyth, 1959.

Jenkins, Geraint H. *The Foundations of Modern Wales: Wales 1642–1780*. Vol. 4 in *History of Wales*. Oxford: Clarendon Press, 1987.

Jenkins, J. Geraint. *Maritime Heritage: The Ships and Seamen of Southern Ceredigion*. Llandysul: Gomer Press, 1982.

Jenkins, J. Geraint. *The Welsh Woollen Industry*. Cardiff: National Museum of Wales, 1969.

Jenkins, Jenkin. *Hanes Unwaith am Siencyn Ddwywaith* (The Singular History of Jenkin Jenkins). Utica, N.Y.: T. J. Griffiths, 1872.

John, Arthur H. *The Industrial Development of South Wales, 1750–1850*. Cardiff: University of Wales Press, 1950.

Johnson, Paul E. *A Shopkeeper's Millenium: Society and Revivals in Rochester, New York, 1815–1837*. New York: Hill & Wang, 1978.

Jones, Anthony. *Welsh Chapels*. rev. ed. Phoenix Mill: Alan Sutton, Pub., in association with National Museums and Galleries of Wales, 1996.

Jones, Evan. *Y Mynydd Bach a Bro Eiddwen* (Mynydd Bach and the Eiddwen Neighborhood). Aberystwyth: Cymdeithas Lyfrau Ceredigion, 1990.

Jones, John Rees. *Sôn am y Bont* (Speaking of Pontrhydfendigaid). Ed. E. D. Evans. Llandysul: Gwasg Gomer, 1974.

Jones, Philip N. *Mines, Migrants, and Residence in the South Wales Steamcoal Valleys: The Ogmore and Garw Valleys in 1881*. Occasional Paper in Geography, no. 25. Hull: Hull University Press, 1987.

Jones, William D. *Wales in America: Scranton and the Welsh, 1860–1920*. Cardiff: University of Wales Press, 1993.

Jones-Edwards, W. *Ar Lethrau Ffair Rhos* (On the Slopes of Ffair Rhos). Aberystwyth: Cymdeithas Lyfrau Ceredigion, 1963.

Jordan, Terry G. *German Seed in Texas Soil*. Austin: University of Texas Press, 1966.

Kamphoefner, Walter D. *The Westfalians: From Germany to Missouri*. Princeton: Princeton University Press, 1987.

Kulikoff, Allan. *The Agrarian Origins of American Capitalism*. Charlottesville: University Press of Virginia, 1992.

Langton, John, and R. J. Morris, eds. *Atlas of Industrializing Britain, 1780–1914*. London: Methuen, 1986.

Lawton, Richard, and Colin G. Pooley. *Britain 1740–1950: An Historical Geography*. London: Edward Arnold, 1992.

Lees, Lynn Hollen. *Exiles of Erin: Irish Migrants in Victorian London*. Ithaca, N.Y.: Cornell University Press, 1979.

Leigh's Guide to Wales and Monmouthshire. London: M. A. Leigh, 1833.

Lesley, J. P. *The Iron Manufacturers Guide to the Furnaces, Forges, and Rolling Mills of the United States*. New York: John Wiley, 1859.

Lewis, W. J. *Lead Mining in Wales*. Cardiff: University of Wales Press, 1967.

Lucassen, Jan. *Migrant Labour in Europe 1600–1900: The Drift to the North Sea*. Trans. Donald A. Bloch. London: Croom Helm, 1987.

Macfarlane, Alan. *The Culture of Capitalism*. London: Blackwell, 1987.

McQuillan, D. Aiden. *Prevailing over Time: Ethnic Adjustment on the*

Kansas Prairies, 1875–1925. Lincoln: University of Nebraska Press, 1990.

Mingay, G. E. *Land and Society in England, 1750–1980*. London: Longman, 1994.

[Moore-]Colyer, Richard J. *The Welsh Cattle Drovers: Agriculture and the Welsh Cattle Trade Before and During the Nineteenth Century*. Cardiff: University of Wales Press, 1976.

Moore-Colyer, Richard J., ed. *A Land of Pure Delight: Selections from the Letters of Thomas Johnes of Hafod, Cardiganshire (1748–1816)*. Llandysul: Gwasg Gomer, 1992.

Morawska, Ewa. *For Bread with Butter: The Life-Worlds of East Central Europeans in Johnstown, Pennsylvania, 1890–1940*. Cambridge: Cambridge University Press, 1985.

Morgan, D. Densil. *Christmas Evans a'r Ymneilltuaeth Newydd* (Christmas Evans and the New Nonconformity). Llandysul: Gwasg Gomer, 1991.

Morgan, Derec Llwyd. *Y Diwygiad Mawr* (The Great Revival). Llandysul: Gwasg Gomer, 1981. Translated by Dyfnallt Morgan as *The Great Awakening in Wales*. London: Epworth Press, 1988.

Morrow, Frank C., comp. and ed. *A History of Industry in Jackson County, Ohio*. Wellston, Ohio, 1956.

Norris, James D. *Frontier Iron: The Maramec Iron Works, 1826–1876*. Madison: State Historical Society of Wisconsin, 1964.

Oliver, David, comp. *Index to the Register of Births and Baptisms of the Welsh Chapel of the Calvinistic Methodist Denomination at Wilderness Row, Clerkenwell, in the Parish of St. John, afterwards at Jewin Crescent . . .*, transcribed from Public Record Office RG4/4400. London: London Branch, Welsh Family History Societies, 1995.

Ostergren, Robert C. *A Community Transplanted: The Trans-Atlantic Experience of a Swedish Immigrant Settlement in the Upper Middle West, 1835–1915*. Madison: University of Wisconsin Press, 1988.

Ostergren, Robert C. *Patterns of Seasonal Industrial Labor Recruitment in a Nineteenth-Century Swedish Parish: The Case of Matfors and Tuna, 1846–1873*. Report no. 5 from the Demographic Data Base. Umeå, Sweden: Umeå University, 1989.

Owen, Meurig. *Tros Y Bont: Hanes Eglwysi Falmouth Road, Deptford a Parson's Hill, Woolwich, Llundain* (Over the Bridge: A History of the Churches of Falmouth Road, Deptford and Parson's Hill, Woolwich, London). London: Eglwys Jewin, 1989.

Parry, Jonathan, and Maurice Bloch, eds. *Money and the Morality of Exchange*. Cambridge: Cambridge University Press, 1989.

Parry, Mary. *Cofiant y Parch. Robert Williams, Moriah, Ohio* (Biography of Rev. Robert Williams, Moriah, Ohio). Utica, N.Y.: T. J. Griffiths, 1883.

Paskoff, Paul F. *Industrial Evolution: Organization, Structure, and Growth of the Pennsylvania Iron Industry, 1750–1860.* Baltimore: Johns Hopkins University Press, 1983.

Phillips, Richard. *Dyn a'i Wreiddiau: Peth o Hanes Plwyf Llangwyryfon* (Man and His Roots: Some of the History of Llangwyryfon Parish). Privately published by the author, 1975.

Redford, Arthur. *Labour Migration in England, 1800–1850.* 2d ed. Ed. and rev. W. H. Chaloner. Manchester: Manchester University Press, 1964.

Rees, Alwyn D. *Life in a Welsh Countryside: A Social Study of Llanfihangel yng Ngwynfa.* Cardiff: University of Wales Press, 1971.

Richard, E. W., and Henry Richard. *Bywyd Ebenezer Richard* (The Life of Ebenezer Richard). London: W. Clowes, 1839.

Roberts, E. O. *Hanes Eglwys Gymreig Jackson, Ohio* (History of the Welsh Church in Jackson, Ohio). Utica, N.Y.: T. J. Griffiths, 1908.

Roberts, Gomer M. *Y Ddinas Gadarn: Hanes Eglwys Jewin Llundain* (The Strong City: A History of Jewin Church, London). London: Pwyllgor Dathlu Daucanmlwyddiant Eglwys Jewin, 1974.

Roberts, J. C. *Hanes Cymdeithas Elusengar Utica a'r Cylchoedd, o'i Sefydliad yn 1849 hyd Ionawr 1, 1882* (The History of the Charitable Society of Utica and Its Region, from Its Establishment in 1849 to January 1, 1882). Utica, N.Y.: Ellis H. Roberts, 1882.

Roberts, Millard F. *A Narrative History of Remsen, New York, Including Parts of Adjoining Townships of Steuben and Trenton, 1789–1898.* 1914. Reprint, Interlake, N.Y.: I-T Publishing, 1985.

Roberts, Rev. Robert. *Cofiant am y Diweddar William Rowlands, Cwrt-y-cwm, Plwyf Llanychaiarn, Sir Aberteifi* (Biography of the Late William Rowlands, Cwrt-y-cwm, Llanychaiarn Parish, Cardiganshire). Aberystwyth: Philip Williams, 1861.

Rothenberg, Winifred Barr. *From Market-Places to a Market Economy: The Transformation of Rural Massachusetts, 1750–1850.* Chicago: University of Chicago Press, 1992.

Salaman, R. N. *The History and Social Influence of the Potato.* Cambridge: Cambridge University Press, 1949.

Salisbury, Harrison E. *A Journey for Our Times: A Memoir.* New York: Harper & Row, 1983.

Schama, Simon. *The Embarrassment of Riches: An Interpretation of Dutch Culture in the Golden Age.* New York: Knopf, 1987.

Sheppard, Francis. *London 1808–1870: The Infernal Wen.* Berkeley: University of California Press, 1971.

Shepperson, Wilbur S. *British Emigration to North America: Projects and Opinions in the Early Victorian Period.* Oxford: Blackwell, 1957.

Shepperson, Wilbur S. *Samuel Roberts: A Welsh Colonizer in Civil War Tennessee.* Knoxville: University of Tennessee Press, 1961.

Sloane, Eric. *Eric Sloane's Sketches of America Past.* 1962. Reprint, New York: Promontory Press, 1986.

Tawney, Richard Henry. *Religion and the Rise of Capitalism*. Harmondsworth: Penguin Books, 1938. Reprint, London: Penguin Books, 1969.

Taylor, Clare. *Samuel Roberts and His Circle: Migration from Llanbrynmair, Montgomeryshire, to America, 1790–1890*. Aberystwyth: Privately published, 1974.

Temin, Peter. *Iron and Steel in Nineteenth-Century America: An Economic Enquiry*. Cambridge: M.I.T. Press, 1964.

Thomas, Brinley. *Migration and Economic Growth: A Study of Great Britain and the Atlantic Economy*. Cambridge: Cambridge University Press, 1954.

Thomas, David. *Agriculture in Wales during the Napoleonic Wars*. Cardiff: University of Wales Press, 1963.

Thomas, Owen. *Cofiant y Parchedig John Jones, Talsarn* (Biography of Rev. John Jones, Talsarn). Wrexham: Hughes & Son, 1874.

Thomas, Peter. *Strangers from a Secret Land: The Voyages of the Brig "Albion" and the Founding of the First Welsh Settlements in Canada*. Toronto: University of Toronto Press, 1986.

Thomas, R. D. *America: neu Amrywiaeth o Nodiadau am yr Unol Daleithiau*. Translated by Clare Thomas as *America: or Miscellaneous Notes on the United States*. 1852. Reprint, Aberystwyth: National Library of Wales, 1973.

Thomas, R. D. *Hanes Cymry America*. Translated by Phillips G. Davies as *A History of the Welsh in America*. Lanham, Md.: University Press of America, 1983.

Thompson, Edward P. *Customs in Common*. New York: New Press, 1991.

Thompson, Edward P. *The Making of the English Working Class*. New York: Vintage, 1963.

Tomlinson, Charles, ed. *Cyclopaedia of Useful Arts & Manufactures*. London: George Virtue, 1853.

Tribe, Keith. *Genealogies of Capitalism*. London: Macmillan, 1981.

Trosset, Carol. *Welshness Performed: Welsh Concepts of Person and Society*. Tucson: University of Arizona Press, 1993.

Tuan, Yi-Fu. *Morality and Imagination: Paradoxes of Progress*. Madison: University of Wisconsin Press, 1989.

Van Hinte, Jacob. *Netherlanders in America: A Study of Emigration and Settlement in the Nineteenth and Twentieth Centuries in the United States of America*. Trans. Adriaan de Wit, ed. Robert P. Swierenga. Grand Rapids, Mich.: Baker Brook House, 1985; originally published in Holland, 1928.

Walker, Joseph E. *Hopewell Village: The Dynamics of a Nineteenth-Century Iron-Making Community*. Philadelphia: University of Pennsylvania Press, 1966.

Waller, William. *An Essay on the Value of the Mines, Late of Sir Carbery Price*. London, 1698.

Weber, Max. *The Protestant Ethic and the Spirit of Capitalism*. New York: Charles Scribner's Sons, 1958.

White, Eryn M. *"Praidd Bach y Bugail Mawr": Seiadau Methodistaidd De-Orllewin Cymru* (The Mighty Shepherd's Little Flock: Methodist Societies in South-West Wales). Llandysul: Gwasg Gomer, 1995.

Wilks, Ivor. *South Wales and the Rising of 1839*. Urbana: University of Illinois Press, 1984.

Willard, Eugene B., ed. *A Standard History of the Hanging Rock Iron Region of Ohio*. 2 vols. N.p.: Lewis Publishing Company, 1916.

Williams, C. J., and J. Watts-Williams. *Cofrestri Plwyf Cymru/Parish Registers of Wales*. Aberystwyth: National Library of Wales and Welsh County Archivists' Group, 1986.

Williams, D. J. *The Old Farmhouse*. Trans. Waldo Williams. 1961. Reprint, Carmarthen: Golden Grove Book Company, 1987.

Williams, Daniel Jenkins. *One Hundred Years of Welsh Calvinistic Methodism in America*. Philadelphia: Westminster Press, 1937.

Williams, Daniel Jenkins. *The Welsh Community of Waukesha County*. Columbus, Ohio: Hann & Adair, 1926.

Williams, Daniel Jenkins. *The Welsh of Columbus, Ohio: A Study in Adaptation and Assimilation*. Oshkosh, Wis.: Privately published, 1913.

Williams, Daniel Webster. *A History of Jackson County, Ohio*. Vol. 1, *The Scioto Salt Springs*. Jackson: Jackson County Chapter of the Ohio Genealogical Society, 1981. Originally published 1900.

Williams, David. *Cymru ac America/Wales and America*. Cardiff: University of Wales Press, 1975.

Williams, David. *A History of Modern Wales*. 1950. Reprint, London: John Murray, 1969.

Williams, David. *The Rebecca Riots: A Study in Agrarian Discontent*. Cardiff: University of Wales Press, 1955.

Williams, Glyn. *The Desert and the Dream: A Study of Welsh Colonization in Chubut 1865–1915*. Cardiff: University of Wales Press, 1975.

Williams, Glyn. *The Welsh in Patagonia: The State and Ethnic Community*. Cardiff: University of Wales Press, 1991.

Williams, Gwyn A. *Madoc: The Making of a Myth*. London: Methuen, 1980.

Williams, Gwyn A. *The Merthyr Rising*. London: Croom Helm, 1978.

Williams, Gwyn A. *The Search for Beulah Land: The Welsh and the Atlantic Revolution*. London: Croom Helm, 1980.

Williams, Jay G. III. *Memory Stones: A History of Welsh-Americans in Central New York and Their Churches*. Fleischmanns, N.Y.: Purple Mountain Press, 1993.

Williams, Michael. *Americans and Their Forests: A Historical Geography*. Cambridge: Cambridge University Press, 1989.

Williams, Stephen Riggs. *The Saga of Paddy's Run*. Oxford, Ohio: Miami University Alumni Association, 1972.

Williams, Rev. William. *The Experience Meeting—An Introduction to the Welsh Societies of the Evangelical Awakening*. Trans. Mrs. Lloyd-Jones. London: Evangelical Press, 1973.

Willigan, J. Dennis, and Katherine A. Lynch. *Sources and Methods of Historical Demography*. New York: Academic Press, 1982.

Other Print Sources

Abrams, J. L. "The Welsh People of Ironton, Lawrence Co., O[hio]." *Cambrian* (1880): 86–90.

"The Accidental Settlement of the Welsh in Gallia and Jackson Counties, O[hio]." *Cambrian* (1883): 129–31.

Allen, Robert C. "The Shift to Mineral Fuel: Ohio Valley Blast Furnaces." Working paper from Cliometrics Conference, Madison, Wisconsin, 26–28 April 1973.

Anderson, Timothy G. "Domestic Industry, Industrialization, and Overseas Migration in Eastern Westphalia, 1840–1880." Paper delivered at the annual meeting of the Association of American Geographers, Atlanta, Georgia, April 1993.

Atack, Jeremy. "Firm Size and Industrial Structure in the United States during the Nineteenth Century." *Journal of Economic History* 46 (1986): 463–75.

Atkins, P. J. "The Retail Milk Trade in London, c. 1790–1914." *Economic History Review*, 2d ser., 33 (1980): 522–37.

Ballinger, John. "Further Gleanings from a Printer's File." *West Wales Historical Records* 11 (1926): 219–25.

Ballinger, John. "Holi'r Pwnc" (Examining the Subject). *West Wales Historical Records* 12 (1927): 225–31.

Bartholomew, Margaret, and Martha Morgan. "The Evan Morgan Story." Undated typescript. Oak Hill, Ohio, Public Library.

Benjamin, Alwyn E. "Melindwr, Cardiganshire: A Study of the Censuses 1841–71." *Ceredigion* 9 (1983): 322–35.

Berthoff, Rowland. "Welsh." In *Harvard Encyclopedia of American Ethnic Groups*, ed. Stephen Thernstrom. Cambridge: Harvard University Press, 1980: 1011–17.

Bowen, Emrys G. "A Clinical Study of Miners' Phthisis in Relation to the Geographical and Racial Features of the Cardiganshire Lead-Mining Area." In *Studies in Regional Consciousness and Environment, Essays Presented to H. J. Fleure*, ed. Iorwerth C. Peate. Oxford: Oxford University Press, 1930: 189–202.

Bowen, Emrys G. "Welsh Emigration Overseas." *Advancement of Science* 17 (1960): 260–71.

Boyns, Trefor, Dennis Thomas, and Colin Barber. "The Iron, Steel, and

Tinplate Industries, 1750–1914." In *Glamorgan County History*, vol. 5, *Industrial Glamorgan,* ed. Arthur H. John and Glanmor Williams. Cardiff: Glamorgan County History Trust, 1980: 97–154.

"A Brief History of Jefferson Furnace." Anonymous typescript (with material by Wilbur Stout submitted to the Ohio State Archaeological and Historical Society in support of a proposal to restore Jefferson Furnace, November 1934.

Brenner, Robert. "Agrarian Class Structure and Economic Development in Pre-Industrial Europe." Reprinted in *The Brenner Debate: Agrarian Class Structure and Economic Development in Pre-Industrial Europe*, ed. T. H. Aston and C. H. E. Philpin, 1985. Reprint, Cambridge: Cambridge University Press, 1990: 10–63.

Burmanje, Piethein. "Trouble in Paradise: The Dutch Reformed Press and Its Views of Calvinist Emigration." In *The Dutch in North-America: Their Immigration and Cultural Continuity*, ed. Rob Kroes and Henk-Otto Neuschafer. Amsterdam: VU University Press, 1991: 25–33.

Carr, Glenda. "William Owen Pughe yn Llundain" (William Owen Pughe in London). *Transactions of the Honourable Society of the Cymmrodorion* (1982): 53–73.

Chidlaw, Rev. Benjamin W. "The Welsh Pioneers in the Miami Valley." *Cambrian* (1884): 248–51.

Chidlaw, Rev. Benjamin W. *Yr American*. Translated by Rev. R. Gwilym Williams as *The American*. Bala: County Press, 1978; originally published in Llanrwst by John Jones, 1840. Pamphlet.

Clark, Peter. "Migrants in the City: The Process of Social Adaptation in English Towns, 1500–1800." In *Migration and Society in Early Modern England*, ed. Peter Clark and David Souden. Totowa, N.J.: Barnes & Noble, 1988: 267–91.

Conway, Alan. "Welsh Emigration to the United States." *Perspectives in American History* 7 (1973): 177–271.

Conway, Alan. "Welshmen in the Union Armies." *Civil War History* 4 (1958): 143–74.

Conzen, Kathleen Neils. "Mainstream and Side Channels: The Localization of Immigrant Cultures." *Journal of American Ethnic History* 11, no. 1 (1991): 5–20.

Conzen, Kathleen Neils. "Peasant Pioneers: Generational Succession among German Farmers in Frontier Minnesota." In *The Countryside in the Age of Capitalist Transformation: Essays in the Social History of Rural America*, ed. Steven Hahn and Jonathan Prude. Chapel Hill: University of North Carolina Press, 1985: 259–92.

Conzen, Kathleen Neils, et al. "The Invention of Ethnicity: A Perspective from the U.S.A." *Journal of American Ethnic History* 12 (1992): 3–41.

Conzen, Michael P. "Ethnicity on the Land." In *The Making of the American Landscape*, ed. Michael P. Conzen. London: HarperCollins, 1990.

Conzen, Michael P. "Spatial Data from Nineteenth-Century Manuscript Censuses: A Technique for Rural Settlement and Land Use Analysis." *Professional Geographer* 25 (1969): 337–43.

"David Evans, Hewitt's Fork, Jackson Co., Ohio, Commonly Called David Evans of Wern." *Cambrian* (1882): 216–18.

Davies, Alun Eirug. "Wages, Prices, and Social Improvements in Cardiganshire, 1750–1850." *Ceredigion* 10 (1984): 31–56.

Davies, Hywel M. "'Very Different Springs of Uneasiness': Emigration from Wales to the United States of America during the 1790s." *Welsh History Review* 15 (1991): 368–98.

Davies, John. "Agriculture in an Industrial Environment." In *Industrial Glamorgan from 1700 to 1970*, vol. 5 in *Glamorgan County History*, ed. Arthur Henry John and Glanmor Williams. Cardiff: Glamorgan County History Trust, 1980.

Davies, John. "The End of the Great Estates and the Rise of Freehold Farming in Wales." *Welsh History Review* 7 (1974–1975): 186–213.

Davies, Margaret M. "The Isaac Family, Llangwyryfon, Wales." Undated typescript. Welsh-American Heritage Museum, Oak Hill, Ohio.

Davies, Phillips G. "The Growth and Assimilation of the Welsh Settlements in Iowa," *Iowa State Journal of Research* 60 (1985): 107–28.

Davis, Dan T. *Early History of Horeb Church*. Oak Hill, Ohio: Privately published, 1938. Pamphlet.

Davis, Dan T. *Us Davises*. Oak Hill, Ohio: Privately published, 1950. Pamphlet.

Davis, Jennie, and Juanita Davis Clyse. "History of the Cooper Davis Family." Typescript, 1971. Oak Hill, Ohio, Public Library.

Davis, Richard Anthony. "A Davis Family History." Typescript, 1988. Welsh-American Heritage Museum, Oak Hill, Ohio.

Davis, W. N. "Out of the Past." Installment no. 84, "Charcoal Burning," *Oak Hill Press*, 26 February 1969.

Duckworth, Christopher S., ed. "The Hanging Rock Charcoal Iron Industry." Typescript, Ohio Historical Society, 1989.

Easterlin, Richard A. "Immigration: Economic and Social Characteristics." In *Harvard Encyclopedia of American Ethnic Groups*, ed. Stephan Thernstrom. Cambridge: Harvard University Press, 1980: 476–86.

Ellis, David M. "The Assimilation of the Welsh in Central New York." *Welsh History Review* 6 (1973): 424–50.

Erickson, Charlotte. "Emigration from the British Isles to the U.S.A. in 1831." *Population Studies* 35 (1981): 175–97.

Erickson, Charlotte. "Who Were the English and Scottish Emigrants in the 1880s?" In *Population and Social Change*, ed. D. V. Glass and R. Revelle. London: Edward Arnold, 1972: 347–81.

Evans, Ben R. "Evans Family History." Typescript dated Jackson, Ohio, 1966. Personal collection of Mr. And Mrs. Richard Isaac.

Evans, D. J. "Welsh Students in the Ohio University." *Cambrian* (April 1887): 105–6.

Evans, Eleanor, and George Morgan Family History. Undated typescript. Oak Hill, Ohio, Public Library.

Evans, Meredydd. "Pantycelyn a Thröedigaeth" (Pantycelyn and Conversion). In *Meddwl a Dychymyg Williams Pantycelyn* (The Mind and Imagination of Williams Pantycelyn), ed. Derec Llwyd Morgan. Llandysul: Gwasg Gomer, 1991: 55–81.

Evans, Mrs. Rees L., and D. Dwight Evans. "John Richards Family—The Nannie Rees Branch"; and Address to 100th Richards Reunion. Undated typescripts. Welsh-American Heritage Museum, Oak Hill, Ohio.

Evans, Virgil H. *The Family Tree of John Jones (Tirbach)*. Columbus, Ohio: Privately published, 1929. Reprint, Oak Hill, Ohio: Cardiff Club, 1984. Pamphlet.

"Funeral Services of David A. Lloyd." Typescript, 1911. Oak Hill, Ohio, Public Library.

Geertz, Clifford. "'From the Native's Point of View': On the Nature of Anthropological Understanding." In *Local Knowledge: Further Essays in Interpretive Anthropology*. London: Fontana Press, 1983: 55–70.

Gjerde, Jon. "Chain Migrations from the West Coast of Norway." In *A Century of European Migrations, 1830–1930*, ed. Rudolph J. Vecoli and Suzanne M. Sinke. Urbana: University of Illinois Press, 1991: 158–81.

Glass, D. V. "Vital Registration in Britain during the Nineteenth Century." In *Numbering the People: The Eighteenth-Century Population Controversy and the Development of Census and Vital Statistics in Britain*. London: Gordon and Cremonesi, 1973: 181–205.

Gould, S. J., and N. Eldredge, "Punctuated Equilibria: The Tempo and Mode of Evolution Reconsidered." *Palaeobiology* 3 (1977): 115–51. ·

Grigg, D. B. "E. G. Ravenstein and the 'Laws of Migration.'" *Journal of Historical Geography* 3 (1977): 42–54.

Gruffydd, R. Geraint. "Diwygiad Llangeitho a'i Ddylanwad" (The Llangeitho Revival and Its Influence). *Y Traethodydd* 146, no. 619 (1991): 95–104.

Henretta, James A. "Families and Farms: *Mentalité* in Pre-Industrial America." *William and Mary Quarterly*, 3d ser., 35 (1978): 3–32.

Henretta, James A. "The Protestant Ethic and the Reality of Capitalism in Colonial America." In *Weber's* Protestant Ethic: *Origins, Evidence, Contexts*, ed. Hartmut Lehmann. Cambridge: Cambridge University Press, for the German Historical Institute, Washington, D.C., 1993: 327–46.

"Henry Hughes Autobiography." Trans. Albert Barnes Hughes. Typescript, 1947. Southern Minnesota Historical Center.

Hickey, Joseph V. "Welsh Cattlemen on the Kansas Flint Hills: Social and Ideological Dimensions of Cattle Entrepreneurship." *Agricultural History* 63 (1989): 56–71.

Hoelscher, Steven D., and Robert C. Ostergren. "Old European Homelands in the American Middle West." *Journal of Cultural Geography* 13 (1993): 87–106.

"Hon. T. L. Hughes, Oak Hill, O[hio]." *Cambrian* (1888), 225–26.

"Horeb, Jackson County, Ohio." *Cambrian* (1885): 45–51.

Howell, David W. "The Impact of Railways on Agricultural Development in Nineteenth-Century Wales." *Welsh History Review* 7 (1974): 40–62.

Hughes, David Wendell. "Davies Family Genealogy." Undated typescript. Welsh-American Heritage Museum, Oak Hill, Ohio.

Hughes, T. Jones. "The Social Geography of a Small Region in the Llŷn Peninsula." In *Rural Welsh Communities*, ed. Elwyn Davies and Alwyn D. Rees. Cardiff: University of Wales Press, 1960: 121–84.

Jenkins, Dafydd. "Dyddiadur Cymro" (A Welshman's Diary). *Heddiw* 6 (1941): 236.

Jenkins, Estella Jones. "History of the 'Brynele' Edwards Family." Undated typescript. Personal collection of Roland L. Edwards.

Jenkins, Geraint H. "'A Rank Republican [and] a Leveller': William Jones, Llangadfan." *Welsh History Review* 17, no. 3 (1995): 365–87.

Jones, Ben A. *Y Byd o Ben Trichrug* (The World from Atop Trichrug). Aberystwyth: Cymdeithas Lyfrau Ceredigion, 1959.

Jones, Edward. *Y Teithiwr Americanaidd: Neu Gyfarwyddyd i Symudwyr o Gymru i'r America* (The American Traveler: Or Advice to Emigrants from Wales to America). Aberystwyth: E. Williams, 1837. Pamphlet.

Jones, Edwin. "Jones-David Clan." Undated typescript. Personal collection of Edwin F. Jones.

Jones, Emrys. "Some Aspects of Cultural Change in an American Welsh Community." *Transactions of the Honourable Society of Cymmrodorion* (1952): 15–41.

Jones, Emrys. "Tregaron: The Sociology of a Market Town in Central Cardiganshire." In *Welsh Rural Communities*, ed. Elwyn Davies and Alwyn D. Rees. Cardiff: University of Wales Press, 1960: 66–117.

Jones, Emrys. "The Welsh in London in the Nineteenth Century." *Cambria* 12 (1985): 149–69.

Jones, Emrys. "The Welsh in London in the Seventeenth and Eighteenth Centuries." *Welsh History Review* 10 (1981): 461–79.

Jones, Gwilym. "The Saga of Cilcennin." *Cylchgrawn Cymdeithas Ceredigion Llundain* (Journal of the Cardigan Society of London) 22 (1966–1967): 19–27.

Jones, Ieuan Gwynedd. "Religion and Society in the First Half of the Nineteenth Century." In *Explorations and Explanations: Essays in the Social History of Victorian Wales*. Llandysul: Gwasg Gomer, 1981: 217–35.

Jones, John E. "Romance of the Old Charcoal Furnace Days of the Hanging Rock Iron District." Paper presented at the Globe Iron Co. sales representatives meeting, Jackson, Ohio, 27–28 July 1934.

Jones, John I. "History of John H. Jones." Typescript, 1928. Personal collection of Cindie Tidwell.

Jones, Llewellyn. "Genealogy of the 'John T. Jones, Bryn Garw' Family." Typescript, 1963. Oak Hill, Ohio, Public Library.

Jones, Maldwyn. "Welsh-Americans and the Anti-Slavery Movement in the United States." *Transactions of the Honourable Society of Cymmrodorion* (1985): 105–29.

Jones, Peter Ellis. "Migration and the Slate Belt of Caernarfonshire in the Nineteenth Century." *Welsh History Review* 14 (1989): 610–29.

Jones, R. Tudur. *Duw a Diwylliant: Y Ddadl Fawr, 1800–1830* (God and Culture: The Great Debate, 1800–1830). Originally delivered as lecture at Hen Gapel, Tre'r Ddôl, 22 September 1984. Welsh National Folk Museum, 1986. Pamphlet.

Jones, Rosemary A. N. "Women, Community, and Collective Action: The *Ceffyl Pren* Tradition." In *Our Mother's Land: Chapters in Welsh Women's History 1830–1939*, ed. Angela V. John. Cardiff: University of Wales Press, 1991: 17–41.

Jones, William Harvey. "Welsh Settlements in Ohio." *Ohio Archaeological and Historical Publications* 16 (1907): 194–227.

Keeler, Vernon D. "An Economic History of the Jackson County Iron Industry." *Ohio Archaeological and Historical Quarterly* 42 (1933): 132–244.

Kenrick, G. S. "Statistics of the Population of the Parish of Trevethin (Pontypool) . . . and Inhabiting Part of the District Recently Disturbed." *Journal of the Royal Statistical Society* 3 (January 1841): 366–75.

Knowles, Anne [Kelly]. "History in a Song." *Y Drych* (The Mirror) (November 1991): 8.

Knowles, Anne [Kelly]. "The Thunder God Is Smiling." *Y Drych* (The Mirror) (April 1993), 16–18.

Kober, George M. "Iron, Steel, and Allied Industries." In *Industrial Health*, ed. Kober and Emery R. Hayhurst. Philadelphia: P. Blakiston's Son & Co., 1924: 176–83.

Kulikoff, Allan. "The Transition to Capitalism in Rural America." *William and Mary Quarterly*, 3d ser., 46 (1989): 120–44.

Liechty, Joseph C. "Humility: The Foundation of Mennonite Religious Outlook in the 1860s." *Mennonite Quarterly Review* 54 (1980): 5–31.

Linnard, William. "Merched y Gerddi yn Llundain ac yng Nghymru" (The Garden Girls in London and in Wales). *Ceredigion* 9 (1982): 260–63.

Lloyd, David. "The Moriah Calvinistic Methodist Church, Jackson County, Ohio." *Cambrian* (1884), 108–12.

Lloyd, James H. Recollections of the Edwards, Brynele clan. Untitled and undated typescript. Oak Hill, Ohio, Public Library.

Lloyd, Lewis. "The Port of Aberystwyth in the 1840s." *Cymru a'r Môr/ Maritime Wales* (1980): 43–61.

Long, Mark W. "The Historic Coal Mining Industry of Jackson County." In *Jackson County, Ohio: History and Families 1816–1991*, comp. Jackson County Genealogical Society. Paducah, Ky.: Turning Publishing, 1991: 30–38.

Meyering, Anne C. "Did Capitalism Lead to the Decline of the Peasantry?

The Case of the French Combraille." *Journal of Economic History* 43 (1983): 121–28.

Moore-Colyer, Richard J. "Farmers and Fields in Nineteenth-Century Wales: The Case of Llanrhystud, Cardiganshire." *National Library of Wales Journal* 26 (1989–1990): 32–57.

Moore-Colyer, Richard J. "The Gentry and the County in Nineteenth-Century Cardiganshire." *Welsh History Review* 10 (1981): 497–535.

Moore-Colyer, Richard J. "Landscape and Landscape Change." Typescript, 1976.

Moore-Colyer, Richard J. "Of Lime and Men: Aspects of the Coastal Trade in Lime in South-West Wales in the Eighteenth and Nineteenth Centuries." *Welsh History Review* 14 (1988): 54–77.

Moore-Colyer, Richard J. "Nanteos: A Landed Estate in Decline, 1800–1930." *Ceredigion* 9 (1980): 58–77.

Moore-Colyer, Richard J. "The Pryse Family of Gogerddan and the Decline of the Great Estate, 1800–1960." *Welsh History Review* 9 (1979): 406–31.

Moore-Colyer, Richard J. "Some Aspects of Land Occupation in Nineteenth-Century Cardiganshire." *Transactions of the Honourable Society of Cymmrodorion* (1981): 79–97.

Morgan, David. "David Morgan's Account of Travel to America with John and Ann Alban." Anonymous translation. Undated typescript copy. Personal collection of William R. Alban.

Morgan, David E. "Background of the Edwards Family, Brynele." Undated typescript. Personal collection of Roland L. Edwards.

Morgan, David E. "Factual Information Regarding Richard Morgan and His Wife, Elizabeth Jones Morgan." Undated typescript. Welsh-American Heritage Museum, Oak Hill, Ohio.

Morgan, Derec Llwyd. "Daniel Rowland (?1711–1790): Pregethwr Diwygiadol" (Daniel Rowland . . . Revivalist Preacher). *Ceredigion* 11 (1991): 217–37.

Morgan, Derec Llwyd. "Pantycelyn a'i Gynulleidfa: Yr Emynydd a Mirandus" (Pantycelyn and His Congregation: The Hymnist and Mirandus). In *Meddwl a Dychymyg Williams Pantycelyn* (The Mind and Imagination of Williams Pantycelyn), ed. Derec Llwyd Morgan. Llandysul: Gwasg Gomer, 1991: 82–101.

Morgan, Derec Llwyd. "Taith i Langeitho, 1762" (Journey to Llangeitho, 1762). In *Pobl Pantycelyn* (*Pantycelyn's People*), ed. Derec Llwyd Morgan. Llandysul: Gwasg Gomer, 1986: 2–15.

Morgan, Gerald. "Adeiladu Llongau yng Ngogledd Ceredigion/North Cardiganshire Shipbuilding 1700–1880." Occasional Papers in Ceredigion History, no. 2. Aberystwyth: University of Wales, 1992. Pamphlet.

Morgan, Prys. "From Death to a View: The Hunt for the Welsh Past in the Romantic Period." In *The Invention of Tradition*, ed. Eric Hobsbawm and Terence Ranger. Cambridge: Cambridge University Press, 1983: 43–100.

Muntz, Alfred Philip. "Forests and Iron: The Charcoal Iron Industry of the New Jersey Highlands." *Geografiska Annaler* 42 (1960): 315–23.

Niday, Mary Elizabeth Walker. "Keeping up with the Joneses." Typescript dated Jackson, Ohio, 1989. Oak Hill, Ohio, Public Library.

Owen, Bob. "O Sir Aberteifi i Jackson a Gallia, Ohio" (From Cardiganshire to Jackson and Gallia, Ohio). *Cylchgrawn Cymdeithas Ceredigion Llundain* (Journal of the Cardigan Society of London) 11 (1955–1956): 17–21.

Owen, Bob. "Ymfudo o Sir Aberteifi i Unol Daleithiau America o 1654 hyd 1860" (Emigration from Cardiganshire to the United States of America from 1654 to 1860). *Ceredigion* (1952–1955): 160–69, 225–40.

Owen, Bob. "Yr Ymfudo o Sir Gaernarfon i'r Unol Daleithiau" (The Emigration from Carnarvonshire to the United States). *Transactions of the Caernarfonshire Historical Society* 13 (1952): 42–67.

Parkinson, A. J. "Wheat, Peat, and Lead: Settlement Patterns in West Wales, 1500–1800." *Ceredigion* 10 (1985): 111–30.

Peet, J. Richard. "The Spatial Expansion of Commercial Agriculture in the Nineteenth Century: A Von Thunen Interpretation." *Economic Geography* 45, no. 4 (1969): 283–301.

Phillips, Richard. "Amgáu Tir ar Fynydd Bach" (Enclosing Land on Mynydd Bach). *Ceredigion* 6 (1971): 350–63.

Pooley, Colin G. "Welsh Migration to England in the Mid-Nineteenth Century." *Journal of Historical Geography* 9 (1983): 287–306.

Pryce, W. T. R. "Migration and the Evolution of Culture Areas: Cultural and Linguistic Frontiers in Northeast Wales." *Transactions of the Institute of British Geographers* 65 (1975): 79–107.

"The 'Pwngc' Sunday at Horeb, Jackson County, Ohio." *Cambrian* (1886): 123–26.

"Rhestr o'r Aelodau" (List of the Members). *Cylchgrawn Cymdeithas Ceredigion Llundain* (Journal of the Cardigan Society of London) 1 (1934–1935): 42–55.

Richey, Harry E. "Isaac-Evans Genealogy." Undated manuscript. Welsh-American Heritage Museum, Oak Hill, Ohio.

Riden, Philip. "Iron and Steel." In *Atlas of Industrializing Britain, 1780–1914*, ed. John Langton and R. J. Morris. London: Methuen, 1986: 127–31.

Roberts, Samuel. "Ffarmwr Careful, Cilhaul-Uchaf." In *Gweithiau Samuel Roberts* (The Works of Samuel Roberts). Dolgellau: Evan Jones, 1856: 73–106.

Salamon, Sonya. "Ethnic Communities and the Structure of Agriculture." *Rural Sociology* 50 (1985): 323–40.

Saueressig-Schreuder, Yda. "Dutch Catholic Emigration in the Mid-Nineteenth Century: Noord-Brabant, 1847–1871." *Journal of Historical Geography* 11 (1985): 48–69.

Stout, Wilbur. "The Charcoal Iron Industry of the Hanging Rock Iron District: Its Influence on the Early Development of the Ohio Valley."

Ohio Archaeological and Historical Quarterly 42 (1933): 72–104.

Strickon, Arnold. "Ethnicity and Entrepreneurship in Rural Wisconsin." In *Entrepreneurs in Cultural Context*, ed. Sidney M. Greenfield et al. Albuquerque: University of New Mexico Press, 1979: 159–89.

Struble, Michael T. "Horeb Chapel: The Evolution of a Welsh Barn Chapel upon the American Landscape." *Material Culture* 25 (1993): 37–45.

Struble, Michael T., and Hubert G. H. Wilhelm. "The Welsh in Ohio." In *To Build in a New Land: Ethnic Landscapes in North America*, ed. Allen G. Noble. Baltimore: Johns Hopkins University Press, 1992: 79–92.

Swierenga, Robert P. "Dutch Immigration Patterns in the Nineteenth and Twentieth Centuries." In *The Dutch in America: Immigration, Settlement, and Cultural Change*, ed. Robert P. Swierenga. New Brunswick, N.J.: Rutgers University Press, 1985: 15–42.

Swierenga, Robert P. "Local Patterns of Dutch Migration to the United States in the Mid–Nineteenth Century." In *A Century of European Migrations, 1830–1930*, ed. Rudolph J. Vecoli and Suzanne M. Sinke. Urbana: University of Illinois Press, 1991: 134–57.

Taylor, Clare. "Paddy's Run: A Welsh Community in Ohio." *Welsh History Review* 11 (1983): 302–16.

Thickens, Rev. John. "Hanes ac Atgof" (History and Recollection). In *Dathliad Agor Capel Newydd Eglwys Jewin, Trefn y Gwasanaeth* (A Celebration of the Opening of the New Jewin Church, Order of Service). London: Eglwys Jewin, 1961. Pamphlet.

Thirsk, Joan. "Industries in the Countryside." In *The Rural Economy of England: Collected Essays*. London: Hambledon Press, 1984: 217–33.

Thistlethwaite, Frank. "Migration from Europe Overseas in the Nineteenth and Twentieth Centuries." In *A Century of European Migrations, 1830–1930*, ed. Rudolph J. Vecoli and Suzanne M. Sinke. Urbana: University of Illinois Press, 1991: 17–49.

Thomas, Brinley. "A Cauldron of Rebirth: Population and the Welsh Language in the Nineteenth Century." *Welsh History Review* 13 (1987): 418–37.

Thomas, Brinley. "Migration into the Glamorganshire Coalfield, 1861–1911." *Economica* 30 (1930): 275–94.

Thomas, Brinley. "Wales and the Atlantic Economy." *Scottish Journal of Political Economy* 6 (1959): 169–92.

Turner, Frederick Jackson. "The Significance of the Frontier in American History." In *The Frontier in American History*, ed. Wilbur R. Jacobs. Tucson: University of Arizona Press, 1986: 1–38.

Van Vugt, William. "Running from Ruin? The Emigration of British Farmers to the U.S.A. in the Wake of the Repeal of the Corn Laws." *Economic History Review*, 2d ser., 41 (1988): 411–28.

Van Vugt, William. "Welsh Emigration to the U.S.A. during the Mid-Nineteenth Century." *Welsh History Review* 15 (1991): 545–61.

"Voices from North America." Two letters by Albertus c. Van Raalte, dated 27 November and 16 December 1846. Trans. John Dahm. Heritage Hall Publications, no. 3. Grand Rapids, Mich.: Calvin College and Calvin Theological Seminary Archives, 1992.

Walters, Judith A. "Thomas, Walters & Related Welsh Families of Southern Minnesota." Typescript dated Lynnwood, Washington, 1972. State Historical Society of Wisconsin.

Williams, Benjamin G. "History of Benjamin G. Williams for His Son, Daniel Webster Williams." Reprinted in *Jackson County, Ohio: History and Families 1816–1991*, comp. Jackson County Genealogical Society. Paducah, Ky.: Turner Publishing Co., 1991: 65–75.

Williams, David. "'Rhyfel y Sais Bach': An Enclosure Riot on Mynydd Bach." *Ceredigion* 2 (1952): 39–52.

Williams, David. "Some Figures Relating to Emigration from Wales." *Bulletin of the Board of Celtic Studies* 7 (1935): 396–415.

Williams, Moelwyn I. "Seasonal Migrations of Cardiganshire Harvest-Gangs to the Vale of Glamorgan in the Nineteenth Century." *Ceredigion* 3 (1957): 156–59.

Williams-Davies, John. "'Merched y Gerddi'—Mudwyr Tymhorol o Geredigion" ("The Garden Girls"—Seasonal Migrants from Cardiganshire). *Ceredigion* 8 (1978): 291–303.

Y Beread

Y Cenhadwr Americanaidd (The American Missionary)

Y Cyfaill o'r Hen Wlad (The Friend from the Old Country)

Y Drych (The Mirror)

Dissertations and Theses

Bert, William Owen. "The Mosquitoes of Minnesota, with Special Reference to Their Biologies." Ph.D. diss., University of Minnesota, 1936.

Fisk, Charles John. "Reconstruction of Daily 1820–1872 Minneapolis–St. Paul, Minnesota, Temperature Observations." M.S. thesis, University of Wisconsin–Madison, 1984.

Knowles, Anne Kelly. "Welsh Settlement in Waukesha County, Wisconsin, 1840–1873." M.S. thesis, University of Wisconsin–Madison, 1989.

Legreid, Ann Marie. "The Exodus, Transplanting, and Religious Reorganization of a Group of Norwegian Lutheran Immigrants in Western Wisconsin, 1836–1900." Ph.D. diss., University of Wisconsin–Madison, 1985.

Saueressig-Schreuder, Yda. "Emigration, Settlement, and Assimilation of Dutch Catholic Immigrants in Wisconsin 1850–1905." Ph.D. diss., University of Wisconsin–Madison, 1982.

Van Vugt, William. "British Emigration during the Early 1850s, with Special Reference to Emigration to the U.S.A." Ph.D. diss., University of London, 1985.

Walters, Gwynfryn. "The Tourist and Guidebook Literature of Wales,

1770–1870: A Descriptive and Bibliographical Survey with an Analysis of the Cartographic Content and Its Extent." 2 vols. Ph.D. diss., University of Wales, 1966.

Non-Print Sources

INTERVIEWS

Don Craig, manager of the historical museum at Buckeye Furnace, Ohio, 7 January 1990.

Evan E. Davis at his home, Oak Hill, Ohio, 7 January 1990, 8 and 28 July 1990.

Gwen Davies (b. 1899), conducted by Edward Wicklein, 26 December 1978, Presbyterian Historical Association, Philadelphia.

Enid Hoffman at her home, Madison, Wisconsin, 18 July 1988.

Dafydd Jones, Bronyfynwent at Bronnant School, Dyfed, 11 April 1995.

Dai Morris Jones at his home, Blaen Beidiog, Trefenter, Dyfed, 13 May 1992.

James H. Lloyd, by telephone, 27 February and 29 May 1993.

Rev. Stephen Morgan at his home, Talsarn, Dyfed, 14 June 1992.

Mildred Hughes Southcott at her home, Wales, Wisconsin, 24 June 1988.

Jean Williams at her home, Tŷ Capel Jewin, London, 21 June 1992.

ASSISTANCE WITH GENEALOGY AND LOCATION OF EMIGRANT FARMS

William R. Alban, Galena, Ohio (Alban family, Evan O. Davies family, John R. Evans family, Daniel Richards family)

Mildred Jenkins Bangert and David Jenkins, Oak Hill, Ohio (David Jenkins family)

Eleanor Cole, Mankato, Minnesota (John Hughes family)

Evan E. Davis, Oak Hill, Ohio (David Davis family, Thomas T. Jones)

Myron E. Davis, Jackson, Ohio (John Lot Davies family)

Dafydd Edwards, Nancwnlle, Dyfed (southern Mynydd Bach)

Roland L. Edwards, Grove City, Ohio (Edwards, Brynele family; Moriah chapel)

Eluned Evans, Madison, Wisconsin (Montgomeryshire)

John Evans, Llanddeiniol, Dyfed (northern Mynydd Bach; David Jones, Penglog family; Stephen Davis family; Thomas Thomas, Travel family; John D. Evans family)

Mary Fontaine, Madison, Wisconsin (Rev. Robert Williams family)

Dafydd Jenkins, Aberystwyth, Dyfed (Cardiganshire Welsh in London)

Edwin F. Jones, Jackson, Ohio (Enoch T. Davis family, David Jabez Davis family, David D. Jones family)

Eirlys Jones, Llanelidan, Clwyd (central Denbighshire, Thomas Llewelyn Hughes family)

Ieuan Gwynedd Jones, Aberystwyth, Dyfed (northern Mynydd Bach, Carmarthenshire)

Ivor Jones, Hillsboro, Ohio (Jones, Benglog family)

Peter Jones, Llandyfrydog, Gwynedd (Anglesey, Llŷn Peninsula)

Thomas J. and Eilonwy Rhys Jones, Groesfaen, Mid Glamorgan (Carmarthenshire)

William D. Jones, Cardiff, Mid Glamorgan (Glamorgan and Monmouthshire iron and coal district, Carmarthenshire)

James H. Lloyd, Oak Hill, Ohio (Edwards, Brynele family; Mary Evans Lloyd Jones family)

E. Gwynn Matthews, Llanrhaeadr, Clwyd (Denbighshire)

Lucille McFee, Madison, Wisconsin (ship manifests)

Evelyn and Islwyn Morgan, Pontrhydfendigaid, Dyfed (eastern Mynydd Bach)

Gerald Morgan, Aberystwyth, Dyfed (northern Cardiganshire)

Rev. Stephen Morgan, Trefilan, Dyfed (southern Mynydd Bach)

John R. Morris, Llanddeiniol, Dyfed (northern Mynydd Bach)

Tony Platt, London (Cardiganshire Welsh in London)

Edward T. Porter, Tacoma, Washington (Gwnnws Uchaf, Lledrod, Ffair Rhos, Caron)

John Roderick Rees, Bethania, Dyfed (southern Mynydd Bach)

Alice Richards, Washington, D.C. (David Richards family)

Cindie Tidwell, Corrales, New Mexico (John H. Jones family)

Index

The University of Chicago
GEOGRAPHY RESEARCH PAPERS

Titles in Print

226. GRITZNER, JEFFREY A. *The West African Sahel: Human Agency and Environmental Change*. 1988. xii + 170 pp.

227. MURPHY, ALEXANDER B. *The Regional Dynamics of Language Differentiation in Belgium: A Study in Cultural-Political Geography*. 1988. xiii + 249 pp.

228–229. BISHOP, BARRY C. *Karnali under Stress: Livelihood Strategies and Seasonal Rhythms in a Changing Nepal Himalaya*. 1990. xviii + 460 pp.

230. MUELLER-WILLE, CHRISTOPHER. *Natural Landscape Amenities and Suburban Growth: Metropolitan Chicago, 1970–1980*. 1990. xi + 153 pp.

231. WILKINSON, M. JUSTIN. *Paleoenvironments in the Namib Desert: The Lower Tumas Basin in the Late Cenozoic*. 1990. xv + 196 pp.

232. DUBOIS, RANDOM. *Soil Erosion in a Coastal River Basin: A Case Study from the Philippines*. 1990. xii + 138 pp.

233. PALM, RISA, AND MICHAEL E. HODGSON. *After a California Earthquake: Attitude and Behavior Change*. 1992. xii + 130 pp.

234. KUMMER, DAVID M. *Deforestation in the Postwar Philippines*. 1992. xviii + 179 pp.

235. CONZEN, MICHAEL P., THOMAS A. RUMNEY, AND GRAEME WYNN. *A Scholar's Guide to Geographical Writing on the American and Canadian Past*. 1993. xiii + 751 pp.

236. COHEN, SHAUL EPHRAIM. *The Politics of Planting: Israeli-Palestinian Competition for Control of Land in the Jerusalem Periphery*. 1993. xiv + 203 pp.

237. EMMETT, CHAD F. *Beyond the Basilica: Christians and Muslims in Nazareth*. 1994. xix + 303 pp.

238. PRICE, EDWARD T. *Dividing the Land: Early American Beginnings of Our Private Property Mosaic*. 1995. xviii + 410 pp.

239. PAPADOPOULOS, ALEX G. *Urban Regimes and Strategies: Building Europe's Central Executive District in Brussels*. 1996. xviii + 290 pp.

240. KNOWLES, ANNE KELLY. *Calvinists Incorporated: Welsh Immigrants on Ohio's Industrial Frontier*. 1997. xxiv + 330 pp.

CPSIA information can be obtained
at www.ICGtesting.com
Printed in the USA
LVHW052204240423
745258LV00029BA/772

9 780226 448534